CW00970975

Queen of the Methodists

Queen of the Methodists

The Countess of Huntingdon and the Eighteenth-Century Crisis of Faith and Society

Boyd Stanley Schlenther

Durham Academic Press

First published in 1997 by
Durham Academic Press
1 Hutton Close
South Church
Bishop Auckland
Durham

British Library Cataloguing in Publication Data.
A Catalogue record for this book is available
from the British Library.

ISBN 1 900838 08 7

Typeset by George Wishart & Associates, Whitley Bay.
Printed and bound by Bookcraft Ltd., Bath.

For Alberta:
the last leaf on the tree

Contents

ILLUSTRATIONS

Jacket Illustration:
Portrait of Lady Huntingdon, by J. Russell. By courtesy of the Cheshunt Foundation, Westminster College, Cambridge.

Following page 82:
1. Portrait of the Earl and Countess of Huntingdon and children Henry and Selina, by P. Soldi, early 1740s. By courtesy of the Cheshunt Foundation, Westminster College, Cambridge.
2. From Lady Huntingdon's memorial to her husband, by J. Rysbrack, 1746, in Ashby de la Zouch parish church. Photograph by Martin Vaughan, by courtesy of Peter W. Gentry.
3. Engraving of life-sized portrait of Lady Huntingdon, by J. Russell, 1773. By courtesy of V. & J. Duncan Antique Maps and Prints, Savannah, Georgia.
4. Engraving of Lady Huntingdon, c. 1780. From frontispiece to Volume 1 of [A.C.H. Seymour], *The Life and Times of Selina Countess of Huntingdon* (London, 1844).
5. 'The Tears of Methodism.' Satirical engraving of Lady Huntingdon, from *Town and Country Magazine*, [1 September] 1791, page 344. By courtesy of the Bodleian Library, Per 2705, e6740.
6. Portrait of Lady Huntingdon's eldest son, Francis, tenth Earl of Huntingdon, by J. Reynolds, 1754. By courtesy of the Huntington Art Galleries, San Marino, California.
7. Portrait of Lady Huntingdon's younger daughter, Lady Selina, by J. Reynolds, 1762. By courtesy of the Courtauld Institute of Art, University of London.
8. Portrait of John Wesley, by N. Hone, c. 1766. By courtesy of the National Portrait Gallery, London.
9. Portrait of George Whitefield, by J. Woolaston, c. 1742. By courtesy of the National Portrait Gallery, London.
10. Drawing of Howell Harris. From Gomer Roberts (ed.), *Selected Trevecka Letters*, Volume 1 (Caernarvon, 1956).
11. Engraving of William Piercy. From the *Gospel Magazine*, Volume 2, 1775.
12. Engraving of Thomas Haweis. From frontispiece to A. S. Wood, *Thomas Haweis* (London, 1957). By courtesy of the S.P.C.K.
13. Engraving of Lady Anne Erskine. From the *Evangelical Register*, Volume 1, 1824-5.

Abbreviations

Baker	Frank Baker (ed.), *The Works of John Wesley*, vols. 25 & 26 (letters)
Black	Countess of Huntingdon Black Folio of Letters, Rylands
CF	Countess of Huntingdon Papers, Cheshunt Foundation, Westminster College, Cambridge
CL	Congregational Library, at Dr Williams's Library, London
CMS	Venn MSS, Church Missionary Society Manuscripts, University of Birmingham Library
CW	Charles Wesley
Doddridge	Geoffrey F. Nuttall, *Calendar of the Correspondence of Philip Doddridge*
Drew	Letters to and from the Countess of Huntingdon (unless otherwise noted), Drew University Library, Madison, New Jersey
Duke	Frank A. Baker Collection (unless otherwise noted), Duke University Library, Durham, North Carolina
EH	Lady Elizabeth Hastings, later Lady Rawdon/Countess of Moira (SH's elder daughter)
FH	Francis Hastings, 10th Earl of Huntingdon (SH's eldest son)
HA	Hastings Family Correspondence, Huntington
HAP	Hastings Personal Papers, Huntington
HH	Howell Harris
HHRS	Howell Harris diary, in Tom Beynon (ed.), *Howell Harris, Reformer and Soldier*
HHVL	Howell Harris diary, in Tom Beynon (ed.), *Howell Harris's Visits to London*
HMC	Historical Manuscripts Commission
HMC *Hast.*	Historical Manuscripts Commission. *Report on the Manuscripts of the late Reginald Rawdon Hastings*
Huntington	Huntington Library, San Marino, California
JF	John Fletcher
JW	John Wesley
LRO	Leicestershire Record Office
Mitchell	Mitchell Library, Sydney, Australia
NLW	National Library of Wales, Aberystwyth
PRONI	Granard Papers (unless otherwise noted), Public Record Office of Northern Ireland, Belfast
Rayleigh	Countess of Huntingdon Connexion Archives, Rayleigh

Rylands	Methodist Archives (unless otherwise noted), John Rylands University Library of Manchester
Select Letters	*A Select Collection of Letters of . . . George Whitefield*
SH	Selina Hastings, Countess of Huntingdon
SMU	Countess of Huntingdon Letters, Bridwell Library, Southern Methodist University, Dallas
SPCK	Society for Promoting Christian Knowledge, London
Telford	John Telford (ed.), *The Letters of the Rev. John Wesley*
TH	Theophilus Hastings, 9th Earl of Huntingdon (SH's husband)
Trevecka	Trevecka Letters, NLW
Ward & H.	W. Reginald Ward and Richard P. Heitzenrater (eds.), *The Works of John Wesley*, vols. 18-23 (journals and diaries)
WP	William Piercy
Yale	Osborn Collection, Yale University Library

Preface

Letters have been called the paste of history. The extant correspondence relevant to the life of the Countess of Huntingdon is extensive. Some 3,000 letters, mainly addressed to her, are in the Cheshunt Foundation, Westminster College, Cambridge. The major collections of her own letters are in the John Rylands University Library of Manchester; Drew University Library, Madison, New Jersey; the Bridwell Library, Southern Methodist University, Dallas; and the Congregational Library, at Dr Williams's Library, London. Of the eighteenth-century Methodist leaders, this correspondence is rivalled in bulk perhaps only by that of John Wesley. But Wesley was not an aristocrat, and the unique feature of Lady Huntingdon's correspondence is the massive collection of Hastings family letters located at the Huntington Library, San Marino, California; the Leicestershire Record Office; and Drew University Library.

These collections contain an intricate web of correspondence weaving together various aspects of the Countess's long life. They offer an unparalleled opportunity to chart the progress of an eighteenth-century evangelical on a map marked by family, social, political and religious contours. The penance has been the necessity of deciphering Lady Huntingdon's own letters, where tortured calligraphy is wedded to a system of punctuation notable for its non-existence.

My debts are numerous. The staff of all the manuscript depositories listed in the Bibliography, together with other institutions, deserve awards for patience and professionalism in suffering my presence and/or my persistence. More especially: Janet Barnes of Dr Williams's Library, London; the Reverend Dr David Cornick of the Cheshunt Foundation, Westminster College, Cambridge; Rosemary Harden of the Bath Museum of Costume; Dr A.P.W. Malcomson, Deputy Keeper of the Public Record Office of Northern Ireland, Belfast; Lavinia Foote Morid, of the Mitchell Library, Sydney, Australia; Dr Peter Nockles of the John Rylands University Library of Manchester; Christine Penney of the University of Birmingham Library; Dr Mary Robertson of the Huntington Library, San Marino; Margaret and Douglas Staplehurst of the Countess of Huntingdon Connexional Archives, Rayleigh; S.J. Taylor, of the Evangelical Library, London; and Christopher Woodward, of the Building of Bath Museum. I thank all the depositories and record offices listed in the Bibliography for kind permission to quote from their manuscript holdings, including the late Earl of Granard: he and, subsequently, Lady Georgina Forbes, have allowed me to quote from the Granard Papers, Castle Forbes, Ireland, cited as from the Public Record Office of Northern Ireland. I thank also the Earl of Dartmouth, for kind permission to quote from the Dartmouth papers in the Staffordshire Record Office. Permission to quote material in the John Rylands University Library of Manchester has been granted by courtesy of the Director and University Librarian. Permission to quote from Howell Harris's manuscript diaries has been granted by the Historical Society of the Presbyterian Church of Wales.

Further thanks are due to the Reverend Dr Oliver A. Beckerlegge, for translating portions of Charles Wesley's shorthand comments from manuscripts in John Rylands; Dr Eveline Cruickshanks for sharing her unrivalled knowledge of Jacobitism; Robert Cooper, Chief of the Inter-library Loans division of the Hugh Owen Library at the University of Wales, Aberystwyth; the Rt Reverend Dr Thomas Butler; Frank Dowling; Dr Martin Fitzpatrick; Pat Fortescue; the Reverend Dr Stephen Mayor; Wanda W. Smith; the Reverend Dr Janet Tollington; Dr Eryn White; and Professor Peter D. Marshall who read the manuscript with constructive care, for which *il est marqué A*. My wife, Elizabeth, provided endless support and nearly endless proofreading.

I have been sustained and stimulated over the past several years by the self-giving friendship and professional assistance of a small (yet appropriately zealous) group of scholars whose own research has opened vistas into various aspects of Lady Huntingdon's career: the Reverend Dr Geoffrey F. Nuttall, Dr Edwin Welch and Dr Dorothy E.S. Brown. Some debts are incapable of being refunded, and mine to them are of such coin.

The initial research was funded by a grant from the British Academy and honed by a paper presented to the Faculty of Divinity, at the University of Cambridge in 1990, resulting in the publication of '"To convert the poor people in America": the Bethesda orphanage and the thwarted zeal of the Countess of Huntingdon', *Georgia Historical Quarterly* 78 (1994), pp. 225-56. It was further developed by a paper presented to the Eighth International Congress on the Enlightenment, at the University of Bristol in 1991, resulting in the publication of '"A great mother in Israel": Selina Hastings, Countess of Huntingdon: the delineation of an eighteenth-century enthusiast', in the *Transactions* of that Congress (Oxford, 1992), pp. 444-49. To the editors of both publications I am grateful for permission to utilise portions of material which, in other forms, appeared in those articles. Subsequent research, funded by a grant from the College Research Fund of the University of Wales, Aberystwyth, led to a paper presented to the annual meeting of the Southern Historical Association, at New Orleans, in 1995.

Introduction

Reader and biographer share complementary responsibilities. Setting forth on a journey of discovery, the reader accepts the obligation of open-mindedness and receptivity to new insights, journeying as traveller rather than as tourist. The biographer's obligation is to direct the traveller's steps, pledging that what is noted and what is quoted is fully consonant with both the letter and the spirit of the original source.

Happy is the historian whose subject is not only an intriguing person but one whose story encompasses a dramatically changing period of our history, in the process directly intersecting with and influencing many of its central events and figures. When this story includes religious and social upheaval, military invasion and political turmoil, hitherto unknown covert support of the Jacobite cause, an aristocratic murderer, London in flames by the rioter's torch, religiously justified loosening of sexual mores, and much more, the mix is a compelling series of insights into a richly fertile culture.

One of the most colourful figures upon the ever-changing canvas of eighteenth-century English religion was the Countess of Huntingdon. Selina Hastings (1707-91) spans an unsettled century not only chronologically but temperamentally. She was a woman endowed with a frightening level of hyperactivity. She held an unswerving belief that the success of her various enterprises was inseparable from her personal success. As a member of the aristocracy, the Countess's social position was one upon which she ever sought to capitalise, continuing as a religious leader to expect from her followers a proper display of deference. As a woman who rejected the propriety of women preachers, she offers a salutary unpredictable test case for those interested in the history of women.

It is hardly surprising that a nation emerging weary from the religious disputations of the previous two centuries appeared in the early eighteenth century to be enjoying a 'cool' rather than a 'warm' religious period. Yet in this context it is a caricature of Anglican theology of the time to claim that its basic teaching suggested Christians to be justified before God by their performance of good works. In fact, the vast majority of Church of England clergymen did not preach works as the cause of salvation, but as the best evidences of a person's salvation. The general Anglican perception of the Christian life was a day by day pilgrimage: a whole life of 'conversion'.

The Methodists, emerging during the 1730s, believed that supine Anglican practice induced a lack of religious vitality. The Methodist remedy was to infuse faith with warm human emotions, emotions they equated with a new birth. For most Anglican leaders, the warmth thus generated threatened to rekindle old religious fires and pose a threat to the very stability of society.[1] However, not all Methodists persisted in rejecting the role of human behaviour in the scheme of salvation. Most notably, John Wesley was to modify his doctrinal position by introducing a belief in human perfection that ironically went far beyond the Anglican theological position he initially had opposed.[2] Just as Wesley was seeking new forms of expression to sustain Methodism, the Countess of Huntingdon fell back on a thorough-going Puritan Calvinism that rejected any role for good works in securing salvation. The main resulting problem was that her call for an experience of instant conversion at the sound of emotive preaching could prove seriously detrimental to a Christian life in progress. There was for her no possibility of a Christian ever securing serenity. One's will (and works) must always be broken before God. Swimming in these cross-currents, she became caught between the demand for instant conversion and the question of how such an awakened Christian could craft a pattern for an ongoing religious life. She expected – she demanded – that the true Christian would by definition have to experience a crisis of faith that would perforce prove a never-ceasing series of crises.

As our journey into the Countess's arrestingly dramatic life progresses, and her devices and desires become ever more pronounced, the link between religious and personal crises becomes inescapably forged. The Countess of Huntingdon never lived life languidly. Her personality and spiritual quest dictated the contours of her ecclesiastical endeavours. Stimulated by visions and extreme 'highs' of intense faith, she never learnt to live without them and therefore constantly sought their repetition. When they failed, as fail they did, she was brought to despair. Her story offers the most detailed and intimate account of the chemistry of conversion of all the eighteenth-century English evangelicals.

Energetically encouraged by George Whitefield, Lady Huntingdon grasped her new role as one would a new life, emerging as a matriarchal figure, known in the argot of evangelicalism as a 'Mother in Israel'. She combined her status in society with the belief that she had been specially foreordained – predestined – by God as an instrument in his hand to pull the Church of England back from apostasy. Extensive new light will be focused on the dynamics of the early Methodist movement: the jockeying for position, the fearful and startling conflicts among its main players, the painful processes of re-shaping, from amorphous beginnings to hardening forms by the latter years of the century.

Notes

1 David Hempton, 'Religion in British society, 1740-1790', in Jeremy Black (ed.), *British Politics and Society from Walpole to Pitt 1742-1789* (London, 1990), p. 202.

2 Jeffrey S. Chamberlain, 'Moralism, justification, and the controvery over Methodism', *Journal of Ecclesiastical History* 44 (1993), pp. 660, 666, 669. For the beginnings of Methodism see John Walsh, 'The origins of the evangelical revival', in G.V. Bennett and J.D. Walsh (eds.), *Essays in Modern English Church History* (London, 1966), pp. 132-62; Walsh, '"Methodism" and the origins of English speaking evangelicalism', in M.A. Noll et al. (eds.), *Evangelicalism. Comparative Studies of Popular Protestantism in North America, the British Isles and Beyond* (New York, 1994), pp. 19-37; Geoffrey F. Nuttall, 'Continental pietism and the

evangelical movement in Britain', in J.P. van den Berg and J.P. van Doren (eds.), *Pietismus und Reveil* (Leiden, 1978), pp. 207-36; Henry D. Rack, 'Religious societies and the origins of Methodism', *Journal of Ecclesiastical History* 38 (1987), pp. 582-95; W. R. Ward, 'Power and piety: the origins of religious revival in the early eighteenth century', *Bulletin of the John Rylands University Library of Manchester* 63 (1980-81), pp. 231-52; Ward, *The Protestant Evangelical Awakening* (Cambridge, 1992), Chapter 8. See also Walsh et al. (eds.), *The Church of England c. 1689 – c.1833* (Cambridge, 1993).

Chapter 1

Dressed like 'a stucco staircase'

'Lord Ferrers's daughters are now come.' Thus was Theophilus Hastings, the ninth Earl of Huntingdon, informed of the arrival at Staunton Harold, Leicestershire, of the three daughters of Washington, Earl Ferrers. The second, Lady Selina Shirley, had been born at Astwell House, in Northamptonshire, on 24 August (n.s.) 1707.[1] Called 'Liny' by her family, little is known of her early life other than the likelihood that some of it was spent in Ireland.[2] She was the child of a broken marriage, her mother leaving her and one sister with their father and taking the other to live on the continent.[3] In this family turmoil, Selina sided passionately with her father and with an equal passion rejected her mother. One of her sisters had no hesitation in describing their mother as 'vile'.[4]

Theophilus's sisters busied themselves in spying-out for him a suitable bride, one whose qualities would encompass amiability with good sense, a rank in society and a solid fortune.[5] Whatever the continuing machinations regarding the selection of his wife, it is clear that his marriage with Selina Shirley was to some extent an arranged one. Earl Ferrers had received but a moderate share of his patrimony, and there were prolonged negotiations before an acceptable financial agreement could now be struck, with Selina's severely financially straitened father forced to borrow £5,000 for the purpose.[6] Of the lawyers' busy action in this enterprise the prospective bride was none the wiser: 'The good Lady looked very pleasant so I believe heard nothing of our . . . discourse.' While Selina Shirley's grandfather, the first Earl Ferrers, had been ennobled only half a century earlier, Theophilus Hastings could boast a direct lineage back to the early sixteenth century and, more circuitously, several centuries earlier. Indeed, the Shirleys were 'sensible of the honour the family has receiv'd by so noble an alliance'.[7] Selina's mother complained bitterly that she had not been informed by her husband of the impending marriage, which took place at Staunton parish church on 3 June 1728.[8] For his part, Selina's father, relieved at the success of his negotiations, sent his new son-in-law at his Donington Park, Leicestershire, seat seventy-two bottles and a double-casked hogshead of the best port.[9] He was however a lonely man, forsaken by his wife and sorely missing the presence of his daughters. Too ill to travel from London to attend the christening of the Huntingdons' first child, and with his wife in the process of taking legal action against him,[10] two days after the christening he was dead.

For her part, the *grande dame* of Theophilus's family, his half-sister Lady Betty, had no doubts who had been responsible for the happy outcome of the marriage. She wrote several months later: 'I wish the filly be in as good order now as when I first design'd her for Donington.' Thus was the twenty-year-old bride warmly welcomed into her husband's family.[11] No less warmly was she welcomed by her husband, eleven years her senior, who upon or shortly after their wedding gave the now Selina Huntingdon a book containing highly suggestive sexual passages.[12] No prude when facing the marriage bed, the new Countess found there constant passionate fulfilment during the early years. The first child was born nine months and ten days after their wedding, the next twelve months later, the third twelve months yet again, the fourth ten months later, the last three at further intervals of two years, up to 1739. (See illustration 1.) From very early in the marriage she developed gynaecological complications, necessitating frequent long periods away from her family as she sought relief, usually at Bath.[13] Her frequent 'breeding'[14] often produced colic, but she was assured that this was to be expected 'of big bellied Ladys'.[15] None the less, her ill-health became so acute and so dangerous that at times she attempted to conceal it from her husband, though it was the theme of much of her correspondence.[16]

The Countess naturally sought the best medical advice and during the 1730s relied most heavily upon Dr George Cheyne. The Scottish-born Cheyne had centred his practice in Bath and developed an extensive clientele amongst the titled and wealthy. Reputed to be the fattest man in the kingdom, his thirty-two stone bulk loomed large in the field of medical practitioners of the age.[17] Scarcely able to walk, owing to this weight, he prescribed for himself and others a milk and vegetable diet, together with a regime of frequent purgings and vomitings. Although she sought additional medical advice, in the early years of the decade Cheyne remained her chief physician, and predictably enough he it was who encouraged her frequent sojourns at Bath, where he assured her that 'he has made my Case quite his studie'.[18] She slavishly followed his dietary regime. 'Let her live on Milk and Vegetables', the doctor prescribed, topped-up with 'Syrup of marsh mallows'.[19] 'I will venture my whole reputation on it, that you in time will be as well as all your friends could wish, and better than ever you was in your life. . . . I send you enclosed a copy of a letter I lately had from a vegetable [eater] of 72 years . . . for your encouragement to persevere.' He went on to describe another man who had thrived for twenty-two years on nothing but two quarts of milk a day and who could zestfully play six hours of cricket. Milk mixed with wheat, oats and barley was the thing, together with tea.[20] Yet not surprisingly, Cheyne's patient was becoming increasingly weary of her physician's prescriptions, not to mention his demand for constant purging.[21] Her initial belief in Cheyne's 'method' gave way to a growing suspicion that neither he nor any of the other doctors she consulted was mapping a road that would lead to her improvement.[22] She came to fear that his basic motive was to retain her as his patient and increasingly sought other medical advice, for which Cheyne chided her, especially when she seriously considered at different times going to France and Holland for treatment. In addition to Bath, the Countess took the waters at Bristol, Buxton and Scarborough.[23] By 1737 she had resumed eating white meat.[24] So concerned was Cheyne at losing Lady Huntingdon as his patient that he dedicated a book to the Earl, published in 1740. In it he stated that the Countess and her husband's half-sister, Lady Betty, had benefited from his treatments.[25] Despite his limitations, Cheyne was a not inconsiderable figure in the medical world of the first half of the century, whose weighty advice was praised by men as disparate as Samuel Johnson and John Wesley.[26]

While the Countess sought good health, absences from her husband only quickened her desire for him. 'I ever loved you to an excess of Passtion but since my absence from you I have felt greater Pains then I ever thought that Capable of giveing.' 'Could I Purpose the least Pleasure to him I should immagine whole days and nights well spent [to] Contribute one moment of satisfaction to my Dearest of lives who I love and doat on to distraction.' 'Nothing Can be more warm' than her feelings towards him: 'I Could eat you.' 'There is nothing in Heaven that I love or adore half so much as' he. She had 'the uttmost impatience to Clasp in my arms my Dear Dear Creature and assure him I am his ever faithfull Affectionate and Passtionate Lover, old Goody'.[27]

At Bath, Selina Hastings tried her luck in a lottery, her hand at the Quadrille table, her foot on the dance floor. She participated in the extensive and excessive tittle-tattle and social gossip of the time.[28] The society in which she moved calculated affairs of state and incubated affairs of heart. Yet the Countess generally complained of the wickedness of the social whirl, whether of Bath or London,[29] and yearned above all for the domestic tranquillity of Donington Park. At Bath, 'there was a grand ball last night which in my way of thinking was very stupid'. She was not impressed with Bath's beau, Richard Nash. She was positively distressed at the presence of the Earl of Breadalbane, 'much the querest wrecth I ever saw and the Dirtyest so much so I am allways affraid of geting creepers with standing near him'.[30]

The Earl and his Countess did not stint on the finery requisite to their position in aristocratic society. On one occasion, he ordered a scarlet suit of clothes and two pair of breeches, which called for large quantities of superfine cloth, 114 'rich gold wire coat buttons' and three ounces of gold thread for the button holes; a crimson damask morning gown; a crimson damask cap; and a Genoa crimson velvet cap.[31] For her part, the Countess received a shipment of over twenty-one yards 'of a most exceeding beautiful Silk of many colours' purchased for her in Paris.[32] In addition to extensive other property, the Earl owned three-quarters of the entire town of Loughborough and, close to Donington Park, nearly the whole of the town and surrounding lands of Ashby de la Zouch, together with estates in Derbyshire and Staffordshire.[33] In 1731 they leased a house outside London, the 'Grove', at Enfield Chase.[34] When in London they stayed during the summers at Enfield, while other seasons were spent in a house they leased at Savile Row, overlooking Burlington Gardens. There the Countess found 'the prettyest watter Closets I ever saw'. The Earl kept a racehorse at Newmarket, and he and his wife attended the Nottingham races. In 1738 she gave a christening party for her newly-born daughter.[35]

The Huntingdons had to grapple with serious difficulties on their Ashby estates, including financial fraud.[36] Lady Huntingdon found herself dealing personally with a number of problems faced by their tenants, as well as generally taking an active role in supervising the details of various estates, including the collection of rents.[37] Much greater anxiety was caused by the death of her father in 1729, with resulting confusion over his estate and her continuing and ever-increasing conflict with her mother. After leaving her husband, Lady Ferrers had spent much time in France, so that she was now 'quite french in all her dress'. A correspondent informed Lady Huntingdon that she had seen her mother and 'had a great deal of discourse about Travelling but she did not name any of her own famely, and yr Ladp may be sure I wou'd not begin'.[38] The enmity between Lady Ferrers and her family was well known, sharpened by the fact that the Huntingdons held high hopes of receiving £15,000 from the estate of Lady Huntingdon's father.[39] Her mother, totally excluded from the will, had other ideas, and conflict over the late Earl's estate would rage on for years. No sooner was he buried than his widow began to lodge demands on her daughters for money. She had run up 'trifling Debts', which her late husband had refused to honour. As it stood, 'one would think that it might not be difficult for ones own Children to have agreed to it without makeing it matter of publick contention'. In the process, Lady Ferrers strove to drive a wedge between her daughters.

Lady Ferrers was incensed that Lord and Lady Huntingdon had laid claim to some portraits and other items from the Ferrers' family home.[40] She wrote in 1730 protesting against Lady Huntingdon's role as one of the three executrixes of her father's estate. The Countess apparently had offered to give her mother £200 but then had reneged. Now Lady Ferrers insisted that she 'either immediately make good the promise you have made in your letter . . . which I have in my possession to produce when there shall be occasion for it, or else that you will give yr final answer to the contrary & then I shall easily determine what I have to do'. Her daughter's 'conduct in this affair will be the condition of our future good intelligence or of our never having any for the rest of our lives. . . . I am . . . resolv'd never to see nor own any of my children as such that deny me the justice that all the Laws both Human & divine entitle me to receive.' She concluded by accusing her daughter of lacking 'gratitude & good manners': it had been eight months since the birth of Lord and Lady Huntingdon's second son; but they had never informed the grandmother of the name of the child.[41] In response, Lady Huntingdon accused her mother of 'a conduct so dishonourable . . . that was . . . not to be accounted for'. In fact, having examined her father's estate, she concluded that his numerous debts made it unlikely that there would be enough money to pay for his funeral. If she would 'coolly examine the situation', her mother would 'be sensible to what straits we are drove'. Her mother was not inclined to coolness in the matter and instituted legal proceedings against her three daughters, filing a bill in Chancery.[42]

The affair had been greatly complicated by additional protestations against the will by members of Washington Ferrers' own family, especially his brother Lawrence Shirley, Lady Huntingdon's uncle. He accused her of being uncivil regarding his claims to the famous cattle at Chartley Park and wrote hotly that 'those who show no favour, nor give any Quarter, can expect but little'.[43] This conflict, entangling several branches of her father's family, issuing suits and counter-suits on both sides of the Irish Sea and involving not only courts but also parliament, continued throughout the 1730s.[44]

During the decade following her marriage, the Countess of Huntingdon gave birth to seven children, experienced frequent upheaval by absences from her family and throughout appears to have maintained an intense and lively devotion to her husband. Yet her life was turbulent, and she faced increasing ill-health, combined with ill-will in the long-running saga of her father's unsettled estate. Two very different events in 1739, separated by only a month and a half, reveal a woman edging towards the brink of some life-altering change. In January, the Prince of Wales' birthday party in London presented a picture of 'much finery'. Lady Huntingdon, bearing erect her five and a half foot frame, was the 'most extraordinary' of all present:

> her petticoat was black velvet embroidered with chenille, the pattern a large stone vase filled with ramping flowers that spread almost over a breadth of petticoat from the bottom to the top; beneath each vase of flowers was a pattern of gold shells, and foliage embossed and most heavily rich; the gown was white satin embroidered also with chenille mixt with gold ornaments, no vases on the sleeve, but two or three on the tail; it was a most laboured piece of finery, the pattern much properer for a stucco staircase than the apparel of a lady, – a mere shadow that tottered under every step she took under the load.[45]

Six weeks to the day later, on 1 March, Selina Huntingdon joined an army of aristocratic women who staged what can only be described as an assault upon the House of Lords. The context was the increasing hostility aroused over Spain's treatment of British merchant shipping which would lead shortly to the outbreak of the War of Jenkins' Ear. The political crisis in England was brought to a head in parliament, with the Walpole-led ministry attempting to win support for accommodation with Spain, the opposition under Pitt eager to push matters to war.

The resulting debates in both Houses were heated in a high degree, with the ministry in the end winning close votes, although that result did not hold for long. Given that her husband was an ardent anti-Walpole Whig, the Countess of Huntingdon, and by extension the other women with her, shared a detestation of the ministry's (and Court's) pacifying position regarding Spain.[46] The scene on the 1st of March was high farce. Given the pitch of debate during the preceding days, the Lords had decided to close its gallery to all but Commons members. However, 'a tribe of dames resolved to shew on this occasion, that neither men nor laws could resist them'. Arriving at the door at nine o'clock in the morning, 'these heroines' – Lady Huntingdon and eleven others, all but two of whom were titled ladies – were told by Black Rod that the Lord Chancellor had ruled against admitting them. The ladies 'pished at the ill-breeding of a mere lawyer' and demanded entrance. Black Rod 'swore by G__ he would not let them in'. The Duchess of Queensberry, 'as head of the squadron', with a 'noble warmth answered, by G__ they would come in, in spite of the Chancellor and the whole House'. The peers therefore 'resolved to starve them out'. Yet 'these Amazons' stood in their place until five o'clock 'without either sustenance or evacuation, every now and then playing vollies of thumps, kicks, and raps, against the door, with so much violence that the speakers in the House were scarce heard'. Then they fell to 'a dead silence of half an hour', and the Lord Chancellor, believing them to have left, had the door unbolted 'upon which they all rushed in, pushed aside their competitors' – members of the Commons who had been unable to enter because of the locked doors – 'and placed themselves in the front rows of the gallery'. They stayed there till near midnight, when the house rose; 'and during the debate gave applause, and showed marks of dislike, not only by smiles and winks . . . but by noisy laughs and apparent contempts'.[47]

One of the other ladies mentioned in that account was Mary Pendarves, and she the very one who had painted the wide-eyed description of Lady Huntingdon's party costume. Now, as a companion of the Countess and the other fervently anti-Walpole ladies, she provided a second account of the raid. The party had all gone to the Lords 'with the same intention', emboldened by their own '*unshaken intrepidity*'. Locked out, they 'bore the buffets of a stinking crowd from half an hour after ten till five in the afternoon'. When the doors had been opened the ladies stepped aside to allow the MPs to enter; then they rushed in, 'and with violent squeezing, and such a resolution as hardly was ever met with, we riggled ourselves into seats'.[48]

The Countess of Huntingdon's amazing caparison at the Prince's birthday celebrations, dressed like 'a stucco staircase', suggests at best a failure to keep abreast of the latest fashions. Her escapade as a political 'amazon' suggests that she was passing into a period of personal upheaval during which she was liable to extreme fluctuations. She was, indeed, fair set to embark on a six-year period of unparalleled and unrelenting personal crisis.

Notes

1 Lady Elizabeth Hastings to TH, 24 June [*c.* 1724], HA 4723 (quotation); G. Baker, *The History and Antiquities of Northamptonshire* (London, 1822), p. 40. The Astwell estates were owned by her father. Thomas Bayly to SH, 28 October 1729, HA 585.

2 Washington Ferrers to SH, 9 April 1728, HA 10846 (quotation); Edwin Welch, *Spiritual Pilgrim. A Reassessment of the Life of the Countess of Huntingdon* (Cardiff, 1995), p. 11.

3 Sir Richard Levinge to Washington, Earl Ferrers, 15 April 1729, HA 8273.

4 Washington, Earl Ferrers to SH, 11 July 1728, HA 10847; Lady Elizabeth Nightingale to SH, 17 July [1729], HA 9713 (quotation). All the sisters became bitterly estranged from their maternal grandparents. Sir Richard Levinge to Washington, Earl Ferrers, 15 April 1729, HA 8273. For the family backgrounds of the Shirleys and the Hastings, see Welch, *Spiritual Pilgrim*, pp. 7-13, 16-19.

5 Lady Elizabeth Hastings to TH, 6 July 1727, HA 4725.

6 Sir Richard Levinge to Washington, Earl Ferrers, 15 April 1729, HA 8273; Marriage settlement, 31 May 1728; Security for payment to TH from Washington Shirley, Earl

Ferrers, 1 June 1728, HAP, Box 29, folders 11 & 12. See also Extract from marriage settlement, 22 October 1728, *ibid.*, folder 13.

7 Leonard Piddocke to TH, [3 May] 1728, HA 10208; Laurence Shirley to TH, 4 June 1728, DE23/1/1421, LRO.

8 Mary, Countess Ferrers to TH, 16 April [1728], DE23/1/1420, LRO; [Evelyn Philip Shirley], *Stemmata Shirleiana; or the Annals of the Shirley Family* (London, 1873), p. 192n.

9 Washington, Earl Ferrers to SH, 16 September 1728, 14D32/57, LRO. He was congratulated for managing to place two of his daughters 'in sufficient prosperity, & above any future danger of all fall'. Sir Richard Levinge to Washington, Earl Ferrers, 15 April 1729, HA 8273. The other daughter was Selina's elder sister, Elizabeth, who was married in 1725 to Joseph Gascoigne Nightingale. The youngest sister, Mary, married Viscount Kilmorey a year after her father's death. On arranged marriages of the upper classes, see Bridget Hill, *Women, Work, and Sexual Politics in Eighteenth-century England* (Oxford, 1989), p. 176.

10 Washington, Earl Ferrers to TH, 14 December 1728, 11 April 1729; same to SH, 12 April 1729, 14D32/58, 62, 63, LRO.

11 Lady Elizabeth Hastings to TH, 16 January [1729], HA 4728 (quotation); Lady Frances Hastings to SH, 4 May 1728, E1/1/2, CF.

12 [William King], *The Art of Cookery In Imitation of Horace's Art of Poetry* (London, [1708]). Far from being a cookbook, its 160 pages contain such morsels as:

> The French our Relish help, and well supply
> The want of things too gross by Decency.
> Our Fathers most admir'd their Sauces sweet,
> And often ask'd for Sugar with their Meat;
> They butter'd Currants on fat Veal bestow'd,
> And Rumps of Beef with Virgin Honey strew'd.
> ....
> Bess Hoy first found it troublesome to bawl,
> And therefore plac'd her Cherries on a Stall;
> Her Currants there and Gooseberries were spread,
> With the enticing Gold of Ginger-bread.

pp. 99-100. See also pp. 43-45. The new bride inscribed the book, now in NLW, 'S: Huntingdon given me by my dear Lord 1728.'

13 For example, SH to TH, 30 March 1731/2, Drew A10.

14 George Cheyne to SH, 28 December 1734, 14D32/367, LRO.

15 Lady Elizabeth Hastings to SH, 16 January [*c.* 1731], HA 4736. See also Lady Susanna Stanhope to SH, 27 November 1738, HA 12634.

16 For example, Lady Frances Hastings to SH, [*c.* 1735], HA 4990; Mary, Duchess of Norfolk to SH, 3 December 1737, HA 6918.

17 On Cheyne, see Charles F. Mullett (ed.), *The Letters of Dr. George Cheyne to the Countess of Huntingdon* (San Marino, Calif., 1940), 'Introduction'; David Shuttleton, '"My owne crazy carcase": the life and works of Dr George Cheyne 1672-1743', Ph.D. thesis, University of Edinburgh, 1992.

18 Lady Elizabeth Hastings to TH, 26 June [*c.* 1730], HA 4732; same to SH, 18 March 1731/2, 14D32/200, LRO; SH to TH, 30 March 1731/2, Drew A10 (quotation).

19 George Cheyne to TH, 29 August 1734, 14D32/366, LRO; same to SH, [*c.* 1730], HA 1380.

20 George Cheyne to SH, 15 April 1734 (quotation), 3 November 1735, HA 1397, 1405; 28 December 1734, 14D32/367, LRO.

21 George Cheyne to SH, 28 December 1734, 14D32/367, LRO.

22 SH to TH, 18 March 1731/2, Drew A9; Lady Elizabeth Hastings to SH, [25 December *c.* 1735], HA 4753.

23 George Cheyne to SH, 25 February 1736/7, HA 1408 (of the thirty or so letters written by doctor to patient, all but five were in the first half of the decade); Lady Elizabeth Hastings to TH, 7 June 1735, HA 4751; SH to TH [Spring 1736], 14D32/78, LRO; David Garrick to Capt. Peter Garrick, 16 June 1733, D.M. Little and G.M. Kahrl (eds.), *The Letters of David Garrick* 3 vols. (London, 1963), 1:4-5; Lady Margaret Hastings to SH, 25 September 1733, HA 5831.

24 George Cheyne to SH, 20 August 1737, HA 1409.

25 George Cheyne, *Essay on Regimen. Together with five Discourses, medical, Moral, and Philosophical* (London, 1740). He wrote to Lady Huntingdon that at first he had designed to dedicate it to her but thought better of it 'because of the uncommonness and abstractedness of many things in it, and because it is chiefly designed for learned and philosophical men'. George Cheyne to SH, 19 May 1739, HA 1410.

26 Mullet, *Letters of Cheyne*, 'Introduction', pp. xxii-iii.

27 SH to TH, 19 February 1731, 8 March 1731/2; 5, 29 April 1732, Drew A3, 7, 14b, 19.

28 SH to TH, 14 February 1731, Drew A1 (quotation); Anne, Countess of Strafford to SH, 22 November 1731, HA 13204; Joseph Nightingale to SH, 24 December 1731, HA 9714; Anna-Maria Brown to SH, 3 August 1734, HA 1067; Countess of Strafford to SH, 29 April 1731, HA 13200; Mary, Lady Curzon to SH, 25 January 1732, HA 1848.

29 SH to TH, 28 February 1731/2, Drew A6; Lady Frances Hastings to SH, 21 January 1730, HA 4985.

30 SH to TH, 12 April 1732, Drew A17; SH to TH, 23 February 1733, HMC *Hast.*, 3:11.

31 Bill of Peter Careme in account with the Earl of Huntingdon, 17 March 1732/3, HMC *Hast.*, 1:416.

32 John Wright to SH, 27 October 1731, HA 13671.

33 William Gardiner to TH, 2 December 1744, HA 3372; Arthur Crane, *The Kirkland Papers 1753-1869* (Ashby de la Zouch, 1990), p. 102; Survey of Estates, 1732, 14D32/471, LRO. In 1732 he received a remarkable letter from Virginia, strongly urging him to seek the governorship of the colony. Mr Corbin to TH, 3 November 1732, 14D32/504, LRO. Corbin was a distant cousin of Lady Huntingdon. [Aaron C.H. Seymour] *The Life and Times of Selina, Countess of Huntingdon* 2 vols. (London, 1839), 1:6.

34 Lady Mary Hastings to SH, 27 December 1731, HA 5828.

35 SH to TH, 29 [August] 1734, Drew A20 (quotation); Lord Gower to TH, 16 November 1734, DE12/1/1426, LRO; Mary, Viscountess Kilmorey to SH, [*c.* 1739], HA 9564; J.J. Cartwright, *The Wentworth Papers* (London, 1883), p. 535.

36 Sir George Beaumont to TH, 15 November 1731, HA 655.

37 For example, George Jennings to SH, 21 October 1729, HA 7798; John Blake to SH, 27 July 1737, HA 770.

38 Anne, Countess of Strafford to SH, 2 November 1730, 14D32/517, LRO; same to SH, 19 November 1730, HA 13197.

39 Will of Washington, Earl Ferrers, P.C.C. 197 'Abbott', Principal Probate Registry, London, printed in Matthew Francis, 'Selina, Countess of Huntingdon (1707-1791)', B.Litt. thesis, University of Oxford, 1957, pp. A150-55. See also Thomas Bayly to SH, 28 October 1729, HA 585.

40 Mary, Countess Ferrers to SH, 26 August 1729, HA 10830; same to James Campbell, 27 December 1729, HA 10831.

41 Mary, Countess Ferrers to SH, 18 or 19 November 1730, HA 10634.

42 SH to Mary, Countess Ferrers, [November or December 1730], HA 5845 (quotation); [SH to same, early 1730s], 14D32/272, LRO; Lawrence Shirley to Leonard Piddocke, 20 January 1733, HA 10819.

43 Lawrence Shirley to SH, 17 December 1729, HA 10818.

44 For example, 'Lords Com[m]ittees appointed to consider of a Bill', 27 March 1730, Hastings Correspondence, Parliament Box 4, folder 42, Huntington; 'Of Wittnesses taken at Carrickmascross...1735...in a Cause depending in his Majestys High Court of Chancery', D 3531/A/4, PRONI; Lawrence Shirley to TH, 9 January 1734, HA 10820; Thomas Bayly to SH, 5 August 1738, HA 617; Between Selina Countess Dowager.Ferrers & others – Mr Laurence Shirley Esqr. & others...Debts, 3 May 1739, Hastings Legal Papers, Box 20, folder 10, Huntington.

45 Mary Pendarves to Ann Granville, 23 January 1738/9, Lady Llanover (ed.), *The Autobiography and Correspondence of Mary Granville Mrs Delany*, first series, 3 vols. (London, 1861), 2:28. Her height has been calculated from a collection of her dresses now in the Bath Museum of Costume.

46 For the Earl of Huntingdon's opposition to the King and his ministry in this affair, which came to a head on the day of the ladies' invasion, see Leo Francis Stock (ed.), *Proceedings and Debates of the British Parliaments Respecting North America* 5 vols. (Washington, D.C., 1924-41), 4:686-88.

47 Lady Mary Wortley Montagu to Lady Pomfret [March 1739], Robert Halsband (ed.), *The Complete Letters of Lady Mary Wortley Montagu* 3 vols. (Oxford, 1965-67), 2:135-37.

48 Lady Llanover, *Autobiography and Correspondence of Mary Granville*, 2:44-45. For the debate see *Journal of the House of Lords*, 25:307-9; William Cobbett (comp.), *Parliamentary History of England from...1066 to 1803* 36 vols. (London, 1806-20), 10:1091-1246; James E. T. Rogers (ed.), *A Complete Collection of the Protests of the Lords* 3 vols. (Oxford, 1875), 1:481-85. See also A.S. Turberville, *The House of Lords in the XVIIIth Century* (Oxford, 1927), pp. 238-40.

CHAPTER 2

'Oh! the distress of my soul'

Nothing is known of Selina Shirley's religious attitudes as a girl, apart from the suggestion that she was 'uncommonly desirous of attending funeral solemnities particularly those of children'.[1] As the Countess of Huntingdon, throughout the first decade of her marriage she pursued a religious life typical in the Church of England, aiming at the performance of good works and living a moral life. She supported religious enterprises on her husband's estates and dutifully busied herself in charities. She ordered a set of communion plate for the family's parish church at Castle Donington and secured Bibles, Books of Common Prayer and other Christian literature, including two dozen copies of *The Whole Duty of Man*, presumably for use on the Huntingdons' estate.[2] She took seriously the nobility's responsibility to help their tenants 'live & act agreeable to their Christian Profession'. She recommended two possible candidates for the Deanery of Windsor. She was asked to give advice to a young man planning to attend Eton on how to protect his morals.[3] At home or away, she regularly attended services of worship.

Lady Huntingdon took under her 'protection' a charity school at Melbourne, Derbyshire, which had been built by her sister-in-law, Lady Betty Hastings. The school was for poor boys and girls aged eight to twelve, to prepare them as servants or apprentices, and the Countess assumed responsibilities from engaging clergymen to inspect the children's progress to providing a house for the Master.[4] She contributed ten guineas for Thomas Coram's London Foundling Hospital. Further afield, she took an interest in foreign missions. Beginning in 1729 she subscribed ten guineas a year to the Anglican Society for Promoting Christian Knowledge and was informed that it was sending books and money to missionaries in Madras and Tranquebar and had hopes of taking useful action in such places as Russia, Poland and Hungary.[5] In the voluminous correspondence of the 1730s the only other reference to her religious interests is a letter from a man who had promised to notify her when a noted Quakeress was to preach near London. However, this does not necessarily indicate anything more than curiosity on the Countess's part, since an invitation to the Quakeress to preach at Court before the Queen six months earlier had created a stir.[6]

Religious conversion never clearly starts with a beginning: there is always an antecedent. What led to Lady Huntingdon's 'conversion' to Methodism was a combination of increasing anxieties – religious, emotional, health, family and financial. It took place during a period when she was telling correspondents that she had 'lived a life so disagreeable' to herself.[7] The unresolved difficulties over her father's estate had finally driven a wedge between her and her two sisters.[8] The matter had come to the Chancery court in 1738, where the sisters and their families had been ordered to pay substantial claims laid by her mother and other members of the Shirley family. All this led the Countess to make dark 'reflections . . . upon human Life. . . . Consideration must shew us the emptiness of all sublunary things without using this life as the way and means to lead us to a better.'[9] These considerations did not however hinder Lord and Lady Huntingdon in their attempt to have the Chancery decision overturned, and the running battle continued well into the 1740s, with increasing tension between the Huntingdons and the Countess's sisters and their families.[10]

These financial conflicts played a significant part in Lady Huntingdon's turning to a more 'unworldly' religious orientation. This conclusion is supported by the crisis surrounding the death of her husband's half-sister, Lady Betty Hastings. Early in her life, Elizabeth Hastings had inherited extensive property, including the family seat of Ledston Park, near Pontefract in Yorkshire, where she permanently resided in benevolent spinsterhood. Her beauty and refinement had been widely eulogised by many, including Congreve and Steele in the *Tatler*. William Law considered her a peculiar example of piety. Lady Betty subscribed widely and liberally, pouring most of her largess on educational and Church of England enterprises. To the Church she was deeply committed and in particular generously supported poor scholars from the north of England in their training for the ministry at Queen's College, Oxford, exhibitions which she established in 1737.[11] Lady Betty had also taken an interest in some of the zealous young Methodists at Oxford. According to George Whitefield, she had in 1736 'allowed some of them two or three small exhibitions'. He too 'partook of her ladyship's bounty'.[12] Yet Lady Betty Hastings increasingly came to view the activities of the Methodists in a less sanguine light. Although Whitefield appeared desirous of serving God, wrote one of her correspondents whom she had asked for 'a character' of Whitefield, 'he is proud, and dont know it, nay has spiritual pride, which is the worst sort'. The correspondent had heard him preach, and 'why Mr Whitfield is so followed for his preaching I cant imagine. . . . I can see nothing in him to be so much admired.'[13]

The relationship between Lady Betty and the Countess had always been cordial, even warm, the two women maintaining a regular correspondence.[14] Lady Betty's letters displayed a kindly yet not overly-pious nature. In fact, her first letter that dwelt on religious sentiments was written precisely at the time when the Countess was altering her religious stance. She observed that Lady Huntingdon and her husband had made a 'vigerous Start' in a new-found religious orientation.[15] The Countess had written of the Earl that 'the scriptures are become his whole study and I do think he has truly a humble heart and I am fully persuaded he does not think himself possessed of the least degree of merit. . . . I feel every day there is no delight and pleasure in this world equal to the conviction of pious souls. It raises the heart so much above all earthly things.' These changes had occurred at the very time, in June 1739, when Lady Huntingdon was suffering from 'extreem illness'.[16] In any case, 'her whole family says she is a new creature'.[17]

To assist in consolidating this religious advance, Lady Betty called upon her close clerical adviser, the Reverend Thomas Barnard, Master of the Leeds Grammar School. For a brief period during the summer and early autumn of 1739 Barnard entered into a supportive correspondence with Lady Huntingdon. Because of the 'full Awakenings, and strong Convictions' she was experiencing, he felt it necessary to attempt to 'provide for your Ladyship's stability'. His letters were models of maturity: he urged her to consider her pilgrimage a gradual growth in grace. She should certainly 'observe Moderation in all Things, nor be hurried on with too much Eagerness in the spiritual combat'. She should take care to avoid being ruled by her passions, whether of grief or joy. She should not attempt to practice prayer and meditation much more than she previously had done, but to 'see that your Heart is toucht with 'em. . . . Cause all your Sentiments, Tempers, Affections, words and actions as near as you can to hold Correspondency with your Prayers.' He counselled her to seek God's will quietly and with patience. 'According to your Ladyship's spirit' will be the progress she would be able to make. She had set 'Rules' for herself, and he called on her to keep them, but only if she did not 'sicken at any part of your external Life'. It was necessary to remain in the same relationship with her former friends and acquaintances.[18] It is suggestive that these letters were written to Lady Huntingdon alone, with no hint that her husband was joining in her spiritual pilgrimage, although his sisters at Ledston firmly believed that he was.[19]

Thomas Barnard's role as spiritual midwife to the reborn Countess of Huntingdon was short-lived. Within less than a month she had ceased actively seeking his advice. From Ledston, gentle words informed her that Barnard mentioned that 'his Correspondence with your Ladyship seems to be in a declining state'. For their part, the Ledston ladies knew of no better 'director in Spirituals than Mr Barnard'. His holy zeal was combined with 'good Judgment', without which they had seen otherwise zealous Christians 'run themselves a ground . . . and in the end have done disservice to Christianity'. Most important, both Barnard and Lady Betty rejected field preaching.[20] These were coded messages, clearly conveying the fear that the Countess's zeal was outrunning her judgement. Barnard had misread Lady Huntingdon's needs. When she wrote to him that she 'wou'd undergoe every Thing to come to the true Knowledge of my only saviour' he replied that it was a generally-held opinion that she had never been at any great distance from God in the first place and that whatever difficulty she would have in becoming a true Christian was probably 'but little'. How little he knew the woman. Barnard came to see – in what appears to be their final exchange – 'that your Spirit now stript of much of its old Cloathing, is become exceeding tender and of most exquisite Feeling, and susceptive of every Harm'. That was the correct reading, but now it was too late for him to assist, especially so when he went on to tell her that he and many others expected her to be a Lady Betty *redivivus*.[21]

The time was fast approaching when the Countess of Huntingdon would have no desire to be associated with Lady Betty Hastings. Not only had the Countess's sister-in-law firmly rejected field preaching but, just as firmly, the nascent Methodist movement as a whole. To Lady Betty the ideal clergyman was a 'Gentleman' who maintained 'very Good Sense' and who led 'an Exemplary Life'.[22] This was not the direction in which the Countess of Huntingdon's religious zeal was pointing. Moreover, it appeared to her that Lady Betty had contrived to deprive the Huntingdons of a rich inheritance. In the spring of 1738 she had had a cancerous breast removed and over the following year and a half suffered increasing medical complications. By the autumn of 1739 it was clear to her physicians and family that Lady Betty was dying. With Lady Huntingdon confined at Donington prior to giving birth to her final child, her sister-in-law died at Ledston just before Christmas.[23]

Prior to her death, Lady Betty had been actively seeking 'a Religious good man' to serve as the Huntingdons' domestic chaplain.[24] Yet whatever spiritual blessings she intended to bequeath them were far outweighed by the paucity of her material bequest. She left the bulk of her vast wealth to her charities, especially schools and Queen's College, Oxford.[25] In a complicated personal will, her remaining estate went to her spinster half-sisters, the Ladies Anne, Frances and Margaret – Theophilus's sisters – to whom she gave the extensive Ledston properties and the contents of Ledston house, together with numerous holdings in Yorkshire. In addition, she left Margaret an annuity, or a lump sum of £3,000 if she married within five years, and £5,000 to the descendants of her late grandfather. Her three half-sisters were to be executrixes of the will. To Lord Huntingdon and his male heirs, Lady Betty left the payment of rents in Sussex and elsewhere. In addition, after the deaths of all her half-sisters, the Ledston estates were to go to the Huntingdons' eldest son, Francis, and his legitimate heirs. If Lady Margaret forfeited her £3,000 by not marrying in time, the Huntingdons' elder daughter, Elizabeth, was to receive £1,000, but 'not otherwise'. The Earl of Huntingdon was named as one of six trustees to administer the provisions of the will.[26]

Theophilus and Selina Huntingdon were shocked and devastated. An unsuspecting correspondent condoled with her at Lady Betty's death and proceeded to comment: 'I hope she has left her estate where she ought to have. . . . I should be glad to know, as it will give me the greatest pleasure to know my Lord has got it.' Lord Huntingdon had not got it, and his wife had no hesitation in writing letters to various acquaintances bitterly complaining about the treatment they had received. 'I am sorry to have one part of Nando's letter that you wrote him. I think the justest charity L[ady] B[etty] could have done was to have it where everybody wished, to my L[or]d: but I never will have a good oppinion of over Religious people.' 'What your Ladyp mention[ed] in your letter has putt me quite out of temper ever since, and though it is now over . . . I . . . must beg all your pardons in calling it a wicked action . . . leading you all along into the beliefe' that Lord Huntingdon would be the main beneficiary of the will. 'When I dye may no such good works follow me.'[27]

Thus any grief felt at Lady Betty's death was balanced by the Huntingdons' anguish over her will. There is little doubt that the Methodistic turning they had taken riled Lady Betty, and Lady Huntingdon nursed the firm belief that her sister-in-law's clerical advisers, including Thomas Barnard, had exerted strong influence over her. After less than four months under Barnard's supervision at Leeds, the Huntingdons removed their second son, George, to join his elder and younger brothers at school in London.[28] Another of Lady Betty's clerical advisers to earn high displeasure was Martin Benson, Bishop of Gloucester. Close to Theophilus for many years, the Earl had made Benson one of his domestic chaplains as early as 1714, and over the years they had remained exceptionally fast friends.[29] During the period of her illness, he frequently visited Lady Betty, 'to the true satisfaction of every body here & particularly of the good Lady who I believe has a great regard for him'. At her death he organised the funeral.[30]

As Bishop of Gloucester it was Benson who had ordained George Whitefield both as deacon and as priest. That latter ordination had taken place at the beginning of 1739, and the Bishop now ruefully regretted the action. Believing that Whitefield had understood he was being ordained to serve a parish, Benson had been shocked at the young ordinand's flouting of church law by his invasion of various parishes and his concomitant vilifying of ministers, men Whitefield considered to be unregenerate. During the summer of 1739 the two had exchanged critical letters. Whitefield said that he had 'written to the Bishop of Gloucester, and have delivered my soul, by meekly telling him of his faults'.[31] Meekness lies in the eye of the reader. If Whitefield was guilty for preaching out of a parish, he wrote that 'your Lordship equally offends when you preach out of your own diocese'. 'I hope your Lordship will inspect into the lives of your other Clergy, & censure them for being Over-remiss, as much as you censure me for being Over-righteous. It is their falling from their Articles, & not preaching the truth as it is in Jesus, that has excited the present zeal of (what they in derision call) the Methodist Preachers.' 'If you & the rest of the Bishops cast us out, our Great & Common Master will take us up.' Benson was shocked: 'I wish I had been able to say any thing at any time to you, as I sincerely wish you well, wch might persuade you to alter your conduct & apply your zeal to the care of that District to wch you were ordained & appointed.' He had expressed his 'dislike & disapprobn of your behaviour & proceedings since the time of your ordination'.[32]

As he visited Lady Betty in her final illness, Benson would certainly have displayed his burnt fingers and have contributed to, or confirmed, her rejection of irregular preachers. Indeed, Lady Huntingdon was in no doubt that her new-found religious orientation and the family's financial misfortune were closely intertwined. Five months after the fateful will, she was writing of Benson to her husband, that 'I wish the power of the Gospel had routed . . . his heart'. Sometime later she was in London with the Archbishop of

Canterbury, John Potter, and 'who should Come [in] but the Bishop of Gloster and I think I never saw such surprize and Confusion in a face when he saw me. . . . By his looks one might believe [he thought] the arch Bishop and I ware . . . the Danger of the Church.'[33] The Huntingdons had no further contact with Martin Benson.

Effectively disinherited by her husband's family, Lady Huntingdon simultaneously clashed with her own. As late as November 1739 she had maintained a friendly relationship with her sister Mary. Yet only months later all turned to bitterness. Mary accused her of colluding with their elder sister against her in the tangle over their father's estate. The Huntingdons' legal adviser was 'a very great rogue', an 'ignorant impertinant solicitor'. Selina was now the butt of many jokes owing to her association with the Methodists. 'I'm concerned to think my dr Sister . . . should encourage such a crashing set of people' who pass 'uncharitable censures on them that are not in the same way of thinking'. She hoped that 'God almighty who once endued you with a very good understanding will disperse the mist that now hangs before you & restore you to yr former right way of judging'.[34] For her part, Lady Huntingdon found her sister increasingly frivolous and worldly, acting like a fifteen-year-old, exhibiting 'extreem folly vanity madness'.[35]

Lady Huntingdon's new religious orientation was being moulded by those Methodistic influences so firmly rejected by Lady Betty just before her death. Ironically, these influences had emerged most vividly within the midst of Lady Betty's immediate family at Ledston. The Reverend Benjamin Ingham, who had been one of the members of John Wesley's 'Holy Club' at Oxford, had come under the influence of the German-based pietist group, the Moravians, and set about to evangelise his native Yorkshire. By 1739 he had established some forty groups of followers.[36] All this excited the particular interest of Lady Margaret Hastings, Theophilus's youngest sister, who often enthused to the Countess over Ingham's work. Thus, when she received word about Lady Huntingdon's religious awakening, Lady Margaret lost no time in writing to that 'Humble good Man', from whom she herself had 'reaped Great advantages'. Ingham spent the entire month of August 1739 at Donington Park,[37] and the Countess arranged for him to preach at the local parish church, probably a sermon on 'the New Birth'. When the Huntingdons' parish minister was offended by it, Lady Margaret hoped that the Countess would 'pray more earnestly for his conversion', while, on the contrary, Lady Betty advised her to 'carry Just the same to him as before this happened'.[38]

Benjamin Ingham had drawn Lady Margaret enthusiastically into support for the Moravians and their foreign missions and now began soliciting such funds from Lady Huntingdon, in return sending her a collection of Moravian hymns. Lady Betty's reservations regarding Ingham's aggressive field-preaching, as well, no doubt, of his Moravianism, combined with the staggering provisions of the will, drew Lady Huntingdon all the more to his support. Lady Margaret bombarded her with further glowing reports of Moravian activities, and Lord and Lady Huntingdon sent twenty guineas for their orphanage at Herrenhut.[39] They sought the prayers of these German

Moravians that they might be truly converted, and the Countess desired a physician of Moravian persuasion to live at Donington and to serve among the ill and the poor.[40]

At the Countess's instigation, she and her husband received visits from other leading Moravians. One, James Hutton, gave a sharp insight into the Huntingdons' religious attitudes towards the end of 1740. The Countess had a 'great liking' of the Moravians. She was 'more eager to hear the Gospel than any one I ever saw before', but of 'poor sinnership and of the Saviour she has not much to say'. 'She does not lack good sense, but has a very violent temper; her lady's maid, however, tells me she has not been in a passion for more than twelve months.' None the less, Hutton still found her to be 'of a choleric and violent temper'. When they were joined by the Earl, Hutton found him 'not yet awakened, being unable to distinguish the difference between the preaching of the clergy and that of ourselves'.[41]

Lady Huntingdon's Ingham-led Moravian orientation was however heading towards an abrupt halt. After Lady Betty's death it had been decided that Lady Margaret would come to live with the Huntingdons at Donington, where they would all 'be united in Christ for Ever'.[42] However, Lady Margaret soon made other plans. By the spring, the Countess told her husband that she had 'some uneasiness upon my spirits about L-y M-te. I fear she will not return to Donington with me but do not speak of this.' That letter was written from Ledston. In the aftermath of the débâcle of the will, Lady Betty's remaining sisters, knowing of the Huntingdons' bitter disappointment, suggested that the Countess assume the management of that estate.[43] The Huntingdons accepted this arrangement and spent extended periods of time at Ledston over the next few years. Lady Betty had left no money for its upkeep and, pressed financially, they nearly sold their Enfield house for funds to maintain Ledston for the future use of Francis. In the event, they gave up the Savile Row house but managed to maintain a base in central London by renting a house in Downing Street, presumed to be what is now the official residence of the Chancellor of the Exchequer.[44] In all these anxious financial and household affairs Lady Huntingdon assumed her share – more than her share – of practical duties. From Ledston she wrote to her husband: 'Can't say but it humbles me very much that I Cannot set foot on a piece of Ground I Can Call yours or yet one of our Childrens.' Lady Margaret had expressed to her the wish that 'God Grant that None of her Surviving relations may displease him by their behaviour on this trying Occasion'. Nothing should be allowed 'to give the least Disturbance to the Unspeakable Happiness' to the spirit of the departed Lady Betty.[45]

Not only did Lady Margaret's part in the immediate inheritance of Ledston offend the Huntingdons: she soon seemed poised to deprive their daughter Elizabeth of her inheritance.[46] Constant letters during 1739 and 1740 had sung Lady Margaret's song of praise for Ingham, who 'seems to abound in Charity to Me'.[47] Charity now took a different turn. As early as May 1740 their relationship was the stuff of gossip. 'The news I have heard from London is, Lady Margaret Hastings having disposed of herself to a poor wandering methodist.'[48] For a year and a half Lady Margaret's family remonstrated with her. Not least did Lord and Lady Huntingdon express their displeasure. Ingham might be a valuable religious guide, but as a member of the Hastings family he was definitely below stairs. Although it would not be sinful, 'prudant it is not'.[49] Constantly the would-be bride attempted to persuade Lady Huntingdon of the propriety of her marriage plans, based on the religious qualities of her intended husband. She mused that 'Jesus Christ came into the world to form unto himself a People . . . yt should be strangers to the Lusts of the flesh by studying in the body the Life of Angels – yet should have no need of divorce as being able . . . to bear with patience all the Evils of a married state'.[50] Meanwhile, rejected by Lady Margaret's sisters at Ledston and their local vicar, the couple desperately sought a clergyman who would grant them a marriage licence.[51] Finally, in November 1741 the forty-one year old Lady Margaret and Ingham, twelve years her junior, were wed. When she wrote to Lady Huntingdon the following month, Lady Margaret Ingham did not 'so much as mention . . . his name' nor that of her sisters.[52] This letter, which reveals Lady Margaret's break in relations with her family, acknowledged that they will 'all live together tho not in time yet in Eternity'. In clear Moravian terminology she appealed to the 'Sufferings of our Dear Lord'. 'May we eat his flesh and drink his Blood . . . His Precious Blood.'[53] Lady Huntingdon found that her sister-in-law's behaviour 'quite shocks one'. 'O how I lament poor Sister Margrate', she wrote shortly after the marriage. The Countess had been bombarded with questions in Bath and found it gave 'great trouble' to 'all the religious people' there, 'as it may prove a stumbling block to the weak'. The scandal was all the more damaging since it was clear that Ingham and Lady Margaret had lived together for some time before they married.[54]

The Huntingdons' lament was monetary as well as moral. Lady Margaret had managed to marry before the deadline set in Lady Betty's will, thus depriving their young daughter Elizabeth of her inheritance. Dispute with Lady Margaret over the matter proved futile.[55] She had obtained a husband, and Ingham had secured the funds necessary to establish a Moravian centre near Halifax and, a few years later, near Pudsey, the Moravian settlement of Fulneck. His wife also provided him with a house at Aberford, about sixteen miles from York. Eight months after their marriage Ingham formally placed all his societies under Moravian control.[56]

The Countess's resentment of Ingham brought her adherence to Moravianism to a halt at the very time Ingham and John Wesley were parting company on theological grounds. Her personal reasons for rejecting Ingham dovetailed neatly into her religious quest. Initially close colleagues from Oxford days, Wesley and Ingham began to sever relations in 1740 over Moravian 'stillness': a person not possessed of total and complete faith should cease from all effort, including worship, and merely wait upon God in contemplation.[57] One of the Moravian leaders was a German bishop who had deeply influenced both Ingham and Wesley. August Spangenberg, fully supported by Ingham, was espousing the stillness doctrine.[58] Focusing now on John and Charles Wesley as potential religious mentors, Lady

Huntingdon initiated a correspondence with John in the spring of 1741. Her first letter appears to have been on the 2nd of April, and he was with her and Theophilus at their Enfield home on seven occasions during the spring and summer.[59] (See illustration 8.) Later in the year the Countess reported to him from London that 'the still ones are not without their attacks. . . . They have by one of their agents pressed me very much to see Span[genberg], but I have taken no sort of notice, as if I had [not] received it.' Concerned lest John's brother Charles be infected with their teaching, she hoped that John would 'approve a step with respect to them your brother and I have taken, no less than his declaring open war with them'. She had given him 'free liberty' to use her name 'as the instrument in God's hand that had delivered him from them'. To Charles she wrote that he must 'trample on man & divils'.[60]

Thus at the very point of rejecting Ingham, Lady Margaret and their Moravianism, the Countess of Huntingdon fervently aligned herself with the Wesleys. John was 'a chosen vessel, and set for the defence of the Gospel'.[61] She desired that he '& your Brother might think on me as you would do on no one else!' She wrote to their mother, a letter accompanied by a gift of Madeira. In reply, Mrs Wesley was 'much pleasd, that they have in any means been serviceable to yr Ladisp'. It was a relationship that held reciprocal advantages. For her part, Lady Huntingdon laid hold on John Wesley's belief in Christian perfection, a notion the Moravians had rejected. Perfection was a doctrine she 'hope[d] to live and die by; it is absolutely the most complete thing I know'. God demanded nothing less 'than entire purification of soul'.[62]

At expense to her health, the Countess was constantly reading religious works to her servants, and friends were concerned that she was attempting 'to make too much haste to perfection'.[63] She asked John Wesley if she had his permission to 'explain the scripture' to those about her and to 'put them in [a] band. May I venture upon such an office?'[64] She wanted to establish a utopian community. 'I am sure it must be a town of our own building [secure?] in property to us alone that the few souls who are . . . now scattered may become a household to the Lord. . . . I have by [me] a plan for this purpose.' God's 'own should not be scattered as sheep that had no shepherd & together be able to make a stand against the powers of Satan'.[65] Farther afield she was witnessing to 'the fine Ladys at Bath', also hoping for the conversion of Beau Nash. Although she had put her medical custom in other hands, she still maintained social contact with George Cheyne, providing him with religious prescriptions. 'The people of Bath sayes I have made him a methodist.' However, Cheyne, who held serious misgivings about Methodism, especially regarding its potentially socially disruptive effects, through his commitment to mysticism probably influenced her own religious orientation. She was being encouraged to 'be an instrument' in God's 'hand to open the eyes of thousands of those whom the God of this world has blinded'.[66] Her religious fluctuation is striking. A school she had supported at Markfield, Leicestershire, she now 'lay aside', dismissing all its masters. She wrote that a school would 'never answer the end of bringing forth any of the Gospel fruits of holiness, till the parents are first made Christians'. She was willing to support a schoolmaster only 'among those people who are awakened'.[67]

During much of the period of her initial association with the Wesleys, from 1741 to 1743, the Countess was frankly fevered. The continuing frantic financial squabbles over Lady Betty's will and the Ferrers family inheritance, further complicated by the death of Lady Huntingdon's mother in Paris at the beginning of 1740 and conflict with her own sisters,[68] produced fertile ground for a deepening of the roots of her personal religious crisis. Further fall-out from Lady Betty's will had involved Lord and Lady Huntingdon in conflict with another of his sisters, the mentally unstable Lady Catherine Wheler. With a devotion to her husband's position in society matched only by her undisguised acquisitiveness, Lady Catherine had been active since before Lady Betty's death in ensuring that she and her husband profited substantially from the estate. In fact, in the end the Ledston properties were to fall to the Wheler family. Lady Catherine's husband, Granville Wheler, who had taken Holy Orders in 1737 and was given a living by Lord Huntingdon, increasingly earned the Huntingdons' displeasure. On one occasion, an invitation to dine was accompanied with a request that the Huntingdons bring their own meat for the meal. More serious was the Huntingdons' resentment towards the Whelers over the inheritance, and, in the Countess's case, because of their rejection of Methodism.[69] Burdened with 'worldly affairs', Lady Huntingdon began judging the Christianity of others by the amount of 'the spirit of this world' she perceived in them.[70]

In addition, the Huntingdons' eldest son, the twelve-year-old Francis, was having serious difficulties with his education, moving schools from Westminster to Winchester and then back to Westminster. Another son was proving extremely dilatory at his school. Moreover, the Countess and her family were injured – she and her husband badly – when their coach overturned.[71] This accident occurred shortly after the death of the daughter of a close friend of the Huntingdons, a death all the more devastating since the young woman and her sister were staying with them at the time. However, the other daughter was well, and their father was grateful to the Earl and Countess for inviting her to remain with them. A year later the Countess wrote to the man: 'May Almight[y] God prepare you for this second great schock'. The other daughter, too, had died while living with the Huntingdons.[72]

Death now stalked the Earl and Countess of Huntingdon. The double-deaths of their friend's daughters were a strange prefiguring. Their second and third sons, George and Ferdinando, were at school together in London when 'Ferdy' contracted smallpox in April 1743 and within days was dead, buried in Westminster Abbey. Although his brother at first appeared to escape the infection, eight months later he too was dead.[73] The Huntingdon family was frantic, obsessed with the fear that their eldest son and heir, Francis, also at school in London, would follow his brothers' footsteps to death. The Earl received well-intentioned advice from his sister Frances, warning him not to have the boy inoculated: she knew a child who had been, and while avoiding death from smallpox yet 'has remain'd an idiot ever since'.[74]

The reaction of the Countess of Huntingdon to these doleful events can hardly be imagined. Her grief was amplified by the ferment of her religious state. Under Methodistic tutelage she did not experience the expected joy of a convert. In fact, she was thrown into unremitting turmoil and confusion. The stripping of the soul left her open during the early 1740s to a myriad of competing religious voices and fluctuating emotions. To John Wesley she wrote:

> He has set my feet in a large room. All but Gods Children seems as so many machines apointed for uses that I have nothing to do with. . . . I am brought to less than nothing. Broken to pieces as the potters vessal. . . . I long to leap into the flames to get rid of my sinfull flesh & that every atom of those ashes might be separate that neither time place or person should say Gods spirit had been ever so clothed.

To John's brother she wrote:

> No soul can conceive the darkness perplexity misery I have constantly surrounds me. I hate the world & the things of it but I am so [ruffl'd?] by outward things so confound'd by a variety of events, that to tell you one quarter of what I feel would fill sheets. Upon the whole I am & have been . . . so ill in body I am scarcely able [to] move about & my mind so distracted that I know not what to do.

'O! the disturb of my soul.'[75] Throughout 1743 her letters to Charles Wesley were particularly fevered.[76]

The Wesleys were shepherds to whom the Countess was playing the role of a devoted, if excitable, sheep. John saw her as one who could provide patronage of methodistically-oriented clergy, using her presumed influence to protect him and his followers from those hostile to the movement; yet he was already becoming exasperated with what he considered to be her use of combined emotional blackmail and imperious demands. She might be known as one of his followers, but Wesley sensed that she posed a challenge to his leadership as well as a drain on his time.[77] In 1741 she apparently had persuaded him to soften his criticism of the University of Oxford in a sermon he was to preach there.[78] In 1742 she had advised him to make certain changes in his journal before publication and had pressed him, against his initial judgement, to preach to colliers in the north of England,[79] an enterprise in which she seems to have taken a particular interest at the time.[80]

The Countess's zeal for seeing the gospel propagated among the staff and labourers at Donington led to David and John Taylor (possibly brothers) being brought to the Wesleys' attention. Although she claimed only to have asked David, one of her servants, to visit some homes in the parish to read a prayer and one of Bishop Thomas Ken's sermons and to sing a psalm, she actually had encouraged his field preaching from the start.[81] Yet she soon began to doubt his capacities. 'He has more pride than I ever saw in man' and 'will have no one to rule over him', and unless he agreed to be guided by the Wesleys she determined to cease her patronage.[82] Taylor's increasingly active support of Benjamin Ingham and the Moravians hardly aided his relationship with the Countess.[83] In John Taylor, who was to assist Wesley with the beginnings of Methodism in Newcastle, she found a much more humble spirit.[84]

As Lady Huntingdon's correspondence with John Wesley all but ceased by the summer of 1742, that with his brother grew more intense. That autumn Charles was with her, and she assured him that in her turbulent spiritual state all the insight she had received 'is due to you, first cause in God's hand for two years of every spiritual blessing I possess'. For his part, he continued to write hymns for her. She wrote to him that she had told his brother John that she was 'sure you lov'd me better than he did & he flatterd me with telling me you only shewed it more'.[85] It would not be the last time she attempted to play the brothers Wesley off against one another. In London, John Wesley established in 1743 his West Street Chapel, Seven Dials, which became the major Methodist centre in the fashionable West End. Here a special seat was kept for Lady Huntingdon. Only if she had not arrived at a service before the Creed was recited, or if she were out of town, would anyone else be allowed to occupy it. John felt that all this showed 'too great' a respect to her, but his brother persuaded him otherwise.[86]

In spite of uneasiness over his brother's catering to her every whim, John Wesley was not shy about capitalising on her name. Commencing in the autumn of 1743 and continuing on a weekly basis for a full year, he published a 'chaste collection of English poems'. In October 1744 all the parts were gathered into three volumes and published under the title *A Collection of Moral and Sacred Poems*, which he dedicated to the Countess. Herein, Wesley claimed that 'a year or two ago' she had expressed a desire to see such a collection published, because for too long poetry had 'been prostituted to the vilest' purposes.[87] However, Lady Huntingdon may have been less than delighted to have her name associated with the enterprise, since within three months Wesley was forced to pay out substantial sums for breach of copyright.[88]

The Countess thought Charles Wesley 'more open and free and freed from a party than his brother John'.[89] Indeed, her early ardour for John Wesley had melted. If he was tiring of her demands, she was particularly frustrated at attempting to live by his doctrine of perfection. 'I find my self weary of all things I do as it is all too little for God. Nothing satisfies me. . . . I am apt to be active at first in undertakings but when I find my self no nearer my end I propos'd by it then I am [timid?].' By June 1744 she was openly speaking out against sinless perfection 'and the instantaneous gift of sanctification as Bro. Wesleys hold',[90] doctrines which less than three years earlier she had determined 'to live and die by'. This theological volte-face was startlingly reflected in her acceptance of predestination, a belief abhorrent to the Wesleys. When she first embraced Wesleyanism in 1741 she had sent to John Wesley 'an humble soul' who 'has been a strong predestinarian' in order to have Wesley cure him of the diseased doctrine. The clash over predestination had bedevilled the Methodist movement from the outset, lodged especially in the different perceptions of John Wesley and George Whitefield. It had marked out a terrain of conflict that over the ensuing years would change from jousting-ground to battlefield.[91] Whitefield was particularly upset early in 1741 by the double-barrelled publication of a sermon by John ('Free Grace') and a hymn by Charles ('Universal Redemption'). Although Whitefield and the Wesleys attempted to keep Methodism together by avoiding any show of public disputation, privately matters were far different. 'Brother Weslies (with grief I speak it) seem to be worse than ever. . . . They have published another hymnbook price three Shillings, wherein are some dreadfully horrid things. We are called advocates of the devil . . . &c. Xtians are to be as completely holy as the angels, & as . . . sinless as Jesus himself.'[92]

The conflict over free will versus predestination would indeed prove to be the rock upon which any hope of a united Methodist movement would be wrecked. To most of the evangelically-minded it was not basically an intellectual conflict. Those who adopted predestination appear to have done so from their personal experiences.[93] This certainly was true of the Countess. Anxious to follow the teachings of her Wesley mentors, she had thrown herself wholeheartedly into a precocious striving for perfection. Yet the more she tried, the greater the personal disasters that seemed to cascade upon her. Therefore, it is not surprising that she wavered and was tempted to find some truth in Whitefield's Calvinistic teaching. The initial test came early in 1742 in Gloucester, at what may have been their first meeting. She told him she thought it right that he and the Wesleys had parted company over this crucial doctrine and 'charged him with some severity about his conduct' to John Wesley. For his part, Whitefield 'held [forth] for above two hours upon the doctrine of election & reprobation'. In the process, reported the Countess, he had 'collected all the choicest flowers' of everything that could be said in favour of the doctrine. He attempted 'to charm me telling withall (or giving me to understand) I was an elect'. Lady Huntingdon then told Whitefield that Wesley's doctrine of perfection was the better way because while Whitefield 'was willing to groan' under the burden of his sin, she could look forward to the day when she would be freed from it. Whitefield, she reported, had a stronger 'prejudice' for predestination than any she had ever encountered. Yet, 'I must say he talked very sensibly', with 'a command of words & smoothly put togeather'.[94]

Into 1743 Lady Huntingdon was still supporting Wesley's teachings,[95] but by early 1744 she was corresponding with Whitefield and clearly moving away from perfection to predestinarianism.[96] John Wesley was now accusing her of acting like a 'Luther', while she complained of Wesley's 'pride'.[97] The fluidity of her thinking during the mid-1740s is manifest. It reflected Methodism's own searching for a theological anchor but was all the more crucial in the Countess's case owing to her traumatic and seemingly endless personal upheavals. In August 1743[98] she met the enigmatic Howell Harris, who combined a rustic Welsh charisma and ardent preaching style with a weathercock personality. (See illustration 10.) Having himself swung behind Whitefield's Calvinistic doctrine, by the spring of 1744 Harris was visiting her frequently in London and preaching to small groups of élite friends she had gathered for the occasion.[99]

Increasingly now under Harris's influence, the Countess began to attend services at the Tabernacle Chapel in London. Whitefield had established the chapel and then left it, during a lengthy visit to America, under the control of a number of helpers, including Harris. Early in 1744 Harris introduced her to James Erskine, a remarkable Scottish Member of Parliament, amateur theologian and frequenter of the Tabernacle, who would have a powerful influence on her religious thinking.[100] Yet 1745 found her in religious turmoil. Harris was informed that she was 'backsliding' and, indeed, during May 'her very sense being taken from her', she had undergone 'a month of the sharpest trials'.[101] It is understandable that during these turbulent years Lady Huntingdon had been sorely tempted merely to retire 'out of the World'. Both she and others voiced concern that she would become a mystic: 'Your fear of mistysesam for me is one of my own fears for my self.'[102] This fear was to surface again, but during the early 1740s it was real enough owing to her interest in the writings of William Law, especially his 1728 publication *A Serious Call to a Devout and Holy Life*. As early as 1739 Law had visited Lord and Lady Huntingdon,[103] and his influence on her spiritual life would continue for many years. She was attracted to Law's teachings because of his otherworldliness and his condemnation of distracting things such as the theatre, his disparaging of human reason, his break with John Wesley and his Jacobitism.[104]

Clearly, this latter point needs amplification. Determining the possible relationship during the early 1740s between Jacobitism and the new Methodist movement is beset with difficulties, yet the common popular fear of Methodism as a socially disruptive handmaid to a plot to overturn the Hanoverian monarchy may have had more substance than is generally supposed. Although John Wesley saw fit to submit a formal Address in March 1744 affirming Methodist loyalty to King George, at the same time he and other Methodist preachers grasped 'the precious opportunity' of the 'general panic [which] ran through the nation'.[105] That 'great preachers are above great Kings' was part of the new evangelical ethos. True fear gripped many that methodistic hands were loosening the bonds of political obedience and social control.[106] Certain it is that the abortive French invasion of 1744 and Jacobite rebellion of the following year had a direct impact upon the already chaotic lives of the Earl and Countess of Huntingdon.

The immediate backgrounds of both were Jacobite. The Countess's Ferrers family had strong Tory and Jacobite leanings.[107] Her husband's father, the seventh Earl, had been a remarkably energetic supporter of James, the Pretender.[108] But this was not merely a Jacobitism of the past. As an eighteen-year-old, the Countess's husband had been regaled with virulent anti-Hanoverian tales by his Leicestershire legal adviser Leonard Piddocke. 'That King George has no more right to the Crowne than my Arse. That King George has the pox and has pox'd the Court and that the Court pox'd the Prince and princess and that they would pox the Nation.'[109] Piddocke, who amused himself with gross scatological references to the King, was to continue as the Earl's trusted steward and close adviser until his death in the early 1740s.[110]

Family background or even Lord and Lady Huntingdon's early personal adherence to Jacobitism hardly constitute conclusive evidence of their continuing support for the cause. Many were the fluctuations and total changes in sympathy for the Jacobites during the first half of the eighteenth century. However, enough fragmentary evidence exists to place the Huntingdons at the very least within the framework of intellectual support during the early 1740s. Personal rejection of George II did not in itself indicate adherence to the exiled Stuarts, but it was a necessary prerequisite. Winchester and Westminster Schools were the leading public schools to which Jacobites sent their sons,[111] and to these young Francis Hastings had been sent. From Westminster, during the early 1740s, he wrote letters to his parents remarkably disparaging of the King. Francis reported that while the King was walking in Ranelaigh Gardens two young men slowly passed by. 'One said to the other, where shall we sup? T'other made answer at the kings arms. O, says t'other, that's too full (for the Countess of Yarmouth was with him). At the kings head then. Oh, no says he, that's very empty, on which the king made out of the Gardens directly.' Young Francis delighted in reporting to his parents gross disrespect shown to the Monarch by mobs who 'swore at him & called all the names yt could be thought of'. He attended a 'poppit show' where the King was made to 'speak broken english' and they 'joke upon him vastly'.[112]

The Huntingdons' direct contact with leading Jacobite sympathisers is more revealing. The Nonjuror Anglican clergyman, Thomas Carte, was one of 'James III's' chief liaison men in England during the 1730s and 40s, and among other services to the 'Old Pretender' Carte lauded his supposed ability to administer the 'king's touch' to the ill. Carte also organised local groups to support Jacobite candidates at parliamentary elections.[113] It is therefore not without significance that he served the Earl as a trusted handler of financial affairs during the 1730s,[114] and before the Earl died he gave Carte a substantial number of the Hastings family papers.[115] Carte also was in high favour with the Countess.[116] Even closer links were forged with other Jacobite sympathisers. Lady Huntingdon's movement towards Calvinism brought her into close contact at the Tabernacle Chapel with James Erskine, a virulent anti-Walpole Scottish Member of Parliament. Over the years, Erskine had openly professed allegiance to the Hanovers while secretly supporting the Stuart cause. He was intimately involved during the early 1740s in negotiations with the 'Old Pretender' and the French government for the restoration of the Stuarts in England. James wrote to Erskine in 1740, thanking him for his 'zealous and loyal disposition'. In June 1745 Erskine informed him that 'there never was and never can be such a favourable opportunity to attempt your Majesty's restoration' and argued for the speedy landing of French troops.[117] During the very same period, in 1744 Lady Huntingdon issued an insistent invitation to Donington to one of the most consistent Jacobite supporters of all, John Byrom. There, he was 'very freely and courteously entertained, and you may guess at our conversation'.[118]

Whatever turn her religious affections took, throughout her life the Countess proved passionate in her Protestantism. It may therefore be wondered how she could associate herself with the Jacobite cause. Yet it was not unusual. Especially with Charles Stuart, Roman Catholicism appeared for a time equivocal, and a number of Anglicans and Dissenters did not find it impossible to support his cause. Some Jacobite sympathisers encouraged the outbreak of the evangelical spirit in England and Scotland as a means of cutting across traditional denominational and political loyalties and thus facilitating the chances of success for the Stuart cause.[119] Moreover, for those, like Lady Huntingdon, who associated the reign of George II with an ungodly worldliness, the prospect of a new monarch shimmered as an answer to prayer. In fact, in the minds of some Jacobite supporters the notion of the Second Coming took on new poignance. A depraved and evil kingdom might well now be ripe for the visitation of God's wrath. God could well be preparing to 'bring ... Plagues of famine, Pestilence, Fire & Sword, & massacre, on these lands, because of our dreadful sins & impenitency', according to James Erskine, who had a particular taste for speculating on the imminent millennium.[120]

Lady Huntingdon herself had heard of a man, 'a most religious worthy man [who] is given to the Spirit of Prophycy'. He was forecasting, she gleefully wrote to her husband, that the King would 'fall soon and that before this summer is over England will be invaded ... and that much happiness and tranquility will follow to this nation but that it will be the most Bloddy Batle that was ever known and that inumarable lives will be lost'.[121] As the Jacobite crisis came to a head, the Countess's interest in prophecies increased in proportion. The defeat of Charles Stuart in Scotland, she was informed, meant that he 'will never Return again to his friends and Country'. There will be 'a Devostation and a Desolation in Christendom in Perticular'. All 'unbelievers' will be 'cutt off ... from the face of the Earth as never has been since the Days of Noah'. 'All the Unbelieving Bishops and Clergy with their people whome they keep in the Dark will Die of a plague. ... It may be ... before the end of this Summer.'[122]

The general panic caused by the threatened French invasion of 1744 and the Scottish Jacobite uprising of 1745 had a direct and ultimately devastating impact upon Lord and Lady Huntingdon. The Earl became obsessive about securing up-to-date details of the progress of events in Scotland and was the recipient of countless letters on the subject. Knowledge that the Countess had actively led in securing the release of at least two Methodists who had been pressed into military service in 1744 to repel a French Jacobite invasion[123] could only increase suspicions regarding the Huntingdons' loyalty to the Hanoverian succession. When the Scottish rebel forces had reached within 120 miles of London, she was asked by a correspondent about her 'sentiments upon the present anxietys',[124] clearly indicating a suspicion of the Huntingdons' proclivities; indeed, during 1745 one man went 'to three different magistrates, to give an oath, that she was guilty of treasonable acts'. She later reflected on how her 'life was combin'd against' in Leicestershire. In the aftermath of the Jacobite uprising 'they called out in the open streets for me, saying, if they had me they would tear me to pieces, &c'.[125] In her fluid religious state the Countess had begun to be influenced by several Quakers, many of whom were firm in their support of the Stuart cause. One, who had many 'hours of Sweet Converse' with Lady Huntingdon, wrote to her in the spring of 1746 of her joy 'to hear that thou hast met with some of our Friends who are Earnestly working out their Salvation' and went on to suppose that Lady Huntingdon in 'these Troubleous Times' was 'very near Danger'.[126]

News of victories over the rebels threw the Earl of Huntingdon into deep despondency. A crisis was reached when in July 1746 he was summoned to the House of Lords to sit in judgement on the Scottish Lords who had been apprehended after the Jacobite defeat at Culloden. He was determined to avoid attending, only increasing suspicions regarding his loyalty to the Crown. There was a supposition that he and his family might suffer to the extent of having their estates confiscated.[127] For their part, Jacobite friends were extremely apprehensive lest he 'shou'd be obliged to attend the Tryals of the Worthy Peers'.[128] Indeed, the severity of the punishments meted out reveals the depth of the fear that the rising of 1745-46 had generated.[129] It was determined that Lady Huntingdon should secure for her husband a medical certificate, stating that he was too unwell to attend the trial. Obtaining it was far from straightforward. While it was observed 'how easily every one had got off with excuses that had not a mind to be there . . . it was not to be so with you', and witnesses testifying to the truth of the Earl's indisposition were very closely examined by the Lords.[130]

The Earl of Huntingdon had no need to feign illness. During 1745 and 1746 his physical condition had suffered a self-induced downward spiral. His despair over the abortive Stuart uprising seems to have squeezed from him all desire to live.[131] In spite of persistent pleas of friends for over a year that he make some effort to preserve his health, he appeared not only resigned to, but desirous of, death. 'For God's sake, My Dear Lord, do not be careless & negligent of yourself . . . for tho' Life may be indifferent to Yourself, yet Preserve it, I beseech you, for the sake of yr Family & Friends.' 'It gives me a real concern yt a person of Ld. Huntingdons good sense, from pursuing a way of living destructive of his health . . . shou'd still continue in the same Dropsical disorder I saw His Lordship in last year.' His disregard for his health led to great fears that 'he cannot hold out long'. One friend would have 'come to Donington Park on his hands & knees, cou'd he prevale wth. my Lord to set in, in earnest, for the recovery of his Health – But that he almost despairs of'.[132]

From London, the Countess reported to her husband the outcome of the trials in the House of Lords. She had already received a letter from a fervent Jacobite, wildly speculating that a French fleet and an army of 15,000 Stuart supporters might yet arrive 'to preserve those Noble Lives'. 'If design'd to serve my King [Charles] God speed it.'[133] Lady Huntingdon's own views become clear in continuing letters to her husband. She expressed extensive sympathy for the three Lords and others who were executed. She highly approved of two of the rebels who refused to apply for clemency since they would have been beholden to the 'E[lector] of H[anover]'. She was shocked to think of the fate of one of the captured Jacobites, a tragic 'return for le[a]ving his wife and family to serve the publick'.[134]

From the end of August through to mid-October the Earl and the Countess appear to have exchanged places constantly between Donington and London. He was in Leicestershire during much of August, expecting her arrival by the 24th. As soon as the rebel trials and executions had been completed, he found himself well enough to return to London. Having made a further journey back to Donington, he returned to London by the beginning of October.[135] Meanwhile, his wife wrote that she had received a visit at Donington from May Drummond, the Jacobite Quaker author and preacher, who had given the Countess 'much light into the affairs of Scotland . . . as she has been their since all the distress's of that people. She is both a sensible well bred and agreeable woman.' The Countess, planning to join her husband in London by the end of October, was appalled, not only by his physical but by his spiritual state. If he could 'see the agonies of mind . . . I suffer on account both of your mortal and im[m]ortal part', it would give him a 'most sensible pain'. She hoped that he would not consider this 'any reproof, but the fruits of my present tears' which sprang from 'the most ardent affection'.[136] Yet indifferent to living and, with his wife and family at Donington, the Earl died at his London home on 13 October, aged forty-nine.

The Countess of Huntingdon erected an elaborate memorial to her husband, upon which the epitaph stated that 'every hour' of his married life had 'passed smoothly away, in the company of one who enjoyed a perpetual serenity of soul'.[137] (See illustration 2.) However tranquil Lady Huntingdon's soul, it was a curious statement on a memorial to her husband. Theophilus's soul had been far from serene. Although joining in her initial evangelical exercises during the summer of 1739, it soon became clear that her religious fervour far outstripped his own. Into the 1740s various Methodist activists had increasingly centred their attention solely on her, with the Earl either on the periphery or totally absent. On a personal level, although she continued to voice a pre-1739 passion for her husband, where he once had been more important to her than heaven, she now began to express reservations. 'I hope that passtion I feel for you will be found acceptable to him as . . . it applys the performance of his Command[ments].' There was nothing she would avoid doing for her husband's happiness, so long as 'it did not become inconsistent' with her duty to God.[138] It is worth observing that after 1739, when she was aged just thirty-two, she bore no further children. In fact, some friction between the Earl and Countess had been noted the following year. A religious visitor was bold enough to speak 'very freely to her respecting her conduct towards her lord; telling her she ought to be obedient, cheerful, and loving'.[139] Perhaps it was at this time when, in an apparent rejection of 'worldly' things, she had her husband's ancient silver mace and family seal melted down into a chocolate pot. It was an action he, perhaps understandably, 'bitterly regret[ted]'.[140]

It is not difficult to believe that the Earl had wearied of the pace being set by his wife in the religious race. As he fell into the background, she was recommending religion with 'ardour'. She highly approved of, and doubtless practised, 'oblig[ing]' servants and workmen 'to attend prayers constantly'. Indeed, in her religious activities at Donington she was 'so strong that I believe many are frightned from me'.[141] By 1745 she was actively engaged in pressing her religious ideas among a small group of women in London and in the process causing serious disruption within their families.[142] With the Earl still at Donington in June 1746 the Countess formed 'a little meeting in my own house . . . and though, with much bitterness to me, in spite of all opposition it increases'. Yet 'so surrounded am I by eyes that long to find fault with all I do, that it makes me cautious to give no offense'.[143] The 'distress' of Lady Huntingdon's soul had in the end added an unbearable weight of distress to that of her husband.

Notes

1 John Henry Meyer, *The Saint's Triumph in the Approach of Death...a Sermon Occasioned by the Death of the...Countess...of Huntingdon* (London, [1791]), p. 31. See also Thomas Haweis, *An Impartial and Succinct History of the Rise, Declension, and Revival of the Church of Christ* 3 vols. (London, 1800), 3:239-40.

2 David Willaume to SH, 18 January 1731/2, 14D32/534, LRO; William Page (ed.), *The Victoria History of the County of Leicestershire*, Vol. 1 (London, 1907), p. 394; George Gell to SH, 5 March 1728/9, 14D32/473; Henry Newman to SH, 15 December 1730, 14D32/476. LRO; same to SH, 28 June 1733, Society Letters, CS 27, SPCK.

3 Lady Elizabeth Hastings to SH, 1732 (quotation); Lady Frances Hastings to SH, 27 January 1729; Lady Mary Hastings to SH, 2 April 1735, HA 4745, 4984, 5832; SH to TH, 13 March 1731/2, 14D32/68, LRO.

4 Philip Burton to FH, 2 November 1756, HA 1147 (quotation); Lady Elizabeth Hastings to SH, 16 January [*c.* 1731], n.d. [1732], n.d. [*c.* 1738], HA 4736, 4745, 4760; Rules for a School, n.d., 14D32/590, LRO.

5 Charles Stanhope to SH, 2 October 1739, HA 12588; Minute Book 13, p. 91 (1 July 1729), SPCK; Henry Newman to SH, 17 December 1730, HA 9593.

6 Thomas Carte to SH, 8 January 1735/6, HA 1238; Philip Doddridge to Mercy Doddridge, 7 July 1735, Doddridge, no. 431.

7 Catherine Walkinshaw to SH, [1739], HA 13035.

8 For example, Thomas Bayly to TH, 26 May 1739, HA 621; Thomas Viscount Kilmorey to TH, 26 June 1739, HA 9569.

9 Lady Elizabeth Hastings to SH, 27 December [1738] (restating reflections made by SH), 14D32/229, LRO.

10 George Middleton to TH, 28 June 1739, HA 9253; Thomas Bayly to SH, 12 July 1739, HA 626; B. Parker to TH, 20 July 1739, HA 9863; Thomas Bayly to SH, 4 August 1739, HA 629; same to TH, 27 March 1740, HA 634; same to TH, 8 July 1740, HA 641; Thomas, Viscount Kilmorey to TH, 20 April 1741, HA 9575; John Sharpe to SH, 8 March 1746, HA 10772; Thomas, Viscount Kilmorey to SH, 8 June [ante-1746], 14D32/354, LRO.

11 L.S. Sutherland and L.G. Mitchell (eds.), *The History of the University of Oxford*, Vol. V (Oxford, 1986), p. 315.

12 George Whitefield, *A Further Account of God's Dealings* (1747), in *George Whitefield's Journals* (Edinburgh, 1960), p. 78.

13 M. Greene to Lady Elizabeth Hastings, 20 January 1738, George Hastings Wheler (ed.), *Hastings Wheler Family Letters 1704-1739* (Wakefield, 1935), p. 156. Though 'the first Reports of the Ways, Declarations, and Pretensions of some young Gentlemen at Oxford, among whom Methodism first began, were very acceptable to her Ladyship', she soon, '(as appears from Minutes under her own Hand) was among the very foremost, who remonstrated against...any Innovations in Practice, any disorderly Assemblies, any

Alienations of the Minds of Men from their settled Ministers'. She definitely was not involved 'in strong Attachments to a new Set of Men amongst us called Methodists'. Thomas Barnard, *Life of Lady Elizabeth Hastings* (Leeds, 1742), pp. xxvi-vii, xxiii.

14 Of these letters, the Countess's do not survive. Before her death, Lady Betty ordered 'great Numbers' of her papers to be destroyed. Barnard, *Life of Elizabeth Hastings*, p. 28.

15 Lady Elizabeth Hastings to SH, 29 July [1739], 14D32/220, LRO.

16 Lady Elizabeth Hastings to SH, 5 June [1739], 14D32/217. See also Elizabeth, Countess of Northampton to SH, 26 July 1739, DE23/1429. The 'conversion' can be placed in June from Thomas Barnard to SH, 12 October 1739, 14D32/528. LRO.

17 Lady Catherine Wheler to Lady Elizabeth Hastings, 11 September [1739], Wheler, *Hastings Wheler Letters*, p. 175.

18 Thomas Barnard to SH, 2[0] July 1739, DE23/1428; 30 July 1739, 14D32/527; 13 August 1739, DE23/1430; 12 October 1739, 14D32/528. LRO.

19 Lady Margaret Hastings to SH, 7 July [1739], DE23/1444; Lady Frances Hastings to SH, [1739], 14D32/242; Lady Elizabeth Hastings to SH, 29 July [1739], 14D32/220. LRO.

20 Henry Hastings to SH, 17, 11 August 1739, HA 5650, 5649.

21 Thomas Barnard to SH, 2[0] July, 23 March 1739/40, DE23/1428, 14D32/529, LRO.

22 Lady Elizabeth Hastings to SH, 25 November 1738, 14D32/228, LRO.

23 Lady Frances Hastings to TH, 13 May 1738, 14D32/240, LRO; Henry Hastings to TH, 1 October, 24 December 1739, HA 5656, 5669.

24 Lady Frances Hastings to TH, 7 January 1740, HA 4993.

25 Barnard, *Life of Lady Elizabeth Hastings*, pp. 154-71; C. E. Medhurst, *Life and Work of Lady Elizabeth Hastings* (Leeds, 1914), pp. 147-210; Beatrice Scott, 'Lady Elizabeth Hastings', *Yorkshire Archaeological Journal* 55 (1983), pp. 109-12.

26 Will of Lady Elizabeth Hastings, 23 April 1739, HAP, Box 30, Folder 9; Granville Wheler to TH, 26 December 1739, HA 13254.

27 Catherine Walkinshaw to SH, 3 January 1740; William Kent to SH, 15 December 1739 [*sic*: early 1740]; F. Fairfax to SH, 10 January 1740, HA 13036, 8046, 9173. See also [Felicia Rant] to SH, 16 February 1739/40, 14D32/373, LRO; Charlotte, Viscountess Howe to SH, 21 February 1740, HA 6933.

28 Lady Elizabeth Hastings to SH, [*c*. 15 December 1739], HA 4760; George Hastings to SH, [February 1740], 14D32/98, LRO; SH to TH, 28 April 1740, A24; SH to FH, 5 July 1740, A32. Drew.

29 Martin Benson to TH, 21 March 1714, HA 690; Lady Elizabeth Hastings to TH, 5 May 1736, 14D32/204, LRO; Martin Benson to TH, 18 April, 14 July 1737, HA 693, 694.

30 Lady Elizabeth Hastings to SH, 25 November 1738, 14D32/228; Granville Wheler to SH, 24 November 1739, 14D32/309 (quotation). LRO; Granville Wheler to TH, 26 December 1739, HA 13254.

31 GW to CW, [August 1739], Luke Tyerman, *The Life of the Rev. George Whitefield* 2 vols. (London, 1876-77), 1:308.

32 GW to Bishop Martin Benson, 10 July 1739, Historical Society of Pennsylvania; Benson to GW, 28 July 1739, PLP 113/1/25, Rylands.

33 SH to TH, 5 May 1740, A25; SH to same, n.d. [early 1740s], A98. Drew.

34 Mary, Viscountess Kilmorey to SH, 2 November [1739], 14D32/351, LRO; same to SH, 9 June [1740], HA 9566 (quotation).

35 SH to TH, 7 December 1741, Drew A37.

36 For Ingham, see Luke Tyerman, *The Oxford Methodists* (London, 1878), pp. 57-154; D.F. Clarke, 'Benjamin Ingham and the Inghamites', M.Phil. thesis, University of Leeds, 1971; Henry Rack, *Reasonable Enthusiast. John Wesley and the Rise of Methodism* (London, 1989), pp. 216-17.

37 Lady Margaret Hastings to SH, 28 July [1739], 14D32/253, LRO (quotation); SH to Lady Elizabeth Hastings, Wheler, *Hastings Wheler Letters*, p. 170.

38 Lady Margaret Hastings to SH, 30 July [1739], [August 1739], 14D32/254, 242, LRO.

39 Lady Margaret Hastings to SH, 17 September [1739], 14D32/258, LRO; Henry Hastings to SH, 13 October 1739, HA 5658; [Lady Margaret Hastings] to SH, [autumn 1739], 14D32/269; same to SH, [1740], 14D32/274. Lady Betty had failed to contribute. Benjamin Ingham to SH, 23 October 1739, DE23/1431. LRO.

40 Benjamin Ingham to Count Nicholas Zinzendorf (in Latin), 26 May 1740, Tyerman/Everett Transcripts, Rylands. See also SH to TH, 7 May 1740, Drew A26.

41 James Hutton to August Spangenberg, 18 November 1740, Daniel Benham, *Memoirs of James Hutton* (London, 1856), pp. 67-68.

42 SH to FH, [18 January 1739/40], Drew A85; Mary, Viscountess Kilmorey to SH, 22 March 1740, 14D32/353; Lady Margaret Hastings to SH, 15 January 1739/40, 14D32/265 (quotation). LRO.

43 SH to TH, [*c.* May 1740], Drew A125; Lady Frances Hastings to SH, 13 March 1740/41, DE23/1434, LRO.

44 SH to Ferdinand Fairfax, [1740 or 41], Black 113; Welch, *Spiritual Pilgrim*, p. 56. In 1745 they took a lease on a house in Chelsea from Sir Hans Sloane, former President of the Royal Society. Philip Miller to SH, 21 November 1745, 14D32/403, LRO. At the same time, they gave up the struggle of attempting to maintain Ledston and leased it out. Lady Oxford's Journey through Yorkshire, 25 April 1745, HMC *Report on the Manuscripts of...the Duke of Portland*, Vol. 6 (London, 1901), p. 182.

45 SH to TH, [c. May 1740], Drew A125; Lady Margaret Hastings to SH, [January 1739/40], 14D32/263, LRO.

46 Since the will stated that Lady Margaret would receive an additional £3,000 from the estate if she married, 'I cant help wishing she will not enter into, since if she does not & not otherwise, one thousand pound is charged upon the Estate to her Niece Lady Betty'. Granville Wheler to TH, 26 December 1739, HA 13254.

47 Lady Margaret Hastings to SH, 20 November [1739], 14D32/261, LRO.

48 Lady Mary Wortley Montagu to Lady Pomfret, 15 February [1741], Halsband, *Complete Letters of Mary Wortley Montagu*, 2:225 (quotation). See also Frances, Countess of Hartford to Countess of Pomfret, 1 May 1740, William Bingley (ed.), *Correspondence between Frances, Countess of Hartford, and...Countess of Pomfret* 3 vols. (London, 1805), 1:234.

49 Elizabeth Hutton to Sarah Hole, [12 November 1740 or 1741], HA 7621.

50 Lady Margaret Hastings to SH, 10 March [1740/1], 14D32/266; [same] to anon., n.d., 14D32, 270 (quotation). LRO.

51 George Legh to TH, 20 October 1741, 14D32/377, LRO.

52 SH to TH, 9 January 1741/42, Drew A43.

53 Lady Margaret Hastings to SH, 24 December 1741, DE23/1/1436, LRO.

54 SH to TH, [January or February 1741/2], A100 (quotation); SH to TH, 9 January 1741/2, A43. Drew.

55 Granville Wheler to SH, 28 June 1742, 14D32/328, LRO.

56 Tyerman, *Oxford Methodists*, pp. 100, 122, 128.

57 For 'stillness' see Rack, *Reasonable Enthusiast*, pp. 202-204. For the separation between the two men see Benjamin Ingham to JW, 3 October 1740, Baker, 26:33-34; Tyerman, *Oxford Methodists*, pp. 100-104.

58 Benjamin Ingham to Philip Doddridge, 6 August 1741, Doddridge, no. 699.

59 Ward & H., 19:458, 463, 464, 466, 467, 470.

60 SH to JW, [24 October 1741], Baker, 26:68; SH to CW, 24 February 1742, Black 2.

61 SH to JW, 15 March 1742, *Methodist Magazine* 21 (1798), p. 642.

62 SH to JW, 24 October 1741, Baker, 26:67; Susanna Wesley to SH, 1 July 1741, DD WF 2/16, Rylands; SH to JW, 15 March 1742, *Methodist Magazine* 21 (1798), p. 643.

63 Magdalene Walmsley to SH, [early 1740s], 14D32/364, LRO. She had 'layed out a considerable sum of money in Books for the good of the Souls about you'. Ann Zouch to SH, 2 April 1741, PLP 116/6/2, Rylands.

64 SH to JW, 29 April 1742, Black 107.

65 SH to CW, 19 July [between 1742 and 1746], Black 85.

66 Lady Margaret Ingham to SH, 27 February 1741/2, DE23/1442, LRO (quotation); SH to CW, 25 October 1743, Black 80; SH to TH, 2 January 1741/2, Drew A42 (quotation); David Shuttleton, 'Methodism and Dr George Cheyne's "More enlightening principles"', in Roy Porter (ed.), *Medicine and Enlightenment* (London, 1994), pp. 334-37; Sarah Perrin to SH, 28 April 1742, 14D32/537, LRO (quotation).

67 E. Ellis to SH, 14 February 1740/1, 14D32/457, LRO; SH to JW, 15 March 1742, *Methodist Magazine* 21 (1798), p. 642.

68 Samuel Levinge to TH, 31 January 1740, HA 8276; John Shadwell to SH, 30 April [1740], 14D32/375, LRO. Needless to say, the Countess did not attend the funeral. SH to TH, 5 May 1740, Drew A25. However, she had to bear the expenses involved. Mary,

Viscountess Kilmorey to SH, 22 March 1740, 14D32/353, LRO; same to SH, 9 June [1740], HA 9566.

69 Lady Catherine Wheler to SH, 26 March 1738, 27 October [1739], 14D32/287, 306; Granville Wheler to TH, 3 December 1740, 14D32/323; [Lady Catherine Wheler] to SH, n.d., 14D32/343; Granville Wheler to TH, n.d., 14D32/337. LRO; SH to TH, 19 August 1745, A 55; [Ann Grinfield] to SH, n.d., B12; A. Barlow to SH, 3 July 1755, B36. Drew.

70 Lady Frances Hastings to SH, 13 March 1740/1, DE 23/1434, LRO; SH to TH, [early 1740s], Drew A98.

71 TH to FH, 23 June 1741, HA 6120; Vincent Bourne to SH, 30 May 1741, 14D32/157, LRO; George Hastings to FH, 3 July [1742], HA 5315; SH to Francis Hastings, 5 July 1742, Drew A50.

72 TH to [William] Cowper, 29 May 1742; SH to same, 21 June 1743, P123/3, 5, LRO.

73 Robert Hemington to TH, 18, 25 April [1743], 14D32/164, 167, LRO; FH to TH, 26 November 1743, HA 5013; *The Complete Peerage of England, Scotland, Ireland, Great Britain and the United Kingdom* 13 vols. (London, 1910-40), 6:661n; Thomas Atherton to TH, 14 January 1743/4, HA 2250. 'The gravestones of the two sons is in the North transept of Westminster Abbey, by the middle pillar on the east side, close by the statues of the two Cannings.' Charles Hole, 'The four Methodist leaders of the eighteenth century' (1875 manuscript), Vol. II, p. 681, Hole MSS, Accession 87 M2, University of Birmingham Library.

74 Lady Frances Hastings to TH, 11 January 1743/4, HA 4996.

75 SH to JW, 9 January 1742; SH to CW, 1743, and n.d., Black 105, 13, 85.

76 For further examples, see SH to CW, Black 7, 8, 9.

77 JW to CW [17 May 1742], Baker, 26:77; Ann Parker Wynter to SH, [*c.* June 1742], DE/1446, LRO.

78 Nehemiah Curnock (ed.) *The Journal of the Rev. John Wesley* 8 vols. (London, 1938. Reprinted.), 2:478-81; Sutherland and Mitchell, *History of University of Oxford*, 5:454-55.

79 SH to JW, 29 April 1742, Black 107; Curnock (ed.) *Journal of John Wesley*, 3:9n. (*c.* May 1742); JW to Mayor of Newcastle, 12 July 1743, Baker, 26:101.

80 Lady Margaret Ingham to SH, 27 February [1741/2], DE23/1442; H. Sparrow to SH, 3 June 1742, 14D32/461; Ann Parker Wynter to SH, [1742?], 14D32/557. LRO. Moreover, her 'hearts desire is that the *poor Tinners*' might be preached to. SH to CW, 1743, Black 15.

81 SH to Vicar of Castle Donington, n.d., 14D32/571, LRO; Diary of John Bennet, 3 July 1743, Rylands.

82 SH to JW, 25 March 1742, Baker, 26:75; SH to JW, 29 April 1742, Black 107. See also SH to JW, [19 April 1742], Baker, 26:75.

83 Richard Parkinson (ed.), *The Private Journal and Literary Remains of John Byrom*, Vol. II, Part II ([Manchester], 1857), p. 374 (January 1744); Tyerman, *Oxford Methodists*, pp. 103, 123.

84 SH to JW, 29 April 1742, Black 107. He had, however, become desperately unstable in his religion, seeking assistance 'that God may restore my inward peace'. John Taylor to HH, 12 October 1742, Trevecka 684.

85 SH to anon., 27 October 1742, D/DF F51, Welsh Methodist (Wesleyan) Archives 870E, NLW; SH to CW, 1743; [1742 or 43]; n.d.; n.d., Black 13, 87 (quotation), 97 (quotation).

86 JW to Elizabeth Hutton, 22 August 1744, Baker, 26:114. For the chapel see Frank Baker, *John Wesley and the Church of England* (London, 1970), p. 85.

87 See dedication, John Wesley, *A Collection of Moral and Sacred Poems* 3 vols. (London, 1744), 1:iii-vii.

88 Baker, 26:115 n. 9, 119.

89 HH diary, 20 December 1744, *HHVL*, pp. 65, 66.

90 SH to CW, n.d., Black 89; HH diary, 9 June 1744, *HHVL*, p. 145.

91 SH to JW, 2 April 1741, Baker, 26:632 (quotation). For the early conflicts between Wesley and Whitefield over predestination, see for example GW to JW, 25 June 1739, 24 May 1740, 25 August 1740, 25 September 1740, 1 February 1741; JW to GW, 9 August 1740, 28 April 1741, Baker, 25:662, 26:622, 626, 32-33, 48-49, 31, 58-61. See also Rack, *Reasonable Enthusiast*, pp. 197-202.

92 GW to HH, 28 October [*sic*: probably November] 1741, PLP 113/1/6, Rylands.

93 Rack, *Reasonable Enthusiast*, pp. 199-200.

94 SH to JW, 19 February 1742, Black 3.

95 See Charles Graves to SH, 12 March 1742/3, 14D32/538, LRO.

96 SH to Philip Doddridge, 10 May 1744, John D. Humphreys (ed.), *The Correspondence and Diary of Philip Doddridge* 5 vols. (London, 1829-31), 4:328; Anne Dutton to Risdon Darracott, 6 September 1744, James Bennett, *The Star of the West; being Memoirs of the Life of Risdon Darracott* (London, 1813), p. 167.

97 HH diary, 12 June 1744, *HHVL*, p. 146.

98 HH diary, 26 August, 6 September 1743, *HHRS*, pp. 50, 52; HH to SH, 31 October 1743, Trevecka 1024.

99 For example, HH diary, 6, 9 April 1744, *HHVL*, pp. 134-35, 136; HH to SH, 25 May 1744, [Howell Harris], *A Brief Account of the Life of Howell Harris* (Trevecka, 1791), pp. 161-62.

100 For example, James Erskine to SH, 30 August, 9 October 1744, 14D32/539, 540, LRO. For the introduction of Erskine and the Countess, together with their close contact with one another and with Harris, see HH to GW, 19 March 1743/4; Erskine to HH, 26 March, and 21 May 1744. Trevecka 1150, 1152, 1186.

101 HH diary, 7, 9 June 1745, *HHVL*, pp. 71, 72.

102 C. Edwin to SH, 3 April, n.y., 14D32/523, LRO; SH to CW, n.d., Black 91.

103 Lady Margaret Hastings to SH, 5 September [1739], 14D32/257, LRO.

104 B.W. Young, 'William Law and the Christian economy of salvation', *English Historical Review* 109 (1994), pp. 313-17.

105 'To His Majesty King George II', Baker, 26:104-6; John Wesley, *A Short History of the People Called Methodists* (1781), in *The Works of John Wesley* 14 vols. (London, 1872), 13:315 (quotation).

106 George Stockwell to GW, 5 January 1760, Letters to George Whitefield, Evangelical Library, London (quotation); Geoffrey Holmes and Daniel Szechi, *The Age of Oligarchy* (London, 1993), pp. 127-28.

107 Shirley, *Stemmata Shirleiana*, pp. 196-97n.; *Complete Peerage*, 1:336n.; Paul K. Monod, *Jacobitism and the English People 1688-1788* (Cambridge, 1989), p. 274; J. Menzies to L. Inses, 6-17 January 1718, HMC *Calendar of the Stuart Papers* 7 vols. (London, etc., 1902-23), 5:393.

108 [Theophilus, 7th Earl of Huntingdon] to John, Earl of Melfort, 23 April 1694, HMC *Hast.* 2:240; Bridget Croft to same, 5 July 1690, *ibid.*, p. 214. He had been one of only ten or so English peers who became Nonjurors after 1688. Monod, *Jacobitism*, p. 142.

109 Leonard Piddocke, 1714/15, quoted in Monod, *Jacobitism*, p. 260.

110 For example, Leonard Piddocke to anon., 13 July 1722, and Thomas Rooke to Piddocke, 25 November 1741, HA 2573, 10566.

111 Monod, *Jacobitism*, p. 274.

112 FH to SH, 24 July 1742, HA 5008; 18 March, 1 April 1742, 14D32/122, 124. See also same to SH, 22 July 1742, 14D32/137. He reckoned that the king had smuggled vast sums out of the country to Hanover. FH to SH, 13 April 1742, 14D32/127. LRO.

113 Monod, *Jacobitism*, pp. 103, 130, 229.

114 For example, Thomas Carte to TH, 22 June [1736], HA 1240.

115 HMC *Hast.* 2:i, n.2, 3:vi, n.3.

116 Thomas Carte to TH, 17 March 1735/6, HA 1239.

117 Romney Sedgwick (ed.), *The House of Commons 1715-1754* 2 vols. (London, 1970), 2:14-17, with the quotations from p. 16. See also John Erskine, Earl of Mar to J. Menzies, 3-11 July 1717, HMC *Calendar of Stuart Papers* 4:420; same to Sir John Erskine, 4 January 1718, *ibid.*, 5:369.

118 Ann Hardinge to John Byrom, 14 September 1744; Byrom to Mrs Byrom, [8 October], 1744, Parkinson, *Private Journal of Byrom*, Vol. II, Part II, pp. 382, 383 (quotation).

119 For example, James Erskine to HH, 19 March 1744/5, Trevecka 1305.

120 James Erskine to HH, 26 January 1744/5, Letters chiefly addressed to the Rev. C. Wesley, Vol. VI, Rylands.

121 SH to TH, 9 January 1741/2, Drew A43.

122 Anon. to his 'sister Cart', 3 May 1746 (enclosed in a letter of 20 May to SH), 14D32/570, LRO.

123 James Erskine to HH, 13 June 1744, Trevecka 1191; John Byrom to Mrs Byrom, 8 October 1744, Parkinson, *Private Journal of Byrom*, Vol. II, Part II, pp. 383-84; Baker, 26:106n.

124 Rowland Cotton to SH, 28 November 1745, 14D32/583, LRO.

125 G[eorge] Waring, *A Sermon Occasioned by the Death of the...Countess of Huntingdon* (Birmingham, [1791]), p. 8; SH to Thomas Haweis, 7 August 1790, SMU 127; SH to Philip Doddridge, 21 May 1747, Humphreys, *Correspondence of Doddridge*, 4:536.

126 E. Cart to SH, 29 July, 25 April 1746, 14D32/548, 544, LRO.

127 John Cooke to TH, 14 August 1746, HA 1596.

128 A. Mundy to SH, 4 July 1746, 14D32/521, LRO.

129 Frank McLynn, *The Jacobites* (London, 1985), p. 127.

130 SH to TH, [August 1746], Drew A101. The medical certificate had been lodged with the Lord Chancellor. John Stamford to anon., 24 July 1746, 14D32/446, LRO; E. Wilmot to SH, 24 July 1746, HA 13405a. For the form of the certificate see E. Wilmot to SH, 17 July 1746, 14D32/467, LRO.

131 It is possible that he was further distraught by a sharp conflict with his elder son and heir, Francis, who appears to have come to reject the Jacobite cause. For example, FH to SH, 12 June [1746], HA 5031. This may have been the subject of the missing contents of the file labelled 'Contains Letters & papers on the difference between Ld Huntingdon and his Son', HA 6994.

132 Gilbert Walmesley to TH, 20 July 1745, HA 13050; E. Wilmot to SH, 17 July 1746, 14D32/467; Magdalene Walmesley to SH, 13 June 1746, 14D32/362. See also Charlotte Pickering to SH, 7 July 1746, 14D32/381; Henry Hastings to SH, 27 July 1746, 14D32/194. LRO.

133 A. Mundy to SH, 4 July 1746, 14D32/521, LRO. Anne Mundy almost certainly was the wife of Wrightson Mundy of Osbaston, Leicestershire (where the Earl owned land). He and his father were zealous Jacobites. Sedgwick, *House of Commons*, 2:280-81. The Countess continued to correspond with and receive visits from Anne Mundy for many years. She referred to herself as the Countess's 'Affectionate Daughter'. Anne Mundy to SH, [1755], Drew B51.

134 SH to TH, [August 1746], Drew A101. The man referred to, 'poor M[ ]ship', may have been James Bishopp, who had been arrested while attempting to smuggle a Jacobite message to France. See Monod, *Jacobitism*, p. 114.

135 TH to SH, 9 August 1746, T3765/M/2/12, PRONI; SH to TH, 9, 12 August 1746, A56, 57; SH to TH, 6 September 1746, A59; SH to TH, 4 October 1746, A58. Drew; EH to TH, 4 October 1746, HA 10411.

136 SH to TH, 8 September, 4 October 1746, Drew A58, 60.

137 Epitaph at the parish church, Ashby de la Zouch, Leicestershire. No family correspondence regarding the Earl's death appears to have survived.

138 SH to TH, 5, 19 May 1744, Drew A25, 53.

139 James Hutton to August Spangenberg, 18 November 1740, Benham, *Memoirs of Hutton*, p. 68. See also SH to William Cowper, 24 July 1742, P/123/6, LRO.

140 EH to [Edward Dawson], 17 September 1800, HA 10436.

141 Robert Goadby to TH, 3 June 1741, HA 4062; SH to TH, [20 December? *c.* 1743], HA 5856; SH to CW, 19 July [between 1742 and 1746], Black 85.

142 Mary Edwards to SH, 5 July 1745, 14D32/541; S. Andrews to SH, 8 July 1745, 14D32/542. LRO.

143 SH to Philip Doddridge, [*c.* 17] June 1746, Humphreys, *Correspondence of Doddridge*, 4:501.

CHAPTER 3

'A leader is wanting'

Whatever had constituted her conversion experience, Selina Hastings clearly had found no inner peace. Her personal crises of the early 1740s, culminating in her husband's death, contributed directly to religious instability. A widow at thirty-nine, she assumed full responsibility for her four children, aged from six to sixteen. Since the Earl had died intestate she now carried the extra burden of attempting to sort out complex personal and financial affairs.[1]

Having cast herself away from Wesleyan teachings, Lady Huntingdon lacked a secure theological mooring. In the immediate aftermath of the Earl's death her own future was totally uncertain. Intentions fluctuated wildly between assuming a bold and active religious role and a contemplative widowly retirement from the world. She proclaimed her dread of 'slack hands in the vineyard: we must be all up and doing'; a month and a half later she was torn between giving 'up all' in retirement, or stepping forward to 'fill her Place'; yet she then 'declared her simplicity and having no will'. She either was going to be 'on fire always' and be active 'to spread the gospel from pole to pole' or she was going to cease 'from care and labour, only to maintain her oneness with God in faith'.[2]

By the end of 1747 it was feared that the Countess was 'warp[in]g tow[ar]ds Quaker[is]m & Mr [William] Law'. That did appear to be her direction. The 'silent looking for God in our selves is the sure way to find him', she had been assured.[3] She was tempted to the 'stillness' or quietism from which four years earlier she had boasted of rescuing Charles Wesley. She now spoke of the 'Revelatio[ns] she had of God', believing that she was 'w[i]th & near the L[or]d continually with[ou]t Interrupt[io]n'. She felt herself 'led by the Spirit & views all there final & then comes w[i]th it to the Word'. In other words, the Countess sought and received immediate direction from God through prayer and only then attempted to test the resulting revelation by reference to the Bible. Howell Harris was horrified by the implications of this approach and found her 'in danger from spiritual pride'. A correspondent boldly (though anonymously) wrote to her: 'Would to God, yr Ladysp was so little in yr own Eyes as to see, self'.[4] She now proceeded to plan retirement at Ashby Place, a house built by the family within the walls of the ruined Ashby de la Zouch castle. There she would be able to spend her remaining years hard by the church where her husband was buried and her memorial to him stood.[5]

It was a plan that did not hold long. Through continuing contact with Howell Harris and James Erskine, Lady Huntingdon was drawn further towards an active role, centred on a Calvinistic commitment. Harris was guarding his followers 'against the Errors and Designs of Bro. Wesley'; and by now the Countess feared John Wesley 'of all men in the world'.[6] For four years George Whitefield had been preaching in the American colonies, and he was persuaded by Harris to return, on the evidence that Lady Huntingdon now was ready to serve Calvinistic Methodism – with the additional intelligence that she wished to make Whitefield her personal chaplain. Correspondents informed him that she 'gives you an encouraging prospect of success upon yr return to Land'. It is highly unlikely that he would have returned to England in 1748 had it not been for these expectations. As soon as he arrived that summer, Whitefield began the process of relinquishing his nominal position as 'Moderator' of Calvinistic Methodism in England and Wales in anticipation of becoming her chaplain. This was effected immediately, with the Countess insisting that when not physically with her he write at least weekly.[7] To make complete her rejection of Wesley's teaching, she gladly embraced Whitefield's Calvinism. It was a theological orientation that provided her with secure belief in election to a pivotal position in pursuing England's redemption. For his part, Whitefield lost no opportunity to underpin her divine calling. 'A leader is wanting. This honour hath been put upon your Ladyship by the great head of the church. An honour conferred on few, but an earnest of a distinguished honour to be put upon your Ladyship before men and angels, when time shall be no more.' He 'rejoice[d] in the prospect of seeing your Ladyship happy amidst a crowd of your spiritual children, who will come to you, from time to time, to be built up in their most holy faith'. To others he wrote that 'good Lady Huntingdon is indeed a mother in Israel'.[8] It was probably at this time that she began to adopt the 'godly twang through the nose' that was the pronounced mark of the Whitefieldian style.[9] (See illustration 9.)

Lady Huntingdon's display of support for Whitefield cut John Wesley deeply. The very day he became her chaplain, Whitefield unkindly wrote to Wesley that 'I suppose you will hear of my preaching to some of the nobility, and I trust the hour is coming when some of the *mighty and noble* shall be called'. He then proceeded to tell him that he considered a union between them 'impracticable', since he had discovered from reading some of Wesley's recent sermons that they 'differ in principles more than I thought, and I believe we are upon two different plans'. A week after Whitefield's appointment, Wesley, who had been studiously avoiding her, visited the Countess on a bright and brittle morning and 'delivered my own soul'. Though 'she received it well', there were 'tears standing in her eyes'. Two days yet again he returned, and her reaction was to sink 'down into a chair'. To Wesley, Whitefield's appointment meant 'warfare'. He knew that Whitefield had poached Lady Huntingdon from him. These disjunctions issued a shrill note that continued to flutter the Methodist dovecotes throughout the formative years. She had furnished Whitefield an entrée into an echelon of society that Wesley now claimed held no interest for him.

Moreover, Whitefield hid his honorific beneath no humble bushel. To a bitter opponent on the episcopal bench he wrote of his right to protest against ill-treatment, 'whether as a chaplain to a most worthy peeress' or as 'a presbyter of the Church of England'.[10]

Two years a widow and despondent at seeing her eldest son and daughter repelled by her religious proclivities, the Countess – like many other evangelicals – turned to her associates in faith to fashion a surrogate family. She emerged as a focal point for the Calvinistic wing of English Methodism. At least in the first decade of this activity she believed her special mission to be the winning of the aristocracy for Christ. To carefully-staged salon services she invited the titled and wealthy to drink tea and to hear the most ardent preachers she could secure, ideally Whitefield himself. Although she maintained throughout her life a taste for a decent wine, guests at these gatherings were offered only tea and lemonade.[11]

What the Countess hoped to build upon was a select group of nobility and other worthies who gathered at times in London. A basic concern was to use such influence to seek protection for the infant Methodist movement. As early as 1744 she was telling the Prince of Wales that 'she was resolved to stand by' the Methodists, and he 'promised there should be no persecution in his father's days or his'. Within half a year of her husband's death, Lady Huntingdon held regular meetings in London with several well-placed men and women.[12] Over the next three years this cabal grew, with one thrust being to muster influence with the Prince of Wales to soften the attitude of the bishops of the Church of England towards the Methodist movement. Philip Doddridge, a favourite of Lady Huntingdon, and far more sympathetic to the Methodists than most of his fellow Dissenters, observed that one of her inner circle, Catherine Edwin, was 'building her self a House at Cookham where I hope she will preach her Neighbour the Prince of Wales into Religion'.[13] It may, in fact, have been the increasing closeness between Catherine Edwin and the Prince that caused Lady Huntingdon to foster a serious resentment towards her. Harris, also, began to find this woman more congenial than the Countess, to the extent that he felt 'willing to lose' Lady Huntingdon's favour. For her part, Edwin resented the Countess's attitude towards Wesley, and perhaps even more to the point, that the Countess refused to show her respect. Harris told Edwin that 'she must expect more of that.'[14] Indeed, what previously had been a close relationship between the two women now became decidedly rocky.

In spite of these nagging jealousies a remarkable band of highly placed women and men had gathered. At various times were to be found Lord Lothian; the Earl of Chesterfield; Chesterfield's former mistress – Lady Frances Shirley (Lady Huntingdon's aunt); Chesterfield's sister, Lady Gertrude Hotham (an old friend of Lady Huntingdon); Chesterfield's sister-in-law, Countess Delitz (a natural daughter of George I); Lord Bath; Lord Bath's father-in-law, Colonel John Gumley; Lord Bolingbroke; Lady Archibald Hamilton (the Prince of Wales's reputed mistress), and her daughter, Lady Frances Gardiner; Charles Stanhope, MP; James Erskine, MP; George (later Lord) Lyttleton; George Bubb Dodington; Lord North;

the Duchess of Queensberry; Sir Luke Schaub; and Alexander Hume Campbell.[15] Lady Huntingdon grasped the opportunity as one of winning at least some of these worthies to her religious orientation, thereby developing the new-birth conversion of England from 'the top'.[16] For some titled guests her drawing room was a hall of judgement; yet in the end blue blood ran thin in the enterprise, and her aunt, Lady Frances Shirley, was her only parlour 'convert'.[17]

An arresting note is that these men and women were already bound together at a very different level: they, and the Countess, were ardent political opponents of the King and supporters of his son, Frederick, Prince of Wales, who from the mid-1730s had appeared in open rebellion to his father. The Countess held a high opinion of Augusta, the Princess of Wales,[18] and had the opportunity of gaining influence in that quarter through her close association with the Princess's housekeeper at Leicester House.[19] In their very differing ways, Lady Huntingdon's public appearances, boisterously in parliament and fantastically at the Prince's birthday party – both on the eve of her religious conversion – had been political statements fully consonant with the orientation of this 'Leicester House' cabal a decade later.

With all hopes crushed of a Stuart deliverance, every effort had now to be refocused on Frederick. To a sardonic Horace Walpole, Lady Huntingdon had emerged as the 'Queen of the Methodists'.[20] She cultivated every possible religious advantage from this political adherence to the Prince. Foremost perhaps was the effort to influence bishops of the Church of England not only to soften opposition to itinerant clergymen but also to be willing to ordain others who were methodistically-inclined. The more disruption the Methodists caused to parish churches, the more distant became this prospect; but the Countess and others in her circle kept hammering the point home to the Prince of Wales, attempting to make him 'sensible of the danger of letting the Bishops have too much power'.[21] Her bitter experience with Martin Benson still rankled. Also in the early 1740s she had attempted to use her influence with the Bishop of Lichfield, but he had proved to be but a 'Scrub Bishop'.[22] And the death in 1747 of John Potter, the Archbishop of Canterbury, 'a true Christian Bishop' with whom she had been on good terms for several years, robbed the circle of an important sympathetic ear.[23] Decided conflict with the Bishop of London, Edmund Gibson,[24] set the note of the general tenor of Lady Huntingdon's subsequent relationships with the bishops of the Church of England. She could hardly expect better relations with Gibson's successor, Thomas Sherlock, a moderate churchman who built bridges with leading Dissenters but who was deeply distrustful of enthusiasts. Moreover, he had been a firm supporter of Walpole, not least in the 1739 Lords debate she and her friends had so noisily attended.

The Countess's role in the leadership of Methodism was further quickened by the departure from the scene of the erratic Howell Harris. A key example of the cult of personality that dogged and damaged eighteenth-century Methodism, Harris boasted that 'I have been the means of beginning all this work in Wales' and called himself 'Father to Wales'.[25] Whitefield's return to

England and his questioning of the quality of Harris's stewardship of English Calvinism left the Welsh exhorter bitter and disillusioned. At first, Harris had been overawed by the circle into which Lady Huntingdon introduced him – pleased, if bemused, by the money and clothes she lavished upon him, while she induced him to speak of his religious experiences to 'a carnal great Lady'.[26] Harris came to feel used and by the end of 1749 was lashing out at the other leaders of the revival, while claiming his own primacy. He now 'saw what I never did before, that I was head in this Reformation, viz. that no one is to control me to send me here or there, to teach and reprove me but the Lord Himself'. Whitefield did not 'honour' him, indeed treated him as a gentleman would a servant. Harris was so stung by this that he fancied it was his 'place to oversee Mr. Whitefield and Wesley' since they were so self-important. What appears to have burned him most sorely was seeing Whitefield's 'spirit jumping over me' in their relationship with Lady Huntingdon. Whitefield had 'got beyond me' in the Countess's 'heart'.[27] Harris did not aid his cause when in the summer of 1749 he 'reproved the pride of the great ones'. As the Countess's chaplain, Whitefield had stiffly upbraided him for that indiscretion. Harris responded by upbraiding Whitefield for not preaching to London's more humble residents, unlike Wesley, who continued to be concerned for their spiritual needs.[28]

Although Harris had considered himself a peacemaker, attempting to keep together Whitefield, the Wesleys and the Countess, his basic concern was for his own authority. He was additionally deeply frustrated by their unanimous rejection of the Moravians, whom he believed were 'the only people I have seen coming up to the Cross'. When he became her chaplain, Whitefield had quickly grasped the Countess's attitude towards the Moravians and immediately repented of his former use of their terminology, such as 'the Bleeding God, Agonizing God, Dying God'. Taking his cue from his patroness, Whitefield began speaking and writing openly against the Moravians, so that, in Harris's view, Whitefield 'is now against our Saviour. . . . The angels do not rejoice now over his work.'[29] During 1749 Whitefield and Harris were 'flying off' against one another, and by the close of the year Whitefield banned his preaching in the Tabernacle Chapel and ordered Harris and his wife out of the adjoining house.[30]

Immediately following Lady Huntingdon's appointment of Whitefield as her chaplain, Harris formed a liaison with a married woman whom he referred to as 'My Eye', 'My Arm', 'My Light' or even 'the eye of Christ's Body'. Whatever he called her, he firmly believed her to be an infallible interpreter of the Divine will, and she was with him everywhere as he travelled throughout Wales preaching in the immediate aftermath of his dismissal from the Huntingdon/Whitefield circle. The affair caused uproar in Wales, where it precipitated a major schism in the Methodist movement. Harris transformed his home at Trevecca into a castellated religious retreat which developed into an early industrial social community.[31] The rupture between Harris and Whitefield was never healed.[32]

The Prince of Wales had told the select group that he 'liked' their religion but at present could do nothing. 'He said if he lived to be King what he then would do.'[33] But, of course, he did not live to be King. Frederick's death in 1751 was immediately followed by Whitefield's departure for America, his remarkable hopes that he might be consecrated a bishop in the Church of England dashed. In 1744 he had been telling others 'of all the scriptures, promises, dreams and providence that have been given him as to his being made Bishop', a hope he maintained as late as 1750.[34] It is possible that Lady Huntingdon had encouraged him in the belief that this would come about through her agency. Whitefield may not have become a bishop, but he had gained much. He had been given a position in society upon which he capitalised boldly. His supporters saw his elevation as the Countess's chaplain as a wondrous opportunity to preach to persons of a high rank at her home. When they both were in London, he regularly preached at her house twice a week 'to the Great and Noble'.[35] Since she provided him with substantial sums of money, he was able to live in some comfort.[36] On the very day she appointed him chaplain, Whitefield had sent his 'thoughts of what scheme seems to be most practicable, in order to carry on the work of GOD, both here and in *America*'. As he returned to America in 1751, Georgia was in the process of becoming a Royal colony. With its government by Trustees removed, Whitefield foresaw a far easier way forward. His desire for legal slavery in the colony had been fulfilled, and the Countess might well be able to exert pressure through some of the noble circle in support of his Georgian ventures.[37]

The effective break-up of the select circle, with the departure of Harris for Wales and Whitefield for extended preaching tours throughout Britain and America, threw the Countess into serious physical and emotional turmoil early in 1751. Ever since Lady Betty's illness and death in 1739, Lady Huntingdon had harboured irrational, if understandable, fears that she too had breast cancer.[38] These fears now became obsessional. She travelled to Bristol seeking medical advice, where the 'unanimous opinion' of the physicians was that her 'pain is only nervous', that 'it is entirely a nervous case'. However, it was 'of no weight with her'. The medical opinion should have lifted her spirits, but 'in her case to be diffident & desponding is part of the distemper'. Whitefield observed that she 'ought always to have a christian friend with her'. 'Mixtures for misery' had driven her, she said, 'even to my wits end'.[39]

Lady Huntingdon was further despondent about the physical health of Philip Doddridge, the eminent Dissenting leader with whom she had corresponded for several years and brought into the orbit of her London salon meetings towards the end of the 1740s.[40] She held him in high esteem, and he in turn was an important stabilising influence on her. In his renowned academy at Northampton, Doddridge insisted that pupils carefully examine all intellectual arguments against Christianity, in order that their own faith might be strengthened, firmly cautioning Christians against being guided by 'any ardent transport of the affections'.[41] In the fateful year of 1751, with so many of her supports removed, the Countess was intent on seeing Doddridge regain his health. By September he was in Bath, in a 'deep consumption'. Being 'much employed in attending' him, she seemed to regain her own health. The plan was to send him to Lisbon's warm climate, and she and a number of her friends provided several hundred pounds for the purpose, of which she contributed £100. For a time she even spoke seriously of accompanying him on the voyage.[42] Yet a fortnight after his arrival in the Portuguese capital he was dead.

Lady Huntingdon was further unsettled by the action of a domestic chaplain, George Baddelley. He had been at the forefront of pressing upon her the authority of the Holy Spirit over the Scriptures, and in her mind 'a piouser or better young man does not live' – until she discovered that he had secretly married her personal maid. They both were dismissed immediately.[43] For two years, since 1750, the Countess had expressed renewed doubt as to what God 'would have me do'. Once again she was uncertain whether to be active in his service or to remove 'from all things in the church militant'.[44] She had yet to find secure theological moorings and was susceptible to renewed speculation regarding the millennium. This dabbling was fostered by Thomas Hartley, a methodistically-oriented Northamptonshire clergyman who later became the leading exponent in England of the teachings of Emanuel Swedenborg. By the early 1750s Hartley was a frequent visitor at her home, where he argued that each individual has several souls: 'He seems to think, three . . . tho' they possibly might be more.' She became so enamoured of Hartley's notions that she undertook to assist him in their publication and introduced him personally to others.[45] Moreover, when in 1754 he published a collection of his sermons, prefixed by a discourse underlining his admiration for mystical writers, he dedicated the entire work to Lady Huntingdon. Hartley went on to publish in 1764 the noted *Paradise Restored; or a Testimony to the Doctrine of the Blessed Millenium*. An ardent supporter of William Law, he was instrumental in maintaining the Countess's support of Law's mystical writings, which she arranged to print in 1755.[46] In the same year Hartley's wife succumbed to 'madness and [a] wild way of talking about the Holy Goast'.[47]

All this points to the inescapable conclusion that Lady Huntingdon was now attempting to find in introspection the inner consolations of faith through mystical speculation. Dabbling in this sort of mysticism was a standard resort of defeated Jacobites. Her keen interest in the writings of William Law did not, however, make him an uncritical observer. Responding to a letter she wrote in 1753, Law advised that

> to be always tampering with Physicians, upon every Occasion, is the Way to lose all natural Soundness of Health; and to be continually talking, and enquiring about the Nature of Distempers, and the Power of Medicines, for the Head, the Heart, the Spirits, and Nerves, is the Way to lose all true Judgment, either of our own Sickness or Health. It is much the same, with regard to our spiritual Health and Constitution, we do much Hurt to it, by running after spiritual Advice on every Occasion, and wanting the Help of some *human Prescription*, for every Fear, Scruple, or Notion, that starts up in our Minds, and so weaken the true Strength of our *spiritual Constitution*, which if left to itself, would do all that we want to have done. . . . The greatest Danger that new Converts are liable to . . . arises from their conceiving

> something great of their Conversion, and that great Things are to follow from it. Hence they are taken up too much with themselves, and the supposed Designs of God upon them. . . . But Piety makes little Progress till it has no Schemes of its own.[48]

An evangelical cleric who spent some time with her was distressed. 'What she talks appears to me a Hotch Potch of Opinions glean'd from every where without direction, which, as she delivers them, encounter each other with continual repugnancies [i.e. inconsistencies]. . . . I judge her to be at present in [the grip] of Self Importance which you know is supercilious as well as Dangerous.'[49]

Now in her mid-40s, the Countess still seems to have failed to make real progress in her personal religious quest. Constantly 'running after spiritual Advice on every Occasion' had indeed produced an unsettled nature. She was, as she acknowledged, 'afflicted tormented & distressed' and, as others observed, experiencing 'tribulation'.[50] She yearned for peace and for a rebuilding of broken relationships. She already had reached a reconciliation with her sister Mary after a seven-year period of bitterness[51] and now, following an unexpected meeting with Benjamin Ingham, began re-establishing relations with him and Lady Margaret[52] – a process facilitated by Ingham's separation from the Moravians.

An attempt at Bristol in the summer of 1749 to secure some form of union between the various methodistic factions had proved futile. Whitefield felt that John Wesley was 'monopolising the name of Methodist to himself only'.[53] Yet even if Whitefield's belief in predestination and Wesley's in perfectionism had not continued to widen the gulf between them,[54] the uncomfortable fact was that Lady Huntingdon's patronage of Whitefield precluded a settlement of the dispute. This was true even though she sincerely sought peace within the Methodist movement and was instrumental in establishing a *rapprochement* early in 1750. Yet the peace was brief, and she went on to caution Whitefield to avoid having much contact with Wesley.[55] Whitefield believed, all too correctly, that Wesley was 'jealous of me', and Whitefield's wife joined the fray by accusing Wesley of 'blackening other mens c[h]aracters to exalt his own'. Wesley was mainly and publicly blackening her husband's.[56] The Countess's hope of peace between the two men was naive,[57] and she seemed unable to comprehend her own role in their differences.

Lady Huntingdon was instrumental in driving a more serious personal wedge between John Wesley and his brother. It has been observed how, from the earliest days of her contact with the Wesleys, Charles had proved her personal favourite. In 1749 he had married a Welsh girl, twenty years his junior. Later that year he literally robbed his brother of an intended wife, Grace Murray, by whisking her away to be married to another Methodist leader. As if in response, eighteen months later John entered into a marriage which became the most notoriously unsuccessful within eighteenth-century Methodist circles, a union which greatly displeased Charles.[58] Thus, an underlying tension between two brothers of very different talents and temperaments now spilled over into open hostility. In the middle of the conflict was Lady Huntingdon. There had been a serious rift between her and Charles, probably when she turned to Whitefield. In mid-1751 Charles received word that she wished to see him, and when he did his 'heart was turned back again, and forgot all that is past'. As she had a decade earlier, the Countess once more longed for his lenitive features. 'Do let me see you soon. You will be a great comfort to me.'[59]

In the summer of 1752 Charles Wesley became highly critical of his brother's extensive use of unqualified lay preachers, as well as of his authoritarian style of leadership. In a lengthy and detailed letter to Lady Huntingdon, Charles poured out bitter complaints, centred on John. It was necessary to 'break his power . . . & reduce his Authority within due bounds; as well as guard against that rashness & credulity of his, which has kept me in continual awe & bondage for many years'. Consonant with the remarkable intrigue frequently present in the feverish rivalries of the Methodist movement in its formative years, this letter was 'intercepted & carried' to John Wesley by one of his agents.[60] Upon reading it, John was livid: 'In what respect do you judge it needful to "break my power", and "to reduce my authority within due bounds?"' He then went on to say that he had never been able to understand how Charles's 'conscience or your sense of honour' could allow him to draw £100 a year for his wife and himself from the proceeds of his hymnbooks and other Wesley publications.[61] Such was the current texture of their relationship, and the Countess moved directly to capitalise on the division. Charles began to spend considerable periods of time with her,[62] and when they were apart there was frequent correspondence: during the period from September 1753 to August 1756 there are extant forty of her letters to him. With the enmity between the Wesleys notched up several degrees, John saw his younger brother falling ever more deeply under the influence of the Countess of Huntingdon: 'Either act really in connexion with me: or never pretend to it. . . . At present you are so far from this that I do not even *know* when and where you intend to go. So far are you from *following* any advice of mine – nay, even from asking it. And yet I may say, without vanity, that I am a better judge in *this [ma]tter* than . . . L[ady] H[untingdon].' 'You do not, will not act in concert with me. . . . For ten years past, and upwards, you have no more acted in connexion with me than Mr. Whitefield has done.' To the Countess, Charles wrote that 'I go on my way as God and men . . . direct, taking no notice' of his brother's complaints.[63]

For her part, Lady Huntingdon was 'charmed' with Charles Wesley's hymns, yet it is doubtful that she ever saw the shorthand verses he wrote on one of the letters into which she had poured her religious anxieties:

Eager to drink her Master up
to fill her Lord's afflictions up
With Jesus crucified . . .
entirely dead,
She languished till she
bowed her head.[64]

Most important, she was solidifying their relationship by acts of friendship and kindness to his wife, whom she frequently saw, especially in Bristol. With Charles absent in London, the Countess in late 1753 tended her when she contracted smallpox. Sally Wesley recovered, but her face was left permanently and grotesquely scarred.[65] Lady Huntingdon's relationship with Charles Wesley and his wife, whom she loved 'with an never failing Love', set the pattern of her subsequent frequent courting of clerical couples. She had rented a house close to them in the Clifton area of Bristol. She devoted considerable time to hand-working a handkerchief for Sally, and there were further such gifts to the couple. For his part, Charles made arrangements for her to receive a pound of her favourite scotch snuff.[66]

Encouraged by the Countess, who was referring to John Wesley's 'ignorant lay Preachers',[67] the division between the Wesley brothers continued to harden. A crisis was reached in the summer of 1755. John correctly supposed that his brother was at her total beck and call. On his side, Charles had been cured 'of my Implicit regard to him'. He no longer could trust John, 'no more than he can me'. 'No quarter do I expect from Him, or his implicit followers.' Charles rejoiced in 'the Hope of my being cast out'.[68] By 1755 this division centred on John's toying with the notion of separation from the Church of England, which both his brother and Lady Huntingdon strenuously resisted. Charles could write to a correspondent that 'you have her thoughts in mine'.[69] John saw the movement of her hand in this conflict. His concern was not whether his preachers or people left the Church of England, but whether they remained faithful to God. 'If (as my Lady [Huntingdon] says) all outward establishments are Babel, so is this establishment.' The Countess solicited support from Whitefield, who then informed her that he had written to John Wesley arguing against any secession. 'O this self-love, this self-will! It is the devil of devils', wrote Whitefield of Wesley.[70]

As was so often tediously true, what underlay the religious squabble was a level more bitterly personal. John Wesley was studiously avoiding any contact with the Countess. He was greatly offended by fearsome attacks on his wife, led by a brother whose 'design is never to speak to her at all. And I suppose this is Lady H[untingdon]'s advice; because he referred me to her for an answer. . . . I do not think she is a competent judge. . . . Neither am I (any more than my wife) willing to refer the matter to her arbitration.'[71] When in the midst of this ecclesiastical and personal strife Charles wrote to his brother about Sally's giving birth, John took no notice. Soon after, when the baby died, Charles refrained from notifying his brother and his wife, on the astonishing reasoning that the news 'of her Death . . . wd . . . give them Pleasure'.[72]

George Whitefield assured his patroness that 'was I not called out to public work, waiting upon and administring to your Ladyship in holy offices would be my choice and highest privilege'. Yet he realised that his prolonged absences were allowing Charles Wesley to gain substantial influence. When Whitefield charged him with 'unforgivingness' towards his brother, Charles informed Lady Huntingdon that he had taken 'the liberty of referring him to YOU for an Answer'. Clearly believing that the Countess's relationship with Charles, especially as it fed upon a mutual antagonism towards John Wesley, was narrowing her religious vision, Whitefield began to re-assert his position as her chaplain. When she wrote to Charles that she would be glad to see him, she added 'tho I must not hear you'.[73]

In fact, 1755 found Lady Huntingdon rejecting all 'establishments' and withdrawing into a life of introspective soul-searching. She found comfort in her belief that 'our Lord keeps my heart as in his sanctuary' and would never forsake her. However, she clearly had not given up personal attempts to influence others' religious outlook. Whitefield had urged her to be instrumental in plucking sinners out of the fire. To the extent that she did, it was proving to be a plucking of individuals. She was, wrote one correspondent, 'the happy Instrument of shewing me the Heavenly Riches, these Divine Treasures unfolded in the Soul'.[74] She was concerned for the religious state of her correspondents, 'even to the most minute circumstances'. Thus one woman could write, soliciting her spiritual guidance while at the same time pleading with her 'not [to] frighten me too much'. It was Lady Huntingdon's practice to attempt to 'infuse' her religious thinking 'into all you converse with'.[75] Although she might be praised, for example, for explaining to an individual the meaning of some verses in St Paul's letter to the Romans, the Countess constantly refused to consider publishing any of her religious notions, even though she now had 'leasure' to do so.[76]

Lady Huntingdon's eye had remained focused on the Court. In 1749 she had managed to have her elder daughter, the eighteen-year-old Elizabeth, appointed Lady of the Bedchamber to Princesses Amelia and Caroline, the King's daughters.[77] It was an ill-fated exercise: within months she had removed Elizabeth, horrified that she was joining in playing cards on Sundays.[78] However, a far better prospect emerged when one Ann Grinfield was appointed to the same post. Mrs Grinfield looked to Lady Huntingdon as her 'most kind Dear and ever bless'd Guide'; yet she felt isolated, shunned by others at Court, 'quite alone' and desperate for the Countess's 'opinion Every moment of the Day'. 'The burden of my [song] is I want my Huntingdon in Town.' She feared lest she 'give prejudices that may do hurt to the Cause. Do tell me what I should do, and how act.' She felt herself 'quite unfit for what your Ladyships warm heart think me designed for'.[79] Over a twelve-month period she wrote a score of such letters to Lady Huntingdon.

The Countess felt that Ann Grinfield's strategic placement was so important that she coached her on how far she should go in attempting to influence the Princesses, wisely cautioning Grinfield not to talk of her too much and directing that all her letters be burnt. She encouraged her to capitalise on the situation boldly with the Princesses in private. Grinfield came to believe that they were willing to receive the Countess: 'The way is prepared.' In reality, the way was prepared for Mrs Grinfield's departure from Court. Lady Huntingdon's agent became far too bold, and in August 1755 the Princesses requested that Ann Grinfield, now clearly mentally confused and emotionally damaged, leave their service. Her conversation with those about her, including the Princesses, was such that they judged her close to madness. She had not furthered the cause when she discussed at Court Lady Huntingdon's practice of holding intimate conversations with God and angels. There, it was hinted publicly that Lady Huntingdon's religion was neither sensible nor reasonable, a verdict in which Mrs Grinfield rejoiced shortly before her dismissal.[80]

The dramatic failure of this further attempt to plant the gospel at the heart of the Court brought the Countess into renewed conflict with her former close religious friend, the wealthy Catherine Edwin, now turned Moravian. Edwin bore a more acceptable witness at Court through a seemingly more rational belief. She rejected Ann Grinfield's religious pronouncements and vigorously dissociated herself from Lady Huntingdon. As the project at Court collapsed, Whitefield reassured his patroness that in heaven Christ 'shall hold You up before the Mighty of the Noble';[81] however, she became decidedly jealous at this time of her chaplain's attentions to other titled ladies.[82]

The abortive venture at Court reveals Lady Huntingdon still careering between contemplative stillness and pregnant activity. She was so stung by the opposition orchestrated by Catherine Edwin that she immediately took and fitted out a more commodious house at Clifton. There she would 'head the little Society' of like-minded religious followers in order to counter the growing Moravian presence in Bristol. At the same time she appears to have perceived this small group of women as contemplatives, 'who live but to devote every hour more and more to the love and knowledge of the Lord Jesus': it was to be a 'retreat'.[83] Comprising the Countess, two other widows and Ann Grinfield, the formation of this cabal 'set Moravians in a flame' and 'Edwin beside Her Self . . . in Her fury'. The Countess's followers knew that she could be 'exceedingly . . . violent . . . against . . . Principles' with which she disagreed.[84] They also knew how different her sentiments were from the Moravians, and she was humbly advised to use 'a little tender treatment' at Bristol in order to win them over. Her view was that correct religion travelled such a narrow path that great confusion was caused if 'the Eye is not single and every moment looking to God'.[85] Yet it is ironic that on the infrequent occasions when she turned from religious speculation and disputation, Lady Huntingdon was capable of rendering to individuals advice practical and encouragement realistic, especially regarding matters legal and financial.[86]

The contemplative retreat at Bristol soon proved to be a mirage rather than an oasis. The Countess became obsessed during this critical year, 1755, with the struggle against Moravians, just then establishing their Bristol congregation. She was assured that their reputation was at rock-bottom in London and that they were ridiculed for looking upon their leader, Count Zinzendorf, as 'the true Apostle, the Pope, the Perfect Pattern, the Paragon'. Howell Harris, cautiously edging himself back from his Welsh retreat into the evangelical movement, continued his constant efforts to effect understanding or even union between Methodism and Moravianism. Visiting the Countess at her Clifton home in 1757, he spent five hours in 'strong Battle' attempting to persuade her to keep an open mind about Zinzendorf and the Moravian Brethren.[87] Indeed, it may have been Harris who induced now in Lady Huntingdon a remarkable, albeit temporary, softening of attitude towards a group she had so strenuously numbered her foes. She was also doubtless sobered by the fact that two of the three select ladies at her Bristol retreat left her, having found Moravianism more suitable to their personal religious quests. By 1760 she appeared to be far more friendly towards the movement. She went so far as to visit their settlement at Bedford, and she also formed a totally different opinion of Count Zinzendorf once she had met him. She liked him 'vastly'.[88] Yet by 1762 the fluctuation had begun to cease, and it would not be long before she returned to as firm and fulsome a denunciation of the Moravians as ever.

Lady Huntingdon proved herself adamant that Methodism should remain within the bounds of the Church of England. She was kept informed of the progress made by Samuel Walker, incumbent clergyman at Truro, who encouraged his people in experimental religion but who vigorously opposed the irregularity of John Wesley's lay preachers. Walker believed that there were many parish ministers throughout the kingdom who were 'speaking the truth'. That is where the effort and energy of Methodism should be expended.[89] With few exceptions, most notably the leading Dissenter Philip Doddridge, the Countess's ecclesiastical connections had been almost solely with Anglican clerics or with those, like Harris, who desperately desired episcopal ordination. During the 1750s she continued to add to her circle of evangelically-minded clergymen, hoping to aid the extension of Methodist influence within the Established Church. To varying degrees these men were of Calvinistic orientation, but it is worthy of note that they generally tended to hold their predestinarian beliefs moderately. Notable among these was James Hervey who initiated a correspondence with the Countess in 1750 at Whitefield's behest. Hervey was a writer of florid poetry and prose, most famously his *Meditations Among the Tombs* (1746). He lived a retired life in his parish, rejecting itinerant preaching, which he considered to be 'repugnant to the apostolical as well as English constitution'.[90] As for predestination, Hervey stated that, 'be it true or false', it 'makes no part of my scheme'.[91] However, John Wesley certainly thought it did and attacked Hervey's writings with vigour, while Lady Huntingdon remained closely interested in and supportive of Hervey until his untimely death in 1758.[92]

Three other noted evangelical Anglican clerics the Countess supported during this period were Henry Venn, Martin Madan and William Romaine. Venn became curate of Clapham in 1754, and by the following year she had heard of his 'glorious' preaching. In a thirteen-paged letter, she encouraged Venn's new-birth commitment, assuring him that she was 'inseparably your companion in this narrow road to Zion. . . . My Dr Friend dont let your heart shrink back from your companion.'[93] She was charmed with Martin Madan,[94] a former barrister who had been converted by the preaching of John Wesley and in 1750 had taken up the London post of chaplain to the Lock Hospital, a refuge for fallen women. William Romaine received her attention and support when he was dismissed from his clerical post as

Lecturer at St George's Church, Hanover Square, in 1755, in favour of a 'moral' preacher.[95] All these men saw their mission not only within the Church but within its churches and almost invariably sought to preach only in those parish pulpits open to them. Romaine went to the length of travelling incognito between his preaching engagements in order to lessen the chance of being taken for an itinerant preacher.[96] These clergymen would ultimately forsake the Countess's service and fall under her disapprobation; but for the present they reflected her devotion to strengthening the sinews of Calvinistic Methodism within the body of the Church of England. All these men were moderate in their Calvinism, which to a degree helped to keep open the possibility of further co-operation with the Wesley branch of Methodism.[97] However, while the Countess continued to find Charles Wesley's preaching a blessing, she judged his brother's to be 'dry'.[98]

Despite her keen religious interests, by the close of the 1750s Lady Huntingdon's leadership in Methodism moved in fits and starts. Tested and tried, it had yet to be proved.

Notes

1 Archbishop of Canterbury, Prerogative Court of Canterbury, to SH, 4 November 1746, Rayleigh. Over a decade later she was still attempting to secure money owed to her husband. Claim of SH, 9 June [1758], Additional Manuscripts 36,190, f. 54, British Library. Her portion of his personal estate was £2,300, which by 1750 she had drawn, together with another £400, 'which is more than her share'. General abstract of personal estate of TH, T3765/c/10, PRONI.

2 SH to Philip Doddridge, 23 February 1747, Humphreys, *Correspondence of Doddridge* 4:524-25; HH diary, 9 April 1747, 26 January 1748, *HHVL*, pp. 137, 178.

3 HH to GW, 17 December 1747, Trevecka 1745; Charlotte Pickering to SH, 12 August 1746, E4/8/10, CF. See also same to SH, 27 May 1746, 14D32/379, LRO.

4 HH ms diary, 5 January 1748, NLW; HH diary, 25 November 1747, *HHVL*, p. 164; anon. to SH, 20 April 1747, Trevecka 1643.

5 Edwin Welch, 'Lady Huntingdon's chapel at Ashby', *Transactions of the Leicestershire Archaeological and Historical Society* 66 (1992), p. 136; SH to Countess of Hertford, 13 June [1718: *sic*. 1747 or 48], HMC, *Report on the Manuscripts of Mrs Frankland-Russell-Astley* (London, 1900), pp. 209-10.

6 HH diary, 5 March 1748, *Journal of the Historical Society of the Presbyterian Church of Wales* 39 (1954), p. 45; 26 January 1748, *HHVL*, p. 178.

7 Thomas Hartley to GW, 15 March 1748, Papers of George Whitefield, Vol. II, no. 12, Library of Congress (quotation); GW to HH, 27 June 1747, Trevecka 1671; GW to SH, 29 September 1748, *Select Letters*, 2:185-86. The appointment as chaplain was executed on 1 September. Rylands Charter 772, Rylands.

8 GW to SH, 30 November, 28 January 1749, *Select Letters*, 2:294, 224; GW to Philip Doddridge, 21 December 1748, *ibid*., 2:216.

9 Francis, Lord Rawdon to FH, 5 August 1776, HMC *Hast*., 3:179. See also Thomas Jones to Robert Lovesgrove, 14 April 1790, F1/901, CF; Seymour, *Life and Times*, 2:204.

10 GW to JW, 1 September 1748, Baker, 26:327; JW to [CW], 15 September 1748, Baker, 26:330-31; GW to Bishop Zachary Pearce, 25 March 1756, Tyerman, *Life of Whitefield*, 2:364.

11 E. Boulton to SH, June 1788, F1/2024, CF; John Knyveton, 4 November 1763, Ernest Gray (ed.), *Man's Midwife* (London, 1946), p. 158.

12 HH diary, 7, 13 March 1744 (quotation); 6, 7, 9, 10 April 1747, *HHVL*, pp. 54, 55, 130, 134-37.

13 Philip Doddridge to Mercy Doddridge, 31 July 1748, Doddridge, no. 1375.

14 HH diary, 29 April 1749, *HHVL*, p. 224.

15 Geoffrey F. Nuttall, 'Howel Harris and "the grand table": a note on religion and politics 1744-50', *Journal of Ecclesiastical History* 39 (1988), pp. 532-41 *passim*. Seymour lists a further twenty-eight 'persons of distinction who attended at Lady Huntingdon's house at this time'. *Life and Times*, 1:108-9. However, as always, extreme caution must be used when approaching his work. Two letters he printed purporting to show that the Duchess of Marlborough (died 1744) became a Methodist 'are almost certainly fabrications designed to enhance Lady Huntingdon's reputation'. Frances Harris, *A Passion for Government. The Life of Sarah, Duchess of Marlborough* (Oxford, 1991), p. 344.

16 She used one occasional attender as a go-between with his brother, the Lord-Lieutenant of Ireland, in an attempt to remove restrictions on the movements of Methodists in that country. SH to [Charles] Stanhope, 30 October 1749, Yale 8.

17 Welch, *Spiritual Pilgrim*, p. 70. See also Paul Langford, *A Polite and Commercial People. England 1727-1783* (Oxford, 1989), p. 254.

18 Lady Elizabeth Hastings to SH, 24 April [between 1736 and 1739], 14D32/212, LRO.

19 See Catherine Walkinshaw to SH, 3 January, 20 February 1740, HA 13036, 13037; same to SH, 19 September, n.y., 14D32/470, LRO. For Walkinshaw, see Linda Colley, *In Defence of Oligarchy: the Tory Party 1714-60* (Cambridge, 1982), p. 257.

20 Horace Walpole to Horace Mann, 4 March 1749, W.S. Lewis (ed.), *Horace Walpole's Correspondence* 48 vols. (New Haven; Oxford, 1937-83), 20:33. The Countess's anti-Walpole opinions are clearly stated in a letter to her husband, 8 December 1744, Drew A54. For the political orientation of those who now attended her religious soirées see Nuttall, 'Grand table', pp. 540-41.

21 HH diary, 13 March 1744, 24 June 1748 (quotation), 30 June 1748, *HHVL*, pp. 55, 199, 200.

22 SH to TH, n.d., Drew A96; Magdalene Walmesley to Mrs Mott, 4 November 1745, 14D32/359, LRO (quotation).

23 SH to TH, n.d., Drew A98 (quotation); Henry Hastings to SH, 17 June 1746, 14D32/190, LRO; HH diary, 9 April 1747, *HHVL*, p. 137. As Bishop of Oxford, Potter had ordained some of the early Methodists, including John Wesley and Benjamin Ingham.

24 HH diary, 9, 12 June 1747, *HHVL*, pp. 145, 146.

25 HH diary, 12 February 1748, 4 March 1752, Tom Beynon (ed.), *Howell Harris's Visits to Pembrokeshire* (Aberystwyth, 1966), pp. 141, 214-15.

26 HH diary, 18 April 1749, *HHVL*, p. 217.

27 HH diary, 28 November 1749; 4, 9 January 1750; 5 September 1751, *HHVL*, pp. 247, 256, 259, 15.

28 HH diary, 5 September 1751 (reflecting on 1749); 20 December 1749, *HHVL*, pp. 15, 252.

29 HH diary, 2 July 1752; 11 November 1753 (reflecting on the change in Whitefield's practice in 1748); 13 June 1753, *HHVL*, pp. 272, 13, 227.

30 Thomas Jackson (ed.), *The Journal of the Rev. Charles Wesley* 2 vols. (London, 1849), 2:63 (3 August 1749) quotation; HH diary, 30 December 1749, 6 January 1750, *HHVL*, pp. 255, 257.

31 Constructed from Alun Wyn Owen, 'Howell Harris and the Trevecka "family"', *Transactions of the Calvinistic Methodist Historical Society* 44 (1959), pp. 8-9; 'Sidney Griffith', *Dictionary of Welsh Biography*, p. 300.

32 HH diary, 10 November 1770, *HHVL*, p. 19.

33 HH diary, 11 July 1748, *HHVL*, p. 204.

34 HH diary, 15 January 1744, 17 January 1750, *HHVL*, pp. 41, 261.

35 GW to Lady ____, 10 November 1748, *Select Letters*, 2:198. See also GW to [James Hervey], 13 January 1749, 2:221; GW to Mr. S____, 18 January 1749, 2:224; GW to Mr. B____, 10 March 1749, 2:244, all *ibid.*

36 James Hervey to his father, June 1750, Tyerman, *Oxford Methodists*, p. 160; Robert Cruttenden to Philip Doddridge, 18 September 1751, Doddridge, no. 1792.

37 GW to SH, 1 September 1748, *Select Letters*, 2:169 (quotation). See also GW to Governor B[elcher], 10 December 1752; GW to SH, 13 January 1753, *ibid.*, 2:461, 475 (where the Countess was planning to write to the Governor of Georgia, obviously on Whitefield's behalf).

38 SH to TH, 7, 14 May 1740, Drew A26, 28; Charlotte Pickering to SH, 7 July 1746, 14D32/381, LRO.

39 Robert Hemington to FH, 1 May, 26 June, 21 March [1751], HA 6297, 6299, 6292; GW to Doctor S____, 4 February 1751, *Select Letters*, 2:398; SH to Thomas Haweis, 6 March 1790, SMU 116.

40 SH to Philip Doddridge, 27 February [1743/4], Yale 1; SH to same, 10 May 1744 (in which she requests 100 copies of one of his printed sermons, 'in order to give away'), Humphreys, *Correspondence of Doddridge*, 4:331; Nuttall, 'Grand table', pp. 535-36.

41 Isabel Rivers, *Reason, Grace, and Sentiment. A Study of Religion and Ethics in England, 1660-1780*, Vol. 1 *Whichcote to Wesley* (Cambridge, 1991), p. 187; Philip Doddridge to Elizabeth Scott, 25 June 1745, Humphreys, *Correspondence of Doddridge*, 4:414 (quotation).

42 Duchess of Somerset to Theophilus Lindsey, 29 September 1751, Thomas Belsham, *Memoirs of the Late Reverend Theophilus Lindsey* (London, 1873), p. 319 (quotation); Seymour, *Life and Times*, 1:449; Robert Cruttenden to Philip Doddridge, 18 September 1751, Doddridge, no. 1792; Robert Hemington to FH, 26 June [1751], HA 6299.

43 SH to Philip Doddridge, 28 March 1750, Yale 3 (quotation); Robert Hemington to FH, [April 1752], HA 6306.

44 SH to CW, 7 October 1752, Black 24.

45 Ann Grinfield to SH, 21 July [1755], n.d. [1755], B16, 17. See also Thomas Hartley to SH, 20 May 1755, C2. Drew.

46 G. Ford to SH, 3 July 1755, B27. See also Thomas Hartley to SH, 24 May 1755, B34; [A. Barlow?] to SH, 25 April [1755], B60. Drew. As early as 1749 the Countess had purchased 100 copies of Law's *The Spirit of Prayer; or the Soul rising out of the Vanity of Time into the Riches of Eternity*, to distribute to her acquaintances. Parkinson, *Journal of Byrom*, Vol. II, Part II, pp. 491-92. See also SH to CW, 27 July 1756, Black 59.

47 Ann Grinfield to SH, [1755], Drew B9.

48 William Law to [SH], 10 January 1754, 'A collection of letters on the most interesting and important subjects', in *The Works of the Reverend William Law* (London, 1762), Vol. 9, Letter VII, pp. 122-24. For SH as the recipient of this letter, see John Byrom diary, 2 April 1761, Parkinson, *Journal of Byrom*, Vol. II, Part II, p. 629. For the flight of some Jacobites towards mysticism, see W. R. Ward, 'Anglicanism and assimilation; or mysticism and mayhem', in W. R. Ward, *Faith and Faction* (London, 1993), pp. 385-96.

49 George Stonehouse to CW, 2 April 1755, Letters chiefly addressed to the Rev. C. Wesley, Vol. VI, no. 75, Rylands.

50 SH to Mrs Charles Wesley, 10 September 1753, Black 22; CW to SH, 22 May, 28 July 1755, Wesley Family (Charles Wesley Division) Papers, 1735-1787, Drew.

51 SH to Philip Doddridge, 29 July 1747, Yale 2.

52 SH to CW, 10 July 1755, Black 42. She visited Aberford during July 1755, where Lady Margaret 'is in vast affliction'. SH to CW, 24 July 1755, Black 43; Lady Selina Hastings to SH, 8 July 1755, Drew B66.

53 HH diary, 2 August 1749, *HHVL*, p. 229.

54 Henry Rack, 'Survival and revival: John Bennet, Methodism, and the old dissent', in Keith Robbins (ed.), *Protestant Evangelicalism: Britain, Ireland, Germany and America c. 1750 – c. 1950* (Oxford, 1990), pp. 12-13.

55 HH diary, 29 April 1749, *HHVL*, p. 224; Ward & H., 20:319 (28 January 1750); GW to SH, 22 December 1752, Tyerman, *Life of Whitefield*, 2:289.

56 GW to CW, 22 December 1752, *Select Letters*, 2:464; Elizabeth Whitefield to John Bennet, 7, 21 November 1751 (quotation), PLP 113.2.2, 3, Rylands.

57 SH to CW, [1753], Black 23.

58 Rack, *Reasonable Enthusiast*, pp. 259-67.

59 Jackson, *Journal of Charles Wesley*, 2:81 (28 May, 1 June 1751); SH to CW, 25 January 1752, Black 21.

60 CW to SH, 4 August 1751, PLP 113.2.5, Rylands. The 'intercepted & carried' was inscribed by CW on his copy of the letter.

61 JW to CW, 4 December 1751, Baker, 26:479-80.

62 GW to CW, 22 December 1752, *Select Letters*, 2:465.

63 JW to CW, 20, 31 October 1753, Baker, 26:527, 528; CW to SH, 15 September 1753, Black 22 (this quotation is from CW's shorthand notes).

64 CW's shorthand note on SH to CW [August 1756], Black 60.

65 SH to CW, 1, 3, 6, 10, 26 December 1753, Black 25, 30, 26, 27, 28; Frederick C. Gill, *Charles Wesley the First Methodist* (London, 1964), p. 156. Later, she and Charles named their

third daughter after the Countess. Luke Tyerman, *The Life and Times of the Rev. John Wesley* 3 vols. (London, 1878. 4th edition), 2:556.

66 SH to CW, 10 July 1755, Black 42 (quotation); SH to Mrs Jones, 7 March 1753, Welsh Methodist (Wesleyan) Archives 870E D/DF F1/52, NLW; SH to Sarah Wesley, 30 June 1757; SH to CW, 1 September 1759, [August 1756], Black 63, 71, 61.

67 SH to CW, 21 October 1754, Black 35.

68 CW to SH, 22 May 1755; 11, 28, 9 June, 26, 28 May [1755] (quotations), Wesley Family (Charles Wesley Division) Papers, 1735-1787, Drew.

69 CW to Walter Sellon, 29 November 1754, Wesley Family (Charles Wesley Division) Papers, 1735-1787, Drew. See also Baker, *John Wesley and the Church of England*, Chapter 10; Rack, *Reasonable Enthusiast*, pp. 296-300.

70 JW to CW, 28 June 1755, Baker, 26:565; GW to SH, 24 September 1755, *Select Letters*, 3:144.

71 JW to Ebenezer Blackwell, 29, 9 April 1755, Baker, 26: 554, 555. See also SH to CW, 4 August 1755, Black 44.

72 CW to SH, 28 July [1755], Wesley Family (Charles Wesley Division) Papers, 1735-1787, Drew.

73 GW to SH, 24 September 1755, *Select Letters*, 3:143; CW to SH, 30 May 1755, Wesley Family (Charles Wesley Division) Papers, 1735-87, Drew; SH to CW, May 1755, Black 40.

74 SH to CW, 29 May 1755, Black 41; GW to SH, 17 February 1750, *Select Letters*, 2:329; ? Flemings to SH, 26 Ma[?] [1755], Drew B50.

75 Ann Grinfield to SH, [*c.* 1755]; Sarah Hodges to SH, 8 December 1753; E. Skrine to SH, 15 May 1755. Drew B10, B54, C7.

76 Countess of Hertford to SH, 5 February 1747/8, B48; Ann Grinfield to SH, [*c.* 1755], B17 (quotation). See also, same to SH, [1755], B9. Drew.

77 Robert Hemington to FH, 11 June [1749], HA 6281.

78 Horace Walpole to Horace Mann, 4 March 1749, Lewis, *Horace Walpole's Correspondence*, 20:33-34.

79 Ann Grinfield to SH, 12 [June? 1755]; [1755]; [1755]. Drew B13, 23, 9.

80 Ann Grinfield to SH, [1755]; [1755]; [1755] (quotation); 16 August [1755]; [1755]; 21 July [1755]. Drew B11, C4, B23, B20, B16.

81 Ann Grinfield to SH, [1755], 21 July [1755], Drew B10,16; CW to SH, 26, 28 May 1755, Wesley Family (Charles Wesley Division) Papers, 1735-1787, Drew; GW to SH, 11 July 1755, Drew B6 (quotation).

82 Ann Grinfield to SH, [1755], 12 [June? 1755], 2 [June? 1755], [1755]; GW to SH, 26 June 1755. Drew B9, 13, 14, 17, 1.

83 SH to Risdon Darracott, [1755], Bennett, *Star of the West*, p. 169.

84 Thomas Hartley to SH, 20 May 1755; Ann Grinfield to SH, [1755] (quotation). Drew C2, B84.

85 G. Ford to SH, 3 July 1755; Ann Grinfield to SH, 21 July [1755]. Drew B27, 16.

86 For example, SH to Mrs Jones, 7 March 1753, Welsh Methodist (Wesleyan) Archives 870E D/DF F1/52, NLW.

87 George Stonehouse to SH, 28 June 1755, Drew B53; HH ms diary, 18 August 1757, NLW.

88 Bristol Moravian Church diaries, 1756-91, Vol. 1, pp. 293, 332, 341, 346, 370, Bristol University Library; SH to Mrs H. Leighton, [November?] 1761, Duke (quotation).

89 A. Barlow to SH, 24 May 1755, Drew B35; Samuel Walker to JW, [20 October 1755], Baker, 26:607 (quotation).

90 James Hervey to SH, 2 February 1750, *Evangelical Register* 1 (1824), p. 7; Hervey to JW, [21 August 1739], Baker, 25:677 (quotation).

91 James Hervey to Lady Frances Shirley, 9 January 1755, Tyerman, *Oxford Methodists*, p. 290. She was Lady Huntingdon's aunt, to whom, in lieu of Lady Huntingdon, who declined the honour, Hervey dedicated his 1755 *Theron and Aspasio*.

92 A. Maddock to SH, 5 January 1759, Trevecka 2244. For the conflict between Hervey and Wesley see Tyerman, *Oxford Methodists*, pp. 301-307, 314-20.

93 G. Ford to SH, 3 July 1755, Drew B27; SH to [Henry Venn], 2 February 1757, C16A, CMS.

94 SH to Mrs A. Barlow, 31 July 1756, AL 2062, Bath Central Library; SH to CW, 27 July 1756, Black 59.

95 A. Barlow to SH, 3 July 1775, Drew B36.

96 Richard Hart to HH, 27 September 1764, Trevecca Group, letter 2838c, Calvinistic Methodist Archives, NLW. For Madan's firm opposition to field-preaching see Walter Shirley to SH, 21 October 1771, F1/1570, CF.

97 'Mr Venn...comforted my heart, by assuring me that Mr Madan is entirely clear of predestination.' CW to Sally Wesley, 10 May, n.y., Jackson, *Journal of Charles Wesley*, 2:216.

98 SH to CW, 7 September 1759, Black 72.

CHAPTER 4

'The children of so many prayers and tears'

One of the basic yardsticks religious movements use to measure effectiveness is the ability to establish their beliefs in the daily lives of their families and thereby to pass on those beliefs to their children. On the basis of this measurement, eighteenth-century evangelical leaders were not conspicuously successful. Howell Harris, George Whitefield and – spectacularly – John Wesley had turbulent marriages and family lives.[1]

Although the Countess of Huntingdon clearly yearned for her family to be a picture of eternity framed in domesticity, her spiritual turmoil spilled over into her intimate family relationships. In one of the many sermons preached and published by her ministers on the occasion of her death, it was stated that 'I have heard our departed friend say there was never known to be one person of the family besides herself, and a cousin, who had the appearance of the fear of God; so that they who were the nearest allied to her had the greatest aversion to her religion'. What this implies about her marriage after 1739 is impossible to gauge, but the Earl's death while creating dreadful personal problems may also have removed the possibility of increasingly serious tension. Another sermon at her death acknowledged that during the early 1740s 'her [religious] distress of mind arose to such a height, that some of the Earl's friends advised him to put her away, but his affection to her prevented him from following this advice'.[2]

There is no doubt regarding the reaction of Selina Hastings' children to the religious milieu she fashioned for them. Although she was certain that it was the duty of children to obey their parents in matters of faith,[3] not one of her own was to accept her evangelicalism. Not a single letter written to her by any of her children at any stage of their lives reveals the slightest inclination in that direction; and lest it be suggested that not all her children's letters can be supposed to have survived, any that would have revealed their religious commitment would have been to her the most prized, and preserved.

All seven of the Countess's children were born within the first decade of her marriage: one, Selina, born in 1735, died in infancy. Two sons, George (1730) and Ferdinando (1732), both died in 1743. Her last child, Henry, was born in 1739 and died in 1758. This left three children living: Francis (1729); Elizabeth (1731); and a second Selina (1737). Francis and Elizabeth soon proved to be strong-willed children whom the Countess found increasingly difficult to influence. Her frustration regarding them was patent: 'The children of so many prayers and tears, I doubt not shall one day be blest.'[4] Such a blessing was to prove elusive.

Naturally enough, Lady Huntingdon's greatest hopes rested upon her first-born, Francis, who at his father's death in 1746 assumed the earldom at the age of sixteen. In his younger school years Francis had been less than punctilious in writing. 'I should have been very happy with a letter from my d[ea]r little Frank but he does not make me a little [one]. . . . He has cost me a thousand uneasie thoughts.' 'It is now so long since your Mama had a letter from you.' 'Write to your Mama, who takes it a little unkind not to have received any letter from you during the time you was at Winchester. . . . Pray don't neglect writing to her by the first post.'[5] It is likely that the young boy did not take kindly to his mother's entreaties to make pleasing God his 'first Care' and to act 'in Obedience to his Commands'. In the early months following her conversion, the Countess ruefully commented that her son George 'seem'd to show no more pleasure in seeing his sister and me than if we had been a Couple of dead doges or Cats'.[6] In the same year that he was criticising a friend for taking Christianity too seriously, the Countess intended to place Francis 'at the Lord's feet'.[7] Yet, remarkably, she placed him at the feet of Philip Dormer Stanhope, Lord Chesterfield. It can be supposed that she was torn between a desire for her son's religious well-being and his potential future in England's leading aristocratic circles. In a confused and despondent state following her husband's death, it perhaps is not surprising that she turned to an eminent man who not only became willing guardian of the young new Earl but was highly placed and capable of giving him the gentle graces of a nobleman.

However, it is amazing that Lady Huntingdon entrusted her son to a man whose mistress had been her aunt. Whatever else this patron offered his young protégé, it was not religious guidance. 'Whoever has lived much in the world and read much of it, will wonder at none of those absurdities and extravagancies, which the mind of man intimidated by fear, invited by interest, or perverted by vanity, is capable of entering very seriously, and even with warmth and acrimony. Witness, most of the systems of philosophy, and most sects of religion.'[8] A noted deist, Chesterfield was determined to shape Francis in his own image, a task in which he was resoundingly successful. (See illustration 6.) Chesterfield was resolved that the young man, a generation younger but none the less his senior in the peerage, should make an early start in becoming a model aristocrat. Therefore, Francis left Oxford early in 1749 after only a few terms to commence a grand tour of Europe which would last for five years, broken only by a year back in England. In the process the young Earl of Huntingdon visited Voltaire, Fontennelle, Duclos, Frederick the Great and the King of Spain. When Mozart came to England in 1764, Helvétius wrote to Francis, addressing him as '*l'Apollone de l'Angleterre*', begging his protection of the '*petit prodige allemand*'. Francis was elected a Fellow of both the Royal Society and the Society of Antiquaries.[9]

Francis also met women – perhaps more than his fair share. According to reports, he drove one young Scottish noblewoman to madness.[10] 'I have met with no one body absurd enough to suppose that you left England a spotless virgin, or to expect, if you had, that you would have returned such to it.' 'Read men and women, but read the latter unbound for some years at least', advised Chesterfield. He further warned Francis to avoid certain French women: 'Singing, dancing, and theatrical girls with Id genus omne are vilifying and dangerous, though much the fashion.'[11] This advice Francis failed to observe, a fashion he failed to resist. He soon was having an affair with the eighteen-year-old Louise Madeleine Lany, the leading dancer at the Paris Opera.[12] The issue of this intrigue was a son, Charles, born in Paris in 1752. Although Francis later acknowledged his illegitimate son and secured him position, he cruelly neglected his mistress. Moving on to Madrid, fully conscious that a lack of constancy towards women was 'unluckily rooted in my nature', he continued his liaisons with various women throughout his European pilgrimage. Towards the end of this continental idyll Chesterfield reckoned that 'you have now been abroad at least twenty years, not by the Calendar indeed, but by the use you have made of your travels, compared with other people's'.[13]

The results of the years abroad in shaping the young Earl put an end to any hopes Lady Huntingdon might have entertained that he could be moulded into an evangelical lord. That, of course, was the last thing that Chesterfield would have desired for his ward. Any entanglements with the Countess's religious orientation would have spelt a far greater threat to Francis's place in society than a permanent attachment to a French dancer. Yet Chesterfield demanded that Francis show an outward filial loyalty and more than once chided him for his failings on that score. 'I have heard it whispered among women that you have not wrote to Lady Huntingdon above once since you left England. . . . Forgive me My dear Lord, if I take the liberty of begging you, for your own sake, to write to her from time to time with marks of affection. I neither know nor inquire how you are together; but be that as it will, my concern is only that you may appear blameless. One must sometimes sacrifice a little to appearances.' 'Your [public] character . . . must not have that little speck, which the least coldness between your mother and you would throw upon it, in the opinion of the majority.'[14] In spite of these injunctions, Francis avoided his mother and greatly upset her by refusing to visit her in Bath. She was ironically glad that he had not had to suffer 'the fatigue you must undergo for a few days upon my account. . . . Disposition only can render any act of kindness acceptable to the heart, let it wear never so costly an appearance. You will therefore find that I can be only thankful to you for a visit when inclination disposes you to comfort the infirmity and revive the declinings' of her 'life'.[15] Another exchange at this time clearly revealed the wall separating them. Francis had written to her, 'preaching' that she should take some pleasure from the world around her. Yet if she did, she felt she would have to take 'this dose of opium' twenty-four hours a day. She now accepted that Francis's 'pleasures ... are real truly earthly' and hoped that he would find 'that it is a mere passing Phantom you are living for, void of every reality to satisfie that demand your heart has of substantial good'. She believed that 'as I am satisfied by heaven and you by earth till one of these are inseficant for our happiness we shall make no Enquirys after them. ... I think I hear you say ... when will this old dull woman have done her Harangue – What has she to do to bring the Ideas of forty seven into those lively ones my present delightful sensations make for me at six and twenty?' She ruefully believed that he doubted her sanity.[16] Sensing correctly that his rejection of her religious stance was hardening into permanency, she renewed her increasingly desperate prayer that he accept her version of the gospel.[17]

Adding to their uneasy relationship was what at first glance might appear a mundane matter: the refurbishment of the family's Leicestershire estate, Donington Park, where the house was 'in a very ruinous condition'. It was so ruinous that 'two of our maids (both old ones) were eaten in their sleep by rats'.[18] Soon after Francis's departure for his prolonged European sojourns, Lady Huntingdon assumed the responsibility for physical improvements, which occupied not a small portion of her time. 'I will stick by your house night and day', she pledged. Here she indulged her special taste for the Gothic. To an unsuspecting Francis she wrote: 'Cannot say I am without my cares how you will approve what is done, but I have the comfort of thinking it is the best I could do.'[19] Upon his return, Francis was devastated by the changes she had wrought to the fabric of his estate. 'My Lord the very moment He cast His eyes on the house condemned the whole proceeding, & put a stop to the work. ... All the windows of the old house are altered to Gothick.' The new part of the house 'tho it touched the old it seemed no part of it: a marriage of a girl of sixteen with an old man of four-score seemed to have as much union in it ... His dislikes out of doors were as great as those within. ... Lady H. took a world of pains & no doubt did all for the best but the success was not answerable to Her endeavours.' As Francis wrote to his sister, 'I dread telling you how ill my intentions have been executed at Donington. I am two thousand pounds out of pocket, & would give five hundred more to have the place in the same situation it was before the alterations were begun.' 'I am undoing a great part of what has been done.'[20] Visitors were dumbfounded. There were 'two tawdry rooms like assemblie rooms at Blackheath, added by the Countess Dowager'.[21] In 1765 Francis greatly upset his mother by refusing to be present at the opening of what was to her the most important project she had yet undertaken: a chapel at Bath. The following year Bath tittle-tattle was that he had 'taken out a Statute of Lunacy against her: that Madness is incident to the family'.[22]

Well before this, Lady Huntingdon's attention had turned to her only other surviving son, Henry, determined that he would be shaped by the religious ethos Francis had so emphatically rejected. She even harboured hopes that Henry would become an evangelical clergyman.[23] Although an observer commented that he had never seen a child 'of such strong passions & so much delighted with the most horrid cruelties', the Countess believed that Henry was growing so much like his late father 'that I look upon him with more delight than I can express'.[24] For his part, Francis held no high opinion of his younger brother's capacities, and Chesterfield felt that giving 'up your brother entirely to her disposal' would permanently deflect the Countess's attentions from interfering with Francis's progress in society. Yet by 1757 Henry's eyesight deteriorated towards total blindness, and his mother rushed him to Brighton, desperately seeking a cure. His death the following year struck her a devastating blow, yet the influence of men like Law and Hartley had had its effect. She began to feel a mystical union with her dead son: 'The inward & the outward . . . are equally real to me.'[25]

Even before she came to realise the finality of Francis's rejection, Lady Huntingdon had experienced a bitter foretaste by the defection of her eldest daughter, Elizabeth. This spirited girl had no intention of being at her mother's disposal. Her resentment at being whisked from Court in 1749 was deep, and she began talking of 'going to heaven with the cards in her hands', while the Countess forbade her reading standard English literature. Exasperated with her mother's religious notions, she argued fiercely against them, on one occasion dressed in 'a red damask & her rational soul'. She refused to be silenced even when her mother's domestic chaplain, George Baddelley, 'pronounced ex Cathedra against her'. In short, Elizabeth's life with her mother was 'void of every thing agreeable'.[26]

A desperate Lady Huntingdon now trained on Elizabeth the biggest gun at her command: George Whitefield. The occasion was the death of Lady Gertrude Hotham's daughter, who apparently was an 'intimate' acquaintance of Elizabeth. Whitefield penned a remarkable letter, which the Countess hoped would nudge the recalcitrant girl towards embracing her religious affections. He wrote that he had prayed at Miss Hotham's bedside, and that ultimately she had uttered such words as 'what a wretch am I'. That had comforted Lady Gertrude, and Whitefield was persuaded that 'the same considerations' would have a like effect upon Elizabeth: 'Methinks I hear your Ladyship add "No – I'll not stop here. By divine grace, I will devote myself to Jesus Christ now & give him no rest till I see the world in that light as dear Miss Hotham did, & as I myself shall when I come to die. I will follow my honoured Mother, as she follows Jesus Christ."'[27]

On the contrary, Elizabeth viewed her mother as 'righteous over-much' and was unnerved by her 'pious ejaculations'. Early in 1752 she ended this 'disagreeable situation' by marrying an Irish nobleman relation, Lord John Rawdon. She would move where it would be unnecessary for her to have 'communication' with her mother.[28] She wrote to her brother Francis that she had 'lived a life of duty with my mother, [but] I own it grew wearisome at length, and was a strong inducement to my marrying. . . . It leaves me governess of my own actions, which shall be such I trust as not to displease a rational mind.' 'Independence' from her mother, she later reflected, 'was my sole inducement' to marry.[29]

Lady Huntingdon turned to the world a brave face, speaking of the good social and financial standing of her new son-in-law, and hoping that his serious character might lead him in time to accept evangelical doctrine. In reality, the Countess reacted to the marriage by denouncing the things of the world and all human affection: the 'doctrine of loving no person or thing is very fashionable with us'.[30] For her part, Elizabeth let it be known that her refusal to accept her mother's version of Christianity was because of her observation of the people who professed it.[31]

Following her marriage, and now in charge of over thirty servants,[32] Elizabeth lived permanently in Ireland and apparently never saw her mother again during the remaining forty years of the Countess's life. It was clear to other members of the family that to do so 'would be disagreeable' to Elizabeth.[33] Only a handful of letters between mother and daughter are extant, and their content would suggest that but a handful were ever written. The passionately anti-Roman Catholic Lady Huntingdon must have been thoroughly shocked at her erstwhile daughter's increasingly active support for Catholic emancipation in Ireland. As early as 1765 Elizabeth was writing to Francis that the Irish Catholics 'naturally preferred the moderate principles of an Englishman's to the early Protestant bigotry a Scotchman or an Irishman imbibes'.[34] In fact, as a leader of Irish society, Elizabeth took an active – even dangerous – part in attempting to apply her Whiggish political principles to aiding the 'Peasantry of the North' who, through the 'Oppression & Tyranny' of 'a wretched Police' were 'reduced . . . to a state of starving'.[35]

Elizabeth's new social activities were also a blatant rejection of her mother's principles. In her new home she was 'very gay' and read a great deal – 'books of all kinds to amuse the fancy as well as improve the mind'.[36] The Countess of Huntingdon had considered grand balls stupid. Now, Elizabeth from her Dublin home, Moira House, made a habit of staging remarkably elaborate costume balls with 'fancied dresses' for as many as 500 guests, including her own children dressed as Cupid and Psyche.[37] It must have been mortifying to Lady Huntingdon that there was extensive talk at Bath of the magnificence of her daughter's house in Dublin, and the 'splendor' of her 'assemblies'.[38] Elizabeth was the most brilliant of the Countess's children, and her stylish and urbane letters sparkle with a keen wit and satirical twist of humour. In recommending to Francis various types of women as possible wives, she suggested that 'your wanderings, nay – even your infidelities, will pass unregarded if you flatter with a childish indulgence – an elegant ring, a diamond fly or beetle for her hair, a rich piece of brocade'.[39]

From the distance of her Irish retreat, Elizabeth continued to view her mother with an irritable eye. The animosity between the two spilled over to servants. One at Donington wrote to Elizabeth's female companion in Ireland that 'all the last summer while Lady H. was at the park I dared not for fear of jealousy & suspicion write a word'. Open communication could be dangerous: 'To answer your Question in a former letter, none have a sight of yours to me. Write what you please.' This same servant informed Elizabeth that her younger sister Selina had not written to her, but that Selina was not to blame. 'I am sure you have sagacity enough to guess. . . . I fear I shall be forced to hear many things said, that will give me pain.'[40] Francis oversaw the education in England of Elizabeth's two eldest sons, but she was hardly pleased when he informed her that they had visited their grandmother, who gave them each a watch chain. 'They both think her a very lively good sort of old woman.'[41] Later, Francis introduced one of Elizabeth's daughters into English polite society and was instrumental in seeing her married. The presence of the Countess of Huntingdon at this wedding, and the general knowledge that she was the bride's grandmother, led to the belief that the bride shared her religious notions. 'Some Methodists in the neighbourhood insist I am one of their sect, which has given great anguish of mind to our vicar, however I have nearly convinced him I am not.' In any case, it was Elizabeth's firm belief that 'Bad Hearts are to be kept at as great a distance as possible',[42] a maxim she maintained without respite in regard to her mother. During the final twenty years or so of Lady Huntingdon's life there appears to have been no communication at all between them. Elizabeth wrote that she was 'totally ignorant' of all her mother's affairs and entered this abrupt note in her memorandum book on 17 June 1791: 'My Mother dyed this day.'[43]

In differing yet decisive ways by the early 1750s the Countess of Huntingdon had lost influence over her two eldest children. She therefore desperately sought to inculcate her commitment into the remaining two. She was advised not to 'break the peace', since 'we cannot honestly direct others' to a power they have lost. The best she could hope for was to maintain the proper forms.[44] That is advice that the Countess was never willing to contemplate. With the death of Henry in 1758, upon which 'nothing can exceed the affliction of heart of the afflicted mother',[45] all her efforts, all her prayers, now were focused on her namesake, the twenty-year-old Lady Selina, 'the idol of her heart'.[46] (See illustration 7.) Lady Huntingdon built upon her daughter's earlier presence at the parlour preaching of men such as Whitefield,[47] but Lady Selina became liable to fall into 'an Hysterical fit'. She was exceptionally close to Francis and Elizabeth – to both of whom she was 'the Kitten' – a closeness clearly conveyed in their letters.[48] Nowhere in those letters is there any reference to God or religion, let alone any hint of the fervent evangelicalism so central to their mother's sense of reality. It is clear that Lady Selina's movements were monitored. On one occasion, one of the Countess's female followers wrote to issue an urgent warning: it had been rumoured that Selina, Francis and Elizabeth were 'to be together in a house in town'. She felt it her 'duty to let you know what I have heard that you may be upon your guard and act accordingly'.[49] Lord Chesterfield referred to Selina's 'perfect beauty', and other men were likewise smitten: 'I have lately seen more of Lady Selina than I ever had opportunity before. I cannot but esteem & honour her the more.'[50] Now left alone with her mother, this charming young woman was to face the full force of the Countess's commitment to save her soul.

Selina was bereft at her sister's marriage and immediate departure from England. Four months later, she wrote to Elizabeth: 'When I am in good spirits the thoughts of Ireland & yr. Distance from me Checks them, & when I am low it gives me the Vapours.' She suffered 'pain, in reflecting the distance that divides us, tho it never can divide our Hearts'.[51] Over the following decade her letters to her elder sister struck the same plaintive note: 'When shall we meet again?' 'I love you too well not to suffer much from the separation we have had ever since I lost you, nor has length of time reconciled me in the least better for it, for I dont find it easy to meet with a friend in all respects such as you my dear Sister ever was to me.' 'My Brother tells me you have dashed all hopes of our seeing you. You must know how great this disappointment must be to us.' She encouraged her sister to write freely, assuring her that their mother would not be able to read the letters. Elizabeth should write such on a separate sheet, and Selina 'can easily avoid' showing it, 'as my letters are brought to me generally early in the morning in my own room'.[52] On her eighteenth birthday, she wrote to her sister's companion – a woman for whom the Countess harboured a hearty dislike – thanking her for birthday greetings. Here Selina reflected at length on growing older, the attachments and disppointments of life – but, as ever, not a single word regarding religion or trust in God.[53]

Apart from expressing deep unhappiness without her, Selina regaled her sister with political news, current London fashions and social gossip. One 'Lady S.L.' had a pet hedgehog which she carries 'about with her, & produces it to everybody. I hear she has renewed her affair with Ld. Newbattle.' Lady Selina's most exciting news was that she had been selected one of the six train bearers for the Queen at the coronation of George III on 22 September 1761. Brother Francis had given her dress, and 'I have borrowed all the Jewels I can'.[54] Following the event, she gave a detailed account of the proceedings, and a footnote to the day caught her particular fancy. One of the ladies came to the room where the train-bearers had gathered and

> clasping to the door in a Violent fit of laughter as soon as she could speake she satisfied our curiosity with telling us, she had bolted upon the Duke of Newcastle, who, had indeed verified the old proverb (that necessity has no law), by coming there [a door out of the apartment, which opened to a 'convenient place'] to relieve his wants. You may imagine how much this Idea diverted us. A consultation was called whether he should be released, or remain under confinement til the Queen went to St. James's.

Selina and the other ladies decided on confinement, and the Duke was trapped for a full hour, since there was no other means of escape.[55]

Only once was the sisters' separation broken, when after a protracted period of beseeching her mother, Selina was allowed to visit Ireland, arriving during the summer of 1757. 'I cannot account for their being together: Nothing was farther from my thoughts than imagining Lady H. would permit it.'[56] It was through Francis's persistent lobbying that his mother finally consented; and in his view the longer the stay, the better: 'I hope you will detain Selina as long as possible. I wish she could pass the winter with you, both for your sake & her own.' In spite of the joy this visit brought to both sisters, they were never to meet again. In 1761 Francis wrote to Elizabeth that 'dr. Sister Selina is well, & loves you as well as I do'.[57] Yet two years later, on the verge of marriage, Lady Selina was dead. Distracted with grief, the Countess's primary purpose was to persuade all about her, and herself, that Selina had finally accepted the religious zeal to which she and her brothers and sisters had hitherto proved immune. Most especially, Lady Huntingdon wished to drive home the point to Elizabeth, who had remained so unmoved by Whitefield's parallel efforts a dozen years earlier. To this end the Countess wrote a letter describing the death of 'my Dearest my altogether lovely child and daughter ... the desire of my eye and constant pleasure of my heart'. The point was that Selina had at the end finally seen light and undergone an unqualified death-bed conversion. In the last stages of her fever, she had 'frequently call'd on the Lord Jesus to have mercy on her', and in the final four days Lady Huntingdon heard her say '"Jesus teach me, Jesus wash me, change me, purify me. ... Two Angels are beckoning me to come and I must go, but I cannot yet get up the ladder."' According to her mother, two days before she died came the crucial words, addressed to her mother: 'Now I understand you.'[58]

That the Countess of Huntingdon experienced grief 'beyond bounds'[59] at this loss was perhaps natural; but the extent of that grief tends to call into question her belief in the efficacy of Selina's dying repentence. Indeed, her distress was such that it shocked a number of her closest evangelical supporters. As the Countess reached a crescendo of despair, John Berridge wrote:

> Is it not better to have your Selina taken to heaven, than to have your heart divided between Christ and Selina? If she was a silver idol before, might she not have proved a golden one afterwards?... Had she crossed the sea and gone to Ireland [as had Elizabeth], you could have borne it; but now she is gone to heaven 'tis almost intolerable. Wonderful strange love this! Such behaviour in others would not surprise me, but I could almost beat you for it, and I am sure Selina would beat you too, if she was called back but one moment from heaven, to gratify your fond desires. I cannot soothe you. ... I am glad the dear creature is gone to heaven before you; lament if you please, but Glory, glory, glory, be to God.

A fortnight later this same correspondent wrote: 'I find your heart was sorely pained, and I pitied you, but durst not soothe you; for soothing, though it eases grief for a moment only makes Lady Self grow more burdensome, and occasions more tears in the end. A little whipping from your Father will dry up your tears much sooner than a thousand lullabies from your brethren. And I now hope you will be well soon.'[60] But Lady Huntingdon was not well soon. In her plangent distraction she discussed vague plans to leave England to settle in Canada, and four months after Selina's death another clergyman was imploring: 'Come, my Lady, let us travel on, sticking close to our heavenly Guide.' Yet still the lament continued: 'I have been hurt & wounded to death.'[61]

However, there might be some compensation. As the Countess had written to Charles Wesley upon the death of his son: 'A dead sorrow is better than a living one. The chance against us parents ... for happiness [is] a hundred to one.'[62] She had been comprehensively unable to secure among her own sons and daughters her passionate religious faith. As she wrote to her 'agent' at Court, Ann Grinfield, 'you do me more credit than any of my children'.[63] The year following Selina's death, the Countess of Huntingdon began to lay plans for a college, an institution which was to become for her a surrogate family, a family with fully obedient and lively children.

Notes

1 See Paul Sangster, *Pity My Simplicity. The Evangelical Revival and the Religious Education of Children, 1738-1800* (London, 1963), pp. 182-83.

2 T[imothy] Priestley, *A Crown of Eternal Glory* (London, 1791), p. 25 (The cousin was Walter Shirley); W[illiam] Aldridge, *A Funeral Sermon Occasioned by the Death of the...Countess...of Huntingdon* (London, 1791), p. 17.

3 HH diary, 29 April 1749, *HHVL*, p. 224.

4 SH to Philip Doddridge, 8 November 1747, Humphreys, *Correspondence of Doddridge*, 5:21.

5 SH to TH, 14 April [*c.* 1745]; TH to FH, 26 March, 27 June 1741. HA 5857, 6117, 6121.

6 SH to FH, 5 July 1740; SH to TH, 28 April 1740. Drew A32, 24.

7 H. Legge to FH, 26 February 1748, HA 8185; SH to Countess of Hertford, [21 December 1718: sic. 1747 or 1748], HMC, *Report on Manuscripts of Mrs. Frankland-Russell-Astley*, p. 211.

8 Lord Chesterfield to FH, 24 September 1750, A. Francis Stewart (ed.), *Letters of Lord Chesterfield to Lord Huntingdon* (London, 1923), pp. 21-22.

9 Willard Connely, *The True Chesterfield* (London, 1939), p. 465; HMC *Hast.*, 3:xi, xii; Lord Chesterfield to FH, 17 May 1753, Stewart, *Letters of Chesterfield*, pp. 76-77.

10 David Murray, Viscount Stormont to FH, 30 August 1754, HA 9494.

11 Lord Chesterfield to FH, 15 November 1750, 26 June 1749, 29 September 1750, Stewart, *Letters of Chesterfield*, pp. 31, 3, 26. Francis had written some rather dreadful love verses 'upon a woman in the warmth of a young passion', *ibid.*, p. 31.

12 Mlle Lany was highly praised as a dancer. Jean G. Noverre, *Letters on Dancing and Ballets* (London, 1930), p. 67; Cyril W. Beaumont, *A Miscellany for Dancers* (London, 1934), pp. 46, 47; Crane, *Kirkland Papers*, p. 4.

13 FH to EH, 20 May 1750, T3765/M/2/14/2, PRONI (quotation); [Viscount Stormont] to FH, 10 April 1755, HA 9498; Lord Chesterfield to FH, 25 October 1755, Stewart, *Letters of Chesterfield*, p. 92 (quotation). Upon his return to England, Francis was appointed in 1756 Master of the Horse in the Prince of Wales' newly-established household and in 1761 Groom of the Stole, an office he held until 1770. Over a decade after the birth of his son, Mlle Lany wrote to ask for money and informed him that she had married an opera singer. Charles Selwin to FH, 16 July 1764, HA 10735. She continued a successful professional career until 1767, a decade before her death. Crane, *Kirkland Papers*, p. 5. Francis died a bachelor. 'I can never believe Lord Huntingdon will marry. He holds women in such a contemtable [*sic*] light that to be sure he never will, never, trust one of us with his honour.' Duchess of Hamilton to Lady Gower, 29 May 1769, Duke of Argyll (ed.), *Intimate Society Letters of the Eighteenth Century* 2 vols. (London, n.d.), 1:136.

14 Lord Chesterfield to FH, 31 August 1749, 9 October 1756, Stewart, *Letters of Chesterfield*, pp. 7, 109.

15 [Ann Grinfield] to SH, n.d., Drew C4; SH to FH, 13 November 1756, Drew A70 (quotation).

16 SH to FH, January 1755, Drew A73.

17 SH to FH, 14 [September?] 1756, Drew A69.

18 Lady Selina Hastings to EH, 23 May 1755; Robert Hemington to [Mary Mott], 8 April [1752]. T3765/M/2/17, 23, PRONI.

19 SH to FH, 21 July 1755, Drew A67; SH to FH, 29 June 1756, HMC *Hast.*, 3:118.

20 Robert Hemington to [Mary Mott], n.d.; FH to EH, 19 May 1757, [summer 1757], T3765/M/2/23, M/2/14/14, 19. It took him nearly a decade to alter the alterations. FH to EH, 4 July 1764, 6 April 1765, T3765/M/2/14/45, 47. PRONI.

21 'Walpole's visits to country seats', *The Walpole Society* 16 (1927-28), p. 64.

22 Lord Chesterfield to FH, 19 October 1765, Stewart, *Letters of Chesterfield*, p. 124; John

Penrose to Peggy Penrose, 27 April 1766, John Penrose, *Letters from Bath* (Glouster [*sic*], 1983), p. 60 (quotation).

23 Lord Chesterfield to FH, 9 October 1756, Stewart, *Letters of Chesterfield*, p. 109.

24 Robert Hemington to FH, [1752]; SH to EH, 27 September 1755. HA 6306, 5840.

25 Lord Chesterfield to FH, 9 October 1756, Stewart, *Letters of Chesterfield*, pp. 108-9; SH to CW, 9 December 1758, Black 67.

26 Robert Hemington to FH, 22 August 1749; 8 September [*c.* 1750]; 26 June, 25 November [*c.* 1751], HA 6283, 6289, 6299, 6294. After Princess Amelia had firmly rejected the Countess's efforts to 'convert' her through the agency of Ann Grinfield, the Princess maintained an affection for and interest in Elizabeth and Francis. FH to EH, 23 October 1766, T3765/M/2/14/53, PRONI.

27 GW to [EH], 22 September 1750, PLP 113.1.15, Rylands.

28 JW to EH, 18 March 1760, Frederick C. Gill (ed.), *Selected Letters of John Wesley* (London, 1956), no. 116; Robert Hemington to FH, 21 March [*c.* 1751], 1 March [1752], 5 January [1753]. HA 6292, 6296, 6307.

29 EH to FH, 13 December 1752, 27 September 1769, HA 10413, 10431.

30 SH to CW, 25 January 1752, Black 20; Robert Hemington to FH, [1752], HA 6306 (quotation).

31 Walter Shirley to SH, 28 September 1760, E4/1/3, CF. See also Shirley to JW, 1 November 1760, *Arminian Magazine* 20 (1797), p. 407.

32 EH to SH, 9 July [1755], Drew B67.

33 Lady Selina Hastings to EH, n.d., T3765/M/2/17, PRONI.

34 EH to FH, 26 January 1765, HMC *Hast.*, 3:144. See also EH to the Countess of Granard, [2 May 1782?], T3765/J/9/1/12, PRONI. Her famous son, Francis Rawdon-Hastings, went on to become an ardent and active supporter of Catholic emancipation. Marianne Elliott, *Wolfe Tone* (New Haven, 1989), p. 166; Frank Mac Dermot, *Theobald Wolfe Tone* (London, 1939), pp. 57, 102, 108, 111, 124; A.P.W. Malcomson, *John Foster. The Politics of the Anglo-Irish Ascendancy* (Oxford, 1978), pp. 409-10.

35 EH to FH, n.d. [early 1772], T3765/M/2/14/89, PRONI. For her lenient views towards Roman Catholics, see also Malcomson, *John Foster*, p. 239; EH to Charles Hastings, 26 March 1804, HA 10437. For her continuing active concern for the poor, see EH to Walter Shirley [junr], 22 January 1801, 26D53/2119, LRO.

36 Mary Delany to Mrs Dewes, 24 February 1753, 25 October 1758, Lady Llanover, *Autobiography and Correspondence of Mary Granville*, 3:208, 526.

37 FH to EH, 30 April 1768, T3765/M/2/14/63, PRONI (quotation); same to same, [*c.* 1770 or 1771], HMC *Hast.*, 3:150-52; Elizabeth Vesey to Elizabeth Montagu, n.d., Reginald Blunt (ed.), *Mrs. Montagu 'Queen of the Blues.' Her Letters and Friendships from 1762 to 1800* 2 vols. (London, [1923]), 1:171-72.

38 FH to Lord John Rawdon, 14 January 1757, T3765/M/2/14/13, PRONI.

39 EH to FH, 13 October 1756, HA 10415. There is a severely damaged portrait of Elizabeth in the Woburn Abbey Collection.

40 Robert Hemington to [Mary Mott], 8 April [mid-1750s]; n.d.; 16 September [mid-1750s]. T3765/M/2/23, PRONI.

41 FH to EH, [1770 or 1771], T3765/M/2/14/61, PRONI.

42 Anne Arksburg to EH, 17 September 1788, T3765/M/2/26A; EH to Countess of Granard, 1 August 1782, T3765/J/9/1/29. PRONI.

43 EH to Walter Shirley [junr], 22 January 1801, 26D53/2119, LRO; EH, Memorandum Book for 1791, T3765/L/4, PRONI.

44 Thomas Hartley to SH, 10 July 1755, Drew B33.

45 Theophilus Lindsey to Lord John Rawdon, 13 September 1758, T3765/M/2/20/6, PRONI.

46 According to Countess Delitz, quoted in Nuttall, 'Grand table', p. 544.

47 HH ms diary, 29 April 1749, NLW. However, when Howell Harris dined with the Countess, Francis, Elizabeth and Selina, he was disappointed that there was 'no evangelical conversation'. *Ibid.*

48 Robert Hemington to FH, 21 March [*c.* 1751], HA 6292; FH to EH [between July and October] 1757, T3765/M/2/14/3/16, PRONI.

49 Ann Grinfield to SH, 22 [January 1754], Drew B24. Apparently Elizabeth and her husband were at this time making a brief visit to England.

50 Lord Chesterfield to FH, 6 November 1756, Stewart, *Letters of Chesterfield*, p. 113; Theophilus Lindsey to Lord John Rawdon, 8 November 1758, T3765/M/2/20/7, PRONI.
51 Lady Selina Hastings to EH, 10 June 1752, T3765/M/2/17, PRONI.
52 Lady Selina Hastings to EH, 12 March, n.y.; 23 May, n.y.; n.d., T3765/M/2/16, PRONI.
53 Lady Selina Hastings to Mary Mott, [1755], T3765/M/2/17, PRONI.
54 Lady Selina Hastings to EH, n.d., [*c.* September 1761], T3765/M/2/17, PRONI.
55 Lady Selina Hastings to EH, [post-22 September 1761], T3765/M/2/17, PRONI.
56 Robert Hemington to Mary Mott, 28 November [1757], T3765/M/2/23, PRONI.
57 FH to EH, [between July and October 1757], 29 January 1761, T3765/M/2/14/16, 20, PRONI.
58 SH to EH, [12 May 1763], T3765/M/2/21/5, PRONI.
59 Lord John Rawdon to FH, 17 May 1763, HA 10441.
60 John Berridge to SH, 23 June, 9 July 1763, Richard Whittingham (ed.), *The Whole Works of the Rev. John Berridge* (London, 1864. 2nd edition), pp. 446-48.
61 John Berridge to SH, 16 July 1763, Letters of Berridge, Rayleigh; JF to SH, 10 September 1763, MAM P4d, p. 93, Rylands (quotation); SH to HH, 27 October 1763, Trevecka 2838a (quotation).
62 SH to CW, 8 January 1754, Black 33.
63 SH to Ann Grinfield, [*c.* 1755], SMU unnumbered.

Chapter 5

'Mistress to a school of prophets'

In the face of a possible French invasion during the early months of 1759, the Countess of Huntingdon held fervent prayer meetings in her London house.[1] Yet her hopes for a renewed role of religious leadership were dealt a serious blow the following year by one of the most notorious public scandals of the age: the arrest of one of her close relations on a charge of murder.

Laurence Shirley had inherited in 1745 the title of Earl Ferrers at the death of the Countess's uncle, who had 'the misfortune to be a lunatic'. Shirley's subsequent marriage unleashed his own ungovernable temper to the extent that in 1758 his wife was granted a legal separation by a special act of parliament, which also vested his estates with trustees. Two years later, at Staunton Harold – the very house in which Selina Shirley had lived for several years before her marriage – he shot and killed a man acting as one of the receivers of Ferrers' estates. The resulting trial before the Lords of Lady Huntingdon's first cousin was one of the sensations of the eighteenth century. Before his execution at Tyburn in May 1760 he was visited frequently by the Countess, who sought to turn a noted crime into an even more spectacular conversion. Charles Wesley was active in supporting her in this endeavour, leading constant public prayers: 'Surely that murderer will be given to us.' The enterprise failed.[2]

Ferrers' trial and execution upheld the premise that all stood equal before the law, yet it seriously if unfairly tainted the Countess's reputation. For thirty years she had been involved in bitter conflict with him over the family's inheritance from her father, and he stood in debt to her for £5,000.[3] She joined other members of the Shirley family in a futile petition to the King for mercy, and the whole affair seriously undermined her health.[4] This tragic episode brought her into closer contact with the executed Earl's younger brother, the Reverend Walter Shirley, an Irish cousin who was being drawn into her London circle in the late 1750s.[5]

The theme of Lady Huntingdon's religious activities during the 1760s was to gather evangelically minded Anglican clerics under her wing, to induce bishops to ordain more of their number and in general to promote thereby the internal invigoration of the Church of England. An important mark of her fostering such clergymen was her invitation to the Swiss-born John Fletcher occasionally to preach and celebrate communion at her house. Soon after, in 1761, she appointed William Romaine and Martin Madan as her chaplains.[6] These appointments ran concurrently with a dramatic new enterprise. The Countess argued that as a peeress of the realm she was entitled to attach to her private residences chapels exempt from episcopal jurisdiction. They might hold several hundred persons, but she reasoned that it would only be an extension of the principle she followed in opening her drawing rooms to religious services. It is clear, however, that she was indulging in a kind of ecclesiastical subterfuge,[7] and though she undoubtedly believed that she remained a faithful Anglican this programme of chapel-building, whatever the legal niceties, was the first, the most visible and most decisive step towards her final separation from the Church of England twenty years later.

The main chapels Lady Huntingdon built during the 1760s were strategically sited, each at major watering places. Borrowing £1,000 from the ever faithful Lady Gertrude Hotham, in 1761 she built a small chapel thirty-six feet by eighteen, in the grounds of her private residence in Brighton.[8] The second main chapel built in this early period was in 1765, at Bath, which was to prove the jewel in her crown of chapels outside London. It was located in the Vineyards area of the expanding and fashionable 'Upper Town'. As its bold physical outlines began to emerge during construction, she was certain that her enemies wished her to die 'before it is finished'. She also was deeply hurt that she had 'not had a line from one creature to rejoice its being built'. The connection to the chapel of her private residence was unmistakable: the two-storey bay house with battlemented parapets fronted the chapel. It was opened for worship in October, with a copiously weeping Whitefield preaching. Howell Harris considered the chapel ostentatious and on the road to 'Popery' and was particularly concerned with the Countess's excessive pride in its ornamentation. For many years, this chapel would be the strongest net cast in the attempt to catch and convert the titled and moneyed classes. She had no doubt that if she could manage the chemistry of combining her favourite preachers with her most sought after converts, it would be impossible for such people to do anything but respond just as she had responded. If, for example, he could only hear Martin Madan, the King would be converted.[9] Moreover, if some Anglican bishops taking the Bath waters could be persuaded from time to time to attend, the beauty of the chapel fabric and the unfailing use of the Book of Common Prayer would persuade them that Lady Huntingdon remained a faithful daughter of the Church of England. However, within five years of the chapel's opening she was informed that her belief that one bishop made a practice of attending 'was ill-founded'.[10] On the other hand, Lady Betty Cobbe, the wife of one of the Countess's first cousins, boasted of smuggling bishops and other worthies into what Lady Betty facetiously called the chapel's 'Nicodemus Corner', a curtained-off area where they could not be seen by other worshippers. How pleased Lady Huntingdon would have been with Lady Betty's efforts on behalf of the chapel if she had known that this young wife and mother was at the same time carrying on a passionate love affair with Francis, can only be imagined.[11]

The fevered activity involved in this chapel-building from 1761 to 1765, especially after the death of Selina in 1763, had taken its toll. Lady Huntingdon's 'perplexitys' and 'disapointments' had 'succeeded each day one another'. She felt herself 'destitute of all friends', and her letters during this period are particularly verbose and irrational. Colleagues were receiving 'light & heat from the burning & shining Countess'. John Fletcher, horrified by an outbreak of 'enthusiasm and offence' among her followers in London, begged Lady Huntingdon to use her influence to 'stop the plague'. Charles Wesley pleaded to like purpose regarding her Bristol followers, entreating her to put a brake on their 'credulity & love of enthusiam'. This she was not minded to do. The Countess had now come to measure the religious commitment of others by the extent of her own passionate zeal. In her new Bath chapel, she wrote, 'some I believe are alive but not enough for me'.[12]

Much of Lady Huntingdon's anxiety centred on Howell Harris's renewed efforts during the early 1760s to re-establish a working relationship between the main players in the new-birth movement. John Wesley, after flirting with secession, was being exposed to the evangelically minded clergy in the Church of England and thus to a degree being called back from a constant obsession with his own movement.[13] It also helped to ease the tension in his relations with his brother. But re-establishing a fruitful working relationship between Lady Huntingdon and John Wesley was pregnant with difficulty. Wesley had been unable to 'learn that your L. has even inquired whether I was living or dead', while many of the Calvinistic clergy she supported, including Whitefield and Madan, seemed to be saying 'down with him, down with him, even to the ground'. Wesley proceeded to write 'an angry letter' to Whitefield.[14] Indeed, it was as a jealous man that Wesley poured out his complaints to Lady Huntingdon. She had never invited him to preach at her Brighton chapel, while her chaplains and other Calvinistic clergy had been 'sent for over and over, & as much notice taken of my Brother & me, as of a couple of Postillions'. The Countess judged Wesley 'as an Eel, no hold of him and not come to the truth';[15] when he wrote to her suggesting that they all seek to work more closely, he unsurprisingly laid at her feet the blame for past divisions. Several people to whom she showed this letter 'laughed' at the suggestion of such a union, considering it 'impossible.'[16]

None the less, some faltering, temporary progress was made towards a *détente*. As late as 1764 the Countess attended Wesley's annual conference, and they both were present at a meeting of Methodist ministers which gathered in August at her large Bristol house on St Michael's Hill.[17] She thought that occcasional meetings between Whitefield, the Wesleys and herself would at least enable them 'to communicate our observations upon the general state of the work'. Moreover, John Wesley should occasionally preach at her Bath chapel – as he did on 26 August 1766. She hoped that 'the old spirit of zeal will yet arise in all the old messengers' and that the Wesleys, Whitefield and Harris would all be present in 1767 when her newly refurbished Bath chapel would be re-opened.[18] She would have been shocked if she had known that this show of open spirit on her part had been misread by the Wesleys: Bath 'and all her chapels (not to say, as I might, herself also) are now put into the hands of us three' – the Wesleys and Whitefield.[19] Indeed, even though Wesley was pleasantly surprised by the invitation from Lady Huntingdon, 'whose heart God has turned again', he was not a little disdainful of the experience of preaching at Bath.[20]

The Countess's attitude towards Wesley remained at best suspicious; at worst, she angrily proclaimed that he would never again be allowed into her presence.[21] This mutual distrust contributed to and in turn mirrored the intensity of the conflict between the mainly lay preachers commanded by Wesley and the evangelical clergy nurtured by Lady Huntingdon, although she was quite capable of entering into angry 'combats' with her own men. Any hope that there could be co-operation or even exchange between the Methodist leaders had collapsed by 1767. While Harris continued to adopt his normal posture of attempting to moderate between the various factions, he could not forbear expressing his own lingering resentment towards Whitefield.[22]

Howell Harris's unrelenting attempts to nudge the Countess to include the Moravian Brethren in her plans proved a trifle dangerous. Now, two or three years following her flirtation with them, she was more vehement than ever in their denunciation. When Harris said that she should admit them to the Bath chapel, 'she was angry'; she would 'never lye att' the feet of Moravians. He was distraught when soon after its opening she in 'hottness' turned out of the chapel a woman who had been one of her hardest working and most faithful Bath supporters. This punishment was owing to the woman's Moravian sympathies; Moravians, Lady Huntingdon now was saying, were 'cunning Papists hold[in]g Transubstantiation'. She refused any contact with them, including, as ever, her *bête noire*, Catherine Edwin.[23] The women who had defected from the Countess's Bristol sisterhood now added Ann Grinfield to their number and were safely in the Moravian fold with Edwin. They all were contributing financially to the Moravian chapel being built in Bath at the very time Lady Huntingdon was struggling financially to build hers.[24] 'Envy, judg[in]g, misrepresentat[io]n, ly[in]g' were all let loose, moaned Harris. He told the Countess that he hoped that she did not consider herself infallible. She told him that Christ came to her and was with her every morning. Harris refrained from telling her that he felt her to be far from spiritual, that her religion was 'outw[ar]d' and that she lived 'in fear' rather than in faith. As ever, he felt that she could not bear to be criticised.[25]

Lady Huntingdon's refusal to follow Wesley's lead in using non-episcopally ordained men clearly reduced the quantity of those upon whom she could call. At the same time, she was certain that the quality of hers was far superior, not only because of their regular ordinations but because of their theological orientation. For his part, by 1768 Wesley was restating with equal vigour his belief in perfection and detestation of predestination. The preaching of all three of Lady Huntingdon's chaplains, Whitefield, Madan and Romaine, Wesley had nearly always found unprofitable, leaving him with a 'dry, dissipated spirit'.[26]

Whatever Wesley's opinion of her clerical team, the Countess's expanding enterprises during the 1760s obviously called out for far more manpower than she was naturally able to attract to her cause. In addition, some who had assisted began to fall away from her service. The central part of that service had been supplying her newly built chapels, together with conducting preaching tours, as when on at least one occasion Venn and Madan had made a progress through Kent for that purpose, accompanied by Lady Huntingdon herself.[27] But even men closest to her, even her chaplains, could not always be depended upon. She was 'hurt and wounded to death' when Madan did not turn up to preach at Bath; and when such a clergyman did not fulfil his engagement, the chapel remained shut, with services cancelled.[28] The opening of her chapel in Tunbridge Wells in 1769, together with the remodelling and extension of her Bath and Brighton chapels two years earlier, further underscored the need for more clerical hands. For a time she even considered establishing a second chapel in Bath. There was 'such a thirst for the preaching that is quite distressing while so few labourers are yet in the vineyard'.[29]

Up to 1768 the Countess had managed at various times to gather under her banner about twenty evangelically minded clergymen, including her three chaplains.[30] She had been successful with some of these men either in securing their ordination or in finding them livings or curates to take their parish places when they preached in her chapels.[31] Yet these men were only sporadically available, and securing additional manpower through further ordinations was severely limited by the few episcopal doors open to her entreaties. For a brief period in 1764 she believed she had discovered the solution: the Greek 'Bishop of Arcadia', 'Bishop Erasmus', whose 'services would be of unestimable value in the creation of a new ministry'.[32] But she soon was persuaded by her leading clerics that the 'bishop' was a fraud. The very visible expansion of her enterprises during the early 1760s had predictably led to increasing caution or even hostility from the bishops she periodically approached to obtain ordination or placement for the evangelically minded. In 1764 the Bishop of Bristol received from her a startling request. Since the present incumbent of Clevedon, west of Bristol, was advanced in years she reckoned that it was safe to expect that he soon would die. Therefore, she made bold to suggest an advance replacement. The man she was recommending already held a living in the Diocese of Bristol, and she fancied that he would become a faithful pluralist. Even more remarkable is her totally undermining the possibility of success in this endeavour, by assuring the Bishop that the man she had in mind would be faithful to his parish duties, notwithstanding the 'differences in sentiment that subsist'. The Bishop replied that he was unable to pledge parishes that already had living incumbents and moreover was 'sorry to hear' from the Countess what 'I but suspected before': that the man she recommended was a Methodist.[33] Lady Huntingdon held the quaint belief that by keeping her distance from Wesleyanism and Moravianism, bishops would be more ready to assist her.[34] This caution made no difference. Her own actions were increasing episcopal suspicion.

Perhaps the Countess's most startling intervention in support of an evangelical incumbent was in the notorious case of the parish of Aldwincle. Her chaplain, Martin Madan, had since 1750 been chaplain to the Lock Hospital, near Hyde Park Corner, established to treat sufferers from venereal diseases. By 1762 a chapel had been erected in the hospital grounds, and Madan secured additional clerical assistance by inviting Thomas Haweis to become his assistant. At the new Lock Chapel the Countess and a number of other evangelical laymen frequently attended services, and soon Haweis was one of about five clergymen regularly filling her Brighton pulpit.[35] Thus commenced her fateful relationship with one of the most enigmatic of the eighteenth-century's evangelical clergymen. (See illustration 12.) Haweis had studied at Oxford without taking a degree and in 1758 was ordained priest. For a time, he served as a curate in one of Oxford's churches, where James Woodforde found his preaching 'very stupid, low, and bad stuff'. Lord Dartmouth, although considering Haweis 'lively', hoped that the zeal was 'prudent'.[36]

Having served as Madan's assistant at the Lock for several months, Haweis was desperate to find a more permanent situation. His presence there was ecclesiastically unofficial; indeed, he had no licence to preach from any bishop, and he attempted twice without success to secure a London living.[37] Thus it must have appeared to him providential when in February 1764 Madan received an unexpected visit. John Kimpton by inheritance and purchase had come to hold the presentative advowson of the vacant living of Aldwincle, Northamptonshire, about seventy-five miles from London. Though purchasable, such advowsons were held in trust under a bishop, in this instance the Bishop of Peterbourgh. If no presentation was made to such a vacant living within six months, that right reverted to the bishop. Kimpton claimed that he had sunk all his money into the purchase and asked Madan, a trained lawyer, for advice. In less than a fortnight the six months would be up, the appointment to the living would fall to the Bishop and Kimpton's ownership of it would be useless. He would be a 'ruined man'. Madan explained that it was not permissible under church law to sell a vacant living. However, given Haweis's ecclesiastical quest, Madan suggested that they lay the matter before him. Kimpton hoped that Haweis would accept the living temporarily, then resign if requested. Whatever agreement was struck that evening, it is clear that Haweis saw the opportunity of securing a regular church living and went so far as to offer to go with Kimpton to request the Bishop to waive the restriction on a clergyman accepting a temporary living. However, when they were alone, Madan told Haweis that this procedure was 'absurd', since a bishop did not have the power to set aside the regulation. It would amount to simony. The following day Madan and Haweis informed Kimpton that the only way that Haweis could accept Aldwincle was that he be given it 'out and out'.[38]

Finding that he had no option, but clearly believing he had struck an understanding with Haweis to resign the living at a future date, Kimpton agreed to give it to him outright. Several months later Kimpton discovered that Haweis had no intention of resignation.[39] By November, he was spreading it about that Haweis had agreed to resign but was reneging. Discovering himself boxed in, Madan, a man of personal wealth, seriously considered giving money to Kimpton, not as an '*injured*, but merely as a *distressed* man'. However, he was strongly advised to avoid doing anything that would appear to be paying 'hush-money'. Madan began now to attempt to distance himself from Haweis, saying that he was certain that Haweis was ready to do what was 'right and honourable'.[40]

As this highly complex affair rumbled on, whatever was 'right and honourable' became submerged in a fearful battle of words. Ten pamphlets were printed, dividing evenly on either side of the conflict but whose cumulative effect was to provide a field day for the opponents of evangelicalism. They portrayed Haweis and Madan as heartless, dishonest money-grubbers. As early as 1766 a horrified Lady Huntingdon considered Haweis's protestations of innocence a 'thunder[ing] against the truth'. Her first inclination was for him to resign the living and be packed off to Philadelphia, where Whitefield thought he could find him a church. Three thousand miles of ocean would prevent Haweis's continued infection of the evangelical cause in England. It would, she reckoned, help to restore Madan's reputation, which she was certain received great 'dishonour' from his connection with Haweis, although she did not consider Madan, her chaplain, without blame. She felt that the Lock ministry was bearing 'little credit . . . to Christianity', and she quickly dismissed her maid when it was discovered that the woman had 'been telling everything out of my house' to Madan's maid.[41] As the crisis deepened the following year Lady Huntingdon told Madan that she 'could not see how Mr. Haweis as an honest man could continue to keep that living'. Madan refused the idea. If Haweis resigned, it would totally blacken both men's names. When she arrived in London in March 1768 the Countess discovered 'a severe scourge indeed upon the Church of God'. Kimpton had been pursued by creditors and thrown into King's Bench prison, leaving his wife and three children on the verge of starvation. Moreover, Haweis was being lampooned at the Theatre Royal, Drury Lane, in a production called *The Hypocrite*. Taking matters into her own hands, and without Madan's or Haweis's knowledge, the Countess proceeded to purchase the advowson herself, giving Kimpton £1,000 and thus freeing him from prison and allowing him to discharge all his debts. Meanwhile she said that Madan and Haweis should make public confession for 'any <u>conscious</u> Infirmity, weakness, Temptation or mistakes stept thro' this Transaction'.[42] Whatever the innocence of their motives in the affair, Lady Huntingdon considered their conduct 'mistaken'.[43]

The men were livid. They took Lady Huntingdon's action 'in a most dreadfull spirit' and proceeded to give 'great offense to many' by openly criticising her. Madan wrote to tell her that they had no sins to confess; Haweis viewed her 'imprudent step' as 'opposite to every wish of ours'. What she had done contributed to branding him 'one of the first of villains, and the basest of Hypocrities', cried Haweis while at the same time he attempted to thrust the main blame onto Madan. A man to whom controversy seemed to be magnetically drawn, Haweis was to find that the 'violence of the abuse' surrounding the Aldwincle affair 'never ceased' throughout the remaining long years of his life.[44]

In the action she took, Lady Huntingdon was participating in a common evangelical practice, but one later to be criticised from within its own ranks. During the eighteenth century approximately half of all advowsons were in the hands of private patrons.[45] In the Aldwincle affair she associated herself with a leading layman, John Thornton, whose regular practice it was to secure livings for evangelical clergymen by purchase: Thornton had 'no favor from the church but what I buy'. At one point in the affair he offered to install Haweis in a more lucrative living if he agreed to resign his claim on Aldwincle; in the event, when the Countess finally determined to purchase the living, she used Whitefield to convey the £1,000 payment to Thornton, who acted as a go-between. However, the transaction made Thornton cautious for the future.[46] Before long, Lady Huntingdon herself, now alienated from Haweis and Madan, was attempting unsuccessfully to find a buyer for her Aldwincle purchase while at the same time officially cancelling Madan's position as one of her chaplains. When in future the Countess set out to purchase an advowson, she commanded that it be done in the 'most perfect confidence'.[47]

The year 1768 proved momentous for the Countess of Huntingdon. At the very time she attempted to remove the sting of the publicity surrounding Aldwincle, a further furore erupted. In March, the University of Oxford expelled six methodistic students.[48] Since his appointment as Principal of St Edmund Hall in 1760, George Dixon had increased the number of his students largely by admitting those of Methodist inclination, several in 1766 and 1767. Matters now came to a head when his Vice-Principal, John Higson, a bitter opponent of the Methodists, discovered that Lady Huntingdon had written to propose another young man, 'a ward of hers at school, whom she designed for the profession of the Ministry'.[49] This discovery was the trigger for Higson's firing off a university enquiry that led to the expulsions.

There can be no doubt that the Countess had been intimately, if quietly, involved in nurturing several if not all these young men for possible ordination.[50] They had held prayer meetings in the home of a humble local couple, George Durbridge and his wife, a family Lady Huntingdon supported financially. In addition to Dixon, her key Oxford contact was James Stillingfleet, a fellow of Merton College, who led the religious exercises at the Durbridge home. Stillingfleet, until his departure for a parish in 1767, through personal meetings and correspondence with the Countess, was deeply involved in her plans for enlarging the evangelical witness at Oxford, plans about which she had committed him to strict secrecy. Moreover, most of the six students had been befriended and encouraged by several evangelical clerics close to her, including Haweis and John Fletcher, together with another she had recently drawn into her circle, Joseph Townsend. Prior to the expulsion, having focused on St Edmund Hall as the cutting edge of evangelicalism at Oxford, she had laid plans for sending further students.[51]

In their defence of the expelled students, Lady Huntingdon's supporters were intent not only to present the young men as innocent victims of harsh and arbitrary treatment but also to support a particular theological orientation. 'What I mean to insist upon', wrote Richard Hill, 'is that the Church of England is certainly calvinistical', a position emphatically rejected by the Vice-Chancellor of Oxford, who led the enquiry which resulted in the expulsion. With Whitefield rushing into the pamphlet war surrounding the affair, John Wesley offered no criticism of his university. Viewing the event not as the expulsion of Methodists, but of Calvinists, Wesley was pleased that the Oxford authorities had cleared the Church of England of official belief in predestination. It was a doctrine 'utterly inconsistent' with its teaching, he said.[52] The expulsion of the six students reopened the ever present theological fault-line within Methodism, which two years later would lead to a convulsion of seismic proportions.

The expulsion fell neatly into place with a plan the Countess had been nursing for four years. Whatever hopes she may have entertained for the easy passage of evangelicals through the universities to Anglican ordination were tempered by bitter experience. As she boldly extended her activities during the early 1760s, she had seen the doors of episcopal palaces and university colleges increasingly closed. For academic training, the Dissenting academies were no option: that would lead to non-episcopal ordination, and her mission was to reform the Church of England. The only alternative she saw was to establish her own institution of learning. By remaining a professing Anglican, she reckoned that she could find at least some bishops willing to ordain the products of such an establishment. 'I wish we had a nursery' for preachers, she wrote in 1764 and early the following year was already discussing plans for a 'college' to be 'established in the true and full primitive spirit'.[53] She reasoned that its location also should be 'primitive', at arm's-length from hostile authorities. Thus she turned to Howell Harris and his mountain retreat in the Breconshire hills of Wales. Though vowing that he would remain his own man and that her establishment must be 'separate from my name', he offered to assist in setting up her 'college' in a farmhouse but a couple of hundred yards from his own religious 'family' of artisans at Trevecca.[54]

The college could never have been built without Howell Harris's active participation. One sacrifice the Countess was forced to make was having to moderate her animus towards the Moravians, who continued to exert a strong influence on Harris. It even meant having to reinstate to her favour the woman she had expelled from the Bath chapel, one Mrs Leighton. Yet Lady Huntingdon was certain that she was still being stalked by her Moravian nemesis, Catherine Edwin, whom she discovered had made 'very free' with Mrs Leighton '& for which I feel angry'. Believing that Edwin had disrupted her Sussex chapels, the Countess had become haunted by the image of a woman she believed to be scouring the country, seeking to expunge all her work. Mrs Leighton and her brother, E.K. Wilson, were to become intimately involved in the details of transforming a dilapidated Welsh farmhouse into a college fit for aspiring clergymen. 'I do lay violent hands upon you both & am determined to look no further for every help my heart can want.'[55] While Harris deputed (at the Countess's expense) twenty-four of his craftsmen to rebuilding, plastering, papering and painting the house and tiling the kitchen, Leighton and Wilson were frantically responding to the Countess's specific injunctions about furnishings: linen, desks, cupboards, candlesticks, plates, china, glassware, kitchen utensils, a cooker. Harris's bill to the Countess totalled £1,000. All this work was done without her presence, and she was distracted by fear that it might not be completed in time for the opening in August. In the event, workmen completed the college chapel late on the night before it opened.[56] (See illustration 14.)

The events at Oxford took place during the height of Lady Huntingdon's preparations for the launching of her Trevecca college. While of course bitterly opposed to the expulsion, she always relished the sense of occasion. Thus Oxford's loss would be Trevecca's gain: those students were 'drove from thence to be the first fruits' of her college. Upon the expulsion, she immediately invited them all to become her students; only two accepted,[57] the least academically qualified of the six.[58] The deliberate christening of her institution as a 'college' was a provocative gesture. No Dissenting academy made so bold until 1786.[59] Moreover, from the outset Lady Huntingdon was determined to give her college as many physical academic trappings as was practical. From the day of its opening, students were dressed in caps and gowns supplied by their benefactress. It was a practice that made bishops and clergy 'murmur against this college'; it was 'assuming one of the privileges of the university'.[60] The Countess, as she made final plans for its opening, reflected – not without a *frisson* of excitement – that she 'must expect fires on all sides kindled for me'. The 'universitys & the bishops with all the outward clamor of order will be employed against me'.[61]

The opening of the college on the 24th of August 1768 was a grand celebration of Methodism. It was also the Countess's sixty-first birthday. She and her entourage of female friends and their servants arrived at the mountain fastness at the end of July, staying and dining each day at Harris's establishment. The day of dedication found many Methodist preachers from Wales and England in attendance, with Whitefield the main preacher. Strikingly absent was John Wesley, though he had been close enough to attend. 'Did you ever see anything more queer than their plan of institution? Pray who penned it, man or woman?'[62]

The Countess had secured John Fletcher, vicar of Madeley, Shropshire, to serve as occasional visitor and overseer. A graduate of the University of Geneva, he held high hopes that the curriculum would include grammar, logic, rhetoric, ecclesiastical history, natural philosophy and geography, together with a place for ancient languages. As an institution whose aim was to produce preachers, Fletcher also saw the need for a 'great deal of practical Divinity'.[63] In spite of valiant efforts, within nine months of Trevecca's opening there were but sixteen students, of very mixed abilities. One of the two expelled from Oxford already had left; the other found himself 'dissatisfied with his situation' and 'wishes to be gone', having found the principles of his fellow students 'so different' from his own. This man, Joseph Shipman – 'nothing but a weather cock' – was to continue to cause the

Countess countless anxieties. Neither he nor the other former St Edmund Hall student found the exchange of Trevecca for Oxford to his taste.[64] The most serious problem was the lack of a suitable teacher. The first, a Welshman, was totally inadequate, not up even to the limited academic standards of some of his students.[65] Upon his dismissal, Lady Huntingdon's desperation led her to an astonishing appointment: a twelve-year-old pupil from Wesley's Kingswood school at Bristol. John Henderson proved a disaster, 'deficient in point of Christian experience', and not 'a proper master'. He was quickly removed.[66]

Although he agreed to be one of the preachers at the first anniversary celebrations in 1769,[67] it was the only time John Wesley ever visited the college. Viewing Trevecca with a sardonic eye, he saw it as direct competition to his own school and a further evidence of Lady Huntingdon's having thrown down the gauntlet in the ongoing struggle for leadership of the Methodist movement. If he were unable to secure competent masters, Wesley was prepared to let Kingswood 'drop'. He would 'have another kind of school than that at Trevecca or none at all'. That was written to Joseph Benson, a Kingswood teacher who was on the verge of being poached by the Countess. Wesley was convinced that she used unworthy inducements to achieve her ends, and there was the additional threat that some of Benson's students at Kingswood would follow him to Trevecca.[68] Benson's defection, although it would last only several months, raised Wesley's pique to new heights: Lady Huntingdon was 'guilty' of great 'narrowness of spirit'. 'Let not the gentlewoman entrench upon the Christian'. Moreover, he claimed that the prime purpose of Trevecca was constantly to send out preachers to challenge his own men.[69]

Meanwhile, the progress of the college was seriously undermined by an increasing rift between its foundress and Howell Harris. In spite of determining to be his own man when assisting in establishing Trevecca virtually in his backyard, Harris soon felt hard done by. The unstable relationship between the two, extending back over twenty-five years, now was set in the direction of total collapse. Not only had he devoted extensive resources in making the college habitable, as well as providing bed and board for her Ladyship and her entourage for several weeks prior to its opening, but the Countess had insisted in claiming seven of Harris's 'family' as her servants. With Fletcher visiting only occasionally and the continuing wide gaps in formal teaching, she called upon Harris to exhort and keep a watchful eye on the students.[70] Yet by the end of 1769 he was complaining openly and bitterly that she made a habit of 'judging my spirit' and constantly maintaining her superiority over others, while she had 'not added one soul' in her management of Trevecca. Brought to a head by a crisis surrounding the college housekeeper being made pregnant by the first college tutor, Harris upbraided the Countess to her face for acting impulsively and considering herself 'infallible'. He started securing separate accommodation for her, so that she would not stay at his house, where she and her party had regularly occupied twenty-one rooms.[71] This physical separation was made permanent early in 1772, when she accused him of attempting to wrest the college from her control.[72] Indeed, Harris was certain that its establishment had been 'my crown', an attitude undergirt by the 'trouble and expenses' to which she had constantly put him. Not for the first time he complained that she 'can't bear contradiction'.[73]

The relationship between Lady Huntingdon and Howell Harris had always been bedevilled by their competing claims to authority in the leadership of the Methodist movement. It now ended in bitter mutual recrimination. She freely told her students that his 'manner was highly censurable'. When she expelled two students, he offered them support. If Harris had known that the college would have come to this, 'I sh[ou]ld never have consented to its coming here'.[74] The Countess discovered upon arrival at Trevecca in the spring of 1773 that one of these she had expelled was 'quite maintained by Harris & is set up to preach against the College'. This former student stood in the lane fronting the college, 'abusing us all & calling all the students . . . preachers of Baal'. On one Sunday he went to nearby Brecon, preached in the streets and, she wrote, 'abused me by name'. All this proved to her that Harris and his followers were 'infamous'.[75] Four months later Harris was dead, but his Trevecca community lived on for many years, now refusing any contact with Lady Huntingdon's Trevecca college.[76]

John Wesley mordantly observed that with Lady Huntingdon it is '*my* College, *my* masters, *my* students'. Indeed, her students, she said, were her 'Rams Horns'. 'The grace & glory that rest on that place ever since the opening must astonish any feeling heart in divine things.' It meant more to her 'than any thing in this whole world'. If it stands fast and faithful, 'I live'. 'Great & glorious days of the church' shall spring forth from Trevecca. Let anyone 'tremble that lets the world or the devil' enter it. 'A day of mighty slaughter it will prove to the base hypocrite & half-hearted spirit.' 'I can cry aloud to my d[ea]r little college courage, courage.' By her devotion to Trevecca, she longed to prove herself 'one of his poor women when all forsook him yet loved him even unto shame & death'. One of her friends addressed her as 'Mistress to a School of prophets'. That was perfect.[77]

Notes

1 Ward & H., 21:176n., 178 and n. (1 January, 27 and 28 February 1759).

2 Jackson, *Journal of Charles Wesley*, 2:228-33, quotation on p. 228. Walpole waspishly commented that 'this horrid lunatic [died] coolly and sensibly....With all the frenzy in his blood he was not mad enough to be struck with his aunt [*sic*] Huntingdon's sermons.' Horace Walpole to George Montagu, 6 May 1760, Lewis, *Horace Walpole's Correspondence*, 9:283-84. For the murder, trial and execution see Crane, *Kirkland Papers*, pp. 6-42, 185-203; *Memoirs of the Life of Laurence Earl Ferrers* (London, 1760); *The Trial of Lawrence Earl Ferrers* (London, 1760); *An Account of the Execution of the Late Lawrence Ferrers* (London, 1760). The quotation regarding the Countess's uncle is from Shirley, *Stemmata Shirleiana*, p. 194.

3 For example, Lawrence Shirley to SH, 17 December 1729; Thomas Bayly to SH, 12 May 1731; Thomas Bayly to SH, 19 April 1737; Thomas Bayly to TH, 27 March 1740. HA 10818, 593, 608, 634; 'By Expences Attending the Administration' (1760), Rayleigh.

4 Thomas Gray to Mr Wharton, 22 April 1760, Duncan Tovey (ed.), *The Letters of Thomas Gray* 3 vols. (London, 1909-12), 2:135; Jackson, *Journal of Charles Wesley*, 2:241 (22 May 1760).

5 Walter Shirley to SH, 20 February 1760, E4/1/1, CF; Theophilus Lindsey to Lord John Rawdon, 30 May 1758, T3765/M/2/20/4, PRONI.

6 JF to CW, 15 November 1759, Luke Tyerman, *Wesley's Designated Successor* (London, 1882), p. 47; Registers of Peers Chaplains, FV/1 Calendar, Vols. XII & XIII (Romaine, 3 January; Madan, 5 October), Lambeth Palace Library.

7 Edwin Welch, 'Lady Huntingdon and Spa Fields chapel,' *Guildhall Miscellany* 4 (1972), p. 176.

8 Statement of loan, 16 February 1762, F1/7, CF; Frank Dowling, 'The Countess of Huntingdon's Chapels', M.Sc. dissertation, Oxford Polytechnic, 1992, p. [91]. It is likely that she sold some of her jewels for £700 to fund the building of this chapel. C9/14/3, CF. The following year she established a satellite chapel about eleven miles north of Brighton, where she leased Great Ote (Oat) Hall mansion. Fitting out the hall as a chapel, she used the remainder as her private residence and as accommodation for preachers visiting Sussex. Ote Hall was to become a focus for her activities in the area.

9 SH to CW, 9 June 1764, Black 75 (quotation); HH ms diary, 6, 7 (quotation) October, 13 December 1765, NLW.

10 Walter Shirley to SH, 19 October 1770, F1/1565, CF. At the Bath chapel there was a separate service at 7 o'clock each Sunday morning 'designed only for the Saints, wherein none of the Church Prayers are used'. [Elizabeth Montagu's sister] to Elizabeth Montagu, [1765], Blunt, *Mrs. Montagu*, 2:27. This procedure may have been followed at the Countess's other chapels.

11 For the affair, which stretched over a number of years until Francis cooled of it, see [Lady Betty Cobbe] to Francis Hastings, 15 October, 15 December [*c.* 1761], 7 December 1775, 9 May 1776, 28 February 1777, HA 1513, 1514, 1516, 1517, 1518; EH to FH, 19 June 1769, HA 10429; Catherine Jones to FH, 27 September 1770, HA 7955. These letters make it clear that the Countess's daughter Elizabeth was colluding in the intrigue, and that she, herself, had an affair with one of Betty Cobbe's brothers.

12 SH to HH, 27 October 1763, Trevecca Group, letter 2838a, Calvinistic Methodist Archives, NLW; SH to anon., 5 July 1766, SMU 73; Henry Venn to Miss Wheeler, November 1766, C11, CMS; JF to SH, 9 May 1763, MAM P4d, John Fletcher Letter Books, Vol. 2, p. 81, Rylands; [CW] to SH, 20 September 1766, photostat copy in Francis, 'Selina, Countess of Huntingdon', plate 40; SH to Judith Wadsworth, 16 January 1766, SMU 63.

13 Baker, *John Wesley and Church of England*, pp. 185-86.

14 JW to SH, 20 March 1763, Telford, 4:206; GW to CW, 17 March 1763, PLP 113/1/20, Rylands.

15 JW to SH, 8 January 1764, E4/3/1, CF; HH diary, 4 November 1763, *HHRS*, p. 205.

16 JW to SH, 20 April 1764, *Evangelical Register* 1 (1824), pp. 38-40; HH ms diary, 5 May 1764, NLW (quotation).

17 SH to CW, 9 June 1764, Black 75; SH to HH, 23 June [1764], F1/1284; HH ms diary, 6-10 August 1764, NLW.

18 SH to JW, 14 September 1766; SH to CW, 4 February 1767, Black 103, 76.

19 CW to Sarah Wesley, 21 August 1766, Jackson, *Journal of Charles Wesley*, 2:247.

20 Quoted in Tyerman, *Life of John Wesley*, 2:557; Ward & H., 22:57 (25 August 1766).

21 HH ms diary, 2 October 1765, NLW.

22 E.K. Wilson to HH, 11 November 1767, Trevecka 2633; HH diary, 4 November 1763, *HHRS*, p. 205 (quotation); HH ms diary, 7 September 1765, NLW.

23 HH ms diary, 2 October, 13 December 1765, NLW (quotations); SH to Judith Wadsworth, 16 December 1765, SMU 56.

24 Bristol Moravian Church diaries, Vol. 1, p. 197; Vol. 2 (2, 9 April 1765), Bristol University Library.

25 HH ms diary, 16 May; 2, 4 October; 13 December 1765, NLW.

26 JW to JF, 20 March 1768, Telford, 5:83.

27 JF to SH, 3 April 1765, MAM P4d, John Fletcher Letter Books, Vol. 2, p. 113, Rylands.

28 SH to HH, 27 October 1763, Trevecca group, letter 2838a., Calvinistic Methodist Archives, NLW.

29 [Edward] Budgen to [John] Jones, 16 July 1769, D.T.M. Jones Collection, no. 1118, NLW; John Fletcher to SH, 12 April 1769, F1/1464, CF; SH to CW, 7 November 1768, Black 77 (quotation).

30 Alan Harding, 'The Countess of Huntingdon and her connexion in the eighteenth century', D.Phil. thesis, University of Oxford, 1992, pp. 54-62.

31 For example, SH to CW, 9 June 1764, Black 75; JF to SH, 3 October 1760, 4 July 1764, MAM P4d, John Fletcher Letter Books, Vol. 2, pp. 49, 105, Rylands; Walter Shirley to Lord Moira, 7 March 1761, T3765/M/3/13/13, PRONI.

32 John Newton to JW, 24 April 1764, quoted in Baker, *John Wesley and the Church of England*, p. 201.

33 SH to Bishop of Bristol, 1 December 1764; Bishop of Bristol to SH, 6 December 1764, MSS 7005C, NLW.

34 HH MS diary, 2 October 1765, NLW.

35 Arthur S. Wood, *Thomas Haweis* (London, 1957), pp. 84-89; JW to SH, 8 January 1764, E4/3/1, CF.

36 W.N. Hargreaves-Mawdsley (ed.), *Woodforde at Oxford* (Oxford, 1969), p. 59 (19 November 1761); Lord Dartmouth to William Rawlings, 17 July 1761, Edwin Sidney, *The Life and Ministry of the Rev. Samuel Walker* (London, 1838. 2nd edition), p. 552.

37 William Romaine to SH, 5 February 1763, *Free Church of England Harbinger* (1868), p. 43; Thomas Haweis, ms autobiography, p. 87, ML B1176, Mitchell.

38 Martin Madan, *An Answer to a Pamphlet, Intitled, a Faithful Narrative of Facts Relative to the Late Presentation of Mr H___s, to the Rectory of Al___w___le* (London, 1767), pp. 5-7.

39 [John Kimpton], *A Faithful Narrative of Facts, Relative to the late Presentation of Mr H——s To the Rectory of AL____W____LE* (London, 1767), pp. 28-29.

40 Madan, *An Answer*, pp. 11, 14, 17.

41 SH to Judith Wadsworth, 15, 17 April 1766, SMU 68, 69.

42 SH to Martin Madan, 2 March 1768, E2/1/6, CF. There are nearly a score of letters regarding the Aldwincle affair in the Countess's papers. See E2/1, E2/2, CF. For the play see [Richard Warner], *Bath Characters* (London, 1808. 2nd edition), p. 113.

43 SH to Lord Dartmouth, 1 March 1768, E2/1/11, CF.

44 SH to Mrs H. Leighton, 11 March 1768, Duke; Martin Madan to SH, 3 March 1768, E2/1/7, CF; Thomas Haweis MS autobiography, pp. 95, 97, ML B1176, Mitchell. See also *Gentleman's Magazine* 38 (1767), pp. 507-10, 591-94; 70 (1800), pp. 560, 1182; 90 (1820), p. 277. And George Redford and John A. James (eds.), *Autobiography of William Jay* (London, 1854), p. 476; William Jones, *Memoirs of...Rowland Hill* (London, 1834), p. 301n.

45 Hempton, 'Religion in British society', p. 205.

46 John Thornton to SH, 7 October 1783, F1/554, CF (quotation); Haweis MS autobiography, p. 97, ML B1176, Mitchell; SH to Thornton, 1 March 1768, and Thornton to SH, [*c.* 3 March 1768], E2/1/8, 9, CF; Thornton to John Venn, 6 February 1790, C68, CMS.

47 Walter Shirley to SH, [1772], E4/1/6, CF; Registers of Peers Chaplains, FV/1, Vol. XIV, f. 158 (14 November 1772), Lambeth Palace Library; SH to Mr E, 29 November 1781, E4/10/25, CF (quotation).

48 S.L. Ollard, *The Six Students of St. Edmund Hall* (London, 1911); J.S. Reynolds, *The Evangelicals at Oxford, 1735-1871* (Oxford, 1953), pp. 35-42; J.N.D. Kelly, *St Edmund Hall* (Oxford, 1989), pp. 61-66; Sutherland and Mitchell, *History of University of Oxford*, 5:458-64.

49 MS St Edmund Hall 56, f. 42a, Bodleian Library.

50 A disinterested contemporary observer commented that they all 'were connected with her ladyship'. Thomas Harmer (1779), quoted in Geoffrey F. Nuttall, *The Significance of Trevecca College 1768-91* (London, 1969), p. 6.

51 James Stillingfleet to SH, 10 November 1766, 3 January 1767, E4/4/2, 3, CF; MS St Edmund Hall 56, f. 4, Bodleian Library; John Thornton to SH, 20 May 1768, E2/2/6, CF.

52 [Richard Hill], *Pietas Oxoniensis* (London, 1768. 2nd edition), p. 82n. (quotation); Thomas Nowell, *An Answer to a Pamphlet, Entitled Pietas Oxoniensis* (Oxford, 1768), pp. 93-94; George Whitefield, *A Letter to the Reverend Dr Durrell* (London, 1768); Ward & H., 22:164 (19 November 1768), quotation. For a discussion of a number of these publications see James E. Hull, 'The controversy between John Wesley and the Countess of Huntingdon', Ph.D. thesis, University of Edinburgh, 1959, pp. 229-30.

53 SH to CW, 9 June 1764, Black 75; SH to HH, 15 January 1765, Edward Morgan, *The Life and Times of Howel Harris* (Holywell, 1852), p. 237.

54 HH ms diary, 15 January 1767, NLW. See also entries for 28 July, 10 August 1764; 18, 20 May 1765; 10 January 1767.

55 SH to Mrs H. Leighton, 4 February, 13 September 1768, Duke.
56 HH to James Easterbrook, 7 April 1768; HH to [E.K. Wilson?], 21 July 1768. Trevecka 2640, 2842; SH to Mrs H. Leighton, 5 August 1768, Duke; Mrs H. Leighton to SH, 29 April 1768, F1/29, CF; SH to HH, 4 June 1768, Trevecka 2642; Lady Huntingdon's Acct balanc'd to March 24, 1769, Trevecka 3227; HH MS diary, 23 August 1768, NLW.
57 SH to Mrs H. Leighton, 11 March 1768, Duke (quotation); John Newton to Earl of Dartmouth, 10 May 1768, HMC, *The Manuscripts of the Earl of Dartmouth*, Vol. 3 (London, 1896), p. 188. Three of the expelled students went on to secure episcopal ordination. For Thomas Jones and Erasmus Middleton, see Ollard, *Six Students*, pp. 39, 45; for Benjamin Kay, see T.E. Owen, *Methodism Unmasked* (London, 1802), p. 105.
58 Nowell, *An Answer*, pp. 28-29.
59 Nuttall, *Significance of Trevecca*, p. 6.
60 HH ms diary, 9 November 1768, 30 March 1769 (quotation), NLW.
61 SH to Mrs H. Leighton, 11 March 1768, Duke.
62 HH ms diary, 29 July 1768, NLW; GW to Robert Keen, 26, 30 August 1768, *Select Letters*, 3:373-74; John Gillies, *Memoirs of the Life of the Rev. George Whitefield* (London, 1772), p. 254n.; JW to SH, 9 August 1768, G2/1/23, CF; JW to CW, 14 May 1768, Telford, 5:88 (quotation).
63 JF to SH, 3 January 1768, MAM P4d, 2:203, Rylands. On Fletcher see Tyerman, *Wesley's Designated Successor*; Patrick P. Streiff, *Jean Guillaume de la Fléchère* (Frankfurt, 1984), in German.
64 Cradock Glascott to SH, 13 October 1768, F1/1448; Joseph Shipman to SH, 6 October 1768, E4/5/6; R. Harman to SH, 19 April 1769, F1/60. CF.
65 JF to SH, 12 April 1769, F1/1464, CF.
66 JF to SH, 1 July 1769, MAM P4d, 2:217, Rylands. After his brief and unhappy time at Trevecca, Henderson later went to Oxford, gaining renown for his knowledge of languages, obsession with the occult, eccentric dress, consumption of alcohol and addiction to drugs. 'Anecdotes of John Henderson, B.A.,' *Arminian Magazine* 16 (1793), pp. 140-44; Dorothy E.S. Brown, 'Evangelicals and education in eighteenth-century Britain: a study of Trevecca College, 1768-1792', Ph.D. dissertation, University of Wisconsin-Madison, 1992, p. 139n.
67 Ward & H., 22:200-201 (23, 24 August 1769).
68 JW to Joseph Benson, 2 January 1769, Telford, 5:123; SH to Benson, 19 March 1770, Duke; Marmaduke Ling to SH, 7 June 1770, F1/96, CF.
69 JW to Mary Bishop, 22 November 1769 (quotations); same to same, 5 November 1769, Telford, 5:162, 154.
70 HH ms diary, 1 September 1768, NLW; JF to SH, 10 November 1768, F1/1449, CF; SH to Joseph Benson [22 April 1770], Duke.
71 HH diary, 9 November 1769, *HHRS*, p. 231 (quotation); HH ms diary, 14 September 1769 (quotation), and note on cover of Vol. 264, NLW.
72 James Glazebrook to SH, 28 March 1772, F1/176, CF; HH diary, 21 September, 1 October 1771, *HHVL*, p. 287.
73 HH diary, 8 October 1769, *HHRS*, p. 229; 24 August, 18 November 1771, *HHVL*, pp. 286, 288.
74 Benjamin Wase to HH, 27 March 1772; HH to Christopher Hull, 8 December 1772. Trevecka 2707, 2728. See also Hull ('your...son in the Gospel') to HH, 26 October 1772, Trevecka 2721.
75 SH to John Hawksworth, 16 March 1773, G2/1/7; SH to John Cosson, 10 March 1773, A3/15/1, CF.
76 See Benjamin La Trobe to Johannes Loretz, 6 January 1786, G.W. Addison (ed.), *The Renewed Church of the United Brethren, 1722-1930* (London, 1932), p. 207.
77 JW to Joseph Benson, 26 December 1769, Telford, 5:166; SH to [Thomas Haweis], 20 February 1777, SMU 93; SH to Mrs H. Leighton, 13 September 1768, Duke; SH to HH, 26 March 1771, Trevecka 2693; SH to Joseph Benson, 12 April 1770, Duke; Lady M. Manners to SH, 14 October 1775, F1/335, CF.

1. *The Earl and Countess of Huntingdon and children Henry and Selina, early 1740s.*

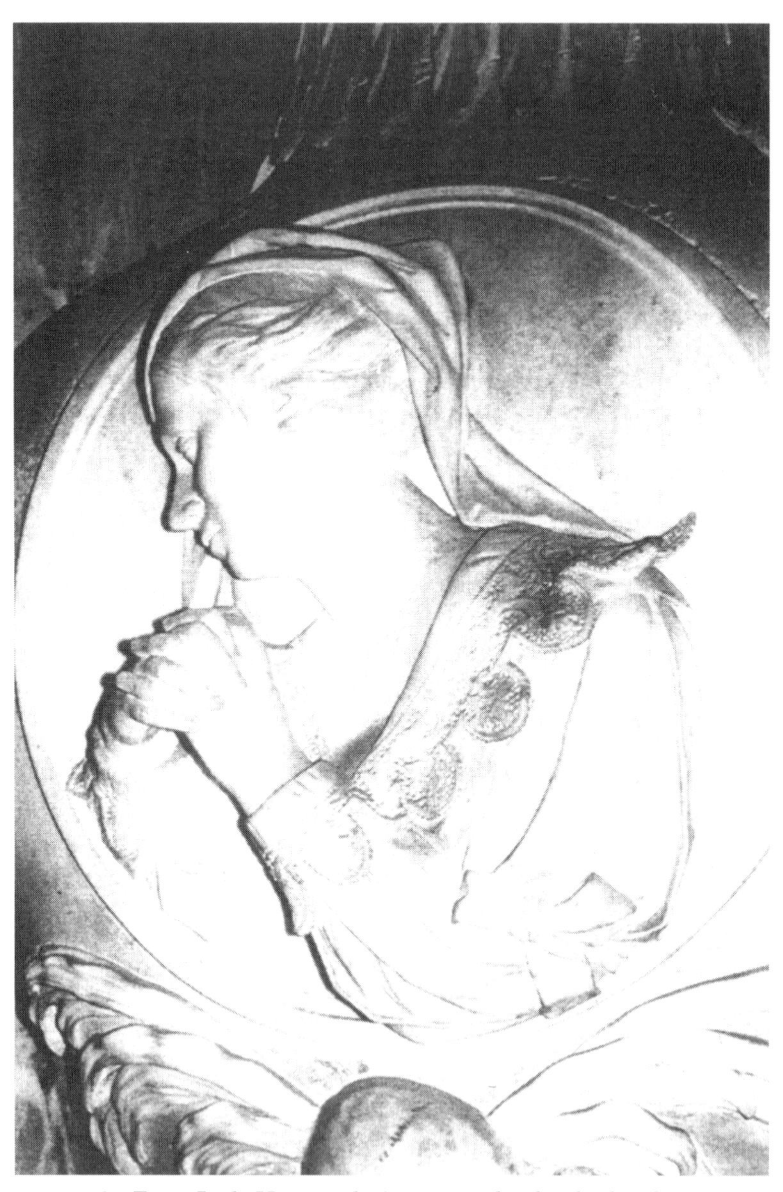

2. *From Lady Huntingdon's memorial to her husband in Ashby de la Zouch parish church, 1746.*

3. Life-sized portrait of Lady Huntingdon sent to bolster her mission to Georgia in 1773.

S. Huntingdon

4. *Lady Huntingdon, c. 1780.*

5. *'The Tears of Methodism' satirical portrayal of Lady Huntingdon, 1791.*

6. Lady Huntingdon's eldest son, Francis, 1754.

7. *Lady Huntingdon's younger daughter, Selina, 1762.*

8. John Wesley, c. 1766.

9. George Whitefield, c. 1742.

10. Howell Harris.

11. *William Piercy.*

12. Thomas Haweis.

13. Lady Anne Erskine.

14. Trevecca College, 1768.

15. Spa Fields Chapel and private residence, London.

My Dr. Lord

I should have been rejoiced to have heard of the good news you have so long wished [illegible] as of Dr. Lady Rawdons being well & happy by the [illegible] of an additional offspring in your family I trust in God that [illegible] [illegible] by & you in his [illegible] [illegible], I own I was more surprised at the news you sent me than you can well imagine. O! [illegible] I could say I was glad but alas! [illegible] [illegible] [illegible] or rather ill judged [illegible] I am still more [illegible] acquainted & a [illegible] unconvinced [illegible] [illegible] [illegible] lightly changing to a view of more [illegible] or [illegible] rather alarms me & makes me tremble at the consequences of such changes in God's sight – the Duke of Shrewsbury

16. An example of Lady Huntingdon's handwriting.

CHAPTER 6

'This opening in America is the astonishment of all that love or fear the Lord'

The romance of overseas missions had always taken Lady Huntingdon's fancy. Before her sister-in-law's marriage to Benjamin Ingham had abruptly aborted the interest, the Countess had been charmed by the details of the Moravians' far-flung missionary enterprise. In 1740 Lady Margaret had written enthusiastically about such ventures in the East and West Indies, Georgia, Carolina, Pennsylvania, Virginia, Ceylon, Lapland, Russia, Constantinople, Guinea, Persia, New York, Germany, Switzerland and Holland, amongst others.[1]

When the Countess first rejected Moravianism, she turned to support the missionary work spearheaded by the noted German pietist establishment at Halle, founded by August H. Francke. Opposed to the Moravians, Halle had backed a mission at Malabar led by several native Indians. One of these, 'Pastor Aaron', so caught Lady Huntingdon's imagination in the mid-1740s that she paid for and distributed large numbers of engravings of the man, including fifty which she gave to the Society for Promoting Christian Knowledge.[2] Increasingly, however, she lost patience with all existing missionary societies. The only way to fashion a means by which true zeal was manifest and firm control exercised was to establish such organs of outreach herself. Trevecca can in fact be understood more accurately as a missionary organisation rather than as a college. Once again, events conspired to sharpen the issue, when in the direct aftermath of the Oxford expulsions the Society for Promoting Christian Knowledge determined not to send academically unqualified methodistic men overseas.[3] In spite of John Fletcher's high hopes for Trevecca as an institution combining practical devotion with solid academic attainment, in practice it was forced by the quality of its students and occasional masters to aim only at teaching the 'rudiments of grammar' rather than 'superiour abilities'.[4]

There has been occasion enough to note how the Countess's Moravian relationships and attitudes fluctuated wildly through the years. Following her 'conversion' she sent money to Germany to support their work, only to drop all involvement in reaction to her sister-in-law's marriage. Then there were the constant battles during the 1740s and 50s, focused on her bitter personal rivalry at Court and in Bristol with Catherine Edwin, who as late as 1768 was going 'about abusing me highly'.[5] Lady Huntingdon had rejected Count Zinzendorf out of hand without ever having met him, only to be highly taken with him when she did. Yet four years later she expelled some of her leading Bath followers for evincing Moravian sympathies. However, securing Howell Harris's crucial support in establishing Trevecca had forced her to mute her anti-Moravianism. Continuing to maintain firm Moravian links, a month after Trevecca College opened, Harris was being supplied with details of the expansion of their overseas missions, from the West Indies to Africa to Greenland to North American Indians to the East Indies to Egypt, Asia and the Labrador Eskimos.[6] Over the following years until his death Harris served as a corresponding member of the Moravian missionary society, regularly receiving notices of its progress and subscribing to its support.[7]

This intelligence regarding renewed Moravian missions spurred Lady Huntingdon into action. With a handful of students now under her supervision, she determined to mount her own overseas campaign, and less than eighteen months after the opening of Trevecca two young men were selected, by lot, for a mission to the East Indies.[8] This was only days before the ship was to sail, and she determined that they must receive episcopal ordination before embarking. After frantic correspondence, the Bishop of London, Richard Terrick, agreed to waive the normal requirement of a three-week period for investigation into a candidate's suitability and proceeded to ordain one of the students, G. Pecore, solely on the basis of her recommendation. Since the other, William Hewer, was under-age, the Bishop refused to act in his case.[9] None the less, the Countess sent both young men on the mission, laying out £600 for the purpose, with her friends trusting that it all would 'answer the cry of your heart in letting your Colledge be made for the furtherance of his Glory to the Isles afar off'. She instructed her Bath chapel to devote a full day to prayer for the mission's success.[10]

It ended in disaster. Pecore reached the East Indies, but earned the Countess's disapprobation by settling as minister to the British garrison in Sumatra – where he was to remain for fifteen years – with the enormous annual stipend of £600. This would end, she said, 'in making him less diligent in his great masters cause'.[11] Hewer cut short his journey, writing that his only hope for 'the exercise of Religion, is by getting back to England again'; upon his return he admitted to Howell Harris that the enterprise had been a catastrophic failure and that he had 'stumbled'. For her part, Lady Huntingdon accused Hewer of certain unrecorded 'crimes'. With others loudly proclaiming him guilty of things 'really shocking', she quickly ended all connection with him.[12]

The dire results of Lady Huntingdon's first thrust into overseas missionary activity made Harris all the more certain that it was Moravians who had the combination of experience, co-ordination and zeal to succeed in such enterprises. On the Countess's side, this failed mission only increased her sense of competition with and disdain for Moravians, whom she now called 'Jesuits, cunning, artful'. She went on to expel two students who had Moravian sympathies and recommenced passing religious judgement on her Moravian inclined Bath supporters, E.K. Wilson and Mrs Leighton – who with Harris had laboured so assiduously and selflessly to prepare Trevecca to her specifications. To Wilson, the Countess was proving 'rash', and he wrote to Harris that since she would be there he would not come to Trevecca: 'I don't find myself at all inclined to pass such another Winter as I did the last.'[13]

At the very time her East Indies project was collapsing, the death of George Whitefield in September 1770 opened a long chapter in Lady Huntingdon's commitment to overseas missions. Whitefield's death signalled a crisis in her life. Never had there been, never would there be, any minister able to approach him in her esteem: 'My heart was unalterably attached to him & I trust ever will be.' This attachment now was reinforced by his will, which left her an orphanage in Georgia. 'Methinks the Mantle droped when the late D[ea]r Founder of Bethesda entered into the Joys above is fell upon yr Ladyship', according to one of her students.[14] Devotion to Whitefield's memory now precipitated her into activity in North America for which she and her followers had scant understanding and for which they made limited preparation.

Britain's last mainland American colony, Georgia had been established and governed by a Board of Trustees with philanthropic motives: to provide a haven for some of London's honest poor. An orphanage had previously been suggested by others, but as soon as he arrived in Savannah in 1738 on his first American tour Whitefield laid plans. Across the years, serious conflict over the nature of the Bethesda Orphanage, its religious ethos and Whitefield's erratic leadership of the venture, together with charges against him of simony, left it hanging in the balance. By the time of his death he had amassed grants of nearly 5,000 acres, all now left to the Countess – together with substantial debts.[15]

Over the years, Bethesda had been a financial and emotional burden to Whitefield. So it would prove for Selina Hastings. In his will he charged her to convert the orphanage into a college; if that were impossible, he called on her to continue it as orphanage and academy. Within three months of learning of his death, she committed herself to send out a man to head the enterprise.[16] Bolstered by the Bishop of London's ultimate agreement to ordain for the East Indies, she now bombarded him hopefully with requests to ordain two of her students for service in Georgia. Bishop Terrick expressed his willingness to ordain any who were 'qualified in point of abilities and in having had a regular education to fit them for the Ministry'. But she and they would have to agree that any such man should 'not think himself at liberty to go from place to place especially where there are resident missionaries' already sent by the Anglican Society for the Propagation of the Gospel. The Bishop was unwilling to be 'instrumental in sending any person to that Province, who may occasion disturbances or give uneasiness to any of our missionaries'. His intention in laying this restraint was 'to prevent that dissatisfaction amongst the Missionaries, and Confusion in the American churches, which has been already too much the Subject of complaint, and which it is my Duty to prevent'. The Countess, in her constant applications to him on this matter was unwise enough to make bitter mention of the 'very great personal Prejudice' she felt that the late Archbishop of Canterbury, Thomas Secker, had harboured towards her. This comment deeply offended Terrick, who assured her that from his own 'intimate knowledge of him' Secker had no 'prejudices against any . . . who were seriously engag'd in the cause of Truth and of Religion'. The correspondence ended with Lady Huntingdon rejecting any restriction on her men itinerating in America wherever they pleased.[17]

Although a bishop's hands would not rest upon the heads of any of her Georgia-bound students, the Countess of Huntingdon's would commission them. She was buoyed by her supporters: 'Bethesda, the Orphans, and the Academy, [were] all to be govern'd wholely unto Thee. Thou art the name, the only name that stand[s] now in the front of that religious band.' Rather than following her initial impulse to dispatch one or two freshly ordained students, she determined to send out several un-ordained students, led by a man already in holy orders. She was certain that the venture was 'the most important event of her whole life' and seriously considered accompanying the students to Georgia.[18] Trevecca was the springboard for her American mission. In October 1772, after days of protracted prayer and preaching at the college, seven young men dedicated themselves. A week later they departed for London amidst astonishing scenes of emotional outpouring. At services in London, they were 'drest in their college gowns', sitting 'in front of the green-seat, Lady Huntingdon at their head'. The ship set sail to words from the pen of her cousin, Walter Shirley:

> Go, destined vessel; heavenly freighted, go;
> For lo! the Lord's ambassadors are there;
> Faith sits at helm, and Hope attends the prow,
> Whilst thousands swell the sail with balmy prayer.[19]

To correspondents she enthused that the 'opening in America is the astonishment of all that love or fear the Lord'. 'America . . . is honoured by the Mission sent over to the Province of Georgia making proposals to build a Church at their own expense & to present me with it. . . . The Invitations I have for our Ministry in various parts of America is so kind & affectionate that it looks as if we are to have our way free thro the whole Continent.'[20]

The launching of the American mission was further fuelled by Lady Huntingdon's millenarianism. Informed now by Thomas Hartley that 'the New Jerusalem church, the Lamb's Wife . . . will shortly appear on earth by descent of Influx from the Lord thro' the Angelical heavens' and that those who were 'in nearest communication with angels' would receive 'the first influx', these exotic predictions placed heightened expectation on her transatlantic task. Soliciting American evangelical opinion on the Second Coming, she proclaimed her own belief in its imminence and encouraged publications relevant to it. The issue was urgent. Bethesda would provide base camp for her 'measures ... to convert the poor people in America'.[21] This zeal was fired by her belief that America was a rocky, reluctant soil, in desperate religious straits. She had been assured that Georgians in particular were religiously 'as dead as stones', and she herself described them as 'miserable neglected, perishing souls, & ... deplorable indeed'.[22] She eagerly emptied her purse to cover all the expenses of her men, men who must remedy this shocking situation in America by the power of their preaching and the freedom of their movement in Georgia, and beyond. Although it never arrived, she purchased and sent out a printing press. One of her supporters wrote: 'I am pleased to hear that you have seen so much of the goodness of the Lord smiling approbation on your American Labors of Love.'[23] It was the first and last time that providence was to smile on any of Selina Hastings' plans for America.

For a start, most of the students were left behind in England, when they got off the ship to preach. Two of them did not bother to renew the effort to go. Only two, together with a domestic housekeeper, made the initial crossing. Early in 1773 the Countess received a string of plaintive letters from the five students who at different times had straggled into Bethesda. All was in chaos: the garden in ruins; no furniture in the house; slaves dressed in rags; buildings and plantation run-down; no prospective students for academy or college. Nor had the head of the mission arrived. The Reverend William Piercy, an episcopally ordained cleric, proved a personnel problem of the highest rank. (See illustration 11.) A product of St Edmund Hall, Piercy had been ordained priest in May 1769.[24] She first met him that year, and a few months later he preached at Trevecca. At the time, he was serving as a curate at Lord Dartmouth's evangelical All Saints Church, West Bromwich. Yet Piercy had caused much dissension by openly criticising the rector (who was also Dartmouth's chaplain), and Piercy had been dismissed from his curacy in the spring of 1770.[25]

From that point forward, Piercy was unable to find even a curacy and, as Haweis before him, offered his services at the Lock Hospital Chapel. However, it was not long before Martin Madan dismissed Piercy because of 'his irregularity of preaching in the fields', and both his falling out with Madan and this reason for his dismissal no doubt endeared him to the Countess. By late 1771 Piercy was writing to her that he 'would most earnestly wish to go from pole to pole preaching Jesus'.[26] He continued in this vein into 1772, seeking by various means to gain her patronage, stressing how he 'adored' field-preaching and 'hopes never to be confined more'.[27] Piercy had not been at the forefront of the Countess's mind as a possible leader; yet when another cleric – whose name had been publicly published as the head of the expedition – was jettisoned by the Countess only days before the students were to sail, she secured Piercy's services. She now claimed to see in him a likely successor to the desperately missed Whitefield: Piercy 'is a beloved friend of mine and one who I truly believe the Lord is raising up in our late Dear Friend's place'. She immediately appointed him one of her domestic chaplains.[28]

When he finally reached Georgia in the spring of 1773, Piercy from the outset exerted such an overbearing air of superiority towards the five students that they petitioned their patroness to overrule him. 'Mr Piercy is the most proud, haughty, cruel, inhumane, oppressive . . . and hypocritical person that I ever was acquainted with in my life', wrote one. It was a unanimous opinion. 'Ten times the honour and respect that your Ladyship is contented with is not sufficient for him.' Piercy responded by branding them all liars, cheats and thieves, active in besmirching his name.[29] This news of mutiny among her men reached Lady Huntingdon alongside further unnerving intelligence. Her leading student, Trevecca's 'closest walker with God', was John Cosson, whom she had made second in command in the Georgia mission. However, for two years he had been engaged in a clandestine affair at Trevecca with the very housekeeper the Countess sent out with her students. The fruit was the birth of a Bethesda child, four months after the couple's arrival. This delighted 'the multitude of enemies that surround us who are gaping on all sides in order to catch at everything to overthrow the great & glorious cause'.[30] It was dangerously true. At the very time she reeled from news of the Cosson affair, Lady Huntingdon learned that numerous Georgians were hostile to the mission. Many in the colony feared that the Bethesda lands ultimately would fall into the hands of Whitefield's relations. She was informed that the plan to convert Bethesda from orphanage to college was wholly misplaced, since America already had several colleges. She should support those institutions instead.[31] In fact, at the very time she dispatched her mission in the autumn of 1772 the Countess personally had ordered the Bethesda orphans 'to be placed out' and no others to be admitted.[32] One student caught the mood with precision: 'The wise and learned despise us as Fools and illiterate persons; the ignorant and the unlearned ridicule and reproach us' and claim that 'we encroach upon the Orphans privilege, and possess ourselves of their property'.[33]

Then it happened. Two months after Piercy's arrival, Savannah's newspaper, the *Georgia Gazette*, published an article highly critical of the Countess's mission ten miles away at Bethesda. Piercy, who had been unable to find an Anglican position in England, now fancied that through the agency of the Countess of Huntingdon he had secured one in America. Attempting to impose his Church of England credentials upon Bethesda, Piercy was ignoring the fact that the greatest part of the Orphan House collection solicited by Whitefield had come from Dissenters. The article stated – correctly – that a Dissenter asked that when she died she be buried at Bethesda next to her husband and that a Dissenting minister officiate. Piercy refused, saying that he was 'certain it would be contrary to Lady Huntingdon's intention, . . . the College being established on the Church of England plan'. That number of the *Georgia Gazette* was published on 26 May 1773. Three days later Bethesda was burned to the ground.[34]

This arson – it is reasonable to infer that it was – achieved its desired ends. The Countess herself saw it as a deliberate act, writing that her plans for Bethesda had 'caused the Curses of the poor to bring that Judgment upon me'. Her students had no taste to attempt its resurrection, one lamenting the destruction as a 'judgement from God' and complaining that they had accomplished nothing. A month later he wrote again: 'O! my God, wilt thou give me such a loving and warm heart full of zeal for thy Glory as thou dost give to that Elect Lady, the Countess of Huntingdon, who is a Mother in Israel. P.S. I hope your Ladyship will not be against my returning home to England with my Brethren.' These ill-trained and ill-starred students did return or drifted into the back country of Georgia and South Carolina, most eventually becoming Dissenting ministers.[35]

The Countess was devastated. 'The disagreeable news each ship brings of our affairs in Georgia were I not to look above all things for comfort must exceedingly discourage all my future attempt.' 'The amazing draft of money that I am called upon for must be for Nigers.' 'The Lord has caused dear Mr Whitefield to suffer much thro this place & indeed myself much more.' She went on to say that 'no trials thro my life have been equal to these', which was a staggering comment. She believed the American débâcle to be negating all her efforts at home – that it had induced bishops to make a secret pact never again to ordain her students, clearly her greatest fear. 'My heart has never fainted till now – indeed I am sinking. . . . I am sure it is such a crisis in the Church of God as has not ever been known.'[36]

Here was a fatal turning point. If Lady Huntingdon had maintained her insistence that Piercy return to England, she might have accepted the futility of attempting to carry on an American enterprise; but taking advantage of her distressed mind, and distance, Piercy fobbed her off. She should entertain no gloomy thought. Like luxuriant flowers, churches would spring up in the Georgia and South Carolina back country, 'built upon our own Plan which will rest in our entire Possession as in England'.[37] This was an astute tactic, given the Countess's belief that through her personally holding deeds to church property, followers – in England and America – would accept her religious injunctions without question. In reality, Piercy's expansive view merely allowed him to abandon Bethesda and attempt to cut a Whitefieldian figure in America. It would not be long before he was observed progressing through the colonies 'with his phaeton & pair of fine horses; with his black boy to fan him in the pulpit while he was preaching, & all at the expense of Lady H'. Was this what her American mission had 'come to?'.[38] As will be seen, after squandering thousands of pounds of her money, Piercy was finally brought to account in England during the mid-1780s.

What is the explanation for this abject failure of her Bethesda plan? Certainly, Lady Huntingdon was impulsive, but she had not acted without some intelligence from America. Unfortunately, her American correspondents were limited in number and far from astute, or disinterested, in the advice they proffered. Whitefield's removal from the scene and the changed political situation in America had contributed to an unravelling of the evangelicals' lines of transatlantic communication. Despite rumours that he angled for appointment as an American bishop,[39] Whitefield had tended to blur 'denominational' divisions between Dissenters and methodistic Anglicans – to the extent that in America he had cut his clerical cloth to suit the colonists' predominantly Dissenting religious culture. On this basis much of the colonial funds for Bethesda had been forthcoming; it was the main reason for such howls of protest after his death when it became clear that Whitefield had bequeathed the institution to a professed Anglican who was moving forward to staff the institution with Church of England men.

The paucity of the Countess's correspondence in the period following Whitefield's death meant that she entertained no knowledge or understanding of American Dissenting attitudes and strength. A letter written after the fire informed her how intolerable it was that a basically Dissenting institution be 'improved entirely to the purposes of Conformity & that with no other reason than that your Ladyship happens to be of the Religion established in England'.[40] Previous correspondence had struck a different note. She received five letters from James Habersham, merchant/magistrate of Savannah, who years before had served with Whitefield at Bethesda. Habersham it was who fatefully insisted she ensure that any minister sent to Bethesda be Anglican. He went so far as to tell her that Church of England clergymen were 'no where more wanted than in America, or in general better received'. It was a patently absurd claim. In reality, the Countess initiated her mission at the height of colonial fears regarding the appointment of bishops for America. A staunch political Loyalist, Habersham was intent on repairing the frayed cords that bound his colony to England; as acting governor of Georgia during the planting of her Bethesda mission, he saw that enterprise as a further means of solidifying his tenuous political position. Indeed, Habersham provided Lady Huntingdon's main window on Bethesda in the months following Whitefield's death and greatly influenced her plans; she went on to press him to transact all the mission's financial affairs in the province.[41] Moreover, she chose to ignore the warnings of Cornelius Winter, Whitefield's young assistant during the evangelist's final American pilgrimage. Upon his return to England in 1771, Winter expressed doubts regarding Bethesda's viability, and his veiled – and occasionally unveiled – criticisms of Whitefield, Lady Huntingdon angrily rejected out of hand. Winter found himself 'under your Ladyship's censure'.[42]

With rare exception, the other correspondence Lady Huntingdon received from America as she mobilised her mission was limited to fawning deference and pious exhortation. Why harbour any doubts, when told that Whitefield frequently had informed Americans of her 'zeal and ardent love for Jesus & Immortal souls'. Why stay her hand, when assured that her 'much applauded fame' had been 'wafted years ago to the British colonies. . . . Go on seraphick Soul you Patroness of serious practical godliness until you assimilate that well adopted metapher of St John pointing to the Church: "I, says he, saw a wonder in Heaven – a Woman cloathed with the Sun, with a crown of twelve Stars on her head and Moon under her feet."'[43]

The Countess's mission to redeem Whitefield's Bethesda drained away substantial financial resources. She lost several thousand pounds and 'during Eight years never had the return of a Shilling'.[44] In the process, huge sums had been devoted to the purchase of slaves. A modern historical truism is that eighteenth-century evangelicals made an important contribution towards the ultimate abolition of slavery in the British empire. True of some of the men in the evangelical/Methodist movement, it was not true of evangelicalism's leading lady. Slave owning was closely intertwined with Selina Hastings' missionary efforts in America. Initially, Whitefield vacillated over slavery but soon concluded that Bethesda must have it to prosper; he became one of the most outspoken objectors to the Georgia Trustees' prohibition of the institution. When in 1750 slavery finally was allowed, Whitefield quickly purchased and was given slaves and at his death left the Countess about fifty.[45] Spurred on by those intimately involved at Bethesda,[46] she proceeded to add more over the years, especially after deciding not to abandon Bethesda after the fire. At one point they numbered about 125,[47] and Piercy would whip them 'for mear trifles almost every day'. The Countess even wrote to her agents in Savannah: 'I must . . . request that a woman-slave may be purchased . . . and that she may be called SELINA, after me.'[48] For several years one can trace in the lists of the Bethesda slaves this black Selina.

Lady Huntingdon's deliberate extension of slavery sharpened the pen of its most articulate opponent in colonial America. The Philadelphia Quaker Anthony Benezet wrote to her in 1774 'from a persuasion that thy love to mankind . . . would induce thee to give what assistance is in thy power . . . of putting a stop to this iniquitous Traffick'. She replied that it is 'God alone, by his Almighty power, who can and will in his own time bring outward, as well as spiritual deliverance'. A further letter from Benezet, enclosing John Wesley's tract against slavery, which called it a 'villainy', surely helped to guarantee her persistence in the ownership, purchase and selling of slaves.[49] Of course, the movement against slavery was but in its formative stage, and Lady Huntingdon cannot be singled out for special censure. Her theology hindered her. Wesley and the Arminian Methodists tended to call for emancipation largely because slaves by definition could not exercise the free will necessary to achieve salvation. The Countess's Calvinism demanded no such freedom. Struggling to be released from the logic of cause and effect, she ever sought to throw on to God the responsibility for any social action.

Lady Huntingdon's concern even for the salvation of slaves was strangely muted, certainly when compared with all her other missionary projects. Apparently, the only positive action she took was to send over a young African, David Margate, to convert them and, presumably, to keep them quiescent.[50] However, Margate burst upon Bethesda in late 1774, creating havoc. He boasted that he was a second Moses '& should be called to deliver his people from slavery' and proceeded to preach insurrection in the nearby colonial bastion of slavery, South Carolina. He also seduced several women slaves at Bethesda. The plantation soon was in disorder '& all the negroes . . . murmuring'. Fear reached frenzy when he was suspected of plotting 'to poison all the white people'. Finally, word was received that a lynching party had been raised in South Carolina, and only quick action secreted Margate on a ship bound for England.[51] The Countess never again made efforts to Christianise her slaves.

The Bethesda mission had ended in catastrophic failure. Its knock-on effects for the Countess's plans in England were extensive. By spending thousands of pounds 'in the service of Bethesda . . . she robbed churches [in England]'.[52] Her supply of students at Trevecca was seriously depleted. The perception that she was intent on mounting overseas missions irrespective of and in competition with established agencies such as the Society for the Propagation of the Gospel heightened the suspicion amongst church authorities. And the experience hardened her own belief that she stood alone in pursuing the gospel trail. The American fiasco only strengthened the certainty that her own hand must control all aspects of her enterprises. In the aftermath of the Bethesda fire she expressed the conviction that only her physical presence in America could have countered the crisis. 'Wonderful things will be accomplished whenever you go there.'[53]

Moreover, Lady Huntingdon was certain that the Kingdom of God would come simply by preachers preaching – regardless of social and political realities surrounding them. Nowhere was this better illustrated than in her headlong plunge into American missions. They were anachronistic, because of her determination to pull every string. She had no inkling that an English Anglican attempting to convert America would raise ecclesiastical hackles. By then, throughout America the dominance of an élite was being aggressively undercut by the exuberant protestations of the powerless claiming their right to control religious movements. The irony was that Whitefield's American evangelistic crusades had played no small part in fuelling this manifestation. This 'democratisation of American Christianity' was beyond her knowledge, and her comprehension.[54] In perhaps the only critical communication received from an American, written in the aftermath of the Bethesda fire, she was accused of adhering to 'the stricktess Forms of the Church of England'; moreover, her plans for an American college meant that students would be '<u>whol[l]y dependent</u>' upon her. 'Perhaps that may ap[p]ear to your Ladyship a Means necessary for the promotion of true Religion – but to those who know the state of the American Churches, it will appear quite the Contrary.'[55] The Georgians believed they had Bethesda, and Whitefield's extensive plantations, within their grasp, only to have it all snatched away by an English woman, an Anglican countess. She activated a religious crusade 'to convert the poor people in America', only to discover that the 'curses of the poor' had wreaked havoc with her plans.

By the time Lady Huntingdon initiated her American mission the transatlantic evangelical network had altered out of recognition. She must have been shocked to discover that, for many, Whitefield's name, once the talisman of American evangelicals, no longer carried the same mystique. 'Were Mr Whitefield himself now to arise & appear with all his former Zeal, his Labours would not be so acceptable as they once were.'[56] Beyond Bethesda there was no focal point for her overseas missions: no American churches or ministers. With the demise of Bethesda she had no men or operations in America, even to attempt to control, and found it impossible to retain any residual presence in the new nation. Her American enterprise had indeed proved an 'astonishment'.

Notes

1 Lady Margaret Hastings to SH, [1740], 14D32/274, LRO: 'You have heard a good deal of this before.'

2 Thomas Broughton to SH, 13 August 1745, 14D32/572. See also Henry Hastings to SH, 13 September 1746, 14D32/196. LRO.

3 Nuttall, *Significance of Trevecca*, pp. 4-5.

4 Cradock Glascott to SH, 13 October 1768, F1/1448, CF.

5 SH to Judith Wadsworth, 5 December 1768, SMU 77.

6 James Hutton to HH, 8 October 1768, Trevecka 2655.

7 See, for example, Trevecka 2661, 2691, 2681, 2692, 2726, 2729.

8 HH diary, 26 December 1769, *HHVL*, p. 283; 14 February 1770, *Transactions of the Calvinistic Methodist Historical Society*, 29 (1944), p. 49.

9 SH to Bishop of London, [December 1769], 9 January 1770, [early 1770]; Bishop of London to SH, 3 January 1770, E3/1/6, 8, 10, 1, CF.

10 John Lloyd to SH, 11 March 1770, F1/1487; T. Godde to SH, 15 January 1770, F1/85 (quotation). CF.

11 SH to Bishop of London, [30 August 1771], E3/1/5, CF; Aldridge, *Funeral Sermon*, p. 22.

12 William Hewer to SH, 25 May 1770, F1/95, CF; HH diary, 22 October 1771, *HHVL*, p. 287; James Glazebrook to SH, 11 May 1772, F1/178, CF.

13 HH diary, 18 November 1771, *HHVL*, p. 288; E.K. Wilson to HH, 17 October, 27 November 1772. Trevecka 2719, 2725.

14 SH to CW, 28 November 1770, Black 79; Joseph Cook to SH, 28 February 1773, A3/1/25, CF.

15 For the earlier development of Bethesda see David R. Poole, Jr., 'Bethesda: an investigation of the Georgia orphan house, 1738-1772', Ph.D. dissertation, Georgia State University, 1978. See also Robert L. McCaul, 'Whitefield's Bethesda college', *Georgia Historical Quarterly* 44 (1960), pp. 263-77, 381-98. These, and other modern historians, are in varying degrees critical of his leadership of the institution. For the most damning, see Neil J. O'Connell, 'George Whitefield and Bethesda orphan house', *ibid.* 54 (1970), pp. 41-62. Whitefield's will is printed in Gillies, *Memoirs of Whitefield*, pp. lxi-ix. For his debts see Extract from Bethesda Accounts, n.d., A4/6/23. More than three years after his death the Countess was still paying off his Bethesda debts. Robert Keen to SH, 26 February 1774, A1/9/11. CF.

16 James Habersham to SH, 15 May 1771, 'The letters of hon. James Habersham', *Collections of the Georgia Historical Society* (Savannah, 1904), 6:129.

17 SH to Bishop of London, 30 August 1771, E3/1/5. See also same to same, n.d., E3/1/9. Quotations: Bishop of London to SH, 2 April 1771; 27 April 1771; 20 May 1771, E3/1/2, 3, 4. CF.

18 William Williams, *An Elegy on the Reverend Mr. G. Whitefield...Presented to Her Ladyship* (Carmarthen, 1771), p. 10 (quotation); James Glazebrook to SH, 12 June (quotation), 28 March 1772, F1/184, 176, CF.

19 *Some Account of the Proceedings at the College of the Right Hon. the Countess of Huntingdon, in Wales Relative to those Students called to go to her Ladyship's College in Georgia* (London, 1772), pp. 19, 56.

20 SH to John Hawksworth, 10 September 1772, 15 June 1773, G2/1/4, 8, CF.

21 Thomas Hartley to SH, 7 November 1770, F1/89, CF; SH to EH, 19 May 1773, T3765/M/2/21, PRONI. For her interest in American opinion see David Vanhorne to SH, 20 October 1772, A3/3/10, CF. American millenianism had sprung from the well of Calvinist revivalism during the 'Great Awakening'. Ruth H. Bloch, *Visionary Republic: Millennial Themes in American Thought, 1756-1800* (Cambridge, 1985), pp. 10-50. For her encouraging publications on prophecy see J. Harmer to SH, 24 October 1770, F1/108, CF.

22 Robert Keen to SH, 24 July 1773, A1/7/10; SH to Bishop of London, 30 August 1771, E3/1/5. CF.

23 Henry Mead to SH, 22 April 1773, F1/219; John Lloyd to SH, 10 November 1772, F1/202 (quotation). CF.

24 BA 2448 Class 778.7322, Hereford and Worcester Record Office. He had been ordained deacon in 1768. Bishop's Subscription Book, B/A/4/36 (17, 19 September 1768), Lichfield Joint Record Office.

25 WP to SH, 15 January 1781, A4/2/21, CF; E.K. Wilson to HH, 15 December 1769, Trevecka 2675; Records of All Saints Church, Smethwick Library; WP to SH, 21 May 1770, F1/1496, CF.

26 Henry Goode to SH, 25 August 1771, F1/1546; WP to SH, 7 September 1771, F1/133. CF.

27 Lady Anne Erskine to SH, 21 April 1772, F1/1599, CF.

28 Robert Keen to SH, 29 September 1772, A1/5/1; SH to James Habersham, 17 November 1772, A3/3/1 (quotation). CF; Register of Peers Chaplains, FV/1, Vol. XIV, f. 159 (15 September, registered 30 October 1772), Lambeth Palace Library.

29 Daniel Roberts to SH, 18 August 1773, A3/6/19; John Cosson to SH, 28 January 1776, A4/2/36. For examples of similar letters see Thomas Hill to SH, 28 July 1773, A3/3/15; Joseph Cook to SH, 1 January 1774, A3/6/6; Lewis Richards to SH, 30 July 1773, A3/6/11. For Piercy's ripostes see WP to SH, 25 February 1774, A4/1/14; 6 January 1775, A4/2/12. CF.

30 JF to SH, 12 April 1769, F1/1464; Charles Stuart Eccles to SH, 10 April 1773, A3/5/11. CF.

31 William Tennent to SH, 10 June 1773, A3/3/9, CF.

32 James Habersham to SH, 26 May 1773, A3/3/2, CF. Just before his death Whitefield boasted of taking in 'about ten orphans. Prizes! prizes! *Hallelujah!*' GW to R[obert] K[een], 16 April 1770, *Select Letters*, 3:418.

33 Daniel Roberts (from 'Bethesda Ruins') to SH, 18 August 1773, A3/6/19, CF.

34 James Habersham to SH, 3 June 1773, A3/3/3, CF.

35 SH to WP, 3 February 1774, A4/3/4; Lewis Richards to SH, 30 July, 30 August 1773, A3/6/11,12. CF. Of the five students who went to Bethesda, all had dispersed by 1775. Four remained in America, two becoming Presbyterian, two Baptist ministers.

36 SH to James Habersham, 28 July 1773, A3/15/2; SH to WP, 11 August, 22 September 1773, A4/3/1, 2. CF.

37 WP to SH, 12 August 1773, A4/1/9, CF.

38 Thomas Rankin, journal, 15 October 1775, Tyerman/Evertt transcripts, Rylands.

39 John Frederick Woolverton, *Colonial Anglicanism in North America* (Detroit, 1984), p. 200.

40 William Tennent to SH, 10 June 1773, A3/3/9, CF.

41 James Habersham to SH, 15 May 1771, 'Letters of James Habersham', p. 130 (quotation); SH to Habersham, 17 November 1772, A3/3/1. For his other letters see A3/1/3,5. CF; 'Letters of James Habersham', pp. 102-111.

42 Cornelius Winter to SH, 20 July 1771, F1/130, CF.

43 John Edwards to SH, 30 October 1773, A3/1/27; John Moorhead to SH, 22 February 1773, A3/1/30. CF.

44 SH to anon., n.d. [*c.* 1784], A4/5/8. From July 1772 to November 1775 alone her Bethesda losses totalled well over £6,000. Notes on Mr Keen's Accounts, 16 March 1781, A4/5/14. See also A4/4/1, 2, 4; A4/6/1. CF.

45 Robert Keen to SH, 3 August 1782, A4/6/24, CF.

46 For example, James Habersham to SH, 5 April 1773, 'Letters of James Habersham', p. 225; Edward Langworthy to SH, 2 January 1773, A3/3/14, CF: 'Nothing can be done here without Negroes, & I wish your Ladyship may increase their Number....Laying out monies any other way, may prove detrimental to your Plan.'

47 For the most detailed accounting, from those she inherited at Whitefield's death up to 1780, listing each slave by name, see 'List of Negroes', A3/8, CF.

48 John Cosson, 28 January 1776, A4/2/36, CF; SH to Josiah Tatnall, John Glen and Nathaniel Hall, n.d., Seymour, *Life and Times*, 2:266. Her attitude towards slavery is ironic, given that the noted black American poet Phillis Wheatley early in the 1770s dedicated to her a book of verses. Phillis Wheatley, *Poems on Various Subjects, Religious and Moral* (London, 1773). See also Susannah Wheatley to SH, 30 April 1773; Phillis Wheatley to SH, 27 June 1773, A3/5/3, 4, CF. Although the poet visited England, she and Lady Huntingdon never met.

49 Anthony Benezet to SH, 25 May 1774, 10 March 1775, A3/1/33, A4/7/9, CF; in the latter he quotes from her letter to him. Wesley's tract was *Thoughts Upon Slavery* (London, 1774), with the quotation from p. 35. It afforded Benezet 'much satisfaction', and he immediately arranged for its American publication. Anthony Benezet to JW, 23 May 1774, *Arminian Magazine* 10 (1787), p. 44.

50 Robert Keen to SH, 22 September 1774, A1/12/5, CF.

51 WP to SH, n.d., A4/2/16, leaf C, CF. These observations of Margate's activities were confirmed by a number of other Georgians, even by those who had been well-disposed towards his mission. James Habersham to SH, 19 April 1775, and same to Robert Keen, 11 May 1775, 'Letters of James Habersham', pp. 241, 243-44; John Edwards to WP, 1 January 1775, A3/6/9, CF.

52 John Johnson to Sir George Houstoun, 9 January 1792, John Johnson's Letterbook, Georgia Historical Society.

53 SH to WP, 11 August 1773, A3/3/1; Lady Anne Erskine to SH, 22 December 1774, F1/1712 (quotation). CF.

54 During this period in America 'young leaders without élite pedigree constructed fresh religious ideologies around which new religious movements coalesced'. The 'wall between gentleman and commoner had been shattered'. Nathan O. Hatch, *The Democratization of American Christianity* (New Haven, 1989), pp. 57, 85. See also Stephen A. Marini, *Radical Sects of Revolutionary New England* (Cambridge, Mass., 1982), pp. 40-59.

55 William Tennent to SH, 10 June 1773, A3/3/9, CF.

56 *Ibid.*

Chapter 7

'Seeing all her friends bow to her'

Not only in America did eighteenth-century social deference produce major pitfalls for a leader of the new-birth movement. In English society, where deference was *de rigueur*, a countess of the realm sat uneasily within the ranks of a religious movement which stressed the freedom of God to choose whom he would. That bespoke an unpredictability of status for Christians. The stage was set for serious complications over ecclesiastical authority, especially in a movement that appealed mainly to those in less exalted ranks of society. Not until after the French Revolution would evangelicalism penetrate English high society.[1]

Conspicuous as an aristocratic Methodist, attention focused sharply on Lady Huntingdon's personal leadership. Passionate personality, together with status in society, combined to make deference doubly imperative for those concerned to win and hold her grace and favour. Time and again followers spoke of her in public or addressed her privately in remarkably fawning terms. Typical were letters telling her that she was 'one of whose notice I am not worthy', 'such a woman that no Body can refues aney thing that she asks them'; or wondering 'how shall we express our selves in terms sufficiently humble . . . we who are so infinitely inferior?'[2] A woman wrote that 'if I look at the great disproportion between Dear Lady Huntingdon and my little Self, I should shrink back from sending this very Familiar Epistle'. A minister wrote of 'the very high veneration' he had for her, which 'almost bordered upon idolatry'. Another man (seeking to secure some placement) wrote that his 'esteem & veneration' for her had been 'raised to the highest pitch possible to be imagined', to the extent that he was persuaded that it was impossible 'for her to do wrong in any instance or upon any occasion'.[3]

For a brief time during her initial years with the Wesleyans, the Countess felt that deference was inappropriate to her new religious style. She wrote to John Wesley: 'I think no distinction of rank ought to be regard'd lest too great a difference should be pay'd . . . more than the Christian [status] of which we make our boast.' Yet two years later the Wesleys were reserving her special seat in their main London chapel. At the same time, John Wesley was dedicating to her his collection of poems, candidly stating that 'it may be an inducement to many to read them. ... Many of them describe what a person of quality ought, and what, I trust, you desire to be.'[4] Lady Huntingdon's attraction to religious egalitarianism was thus short-lived. It had made theological sense while she was heartily committed to perfection, a state presumably open to all. But when her ardour for that doctrine began to wane in 1744 and 1745 the implications of predestination and election came to the fore. Few were chosen. Her new-found mentors certainly left no doubt as to where she stood in the divine scheme of salvation.

> Therefore go on, dear Madam, in the power of His might, and the Lord whom ye seek shall suddenly come to His temple and subdue those enemies that are yet unsubdued in your happy soul. But whither am I going? Do I consider to whom I am writing? Is it not to a King's daughter? ... I am persuaded you shall be caught up with a shout to meet the Lord in the air, and shall be for ever with Him.

Thus, Howell Harris – who continued in like vein: 'May He still animate your seraphic soul with zeal and divine wisdom as He has done hitherto, that you may be the happy means of bringing the savour of his knowledge to Court among our great ones.' In these early years of their relationship, Harris told Lady Huntingdon 'how insignificant I see myself', compared to her. He was constantly 'fearing to offend the Countess'.[5]

George Whitefield proved the most deferential of all. Shortly before his 1748 return from America and his destiny as the Countess's chaplain, Georgians were taken aback at a decided alteration. 'Tis an observation that I believe every body makes ... that Mr Whitefield is much changed from what he was or would seem to be, and become exceeding stately, relishing only the Company of the greatest, which is the opposite extream to that he was in when I first knew him.'[6] Whitefield never ceased to elevate and bolster the Countess's estimation of her own position. 'When your Ladyship stiled me "your friend", I was amazed at your condescension.' 'Surely your Ladyship will never know, till the day of judgment, the great ends God had in view in calling your Ladyship to *London*.' Her conduct was 'truly god-like'. She was 'placed upon a pinnacle'. 'Tears trickle from my eyes, whilst I am thinking of your Ladyship's condescending to patronize such a dead dog as I am. ... He will, he will reward your Ladyship openly. Ever-honoured Madam excuse me.'[7]

Not only did Whitefield make it a practice to pray for the Countess in public,[8] but most breathtaking of all was his announcing to her that at his London chapel 'thousands' had 'heartily united in singing the following verses for your Ladyship':

> Gladly we join to pray for those,
>   Who rich with worldly honour shine;
> Yet dare to own a Saviour's cause,
>   And in that hated cause to join:
> Yes! we would praise Thee that a few
>   Love Thee, though rich and noble too.

Uphold this star in thy right hand,
Crown her endeavours with success;
Among the great ones may she stand,
A witness of thy righteousness!
Till many nobles join thy train,
And triumph in the Lamb that's slain.

This remarkable contribution to Christian hymnody was not unique in singing the Countess's praises. In 1771, after her people at Dover had lifted their voices to sing a specially-composed paean to her praise, they concluded with 'many many prayers . . . put up for your Ladyship, which I doubt not pierced the skyes and entered into the ears of the Son of God'. At her death, her Bristol chapel joined in singing:

Thy handmaid, through favor divine,
Thou hast took to thy bosom of love;
Translated from earth, but to shine,
With far greater lustre, above;
Her animal frame shall no more
Be clog'd and obstructed with pain;
The spirit hath left it, to soar
Where pleasure, for ever, shall reign.[9]

While she lived, the Countess was frequently assured that she was the subject of public prayer. 'I have the pleasure of telling your Ladyship that I have hardly been two days together since I came home without hearing your Ladyship prayed for either in public or private.' 'Your Ladyship is not forgotten in public, nor private: and hearty amens are heard when we pray for your Ladyship.'[10]

The Countess ascribed clear categories of rank to her various ministers. At the top stood episcopally ordained clergymen, at the bottom her student ministers, in the position of dutiful children. On occasion it was literally so. When they embarked for Georgia, the students were cramped into steerage, William Piercy sailing as a very comfortable cabin passenger.[11] Whereas Charles Wesley felt that rough-hewn, uneducated preachers should return to their trades and forget about striving to become refined,[12] one of Lady Huntingdon's explicit directions was that her Trevecca students be taught deference. They were 'sensible of their awkwardness & the need of being a little poli[s]h[e]d' and had no doubts regarding their place. Thus, in addition to study and practise in preaching they were instructed how 'to make a bow'. It was a deference which could be and was practised by the students on their benefactress. One letter written jointly by them all, soon after the establishment of Trevecca, stated that because of their 'utmost gratitude springing from the deepest sense of your Ladyship's tender affection & unmerited love to us all, we lay these few lines at your Ladyship's feet'. One told her that 'a sense of my own unworthyness and inability to write to a person of your Ladyship's rank and dignity' made him loath to fashion a letter to her. Another wrote to her that he and his fellow students were 'very well pleased with your Ladyship's orders', since they came from one who was 'closer than a Mother. O my Lady begging is a charming trade.'[13]

It is no surprise that the Countess of Huntingdon's favour was directed primarily to select folk. To certain of her social circle she was on occasion willing to defer, as she was on some religious points to a small group of clergymen, usually her chaplains. She had, of course, early on established her homes for 'large assemblys . . . of the mighty the noble the wise and the Rich to hear the Gospel, a great many Ladies & people of Fashion as well as Quality'. Whitefield had described those who attended the salon gatherings as 'brilliant ones indeed. The prospect of catching some of the rich in the gospel net is very promising.' It even was considered that such occasions tamed Whitefield's more excessive flights of preaching fancy. He 'preaches more Considered among persons of a Superior Rank who frequent your Ladyship's Lodgings'.[14]

Beyond her drawing room, Lady Huntingdon's chapels in locations such as Bath, Brighton and Tunbridge Wells were known at first as places where an 'Elect Circle' might gather.[15] She directed one of her most trusted clerics to 'have a word to the fine world at Brighton'. In other words, the attenders at such chapels often were not necessarily of the religious, but of the social elect. When the Tunbridge Wells chapel was opened in 1769 it was observed that many 'amused' themselves by attending. Indeed, such 'elect' chapels tended to make clear-cut distinctions in their seating arrangements and even in the nature of the services provided. Lady Huntingdon was implored to send a suitable minister to Bath to conduct Christmas services, since 'a vast number of Quality always attend the Chapel at Christmas'.[16] At Bath the general practice was to limit admission at morning services to the higher ranks of society, while the humbler classes attended in the evening. Only the best preachers were booked for the former, while those of lesser talents held forth in the latter.[17] When the Countess was in the process of taking over the chapel which was to become her London showpiece, it was observed that the ministers who celebrated Communion there 'administered the elements with the same polite *dégagée* air that they would hand cups of tea to the ladies, offer pinches of snuff, or pick up dropped fans'.[18] To Whitefield, the Countess was 'mounting on her high places'. To Wesley, she was at the head of 'genteel Methodists' who 'are (almost all) salt that has lost its savour, if ever they had any'. With a theology that dictated inclusiveness rather than exclusiveness, Wesley rejoiced that God 'is higher than the highest' and concluded that persons of quality 'do me no good, and I fear I can do them none'.[19]

When a relationship with the Countess crumbled the hollowness of previous obsequiousness frequently was revealed. This was sharply true in the case of Howell Harris. A man without ecclesiastical credentials, Harris had been a curiosity in the early years of Lady Huntingdon's parlour meetings. The social distance separating them is starkly revealed by its being several years after he had begun to assist her on a frequent basis that she enquired whether he had a family. Over the years this condescension increasingly rankled, and he often complained of her pride, that she 'does not love reproofs & to be told of faults'. He began to 'turn away when any gave themselves such airs'. Harris believed that she considered herself 'infallible'. By the time of their final separation, he had reached the conclusion that 'Lady Huntingdon seeing all her friends bow to her . . . she can't bear contradiction'.[20]

Those who retained the Countess of Huntingdon's favour were favoured indeed. Not only did she desire close personal friendships; from a select few she demanded them. In these relationships she frequently was self-giving and impulsively warm-hearted. Yet the price to be paid was obedience, or at least acquiescence. It had not always been necessarily thus. In her earliest Methodist years she had yearned for religiously vital men to guide and direct her. Especially had this been true of her relationship with the brothers Wesley. However, it had not been long before she and John Wesley had detected in one another serious rivals in the new-birth movement. Whatever the complex chemistry in the relationship between the brothers, Selina Hastings soon had nurtured a bond with Charles that would never have been possible to form with his elder brother.

Given that she inhabited a position in society with which she neither felt uncomfortable nor rejected, Lady Huntingdon's personal relationships developed on clearly stratified levels. From whatever level, her friends had to tread carefully. Responding to expressions of unease and anguish regarding her own spiritual or physical health, or the difficulties in her personal relationships, or the highs and lows of the progress of her religious ventures, those of her own social circle attempted, through a mixture of calming words and deference to her wishes, to lead her to more peaceful plateaux. 'We shall be careful not to mention any thing you forbid, for which reason I shall say nothing of your letter to dear Lady Anne, tho' I know you will have no secret from her when you meet, nor shall I say any thing of your dear kind letter to Lady Gertrude for the same reason.'[21] Such letters – and frequent they were from many of her well-placed female correspondents – moved round the Countess carefully yet cheerfully, never taking offence and ever humouring and encouraging. They might even gently attempt to smooth the passage for a reconciliation between her and the numerous casualties in her relationships with clerical colleagues.[22] These were the friends she needed – never hysterical, and striking just the right religious notes to persuade her of their support. In 1777, when undergoing an especially critical period of personal and professional despair, she wrote to such a friend that her life had been useless. 'Pray give me leave', came the response, 'to tell my Opinion tho Contrary to yours. In this respect, for Indeed (my Dear Ldy Huntingdon) allow me to say, that if you Have lived to no Purpose, there is no Individual who must not give up all Pretensions to serve the Lord in this world.' Another 'loves you dearly' and 'will come to you the first moment she can'.[23] How right George Whitefield had been to observe that she must not be left dangerously alone.

Lady Gertrude Hotham, Lord Chesterfield's sister, had been the Countess's 'excellent friend' since 1734.[24] Her own Methodist inclination had antedated Lady Huntingdon's, and it was to Lady Gertrude that

Whitefield appealed for assistance when the Countess was 'in the furnace'.[25] It was she who supplied the crucial loan to build the chapel at Brighton and later paid the debts of David Margate, apparently just before his fateful journey to Georgia. In 1764 she travelled with Lady Huntingdon to Wales, a visit that was to plant the seeds for establishing the college at Trevecca. In 1766, during a period when Lady Huntingdon's letters reveal an especially tormented spirit, she sought comfort by going to stay with Lady Gertrude in London, at Grosvenor Square.[26] Her son, Sir Charles Hotham, also was a member of Lady Huntingdon's inner circle. The Countess surely must have appreciated his presence with her when they were robbed of their money and watches by a highwayman, although the robber had the grace to execute the deed in a very 'genteel' manner.[27] All participants in the event appear to have behaved with a proper dignity. On the other hand, a calming approach to Lady Huntingdon carried its dangers. The personal friends she demanded were those 'who will ever contend with every false rest'.[28] This was a voice of shimmering intensity her own restlessness demanded. Thus, even when all might appear calm, there was no doubting the volcanic nature beneath the surface. She showed great concern for the health of the son of one of her closest confidantes in Bath but, when she began to suspect the woman of finding inner comfort in Moravianism, condemned her 'unheard', turned her out of the chapel, and all contact was broken off for several years.[29]

Some of Lady Huntingdon's most affectionate words were reserved for the few clergymen upon whom she most depended. One she addressed as 'chief in the esteem of your ever faithfull & affct. friend S. Huntingdon'. To another and his wife: 'My dear & kindest friends, What must I say, what can I do, to explain the thousand part of my feelings to you both.'[30] Although she bore all the basic costs for her students and provided them with carefully accountable pocket money, to properly ordained clergymen her hand could prove remarkably open. 'I am miserable least he should be ill. My dr. Friend do let me know what money you will want that I may send you a note by the return of post.' While she refused to countenance the marriage of her students, she accepted and even nurtured relationships with the wives and close relations of episcopally ordained clerics, as she had done when Charles Wesley and his wife were particular favourites. To the sister of a cleric she desperately wanted to serve her chapels, the Countess wrote: 'O! my dr. creature take care of yourself. You are each hour I live of infinite value to me.' 'What should I do had not the Lord raised you up as a friend for him [i.e. God] & his poor widow. O! my heart loves you most tenderly.'[31] Frequently, wives of these men would take up pleading pens to defend their husbands' causes when difficulties arose or to trumpet their husbands' successes and to keep them in the Countess's favour.[32] Moreover, it is remarkable how ingrown were the networks of Methodist relationships. Not only was Benjamin Ingham married to the Countess's sister-in-law, but among the ranks of her own immediate clerical followers was her cousin, Walter Shirley, while one of Lady Huntingdon's nieces married a clergyman she depended upon for many years. There were numerous other such inner linkages. A clear warning was incubated in all these relationships: 'I will give up every friend on earth rather than depart from the one point of our saviours great love & glory to poor sinners displayed in his appearance to their miserable hearts.'[33]

Rare it was when those courting the Countess's favour or friendship did not find obsequiousness necessary. One exception was John Berridge. Eighteenth-century evangelicalism could have done much worse than to produce this delightfully provocative and eccentric vicar of Everton, Bedfordshire. Ever ready to puncture pomposity, Berridge it was who wrote the series of caustically practical letters during the height of her distraction over the death of her daughter Selina. Deeply committed to the work of his own parish, he frequently fended off imperious demands to drop everything to fill her chapels' pulpits. 'Don't grumble when you read this, I pray; & yet I am terribly afraid you will, because you have been in a sad grumbling fit of late. I expect a storm when I see you, & it may be a heavy one. . . . However pray let it out as soon as I enter yr. doors, that it may be presently over. For a hasty tempest with sunshine after it, is much preferable to a whole lowering hazy day.' When she did scold him, 'I must inform you, that I am mightly apt to laugh when a scolding is over'. He refused to obey her '*Vatican Bull*' to come to Brighton. 'You threaten me, Madam, like a Pope, not like a Mother in Israel, when you declare roundly, that God will scourge me, if I do not come.' 'Verily, you are a good piper, but I know not how to dance. I love yr. scorpion-letters dearly, tho' they rake the flesh off my bones. . . . All marching officers are not general officers . . . and my instructions, you know, must come from the Lamb, not from the Lamb's Wife.'[34]

Berridge was particularly concerned by the Countess's refusal to provide settled ministries in her chapels. The result was that her unattended congregations were breeding grounds for schism. Unless she left a 'good barking-dog behind you' when she was personally absent, disruptive souls 'will make fine work with yr. poultry by & by, clipping many of their wings, stripping some of their feathers, & brooding others to death'. He had discovered to his cost that whenever he absented himself from his parish, on his return he found 'his family scolding & fighting, with maimed limbs, broken heads, & bloody noses in abundance'. Therefore, Berridge was far from impressed by the peripatetic preachers she forced her students to be. Although he had occasionally preached in her chapels during the 1760s, her increasingly acrimonious nature and support of a rigid Calvinism during the 1770s brought an end to such activity. His task now was to continue an idiosyncratic role as pawky adviser; yet when he proceeded to criticise Trevecca he had gone a step too far. 'I doubt the success of the project, & fear it will occasion you more trouble than all yr. other undertakings besides.' He hoped that it would be 'Christ's College', but if it were, 'a Judas will certainly be found amongst them'. He was highly wary of her constant appeals to emotionalism, 'transports' which he felt had 'almost turned our heads'. What was needed was a 'spirit poured forth of triumphant faith, heavenly love, and steadfast cleaving to the Lord', but Trevecca he found 'little better than "seeking to familiar spirits, and to wizards that peep and mutter"'. 'Where is faith? Buried under [Welsh] mountains and not removing them.' By the late 1770s he was incisively pointing out that she could not forever hold her students rigidly to her will. Although he knew that she abhorred Dissenters, he candidly observed that her students 'are virtual dissenters now, and will be settled dissenters' when her death freed them. 'The Bishops look on your students as the worst kind of dissenters; and manifest this by refusing that ordination to your preachers which would be readily granted to other teachers among the dissenters.'[35]

John Berridge's basic principle was that 'I must not flatter you'.[36] The Countess of Huntingdon needed the sagacious voices of such men around her: the tragedy is that, apart from his, there virtually was none.

Notes

1 David Bebbington, *Evangelicalism in Modern Britain* (London, 1989), p. 23.

2 William Aldington to SH, n.d., F1/1290; James Nicoll to SH, 3 May 1773, F1/221; Jane Cave to SH, 27 June 1773, F1/233. CF. Aldington was a Trevecca student, Nicoll a labourer, Cave a shopkeeper's wife.

3 E. Cart to SH, 25 April 1746, 14D32/544, LRO; *Memoirs of the Life of the Rev. Thomas Wills* (London, 1804), p. 229; George Green to SH, 16 November 1773, 9 July 1774, F1/1664, 1703, CF.

4 SH to JW, 4 August 1742, Black 117; JW to SH, [22?] August 1744, Baker, 26:115.

5 HH to SH, [*c.* 1744], 25 May 1744, Hugh J. Hughes, *Life of Howell Harris the Welsh Reformer* (London, 1892), pp. 276- 78; HH ms diary, 7 April 1744, 5 July 1748, NLW.

6 John Dobell to the Georgia Trustees, n.d., Allen D. Candler et al. (comps.), *The Colonial Records of the State of Georgia* 26 vols. (Atlanta, 1904-1916), 25:52.

7 GW to SH, 22 August 1748, 28 January, 24 February, 27 May 1749, 27 May 1755, *Select Letters*, 2:167, 225, 238, 258; 3:120. Even Whitefield's most uncritical biographer cannot avoid cringing at his unremitting servility towards her. Arnold Dallimore, *George Whitefield* 2 vols. (Edinburgh, 1970, 1980), 2:279.

8 GW to SH, n.d., T.1839, p. 255, PRONI.

9 GW to SH, 30 November 1749, *Select Letters*, 2:293-94; Joseph Cook to SH, 24 December 1771, F1/158, CF; William Francis Platt, *The Waiting Christian: being the Substance of a Discourse Occasioned by the Death of the...Countess Dowager of Huntingdon* (Bristol, 1791), p. 23.

10 Thomas Maxfield to SH, 7 December 1769, F1/1480; James Glazebrook to SH, 20 May 1772, F1/181. CF.

11 Agreement with ship's captain, 19 November 1772, A2/6/9, CF.

12 CW to SH, 4 August 1751, Hull, 'Controversy between Wesley and Countess of Huntingdon', p. 180.

13 JF to SH, 12 April 1769, F1/1464; Trevecca students to SH, 27 June 1769, E4/4/4; John Cosson to SH, 1 December 1769, F1/81; William Aldington to SH, 7 April [1773 or 1774], F1/1291. CF.

14 SH to Philip Doddridge, 30 August 1748, HM 26630, Huntington; GW to Lady B___, 30 December 1748, *Select Letters*, 2:220; James Robe to SH, 18 October 1748, Drew B46.

15 Anon. to SH, 26 May 1768, E2/2/4, CF.

16 SH to Thomas Wills, n.d., II. c. 7/26, CL; [Edward] Budgen to [John] Jones, 16 July 1769, D.T.M. Jones Collection, no. 1118, NLW; R. Carpenter to SH, 16 December 1787, F1/675, CF.

17 Walter Shirley to SH, 22 May 1773, E4/1/18, CF.

18 Letter to the *St James Chronicle*, 8-10 October 1778, William Pinks, *The History of Clerkenwell* (London, 1865. New edition), p. 644.

19 GW to [Robert Keen], 17 March 1766, *Select Letters*, 3:335; JW to JF, 20 March 1768, 26 February 1774, Telford, 5:83, 6:75; JW, quoted in Maldwyn Edwards, 'John Wesley,' in Rupert Davies and Gordon Rupp (eds.), *A History of the Methodist Church in Great Britain* 4 vols. (London, 1965-88), 1:57.

20 HH ms diary, 3 May 1749, 4 October 1765, 14 September 1769, 22 September 1771, NLW.

21 B. Carteret to SH, 19 March, n.y., F1/1128, CF.

22 For example, B. Carteret to SH, 4 January 1777, F1/374, CF.

23 Lady Frances Montagu to SH, 12 June 1777, F1/394; Lady Anne Erskine to SH, 27 November 1772, F1/1625. CF.

24 SH to Lord John Rawdon, April [1759], T3765/M/2/21/4, PRONI; SH to Mrs Barlow, 31 July 1756, AL 2062, Bath Central Library.

25 GW to Lady G__H__, 15 December 1757, *Select Letters*, 3:225. She frequently stayed with Lady Huntingdon during periods of the Countess's deep anxiety. SH to CW, [August 1756], Black 63.

26 Henry Peckwell to SH, 9 January [1774?], F1/1350, CF; FH to EH, 4 July 1764, T3765/M/2/14/45, PRONI; John Berridge to SH, 28 July 1766, Berridge letters, no. 11, Rayleigh.

27 Lady Selina Hastings to EH, 7 February 1762, T3765/M/2/17, PRONI. Sir Charles opened his London house to preaching in 1767. HH ms diary, 16 January 1767, NLW.

28 SH to [Mrs Powys], n.d., Miscellaneous letters 5, Rayleigh.

29 SH to Mrs Leighton, 5 September 1760, 30 November 1765, Wesley Family Papers, Item 18-H, Duke; HH ms Diary, 13 December 1765, NLW; E.K. Wilson to HH, 9 December 1765, Trevecka 2613 (quotation).

30 SH to John Hawksworth, 13 September 1777, G2/1/18, CF; SH to Thomas and Janetta Haweis, 29 January 1790, SMU 112.

31 SH to Judith Wadsworth, 5, 7 April 1766, SMU 66, 67.

32 For example, Henrietta Shirley to SH, n.d., E4/1/25; Bella Peckwell to SH, n.d., F1/1243; same to SH, 1 March 1774, F1/275. CF.

33 SH to Judith Wadsworth, 7 April 1766, SMU 67.

34 John Berridge to SH, 20 July [1763], Berridge letters, no. 28, Rayleigh; Berridge to SH, 16 November 1762, Whittingham, *Whole Works of Berridge*, p. 445; Berridge to SH, 26 December 1767, Berridge letters, no. 12, Rayleigh.

35 John Berridge to SH, 6 March, 28 July 1766, 26 December 1767, 30 December 1768, Berridge letters, nos. 10, 11, 12, 17, Rayleigh; same to SH, 9 January, 23 March 1770, 26 April 1777, Whittingham, *Whole Works of Berridge*, pp. 506, 507, 516-17.

36 John Berridge to SH, 23 June 1763, Whittingham, *Whole Works of Berridge*, p. 447.

CHAPTER 8

'A papist unmasked, a heretic, an apostate'

Lady Huntingdon's students had arrived in Georgia boasting that 'they w[oul]d soon drive all the [Wesleyan] Meth[odis]t Preachers from the continent'. Leaders in the Wesley camp were horrified by the selection of William Piercy to head the mission, he 'who has set West Bromwich together by the ears. . . . In all probability they will sow the seeds of discord and make a breach in the rising [American Wesleyan] Societies.'[1] It is breathtaking to realise how vital a part the Countess's antipathy towards John Wesley played in fuelling her American plans. Establishing an unmistakably Calvinistic college in Georgia could exact revenge against Wesley, who the Countess now was certain preached a totally un-Christian gospel. The running skirmishes between the two strong-willed leaders, punctuated by brief temporary cease-fires, had in 1770 erupted into full inter-evangelical warfare. From the very founding of Trevecca, Wesley had scarcely been able to restrain his ridicule. Trevecca was the target, the Countess the goal. Stung by Joseph Benson's willingness to leave Kingswood for Trevecca, Wesley did not have to wait long before his warnings to the young man were to prove true.

The theological debate raised by the Oxford expulsion in 1768 had centred on whether the Thirty-Nine Articles of the Church of England taught predestination. Wesley had been pleased at the line taken by the university authorities in the affair: Calvinistic predestination had no part in official Anglican teaching. This position was fiercely challenged in the pamphlet war surrounding the expulsions, most especially by the rigid Calvinist polemicists Richard Hill and Augustus Toplady, who happily dug their chisels into Methodism's most jagged fissure. For some time past Wesley's Arminian views had become even more fixed, and he reflected that 'a pious churchman who has not *clear conceptions* even of *justification by faith* may be saved'. Since the Countess had now raised the stakes in their personal and theological contest, Wesley threw caution to the winds. In August 1770, at the annual conference of his movement, the official minutes asserted that there is no such thing as instant sanctification; continuing good works are a condition of a Christian's salvation.[2] By intent and result these minutes loudly slammed the door against any possible accommodation between the Wesleyan and

Calvinistic wings of English Methodism, while throwing open a wide door through which the ecclesiastical furies sprang free. Once the minutes of Wesley's conference were published, events tumbled forward at a frantic pace. Their public proclamation was aimed directly at the Countess's theology, and Wesley followed this by writing to her a 'bitter' and provocative letter, 'charg[in]g her w[it]h self and having fall[e]n to Pride'.[3] Wesley said that for several years he had felt he ought to confront her with these failings. It was his '*business*' to do so, 'as none else either c[oul]d or w[oul]d do it. . . . If she is not *profited*, it is her own fault, not mine; I have done my Duty.' He told her that 'you think yourself of *more importance* than you are'. He said that she replied, 'in effect, "Nay, you think *yourself* to be of more importance than *me*". Indeed I do; to be of ten times more, yea an hundred times more. . . . I *know* her perhaps better than any other person in Engl[an]d does. And I c[oul]d do her more good. But she rewards me evil for good. So fare her well.'[4] Her first action upon reading the minutes was to weep copiously, next to proclaim publicly that she 'abhorred' Wesley 'worse than any creature in the creation, repeating it again and again'. John Wesley and the Countess of Huntingdon were all the more confirming themselves as ecclesiastical prima donnas, resentful of the other's position in the leadership of the methodistic movement. However, their theological differences were real enough. She had charged him with '"establishing another Foundation repugnant to the whole plan of Man's salvation"'. He responded that 'zeal against those principles' in the minutes 'is no less than Zeal against the Truth, & against the honour of the Lord'.[5]

The Countess was stung into action, seeing her most urgent task to cleanse Trevecca of any lingering Wesleyan influences. From its founding, students had been carefully and ardently examined regarding their commitment to preaching forgiveness of sins, with a constant and agonising testing and re-testing of their own personal salvation in Calvinistic terms. Now they were compelled to produce in writing a renunciation of Wesley and all his works, a requirement she proved endlessly thorough in enforcing. She watched hawk-like for any hint of wording that she could construe as sympathetic to Wesley's despised doctrine.[6] Perhaps too angry to think clearly, Lady Huntingdon addressed her students and denounced his teachings, calling the 1770 conference minutes '*horrible*, *abominable* and *subversive*'. She said that 'she must *burn* against' all who did not exuberantly reject those views, and that 'whoever did not fully disavow them should quit the College'. It was a turbulent and painful process for many of her students. When she charged one with unorthodox preaching and being an Arminian, he replied: 'I am not an Arminian; neither am I a Calvinist. Perhaps I am a weathercock for . . . I endeavour . . . to recommend myself to every mans conscience in the sight of God.'[7] In this testing theological period she not only lost her tutor, Joseph Benson, but also the superintendent of Trevecca, John Fletcher, who had faithfully and arduously made frequent visits and had been received by the students 'as <u>an Angel of God</u>'.[8] Fletcher wrote to Wesley that he had told his 'mind to our Deborah, about bigotry, partiality, prejudice. . . . I have insisted and do insist . . . if every Arminian must quit the college, I am discharged for one.' She charges 'you with tergiversation, and me with being the dupe of your impositions'. Fletcher told her that her action 'may appear to many zeal for truth &c but seems to me a spirit of prejudice and needless division'. When Benson left on New Year's Day 1771, he saw Trevecca 'as a scene of great trial and affliction', and her own supporters were referring to the 'melancholy state of the College'.[9] Fletcher himself was melancholy, since his gentle spirit had always seen the good in Lady Huntingdon, whom he considered 'an honest, gracious person, but . . . where prejudice misleads her, her warm heart makes her go rather too fast'. 'What are our dear L[adyship]'s jealousies come to? Ah! poor College.' The result of her exertions was 'the boisterous & troubl'd Waters of the College'.[10]

To her credit, Lady Huntingdon provided Benson with a brief testimonial stating that during nine months as tutor he had shown 'capacity, sobriety, and diligence'. Yet this only emphasised for Benson that he had been dismissed 'wholly and solely, because I did not believe the doctrine of Absolute Predestination'.[11] Both he and Fletcher shared the Wesleyan belief in the possibility of salvation for all. Therein lay the roughest theological rub. Lady Huntingdon had fallen under the sway of England's most vociferous exponents of full-blooded predestinarianism. Wesley's 1770 conference minutes had indeed gone far beyond his and Whitefield's earlier juggling of this theological time bomb. In fact, Whitefield's death, the month following that conference, removed a moderating Calvinistic voice from the ensuing conflict. When the Countess had altered her theological orientation during the mid-1740s, she imbibed Calvinism from those whose views, particularly on predestination, were expressed with a degree of moderation. Men like Whitefield and Harris, while adherents of the doctrine, had refused to let it dictate their religious enterprises.[12] Yet with Whitefield dead and Harris on the verge of exclusion from her presence, Lady Huntingdon was subjected to the full blast of those who blew no uncertain predestinarian trumpets. Whereas in the recent past she had boasted of leaving 'all to the spirit', she now opined with her new advisers that the gift of the Holy Spirit had been completed at Pentecost. Her former affection for writings on the spiritual life, such as those of William Law, was substantially curtailed.[13] The implied rejection of the Christian life as a growth in grace only strengthened the perception, both of the Church of England and of Wesleyan Methodists, that 'your Ladyships Name is made use of to countenance the rankest Antinomianism, & the most ungodly practices'. When she and Howell Harris bitterly parted company in 1772 he invited Wesley to preach to the people at his Trevecca settlement. Harris told Wesley that 'I have borne with those pert, ignorant young men, vulgarly called "students", till I cannot in conscience bear any longer. They preach bare-faced reprobation and so broad antinomianism that I have been constrained to oppose them to the face, even in the public congregation.'[14]

A decade before, the Countess's cousin, Walter Shirley, had been on extremely close terms with John Wesley;[15] yet now Shirley abruptly, and perhaps opportunely, adopted a Calvinistic position and was at the forefront of the conflict with the Wesleyans.[16] Indeed, Lady Huntingdon enrolled him as one of her chaplains only days after learning of Whitefield's death.[17] She and Shirley then joined in supervising a remarkable composition, sent widely throughout the country. With her name 'at the head of the opposition',[18] this printed letter called on Calvinistic supporters, in either the Church of England or Dissenting denominations, to descend *en masse* upon Bristol on 6 August 1771, the date of Wesley's next annual conference. 'It is proposed, by Lady Huntingdon, and many other Christian friends, (real protestants,) to have a meeting at Bristol at the same time.' Since the minutes of the 1770 conference 'are thought injurious to the very *fundamental* principles of Christianity', the proposal was that those responding to this circular letter should 'go in a body' to Wesley's conference 'and insist upon a formal recantation of the said minutes'.[19] In the event, the Calvinistic troops failed to muster at Bristol, yet led by Shirley a tiny delegation to the conference believed they had secured a Wesleyan recantation. It was a belief quickly dispelled by Wesley's publication several days later of a 100-paged pamphlet by Fletcher vindicating Wesley's theology and attacking Shirley. Shirley leapt into print the following month with his *Narrative*,[20] its Introduction and Conclusion composed by Lady Huntingdon herself.[21]

A highly acrimonious pamphlet warfare, which lasted many years, had been launched into already turbulent waters. Although the Countess desperately wished to think well of Fletcher[22] and to lay full blame at Wesley's feet, she was assured that Fletcher had proved himself 'a complete Don Quixote', a mystic, whose congregation at Madeley was 'as dead as Ditch-Water'.[23] Further expanding the printers' trade, Wesley commenced a revision and republication of his previous works. From the other side, the provocatively titled *Gospel Magazine*, supported by Lady Huntingdon and edited by the virulent Calvinist, Augustus Toplady, turned its guns on Wesley, railing against his 'apostasy from the genuine faith of the gospel, an awful proof that evil men and seducers wax worse and worse'. His teachings were 'the very doctrines of Popery, yea, of Popery unmasked'.[24] Wesley went on to establish his even more provocatively titled *Arminian Magazine*. The methodistic publications, which had previously been directed towards fostering general tenets of the evangelical revival, had now become narrowed organs broadcasting the propaganda of warring camps.[25] Rival chapels served as distribution centres for these unhappy outpourings.[26]

Augustus Toplady was a young Anglican cleric whose full-throated espousal of the doctrine of predestination invited no competitor. He had published in 1769 *The Doctrine of Absolute Predestination Stated and Asserted*, and his decisive influence on the Countess during the 1770s is the clearest indication of the freezing of her Calvinistic orientation. At the first opportunity, he eagerly offered his services to her and Shirley in the conflict over the 1770 minutes.[27] Toplady preached regularly in her chapels, and the two maintained a regular correspondence. At his death, Lady Huntingdon wrote that 'never a happier soul lived or died' and spoke of 'the sweetness & simplicity of that heavenly spirit'. He had been a 'great servant of God' and 'so valuable a friend . . . that I so loved & honoured'. 'O! what a loss to the

Church of Christ.'[28] Toplady's influence continued through her avid reading of his printed works.[29]

Lady Huntingdon's convictions were further undergirt by ultra-predestinarian laymen. Richard Hill, who had proved his Calvinistic credentials during the pamphlet war over the 1768 Oxford expulsions, now sharpened his pen against Wesley and Fletcher in a number of vitriolic productions.[30] But perhaps the most effective unordained voice commanding her attention was that of Thomas Powys, like Hill a Shropshire layman. She had known Powys and his wife for several years and was in close contact with them into the fateful year of 1770.[31] Powys's leading role in the present furore was in conceiving the infamous circular letter sent out under the names of Shirley and the Countess.[32] Bolstered by some of England's most outspoken defenders of a rigid predestination, the Countess's commitment to the doctrine became total. What previously had served as personal consolation now became for her not only a badge of orthodoxy but also a litmus test of loyalty. Moving ahead to build further chapels, she issued firm instructions that 'no Ministers are to be admitted . . . but such as preach the pure Gospel, & the true Calvinist Doctrine'. She became, as she said, 'remarkably carefull' that her Trevecca students not 'suffer from any supposed union which may not be altogether in life & doctrine what I require from them'. One clergyman explained to her in 1774 that his recent connection with Wesley had only been to gratify the wishes of his dying wife, who had an 'infatuated prepossession' to Wesley and had been 'fast bound in the Fetters & Irons of their horrid opinions'. Since her 'Exit', he now was free to reject Wesley.[33]

All ministers and students who preached for the Countess were thrown on the defensive, for fear that she would receive reports of their not toeing a clear Calvinist line. Many evangelical clergymen who previously had moved with some degree of freedom between Methodism's two camps attempted to keep their heads down to avoid the direct volleys fired from both sides; others proclaimed their allegiances openly. One such was Vincent Perronet, the venerable Vicar of Shoreham, who earlier had stood on friendly ground with the Countess. Horrified by the virulence of her reaction to the 1770 minutes, he was even more aghast at the vehemence of her predestinarianism. 'May God give repentance to the broachers of such blasphemies!'[34] Another was Walter Sellon, a former baker, who over a period of two decades had earnestly sought Lady Huntingdon's patronage. On occasion she had enlisted his preaching services. Ironically, two months before the fateful 1770 Wesleyan conference, her son Francis had at her request presented Sellon with the living of Ledsham, Yorkshire. However, since 1766 Sellon had anonymously published several works defending Wesley and his doctrines, and now Sellon openly unfurled his true theological colours, accusing her preachers – and by implication herself – of tilling fertile fields for antinomianism by their adherence to predestination. He contributed to the printed conflict with a scurrilous attack on Toplady.[35]

The Calvinists' reaction to Sellon's attacks was one of disdain that a man of such plebeian background should presume to challenge the theological position of his betters. They took a similar line towards others in Wesley's camp. Another of humble background was dismissed as 'a journeyman cordwainer'. His Calvinist opponent would 'not take the least notice of him, or read a line of his composition, any more than, if I was travelling, I would stop to lash, or even order my footman to lash, every impertinent little quadruped in a village, that should come out and bark at me'.[36] Wesley was thus being castigated not only for his theology but for his stooping to employ those of inferior social origin to challenge the teachings of England's elect.

For Lady Huntingdon there were painful personal implications in these partings of Methodist ways. Her theological cleansing could not even stop short of her affection for Charles Wesley. She foolishly provoked this old friend by sending him a copy of the circular letter ('the first sent out by me to any one') together with a personal covering message. Here she re-emphasised her belief that the 1770 minutes were properly described as 'Popery unmasked'. All 'ought deservedly to be deemed papists who did not disown them'. Thus she had

> readily complied with the proposal of an open disavowal of them. . . . You must see in this view that neither partiality nor prejudice has any thing to do in this whole affair. Principles that does make shipwreck of Faith & of course of a good conscience is what I have to object to & no gloss ever so finely drawn over these apostate sentiments can alter their nature or consequence to me. . . . [John Wesley's] principles set up an other Gospel . . . and exclude that of Jesus Christ & thus expose thousands of immortal souls to the just suspicions of denying the only Lord God. . . . None can blame any who from such withdraw themselves.

She concluded by telling Charles that she had laid all this before him 'in order that with the greatest of openness your Brother might be informed by you'. Charles's reaction to this bold attempt to drive new wedges was to scrawl on her letter an endorsement: 'L. Huntin[g]don's LAST.' 'Unanswered by J.W.'s Brother!'[37] Although the shrill anger ultimately subsided, her relationship with the Wesleys was never repaired. Some years later Charles wrote to his daughter, referring to the Countess: 'A sensible Roman-catholic is above a match for any Calvinist.' When the Countess wrote to Charles on hearing of his brother's serious ill-health, she did so on the basis of the 'relenting of . . . Christian affection'. However, she could not forebear mentioning her 'JUST differences' with them. Charles produced a short, polite but studiously reserved reply in which he informed her that 'we shall be in our death not divided'.[38]

Charles Wesley's hymns now became an obvious target for the Calvinists. In the year of its opening, Lady Huntingdon had authorised – and probably had taken an active hand in preparing – a hymn book for her Bath chapel. Not surprisingly, the collection contained several of Wesley's hymns, with which she had long been 'charmed'.[39] But now that the methodistic streams had permanently divided, such inclusions were no longer possible. As the Countess's doctrine sharpened so her hymnody narrowed, and she became 'very urgent for the publication' of a new hymn book. Wesley's hymns either must be excised from the new collection or at least severely altered, since they 'savor so very strongly of Perfection that we cannot retain them without the most palpable Inconsistency as all your Ladyship's Ministers oppose this Doctrine to a Man'. Lady Huntingdon now exercised total control over the 'omitting or adding any' hymns,[40] though there is no evidence that she ever herself engaged in their composition.

Although the printed warfare that produced upwards of fifty pamphlets trailed off following Toplady's death in 1778, the practical effects of the controversy bit deep into the methodistic cause in England. It was a conflict in which claims had been pitched at their highest and the language of denunciation stretched to its limits. Her Trevecca 'college', now narrowly affixed to the Calvinistic camp, was thereby greatly crippled in its potential to serve the whole evangelical enterprise and was to limp from crisis to crisis over the following years. Relations with a number of local laymen who previously had assisted Trevecca became strained or broken. A lawyer in Hay-on-Wye, nine miles to the north-east, was informed by the Countess that there would no longer be any contact between him and her students because of his support of Wesley. He went on to lament the increasingly 'unwieldy affairs' at her 'mysterious Seminary'.[41] To the Countess it must have appeared that Wesley was attempting to surround Trevecca. He had taken care to send his best qualified preachers to Brecon, six miles to the south-west. With so many drained away by the mission to Georgia, only a handful of young and highly inexperienced students were left at Trevecca. This made it impossible for the Countess to counter Wesleyan activity virtually on the doorstep of her citadel. Yet she penned letters to Scotland, warning evangelicals like Lady Glenorchy and Lord Hopetoun that the Wesleyans were '*dreadful heretics*, to whom no countenance should be given'.[42]

Lady Huntingdon denounced Wesley as '*a papist unmasked, a heretic, an apostate*'.[43] Preachers in her chapels dutifully followed suit. She was delighted to hear that at Tunbridge Wells one such 'was very severe on John Wesley last Sunday & mentioned him by name in the pulpit & said the mask was at last fallen from his face'.[44] Driven by the engine of Calvinistic doctrine, the Countess's theological anxiety was fuelled by urgent reports of heterodoxy. 'Arianism is spreading over all these parts & your Ladyship knows wherever that is there must be death upon the people.' Her preachers assured her of their doctrinal (and personal) loyality. 'I could not profitably labor with any one that's tainted with Wesleyism, for I believe it to be the bane of Religion', wrote one.[45]

The Countess and Wesley sent out their preachers as soldiers girded for battle. In the process, and given the urgency, it may be supposed that her students occasionally were less than clear as to whose service she had called them: 'I have fully secured and taken the place in her Ladyships name', one assured her.[46] For some time the target of her activities was not areas previously untouched by the Methodist message but those where Wesley's men had been active. At Dover, Wesley found that her 'preachers had gleaned up most of those whom we had discarded. They call them "My lady's society" and have my free leave to do them all the good they can.' Again at Dover:

'The raw, pert young men, that lately came hither (vulgarly, though very improperly, called "students"), though they have left no stone unturned, have not been able to tear away one single member from our society.'[47] As far away as Dublin, where Lady Huntingdon was planning to build a chapel, 'the spite of Mr. Wesley's people has been most amazingly wicked'.[48] It may be doubted that the Countess learned of Wesley's visits to her estranged daughter Elizabeth in Ireland, where he was entertained 'very agreeably'.[49] In London, Wesley's followers 'spake very disrespectful of your Ladyship, and say your Ladyship must shut up some of your chapels very soon for nobody will preach for you because of opposing Mr Wesley'. Wesley opined that her preachers were 'wholly swallowed up in that detestable doctrine of Predestination, and can talk of nothing else'. He was certain that what '<u>they</u> do is <u>her</u> act and deed'. Her 'young men . . . act by her instructions'.[50] During the 1772 Wesleyan annual conference in Hull, she sent a student to preach against them.[51]

By 1776, though unrepentant, Lady Huntingdon apparently was distressed by the seemingly unquenchable combustibility of the conflict as its flash points spread across the country. She wrote to John Wesley to assure him of her strenuous efforts to ensure that her students when on their preaching rounds 'avoid all disputes or casting the smallest reflection upon you or any of your friends'. He immediately replied, 'persuaded your Ladyship is not sensible of the manner wherein many of the students have treated me. But let that pass: If your Ladyship will be so good as to give them a caution on that head, I know it will not be in vain.'[52] Yet in vain it proved. What she told him may have been true but, if so, the Countess had lost control of a conflict that had taken on a life of its own. Too many had been cut by the sharp crystals of this theological disputation. In fact, her assurances rang rather hollow. She had travelled to Cornwall the previous year 'to spy out the land where our standards may be best establish'd', with Toplady preaching at her Bath and Bristol chapels on route.[53] Her sympathies were deeply touched by the conditions of the tin miners, whose 'souls is become the object of my loving care for them'.[54] However, Cornwall was an area where Wesley's preachers had long been active, and the resulting conflict was predictable. Certainly, Wesley had little cause to accept her assurances. At St Ives: 'Those who styled themselves "my Lady's preachers", who screamed and railed and threatened to swallow us up, are vanished away. I cannot learn that they have made one convert – a plain proof that God did not send them.' Elsewhere they apparently were more effective. At Grimsby, 'and many other parts of the kingdom, those striplings who call themselves Lady Huntingdon's Preachers have greatly hindered the work of God. . . . Wherever we have entered . . . they creep in and by doubtful disputations set everyone's sword against his brother.' At Belton, Wesley grieved that '"My Lady's preachers", so called' had been successful in breaking up his work.[55] Into the 1780s it continued, with one of her preachers boasting in print that wherever he preached he had given the Wesleyans a black eye, while from Norwich she was informed triumphantly that forty of Wesley's followers had converted to her chapel.[56]

In this acrid and ugly conflict, John Wesley and his men seem to have given as good as they got. One of Lady Huntingdon's chapels pleaded for an able minister 'to keep our little Flock from being stolen' by Wesley, whose 'preachers make it Rule to preach against us almost every where'. Wesley himself, it was reported, had delivered at Penzance an 'extraordinary Harangue & Exhortation' in which he spoke 'very disrespectful[ly] of Mr Whitefield, Mr Shirley and of yr Lps. College & Collegians'. The Countess was especially mortified to learn that her Bath congregation was 'tearing to pieces & Mr Wesleys gathering immensely'.[57] In lulls between battles over the succeeding years, both she and Wesley engaged in a programme of pushing and probing one another's ecclesiastical defences. They eyed one another either bitterly or warily across a divide they themselves had done not a little to create. And Wesley wrote to an acquaintance: 'From the time I heard you were rejected by Lady Huntingdon, I have had a tender regard for you.'[58]

Trusting no other hand to impress theological purity, the Countess took full control of Trevecca. John Fletcher had been the first superintendent, and he was the last. Thenceforward, she assumed supervision. She had spent only a few weeks at the college in its first two years; but, following Wesley's 1770 conference, for many years it virtually became her home. From then until the mid-1780s she spent, on average, at least six months of each year at Trevecca.[59] With a frequent turnover of teaching masters, she found herself on occasion supervising all aspects of the students' education.[60] Her responsibilities were such that she had to be there 'continually . . . till absolute necessity constrains my removal'. For perfect order, she should be present to lead and to take decisions. 'One word from your Ladyship will go as far as a Thousand from any other person.'[61] As long as a student was there she provided 'every necessary of life', including a new suit of clothes annually.[62] In return, Lady Huntingdon 'claimed implicit obedience'. She was

> a stern disciplinarian, in the government of her students – as they all found – in the domestic as well as the scholastic arrangements of the college. They rose at five o'clock, and were expected to appear in the hall for divine worship punctually at six; at which hour the prayer-bell rang, and she herself was always present. She cast a searching glance around her, to satisfy herself that none appeared in negligent attire, or betrayed an inattention to the requirements of cleanliness and neatness, on which she was wont to lay great stress.[63]

To be at Trevecca was to be 'amongst your Sons'. 'Mother Huntingdon' – for such she was called[64] – finally had found a number of obedient children. She, in turn, exercised maternal care, seeking medical advice for students, who frequently fell ill in Trevecca's bracing climate. On one occasion she went on her knees to dress a student's injured legs.[65]

It was not only life at Trevecca that was under Lady Huntingdon's close supervision. She also undertook to organise all the students' far-flung preaching assignments. Over the years they roamed every English county, especially through the south-east (focusing on Kent and Sussex), the west (especially Somerset, Gloucestershire and Worcestershire), the north (primarily Yorkshire and Lancashire), and Cornwall, Berkshire, Hertfordshire, Staffordshire and Norfolk, as well as London and the anglicised areas of south Wales.[66] Under her 'immediate direction', students would receive specific commands:

> Collingham shall succeed you there, when you come off for the college, and he may easily change with Jones, as Whitefoot is in Sussex. _____ is just arrived out of Lincolnshire. Do hurry Hall down if he is not gone; and on Williams's return (which will be soon) he shall go there also, and if Wilks wants help, Tyler or Thomas Jones may go, and I think Moody to Harwich, and some one sent to Maidstone or Dover, or Kinfer to Maidstone, and some one to Dover.

'We are quite wore out with the labours.'[67] Nearly until the end of her life, whether resident at Trevecca or at some distance, the Countess personally supervised exactly which students preached where and when. What she demanded of these young men was staggering. 'I have no less than four new establishments for the College labours within this few weeks Hull ... Woolwich ... Gravesend & Lincolnshire. ... They may but be supplied from the College.'[68]

One of the visibly distinctive features of the students sent out to preach was their wearing of the gowns and caps Lady Huntingdon provided. Howell Harris had warned her that it was sharpening Anglican leaders' opposition to Trevecca: yet it had its uses. One student informed her from Hampshire that a local curate had preached against his activities, but 'I found my Gown & band was look'd upon by the poor people as a sufficient refutation of the curate's sermon'. An itinerating student candidly assured his fellows at Trevecca that 'those that the gospel won't draw the college gown will'.[69] When she disowned students, the action was signified by the demand that they surrender these collegiate badges. Wesley voiced his opinion of Trevecca by openly criticising those 'gowns to which they had no Right'.[70] Similar symbols of her authority, in the form of preaching scarves, were provided for clergymen who served in her chapels. One wrote that his scarf 'reminds me of a kind of duty' to her; another that he 'thankfully obey[s] your Ladyship's Injunctions concerning the wearing of the Scarf at Chapel. That and every other badge of my connexion with your Ladyship does me greater honour than I deserve.'[71]

The progressively daunting distances students had to travel to fulfil their preaching assignments called for increasing amounts of money, not least of all for horses. Horses were a constant source of concern for the Countess: how to get them, how to get rid of them, their cost, whether they would be standing in the right place at the right time. 'We are now fourteen students and seven horses at College.' 'I have now settled that [Short?] shall return upon your Horse into Sussex by the second Sunday in Feb: if you leave Brighton upon Monday the 6th this may be done as otherwise I must buy him another horse.'[72] The problem was such that on occasion they resorted to horse stealing in order to complete their preaching postings.[73] In the minute supervision of details, Lady Huntingdon cast a constantly critical eye on her students' expense claims, demanding an exact itemising. It would appear that she had reason to suspect that some of her charges were taking advantage of her largess. Regarding one student she wrote that 'if this propensity of extravagance continues he cannot continue. Sedan chairs & barbers accounts wont do. I am quite amazed.'[74]

None the less, all the burdens she now bore of a purified Trevecca, and the expanding missions sent thence, gave the Countess of Huntingdon a true sense of destiny. Her students referred to her as their 'commanding Officer'. She commanded 'Jesus' College'.[75] Moreover, she seemed to glory in the fact that these were burdens she bore alone. 'I have none to help me.' Increasingly, she came to believe that was her destiny; yet God had told her that he would 'never never leave thee nor forsake thee'.[76] 'Happy shall I lay down my worthless weary head in rest while I can leave behind me my dr. college, who will let the Lord have no rest till he makes our Jerusalem a praise upon earth.'[77]

Notes

1 Thomas Rankin, journal, 15 October 1775, Tyerman/Evertt transcripts, Rylands; JF to Joseph Benson, 12 February 1773, quoted in Telford, 6:20.

2 Ward & H., 22:114 (1 December 1767), quotation; *Minutes of the Methodist Conference 1744-* , Vol. 1 (London, 1862), p. 96.

3 HH ms diary, 12 October 1770, NLW.

4 JW to Joseph Benson, 30 November 1770, Wesley Family Papers, item 18-H, Duke.

5 JF to Joseph Benson, 10 January 1771, John Fletcher Letter Books; JW to SH, 14 August 1771, MAM. JW.3.69. Rylands.

6 William Aldridge to Trevecca students, 20 April 1774, F1/2202, CF; 'An account of John Fletcher's case', Tyerman, *Wesley's Designated Successor*, p. 184.

7 James Glazebrook to SH, 5 December 1770, F1/1521, CF.

8 JF to Joseph Benson, 22 March 1771, James Macdonald, *Memoirs of the Rev. Joseph Benson* (London, 1822), pp. 18-19; Joseph Benson to [JW], 15 October 1785, PLP 7/8/13, Rylands (quotation).

9 JF to JW, 20 February, 24 June 1771, Tyerman, *Life of Wesley*, 3:88, 95; JF to SH, 7 March 1771, E4/7/1, CF; Joseph Benson's journal, Macdonald, *Memoirs of Benson*, p. 26; Henry Mead to SH, 22 December 1770, F1/115, CF.

10 JF to JW, 18 March 1771; JF to Joseph Benson, 24 August 1771, Tyerman, *Wesley's Designated Successor*, pp. 178, 209; Walter Shirley to SH, 17 February 1772, E4/1/8, CF.

11 SH to Joseph Benson, 26 November 1770, 17 January 1771, Duke; Joseph Benson, *The Life of the Rev. John W. de la Flechere* (London, 1838), p. 151. See also Marsh W. Jones, 'Pulpit, Periodical, and Pen. Joseph Benson and Methodist Influence in the Victorian Prelude', Ph.D. dissertation, University of Illinois at Urbana-Champaign, 1995, pp. 49-58.

12 'Doctrines, (I am more and more convinced) are of no service to believers.' GW to SH, 10 November 1755, *Select Letters*, 3:150; 'I am betw[ee]n Calvin[is]m & free will.' HH ms diary, 19 January 1767, NLW.

13 HH ms diary, 28 July 1764, NLW (quotation); JF to Joseph Benson, 22 March 1771, Macdonald, *Memoirs of Benson*, p. 18; Henry Venn to Miss Wheler, [*c.* 1772], C11, CMS.

14 Walter Sellon to SH, 20 November 1771, E4/4/6, CF; Ward & H., 22:346 (14 August 1772).

15 For example, Walter Shirley to JW, 27 May 1760, *Arminian Magazine* 20 (1797), p. 459.

16 'Mr Shirley...is the last man that should attack you. His sermons contain propositions much more heretical and anti-Calvinistical than your minutes.' JF to JW, 24 June 1771, Tyerman, *Life of Wesley*, 3:96.

17 Walter Shirley to SH, 19 November 1770, F1/1568, CF.
18 Richard Hill to [Walter Shirley], 10 January 1772, F1/1386, CF.
19 Circular letter, [June 1771], Tyerman, *Life of Wesley*, 3:93-94.
20 James Glazebrook to SH, 24 December 1771, F1/159, CF; Walter Shirley, *A Narrative of the Principal Circumstances relative to the Rev. Mr. Wesley's Late Conference, held in Bristol, August the 6th, 1771* (Bath, 1771).
21 Walter Shirley to SH [September 1771], F1/1569, CF. It is presumed that she supplied the following:

> To prevent any false Representations of what past [*sic*] on the Objections made by me and others to the doctrinal Points of the Minutes of *Mr. Wesley's* Conference, held in *LONDON*, August the 7th, 1770; a short Narrative of Facts will be the best means to clear up the whole most fully to you, Sir, and to any who may impartially wish for Information; and is particularly due to those Ministers of the GOSPEL, who by Letter or Protest, expressed their united Sentiments with ours, in supposing those Minutes dangerous to the fundamental Truth of Christianity. I shall therefore begin with presenting you with the Extract itself, that gave us the Alarm.
> ....
> Thus we faithfully and earnestly commit into the Hands of the Lord this Testimony for his own Free Grace; submitting ourselves as his poor unworthy Servants; and hoping it may be for his Glory, and the Preservation of his great and inestimable Truths; and begging that, thro' his infinite Mercy, we may become truly devoted Souls, to the *one* Purpose of his Praise in Time, and the Monuments of our Glorious IMMANUEL's Mercy to all ETERNITY!

Shirley, *Narrative*, pp. 3, 24.
22 JF to James Ireland, 6 February 1774, Tyerman, *Wesley's Designated Successor*, p. 300.
23 James Glazebrook to SH, 20 January 1772, F1/167; Walter Shirley to SH, 9 January 1772, F1/1576. In later years, Fletcher destroyed all the Countess's letters to him, believing that it would have been 'unjust to deliver them to strangers'. JF to SH, 28 May 1777, A1/13/11. CF.
24 *Gospel Magazine*, August and May 1771, quoted in Tyerman, *Life of Wesley*, 3:105, 91. Wesley was 'the most rancorous hater of the gospel system that ever appeared in England'. Letter of Augustus Toplady (1773), quoted in *ibid.*, 3:159.
25 See Diane Susan Durden, 'Transatlantic communications and literature in the religious revivals, 1735-1745', Ph.D. thesis, University of Hull, 1978, p. 239.
26 For example, John Lloyd to SH, 15 February 1772, F1/1586, CF.
27 Augustus Toplady to Walter Shirley, 26 July 1771, F1/1572, CF.
28 SH to [Thomas Haweis], September 1778, SMU 100; SH to [Thomas] Beale, 6 April 1778, G2/2, CF; SH to [Mr & Mrs Thomas Wills], 8 August 1778, Letters of SH, 1774-1784, English MSS 338, Rylands.
29 W. Walsh to SH, 29 July 1780, F1/468, CF.
30 Richard Hill to [Walter Shirley], 10 January 1772, F1/1386, CF. See also Tyerman, *Life of Wesley*, 3:159-61.
31 SH to Judith Wadsworth, 7 April 1766, SMU 67; Henry Venn to Mrs Medhurst, 2 January 1770, C11, CMS.
32 'Lady H___ & I were mere Accessories to Your Proposal.' Walter Shirley to Thomas Powys, 2 January 1772, F1/1388, CF.
33 John Forman to SH, 5 September 1783, F1/545, CF; SH to Mr Longston, 18 February 1784, Letters of SH, 1774-1784, English MSS 338, Rylands; Edward Davies to SH, 18 June 1774, F1/302, CF.
34 Vincent Perronet to JW, 9 July 1771, 22 November 1777 (quotation), *Arminian Magazine* 20 (1797), pp. 254-55.
35 SH to Judith Wadsworth, 22 May 1766, SMU 71; Walter Sellon to SH, 6 June 1770, E4/4/5, CF; same to FH, 14 June 1770, HA 10731; Baker, 26:122n.; Sellon to SH, 20 November 1771, E4/4/6, CF; Sellon, *The Church of England Vindicated from the Charge of Predestination* (London, 1771).

36 Richard Hill, *Three Letters...to the Rev. J. Fletcher*, quoted in Tyerman, *Life of Wesley*, 3:161. See also Augustus Toplady, *More Work for Mr. John Wesley*, quoted in *ibid.*, 3:140.

37 SH to CW, 8 June 1771, DD WES 1: Wesley Family Letters and Papers, Folio Vol. 1, p. 120, Rylands.

38 CW to Sally Wesley, 27 May [*c.* 1780], DD WES 4: Wesley Family Letters and Papers, Folio Vol. 4, p. 24, Rylands; SH to CW, 28 June 1775, and CW to SH, 2 July 1775, Black 81.

39 SH to CW, 7 October 1752, Black 24.

40 Walter Shirley to SH, 12 June 1773, E4/1/19; SH to John Hawksworth, 15 June 1773, G2/1/8. CF.

41 SH to Walter Churchy, 18 February 1772, Black 143; Walter Churchy to [CW?], 24 July 1774, Letters chiefly addressed to C. Wesley, Vol. VI, no. 15, Rylands (quotation).

42 John Cave to SH, 20 October 1772, F1/195, CF; Lady Willielma Glenorchy to SH, 10 January 1771, Seymour, *Life and Times*, 2:110-11; Ward & H., 22:323 (12 May 1772), quotation.

43 JF to Walter Shirley, 11 September 1771, Tyerman, *Wesley's Designated Successor*, p. 195.

44 Lady Anne Erskine to SH, 13 November 1772, F1/1623, CF.

45 Christopher Hull to SH, 16 September 1771, F1/135; Henry Mead to SH, 16 November 1771, F1/140. CF.

46 J. Thomas to Thomas Jones, 25 June 1772, Trevecka 2710.

47 Ward & H., 22:299, 354 (4 December 1771, 7 December 1772).

48 Walter Shirley to SH, 14 March 1772, E4/1/12, CF.

49 Ward & H., 22:284 (6 July 1771), quotation; 446 (6 April 1775).

50 John Cosson to SH, 14 September 1771, F1/134, CF; JW to Mrs Woodhouse, 22 October 1773, Telford, 6:51; JW to JF, 26 February 1774, *ibid.*, 6:75.

51 Joseph Benson to CW, 16 August 1772, PLP 7/6/3, Rylands.

52 SH to JW, 8 September 1776; JW to SH, 15 September 1776, E4/3/2, 3, CF.

53 SH to Judith Haweis, 7 September, 7 October (quotation) 1775, SMU 85, 86.

54 SH to John Hawksworth, 23 September 1775, G2/1/16, CF.

55 Ward & H., 23:103-104 (28 August 1778); 138 (3 July 1779); 179 (24 June 1780).

56 T[homas] W[ills] to SH, 2 August 1781, *Extracts of the Journals of Several Ministers of the Gospel...in a Series of Letters to the Countess of Huntingdon* (London, 1782), p. 44; Committee of Norwich Chapel to SH, 27 February 1784, F1/604, CF.

57 John Child and Thomas Skinner, 3 June 1788, F1/731; John Eyre to SH, 14 January 1777, F1/376; Robert Keen to SH, 3 August 1775, A1/13/4. CF; SH to anon., 17 September 1779, SMU 102.

58 JW to Mary Bishop, 18 August 1784, Telford, 7:227-28.

59 For a detailed reckoning, see Harding, 'Countess of Huntingdon', p. 250n.

60 SH to Mr and Mrs Thomas Wills, 26 September 1780, Letters of SH, 1774-84, English MSS 338, Rylands.

61 SH to anon., 17 September 1779, SMU 102; Thomas Molland to SH, 18 January 1774, F1/269, CF.

62 Benson, *Life of Flechere*, p. 144 (quotation); SH to John Clayton, 1 December 1774, HM 44038, Huntington; Robert Harris to SH, 9 February 1772, E4/3/4, CF.

63 Thomas W. Aveling, *Memorials of the Clayton Family* (London, 1867), p. 17.

64 Thomas Davies to SH, 15 September 1777, F1/405; Joseph Cook to SH, 24 December 1771, F1/158. CF.

65 Benjamin Wase to SH, n.d., E4/3/6, CF. Unfortunately, she soon angrily expelled him. Wase to HH, 24 October 1772, Trevecka 2720.

66 Brown, 'Evangelicals and education', p. 216.

67 SH to John Clayton, 22 April 1777, Aveling, *Memorials of Clayton*, pp. 29, 30; SH to John Hawksworth, 16 March 1773, G2/1/7, CF.

68 SH to John Hawksworth, 3 February 1773, G2/1/6, CF.

69 Anthony Crole to SH, 13 July 1774, F1/311, CF; Matthew Wilks to Trevecca students, 6 May 1774, *Evangelical Register* 3 (1828-29), p. 205.

70 Jehoiada Brewer to SH, 29 May 1775, F1/328; Isaac Billing et al. to JW, n.d., F1/1347. CF.

71 Henry Peckwell to SH, 5 May 1774, F1/288; Richard De Courcy to SH, 8 July 1769, F1/73. CF.

72 William Aldington to SH, 31 May 1775, F1/1716, CF; SH to [Mark or Matthew] Wilks, 5 January 1775, Collection 100, Box 2, John Wesley Collection, Emory University Library.

73 SH to Mr Tanner, 21 September 1779, HM 39808, Huntington.

74 SH to John Hawksworth, 2 April 1774, G2/1/11, CF.

75 William Aldington to SH, [1773 or 1774], F1/1290; John Lloyd to SH, 26 July 1779, F1/436. CF.

76 SH to John Hawksworth, 9 February 1773 (quotation), 5 December 1778, 23 September 1775 (quotation), G2/1/6, 20, 16, CF.

77 SH to Joseph Benson, 12 April 1770, Duke.

CHAPTER 9

'More like a playhouse than the House of God'

The eighteenth century provided a fertile field for the satirist. Clamorous political and religious developments provided the material. The burgeoning print culture, combined with a vibrant stage, furnished the means. With the art of personal invective well-developed, the satirical pen was frequently pointed at Methodism.

While the Countess of Huntingdon and John Wesley and their followers had increased the heat of their controversy, those at a safer distance took opportunity to bring things to the boiling point by lampooning the entire Methodist movement. Wesley received his fair share, but perhaps because his Arminian teaching did not run directly counter to the spirit of the age it was the Calvinistic version of the revival movement that was to bear the brunt. The stress on the doctrine of election appeared to challenge a humane and stable society, and satirists were especially active in debunking a theological position which was perceived as severe, and one which apparently both nurtured pride and bore antinomian fruits. By picturing seemingly eccentric individuals to be ridiculous, satirists portrayed these beliefs as being decidedly dangerous.[1]

George Whitefield offered a tantalisingly tempting target, and that from the outset. In his early *Journals* Whitefield had drawn an explicit parallel between himself and 'my dear Saviour' by pointing out that both had been 'born in an inn'. The depiction of a self-serving preacher would remain constant throughout the remainder of his life. A Welsh cleric wrote of the *Journals* that 'such an Inundation of Commendation from a Man's own Mouth is surely unexampled. No Man ever so bedaubed himself with his own Spittle.'[2] As early as 1746 disparaging reference was being made to Whitefield's character in the Drury Lane production of Charles Macklin's *A Will and No Will*. But the fullest treatment was in the 1760s, when he found himself lampooned upon the London stage by the leading theatrical satirist of the day. In Samuel Foote's most famous play, *The Minor*, Whitefield was referred to as 'Squintum' – occasioned by the decided squint in his left eye. 'Squintum' was thenceforth the satirists' usual appellation for Whitefield, with the suggestion that he focused on the carnal while gazing heavenward. Foote's claim that Whitefield had been detected robbing the Countess led the preacher for a time to his sick-bed.[3] In spite of frantic efforts, Lady Huntingdon failed in her interventions with the Lord Chamberlain and David Garrick to have the play suppressed, and by September it had graced stages as far afield as Newcastle.[4] It later crossed the Atlantic to be performed in New York City and Charles Town, South Carolina, and in England was even performed after Whitefield's death. The net thus flung about Whitefield in *The Minor* was tightened further in *The Spiritual Minor* of 1763. Whereas Foote's characters had only made belittling comments concerning the preacher, now Whitefield, as it were, assumed centre stage as the main – hypocritical – figure of the plot. Whitefield was convinced that his being 'mimicked and burlesqued' upon the public stage was clear evidence that 'Satan is angry'.[5] Referring to Whitefield's London chapel, one satirist wrote of 'Squintum's Schism Shop':

> A Road there leads, as men report,
> Not up to Heav'n but Tott'nham Court;
> O'er which on Sundays crowds are driv'n,
> Of new coin'd Saints Cock-sure of Heav'n.[6]

A satirical print of Whitefield, by Hogarth, was widely available at five shillings,[7] and later an article in a London magazine claimed that Whitefield's Bethesda orphanage had been built to house his illegitimate children.[8]

Perhaps for a time Lady Huntingdon's position in society offered her some protection. It is true that in the furore caused by *The Minor* she had already been depicted in print as one who would condone Foote's murder.[9] But with her increasingly exuberant and public activities during the 1760s and 70s it was hardly to be expected that she could avoid the full virulence of flowing satirical pens. In 1766 the following appeared:

> H——, cloy'd with carnal Bliss,
> Longing to taste how Spirits kiss,
> Bids Chapels for her Saints arise,
> Which are but Bagnois in Disguise.[10]

In 1773 she was portrayed in a novel, *The Spiritual Quixote*, as 'Lady Sherwood', whose 'lively fancy' could not be satisfied with the 'plain rational scheme of the established religion'. Therefore, she had turned to listen 'with the same attention to the enthusiastic doctrines of these itinerant preachers, as a person labouring under a hypochondriacal distemper does to the extravagant pretensions of a mountebank'. The same year brought a satirical poem on the nobility, in which the anonymous author vowed that 'You I love my dearest life . . . More than Dartmouth loves field preachers, More than Huntingdon her teachers'. Five years later, in 1778, she was the '*Lady of Trevecka*', in full flow as the financier of Calvinistic Methodism.[11] On the stage, the Countess was portrayed as the 'Duchess' in Charles Johnstone's *Chrysal: or the Adventures of a Guinea*.[12] After she founded her main London chapel, an item appeared in *The Times* entitled 'The Cuckoo'. It described how 'Lady Wallis' had smuggled into a service a 'little piece of machinery' secreted in her muff. All during the preacher's sermon a repeated 'Cuckoo' sounded through the chapel. 'The preacher went on with his discourse – "fornicators and adulterers shall not enter the kingdom of heaven" – Cuckoo! repeated the machine.'[13]

Lady Huntingdon's death induced a bitingly satirical engraving in the *Town and Country Magazine*. She is depicted wearing the robes of a nun, seated in a Gothic church, with clasped hands and upturned eyes. Beside her are a skull, books and writing materials. (See illustration 5.) But though the picture is satirical, the accompanying article, 'The Tears of Methodism', was far more direct.

> Mourn all ye hypocritical preachers, who, regardless of the practice of good works, prescribe faith only to your deluded patients! Mourn all ye empirics who dare to distribute nostrums for the cure of souls; your well-meaning misguided countess is no more! Long have you fed upon the fanaticism of your patroness; long have you fattened on the effects of her enthusiasm, but she now ceases to be the dupe of her credulity; she can no longer be the prey of the reverend vultures which she has reared!
>
> . . . .
>
> The misguided patroness of young ecclesiastics has now finished her terrest[r]ial career, and taken her passage into the world of spirits; where she is doubtless happy. Death, on which she often meditated, has conducted her from this vale of tears to the mansions of the blessed, as a reward for the purity of her intentions! By her death, however, methodism will probably receive a check.[14]

One target the Countess did not provide for satire was public preaching. Although a woman assuming the leadership of men, she refused for herself a preaching role. There are, however, clear indications that she was tempted. Certainly some of her followers pressed her to do so: 'I had repeatedly many many of very dear friends & even ministers who had reasoned with me on this subject', who assured her that God had granted her the appropriate 'zeal, knowledge & abilities'. Yet the firm belief that it would be unscriptural constrained her. She reconfirmed the opinion she had held even from her earliest Methodist days: 'I by no means approve the woman preacher.' The Countess did allow herself to speak on occasion to her gathered students at Trevecca, but rather than preaching she confined herself to giving them 'most excellent advice how to preach'.[15]

Although restricting her writing almost wholly to a constant flow of letters, Lady Huntingdon did not hesitate to prepare a two page Preface to a reprinting of some of the works of the seventeenth-century Puritan writer William Bridge. These sermons she selected herself, and their tone and substance further affirmed her Calvinistic orientation. The Preface stated that readers must 'never cease to remember, that without' faith 'it is impossible to please GOD. . . . As a divine pledge of future glory, it is a rich compensation to us for all the misery and various afflictions which are connected with our fallen state in Adam.' She appealed to the reader that, after perusing the sermons, 'no lukewarm pursuits after less powerful truths, may ever engage your attention'.[16]

John Wesley's tentative yet unmistakable acceptance in his movement of a number of women preachers only confirmed Lady Huntingdon's view of his unfaithfulness to the Bible.[17] It is however remarkable that in an age when religiously sensitive women increasingly recorded their personal pilgrimages, she never indulged in spiritual autobiography, or diaries of any sort.[18] Moreover, in contrast to the Wesleyans, the Countess's branch of Methodism never produced a body of women who recorded their religious stories. Perhaps such activity would have appeared a form of competition to their movement's aristocratic lady. And when the wives of some of her clergymen assumed the role of leaders in local chapels, they constantly deferred to the Countess. However, by fulfilling the ambiguous and, for the period, unique role of member of the laity, woman and aristocrat directing the movement and activities of ministers, she provided fodder enough for satirical treatment.

The 'Tears of Methodism' engraving gives a vivid illustration of a favourite theme for those who criticised Lady Huntingdon: her romanticism. Its most visible statement was her obsession with Gothic architecture, the results of which at Donington were painfully obvious to her son. The Countess's Bath Chapel, opened in 1765, was the town's first Gothic building, running directly counter to the cool classicism growing up around it. The castellated chapel was designed with ogee-headed windows and battlemented parapets. When she turned her attention to Trevecca in 1768 she lavished this same enthusiasm for ogee-headed Gothic, with apparent 'Strawberry Hill' influences. The following year saw similar designs for her Tunbridge Wells Chapel. There was a battlemented front gable, with windows again having interlacing tracery. At Bristol in 1775 she took over the lease of a defunct theatre and installed Gothic traceried windows.[19]

Once the chapels were built, they were frequently decked out internally in elaborate style. Although the Countess could boast no special interest in or knowledge of art, she sought to use artistic artifacts to 'beautify' her chapels. She appears to have been especially fond of eagle lecterns. Bristol had a trio of reading desks supported by such birds, with outstretched wings, and they sprang up in a number of other chapels.[20] One of the punishments Lady Huntingdon prescribed for a preacher who displeased her was to forbid him standing 'behind the eagle'. At Hereford a 'very elegant' sounding board was installed above the pulpit, suspended by a cord from which 'sallies a Dove with an Olive branch, to form a canopy'.[21] It was not long after the opening of her Bath Chapel that she decided it needed further fittings,[22] and Horace Walpole described its neat mahogany 'branches and brackets', together with the eagle lecterns and red cushions for preacher and clerk. 'Behind them rise three more steps, in the middle of which is a third eagle for pulpit. Scarlet armchairs for all three. On either hand a balcony for elect ladies. The rest of the congregation sit on forms.' Howell Harris complained bitterly that she was obsessed with 'the outw[ar]d Chappel ornament'. Wesley waspishly observed that God had shown a 'marvellous condescension' in providing 'such places as ... Lady Huntingdon's chapels, for these delicate hearers, who could not bear sound doctrine if it were not set off with these pretty trifles'.[23] Within these settings Lady Huntingdon called for the use of the

Anglican Book of Common Prayer. This was true not only in her more 'fashionable' chapels such as Bath (where a clergyman was permanently employed to read prayers) and Bristol, but in places as far-flung as Hull, Brecon, Maidstone, Wigan and Guernsey. Not only did it cater for her personal preferences in worship, but its use made visible her professed devotion to the Church of England and aversion to the Dissenting ethos. Although she met some resistance from those in her chapels whose evangelicalism suggested to them freedom from set forms, most joined her in wishing to maintain the drama of the liturgy, or at any rate to retain her favour. The use of the liturgy became a distinctive feature of her 'Connexion' in later years. It provided both respectability and doctrinal orthodoxy.[24]

A taste for Gothic style in building does not of itself a romantic make. The Countess of Huntingdon's preoccupation with death is worthy of note, and her provision of a bust of herself to adorn her husband's tomb, 'embracing his urn', is suggestive of the baroque world her mind inhabited.[25] It has been noted that during the period following Theophilus's death for a time she fancied living in permanent retreat near the church where he was buried. Her house was to be within the ruins of Ashby Castle.

> I am fitting up a little retreat close by the ancient walls of mouldering pomp, and which now serves as a perpetual monument of that better part I have chosen. The towers of these remaining ruins cast a solemn gloom over my little habitation on one side, and on the other, I am within the sound of those echoes praise lends to the venerable walls in which my repository is prepared, and where my slumbering dust will wait the archangel's summons. It is to be as primitive as possible.[26]

It was not only that Lady Huntingdon had experienced so many and so frequent personal losses. Nor was it simply that she, like so many evangelicals, viewed a Christian's good death as one of the best means of converting others. It was the dramas that surrounded such deaths, dramas which lost nothing in their repetition, frequently in print, that were pregnant with evangelical opportunity. On the occasion of the death of one notable, his body was displayed at the Countess's Bath Chapel for a week, with the family on the first day receiving Communion while 'seated . . . at the feet of the corpse' and services and preaching conducted twice a day thereafter.[27] Perhaps the most remarkable, not to say macabre, passing was that of her sister's husband, Thomas Needham, Lord Kilmorey. It fully fitted the Countess's sense of drama and occasion that he died the very day she arrived in London in February 1768. But her sense of the grotesque and bizarre was even more quickened by the fact that her brother-in-law had 'taken a tomb but 2 days before, which he was got into & on the third died in it'.[28] A fervent admirer of James Hervey's florid *Meditations Among the Tombs*, Lady Huntingdon had gladly received a moving account of his death.[29] His *Meditations*, with its obsession with coffins, winding-sheets and worms, had a direct influence on men like William Cowper and contributed to the growing Romantic movement, both in Britain and Germany.[30] The 'Tears of

Methodism' engraving was not misleading in its placing next to the Countess the symbol of death.

In an age when Enlightenment thought was struggling to overcome superstition, Lady Huntingdon, predisposed by a highly-strung personality to frequent flights of fancy, retained the inclinations of an earlier superstitious age. During one of her frequent illnesses, she determined to take the waters at Glastonbury, insisting that 'the water runs through the monastery of Glastonbury & washes the bones of the saints & martyrs & that great regard ought to be had to the supernatural manner in which they were made known, which was no other than a revelation from heaven'.[31] Shortly before the opening of Trevecca, she engaged Lady Anne Erskine as her permanent companion, a decision that was to have fateful effects throughout the remainder of her life. (See illustration 13.) A relation of James Erskine and, like him, a Scot, Lady Anne made a significant contribution to the hardening of the Countess's Calvinism. She also bolstered Lady Huntingdon's commitment to decision-making by the drawing of lots. As was the practice of many Methodists of the period, the Countess had a 'Lot Book' in which she kept biblical 'prophesies'. Frequently, Lady Anne 'drew sweet lots for you', in order to discover the will of God.[32]

Although directed by a zealous spirit of mission, Lady Huntingdon's overseas enterprises were decidedly tinged with a colourful romantic vision. The composition of the life-sized portrait she had specially painted and transported to Georgia to bolster her students is a breathtaking testimony to her favourite self-image.[33] (See illustration 3.) A romantic prospect stirred her to plans for American Indians, but late in her life the mission would be even further afield. She became caught up in the heady prospect of seeing the missionary footprint planted in the South Sea Islands. While a general romantic view of Oceania had progressively taken shape, not least through the voyages of James Cook and the writings of John Hawkesworth, theirs was a view of unspoiled natives in an earthly paradise. That was not a perspective the Countess shared. Regarding a 'plan for the Heathen mission', she was determined to do all 'I can do to get some precious souls out of the Devils fingers'.[34] A romantic vision could be experienced closer to home if there was a whiff of virgin territory. On one occasion when she was in Devon, recuperating from an illness and accompanied by a Trevecca student, she 'made' him stand on the Teignmouth sands to preach. Her excitement was induced by the belief that there 'never never the Gospel had been preached'.[35]

Fortifying Lady Huntingdon's romanticism was her decision to locate her college in the wild solitude of mid-Wales. There, Howell Harris earlier had established his enterprise, and perhaps she herself was rather a Celt in spirit. She was charmed with the simple Welsh women she saw. 'O! that I had the Grace many of them have.'[36] When present at feasts of Trevecca preaching and prayer, those were 'days of my life in which my days of heaven on earth was numbered'. There she found 'unaffected simplicity . . . the very soul of the Primitive church'. There 'the most pure Gospel is preached'.[37] Certainly, for many years Trevecca was her 'most hidden retreat', her 'Utopian Academy', her 'Welsh family'. There on her 'holy ground' she could attempt to escape the throbbing crises of her chapels.[38] There she could muse over reports that she had appeared in dreams to strengthen the weak-hearted.[39] There her 'prayers and tears' could be 'poured out in the greatest fervour', to be witnessed by her students.[40] There, as the tours of the picturesque began to be popular, travellers came to gaze through eyes of curiosity at what was perceived to be a romantic, if eccentric, enterprise.[41] When the aged Lord Chesterfield lay ill in 1773 she visited him, extending an invitation to come to Trevecca, where there were 'such charming mountains'. 'I don't love mountains', he replied. When her faith had removed them, he said, he would be happy to come.[42]

There is an ironic footnote to Lady Huntingdon's romanticism. Eric Gill, probably the most famous person ever produced by the Countess of Huntingdon movement, was born in Brighton, the son of one of the ministers at the Countess of Huntingdon Chapel. In his early years this chapel had been the 'unshaken and unshakeable centre' of Gill's religion, and in their home his father pinned up a large card depicting a great eye, with the text 'Thou God seest me'.[43] Many years later and well after he had cut the cord of this religious upbringing, Gill sought romantic inspiration in the very area it had been found by Lady Huntingdon. It had also been discovered there in the nineteenth century by Walter Savage Landor, the curious self-styled Anglican monk Father Ignatius and the diarist Francis Kilvert. A century and a half after she had established her Welsh retreat, Gill settled his own 'family' seven miles from Trevecca, at Capel-Y-Ffin. There the Romantic movement, which the Countess's hand had played its own part in fostering, achieved a full artistic flowering, led by this astonishingly sexually errant product of her religious endeavour.

The rise of Methodism contributed to and was itself facilitated by the burgeoning eighteenth-century marketplace. There was no better example of this than Whitefield himself, who constantly conceived of his mission in commercial terms. His brothers and sisters all followed their father into the world of commerce, and Whitefield had early indicated that he would not break the succession. In the event, he applied commercial vocabulary and techniques to his preaching enterprises, in both England and America.[44] Indeed, he began his first American mission by hawking a shipload of manufactured goods he had brought with him from England. Most important, he was himself deliberately and carefully marketed. 'The devotion and business of a Methodist go hand in hand', wrote Whitefield. Departing on one of his American visits, he wrote to a merchant: 'I am travelling and you are trading for Jesus Christ.'[45] To enterprising businessmen, especially printers, Whitefield offered the prospect of rich returns since he commanded an enormous market.[46] By plunging into the priorities of the marketplace, Whitefield placed further distance between him and the Wesleys, who rejected such techniques. It also offered satirists further ammunition. Squintum, wrote Foote, was a 'blockhead deal[ing] in scripture as a trade'.[47] Soon after appointment as her chaplain, Whitefield wrote to her ladyship regarding a man who had 'ventured his little all for Christ; and last week a saint died who left him and his heirs two hundred pounds in land. Did ever any one trust in the Lord and was forsaken?'[48]

For her part, the Countess of Huntingdon contributed to the commercialisation of Christianity in three basic ways: by her constant insistence on itinerant and field-preaching and its necessary 'selling' of religion; by her direct involvement in the booming market for the building, buying, selling and renting of chapels and the land connected with such enterprises; and by generally making those who attended her chapels pay for entrance.

The type of preaching encouraged by Lady Huntingdon and other evangelicals was directed towards individuals making an active choice. Rather than a faith accepted as a natural inheritance, here was on offer a religion demanding a decision not unlike one made in the marketplace. Rowland Hill wrote that he was actively engaged in 'crying my wares at the lowest price'.[49] It is little wonder that those who served her as preachers were frequently accused of avarice.[50] They often were regarded as no better than low-paid travelling salesmen.[51]

As the scope of her preaching enterprises expanded in the 1770s and 80s, the Countess was inexorably sucked into the commercial whirl of ecclesiastical economics. As soon as word was out regarding her mission to Georgia, at least two merchants were quick off the mark in offering to supply suits of clothing for the missionaries. She was praised by one merchant not only for her provision of preachers but 'for the good you did . . . to we your Ladyship's Tradesmen'.[52] Entrepreneurs were attracted by what they supposed was her boundless wealth, and at the chapel level the bargaining could be hard. Her people at Worcester pleaded poverty, unconvincingly when they added that they would increase their contributions to her chapel if she would send better preachers.[53] She believed that maintaining a 'hiring ministry' was a great trust which had been thrust upon her, and she felt it necessary to keep these preachers 'in the Lords Hands', which in practice meant her own.[54] Yet few were satisfied with her firm demand for constant itinerating, and the tendency was for such men, having enjoyed the Countess's largess for a season, to seek and secure their ecclesiastical futures in the service of a single Dissenting chapel. Few of her students had doubts that they would always be able to find greater financial rewards outside her religious orbit. On the other hand, a failed businessman who had run up extensive debts might well be attracted to serve a patroness who would at least provide his basic needs.[55] Preaching her funeral sermon in her main London chapel, the minister remarkably used the occasion to assure mourners that although he had been 'a pensioner on her bounty for many years . . . every farthing she gave me has been faithfully applied for the interest of the Gospel'.[56]

It was the provision of meeting places for her congregations that was the focus of Lady Huntingdon's involvement with marketplace religion. The funds for building her initial chapels during the 1760s flowed from her own purse, or from loans she assumed. But, increasingly, there was an extensive trade in meeting houses. Chapels had become speculative ventures which could provide significant financial rewards for those who built, bought and sold or rented them to the highest bidders. One London chapel was being advertised 'for any sect that will hire it'.[57] When she proposed making a contribution to the formation of a chapel in Dublin, she was shocked at the ground rent being demanded, the 'most exorbitant thing I ever heard of & what no instance in England can be found of the like'. It was a 'shocking figure'. When considering bidding for a London chapel, she was informed that the owner of the building wished her to have it, 'either at a yearly Rent fitted up as you please, or to purchase the whole entirely'. But someone else had been interested, 'thinking it might be a very profitable thing let out in Pews'. She had better act quickly. Everywhere the competition was fierce. Chichester begged her for more money. If they did not receive it they would have to abandon the chapel, which would cause their 'adversarys [to] Rejoice, saying ha. ha. so would we have it'.[58]

The Countess continued throughout her remaining years to be intimately caught up in such negotiations, as with a prospective chapel in Oxford Street whose proprietor was expecting an 'enormous rent' but who might be willing to accept a knockdown sum for an outright purchase. Prospective property for a Hereford chapel caused constant headaches, mainly because the owner, though professing to favour her religious principles, yet 'endeavours to make as much as he can' from the sale. Her Hereford followers laid out an elaborate plan of deception in order to secure funds left by a local benefactress to another chapel. The scheme, wrote one proposer, 'will be shewing some of the Wisdom of the serpent, but for my part I think it justifiable'.[59] A prolonged financial tug-of-war persisted between Lady Huntingdon and her Birmingham Chapel, which the people had built on the assumption that she would pay for it. The builder was threatening the chapel leaders with arrest: 'Our Commercial character wd. receive a shock not easily overgot.' From Sussex, she was informed that if she would just pay the money they still owed on the building, the chapel would 'gladly' give her all the 'rights & title' to it.[60] Several laymen in Barton, Lincolnshire, offered to build a chapel in her name if she advanced a substantial sum; but they wanted to be certain that they would control it after her death.[61] The Countess herself dabbled in speculative chapel ownership, as when she and her cousin, Walter Shirley, became joint proprietors in Norwich.[62] In the year after her death, Lady Huntingdon's two leading trustees planned to purchase land for a burial ground at the Tunbridge Wells Chapel. 'Consecrated ground seems to have wonderfully abated in its value, & will grow lower.'[63]

Another way forward was to purchase or lease defunct theatres and other houses of entertainment. This procedure not only held out the prospect of securing premises at potentially bargain prices but would exact sweet revenge on the whole world of secular entertainment and such persecutors as Samuel Foote and David Garrick. There was an abortive attempt to secure the theatre at Richmond, Surrey, during the early 1770s,[64] but at least five playhouses fell to the Countess in subsequent years.[65] Ironically, her romantic taste often resulted in chapels bedecked in a fashion that made them redolent of theatres. At Bristol she installed the obligatory Gothic traceried windows and a trio of lectern-bearing eagles with outstretched wings. Three years after this former theatre had been thus converted, she received a bitter letter from some of the members, complaining that 'your Ladyships Chappel here . . . is now become more like a Play House than the House of God'.[66]

The Methodist movement was dramatic. Although Whitefield fervently preached against the theatre and other public amusements and forbade his followers in England and America attending such performances,[67] he has rightly been called the 'Divine Dramatist'.[68] Fitting well Lady Huntingdon's own sense of drama, Whitefield had been the star performer upon a stage of her own setting at her London house meetings. This she wished to replicate on a larger stage in her main chapels. Attempting, insofar as they were able, to emulate his example of theatricality – often even adopting his distinctive emotive intonation – others of her preachers followed suit, using their sermons to act out the divine drama of salvation for lost sinners. To critics, they were presenting 'Gospel shows'. After the Countess opened her Bath Chapel, Lord Chesterfield observed that it and Martin Madan's 'acting in it, is now the great Spectacle' of the town. 'Saints and sinners equally crowded to see the one and hear the other.'[69] This was carried to such an extreme that on occasion her chapels reacted negatively to her appointing certain men to preach, owing to their 'theatrical airs'.[70]

Theatrical and marketplace religion came together in the Countess's insistence that seating at her main chapels be by ticket only. This means of reserving seats was a marketing technique designed to provide a constant source of local finance. The use of chapel tickets was hardly unique, but whereas Wesley's societies issued them as badges for those deemed worthy of continued membership, for the Countess their use was purely a money-raising device, or on special occasions to induce notables to attend by supplying them gratis.[71] Lady Huntingdon took personal responsibility for preparing the copper plates used to print these tickets, either for individual chapels or, alternatively, as a special 'season ticket' whereby those subscribing money to purchase a seat in any one chapel could gain admittance to services in all.[72] These tickets were engraved with the initials 'S.H.', together with the Countess's coronet, and those for her main London chapel were sold publicly from her adjoining residence.[73] Many people, especially in London, paid for seats in order to hear particular preachers and complained bitterly if those men did not appear in the pulpit.[74] After she disowned one of her most faithful ministers, many people began to vote with their pocketbooks: 'There never was so many tickets ret[urne]d unsold as the last Quarter.' Another minister informed her that he had high hopes his chapel would sell a hundred more tickets than previously; if so, he expected the receipts therefrom to be used to pay for improvements at his 'badly furnished' house.[75]

The use of tickets solely for the purpose of fund raising had the inevitable result of limiting attendance of the poor, especially at those chapels Lady Huntingdon patronised with her presence. At her main London chapel the only recourse for those who could not afford to pay for seats was to stand, or sit on the stairs which led to the gallery.[76] In practice, attendance at her chapels of those of high birth was unusual enough to warrant special mention.[77] Members of newer chapels in remote places such as Ely tended to be 'but very poor',[78] but the backbone of her chapels was formed of artisans and small business entrepreneurs. At the Birmingham Chapel, leaders were a cabinet-maker, a grocer, a plater, a gilder and a leather box-maker; at Norwich, members' occupations ranged from baker, bricklayer, stay-maker to weaver; at one London chapel, from hatter, draper to glass-cutters. Even at Bath the leading men were a builder, a currier, a tallow chandler and a haberdasher.[79] For many upwardly-thrusting artisans, being associated with one of her chapels provided a degree of vicarious social standing. They could claim membership in the 'Countess of Huntingdon Connexion'. This, combined with the marketplace economics which prevailed in these chapels, meant that they were usually unhappy to see seats provided for worshippers who could not pay. At one chapel, where 'the poorest' were attracted, the leading men in the congregation 'oppose . . . and abuse the poor people that come'.[80] Such men proceeded in their chapel life with a zeal fuelled largely by their own ambitions.

The Countess's chapels therefore left themselves open to the charge of 'trading in souls'. Designed as places of worship, they were accused of being 'objects of profit', where those who were unable to pay for seats were 'crouded into a narrow space, and obliged to hear standing'.[81] There appear to have been no qualms regarding the practice in London, but elsewhere there was unease. At Bath, her personal insistence on the procedure was threatening to force the poor to pay or else be denied admittance, and her refusal to alter the system caused the chapel trustees to resign *en masse*.[82] From Bristol, those who complained of the chapel's resembling a playhouse went on to observe that ushers followed the practice of diligently shutting-out those who were not possessed of tickets. There was 'no place free now in the Chappel but a dark dismal hole under the Gallarie more like a corner of New Gate than any Part of Gods House'. The poor had nowhere to sit, all of which appeared to smack of 'private interest and not at Gods Glory and the good of souls. . . . We humbly pray your Ladyship will so consider it, that the few Benches for the Poor might be free.' She must end these 'mercenarie proceedings', which were 'making Merchandize of Gods Sabbaths'.[83]

Notes

1 Albert M. Lyles, *Methodism Mocked. The Satiric Reaction to Methodism in the Eighteenth Century* (London, 1960), p. 112.

2 *Whitefield's Journals*, p. 37; Theophilus Evans, *The History of Modern Enthusiasm* (London, 1757. 2nd edition), p. 111.

3 Lord John Rawdon to anon., 2 April 1761, T.1839, p. 100, PRONI. Making the rounds was the claim that he had tricked her into giving him her watch and other 'trinkets'. 'She tells the story herself.' Horace Walpole to Lord Strafford, 5 July 1761, Lewis, *Horace Walpole's Correspondence*, 35:309.

4 George Taylor (ed.), *Plays by Samuel Foote and Arthur Murphy* (Cambridge, 1984), pp. 8-9; John Grayson to GW, 28 September 1760, Papers of George Whitefield, Vol. 1, no. 29, Library of Congress.

5 GW to Mr D___, 15 August 1760, *Select Letters*, 3:262. For these plays, together with a full discussion of the conflict over *The Minor*, see Mary Megie Belden, *The Dramatic Work of Samuel Foote* (New Haven, 1929), Chapter 3.

6 [James Makittrick Adair], *The Methodist and the Mimick* (London, 1766), p. 5.

7 Hargreaves-Mawdsley, *Woodforde at Oxford*, p. 80 (5 April 1762). This 'Credulity, superstitition, and fanaticism' was a toned-down version of the unpublished 'Enthusiasm Delineated' of about two years earlier.

8 *Town and Country Magazine*, 1769, p. 675. For a general discussion of the satire directed against Whitefield see Lyles, *Methodism Mocked*, Chapter 8.

9 *A Satirical Dialogue between the Celebrated Mr F—te, and Dr Squintum* (London, 1760), p. 25.

10 Evan Lloyd, *The Methodist. A Poem* (Los Angeles, 1972. Original edition London, 1766), p. 37.

11 Richard Graves, *The Spiritual Quixote* (London, 1926. Original edition London, 1773), p. 204; *The Complete Peerage*, 1:497-98; *The Love-Feast, A Poem* (London, 1778), p. 16.

12 Belden, *Dramatic Work of Foote*, p. 97.

13 *The Times*, 1 January 1788, p. 3. 'Lady Wallis' was probably Eglantine Wallace, the comic author.

14 *Town and Country Magazine*, [1 September] 1791, p. 344. See also Mary Dorothy George, *Catalogue of Political and Personal Satires*, Vol. 6 (London, 1938), item 7962.

15 SH to Judith Haweis, 7 October 1775, SMU 86; SH to CW [early 1740s], Black 89; Samuel Pierce, *A True Outline and Sketch of the Life of Samuel Eyles Pierce* (London, 1822), p. 57.

16 *Seven Sermons, by that Learned and laborious Servant of Christ, The Rev. William Bridge...Particularly Recommended by the Countess Dowager of Huntingdon, to the Congregations in Connection with her Ladyship* (London, 1789), p. ii. See also B. Carteret to SH, 27 December, n.y., F1/1112, CF.

17 For Wesley and women preachers see Paul W. Chilcote, *John Wesley and the Women Preachers of Early Methodism* (Metuchen, New Jersey, 1991); A.B. Lawson, *John Wesley and the Christian Ministry* (London, 1963), pp. 176-81; Felicity A. Nussbaum, *The Autobiographical Subject. Gender and Ideology in Eighteenth-Century England* (Baltimore, 1989), pp. 173-75.

18 For such writing see Nussbaum, *Autobiographical Subject*, Chapter 7.

19 Dowling, 'Countess chapels', pp. 8, 44, 54, 113.

20 *Ibid*., p. 45; John Lloyd to SH, 25 May 1788, F1/2020, CF.

21 SH to Judith Wadsworth, 5 December 1768, SMU 77; John Hornby to SH, 19 January 1790, F1/880, CF.

22 SH to CW, 4 February 1767, Black 76.

23 Horace Walpole to John Chute, 10 October 1766, Lewis, *Horace Walpole's Correspondence*, 35:119; HH ms diary, 7 October 1765, NLW; Curnock (ed.), *Journal of John Wesley*, 7:485 (10 April 1789).

24 See Alan Harding, 'The Anglican prayer book and the Countess of Huntingdon's Connexion', *Transactions of the Congregational Historical Society* 20 (1970), pp. 364-67; Harding, 'Countess of Huntingdon', pp. 150-54. Even after her death it was observed that the Book of Common Prayer was in use 'in all principal chapels of the Connexion'. Haweis, *Impartial and Succinct History*, 4:268.

25 Cyril B. Andrews (ed.), *The Torrington Diaries* 4 vols. (London, 1934-38), 2:70.

26 SH to Countess of Hertford, 13 June [1718:*sic* 1747 or 1748], HMC, *Report on Manuscripts of Mrs. Frankland-Russell-Astley*, pp. 209-10.

27 GW to Lady S__ S___, 9 December 1767, *Select Letters*, 3:363-65.

28 SH to Mrs H. Leighton, 4 February 1768, Duke.

29 A. Maddock to SH, 5 January 1759, Trevecka 2244.

30 Frederick C. Gill, *The Romantic Movement and Methodism* (London, 1937), pp. 72-79.

31 Robert Hemington to FH, 26 June [*c*. 1751], HA 6299.

32 Lady Anne Erskine to SH, 13 (quotation), 18, 27 (quotation) November 1772, F1/1623, 1624, 1625; 29 November [1772?], F1/1311. CF.

33 'With much pompous humility, she looks like a old basket-woman trampling on her coronet at the mouth of a cavern.' Horace Walpole to Earl of Strafford, 24 September 1773, Lewis, *Horace Walpole's Correspondence*, 35:346. To a later art historian the cavern was (as is

more likely) a 'sepulchre' and the portrait therefore 'really blasphemous'. John C. Smith, *British Mezzotinto Portraits* 4 vols. (London, 1883), 4:1733-34.

34 SH to Thomas Haweis, 29 January, 2 September 1790, SMU 112, 129.

35 SH to [Thomas Haweis], September 1778, SMU 100.

36 SH to John Hawksworth, 15 June 1773, G2/1/8, CF.

37 SH to Thomas Haweis, 17 September 1779, 6 March 1790, SMU 102, 116.

38 Cradock Glascott to SH, 18 April 1774; William Taylor to SH, 1 March 1783; B. Carteret to SH, 15 July 1780, F1/285, 1883, 459, CF; SH to Joseph Benson, 12 April 1770, Duke.

39 Elizabeth Thomas to SH, n.d.; Daniel Lake to SH, 26 August 1783, F1/1271, 538. CF.

40 John Cottingham, *The Righteous Shall be in Everlasting Remembrance* (London, 1791), p. 17.

41 [Sir Thomas Gery Cullum], 'Synopsis of...[tour] made in Wales in 1775, *Y Cymmrodor* 38 (1927), pp. 54-55. For the early fascination of the area to the romantic mind see Malcolm Andrews, *The Search for the Picturesque* (Aldershot, 1989), pp. 85-107.

42 Quoted by Walpole in Horace Walpole to Horace Mann, 17 April 1775, Lewis, *Horace Walpole's Correspondence*, 24:91.

43 Eric Gill, *Autobiography* (London, 1940), p. 68; Fiona MacCarthy, *Eric Gill* (London, 1989), p. 13.

44 On this theme see Frank Lambert, *"Pedlar in Divinity"; George Whitefield and the Transatlantic Revivals, 1737-1770* (Princeton, 1994), where Whitefield is described as a 'pioneer in the commercialization of religion', p. 8.

45 George Whitefield, *Sermons on Important Subjects* (London, 1825), p. 654; GW to Mr K__, 26 June 1750, *Select Letters*, 2:361-62.

46 Frank Lambert, 'Subscribing for profits and piety: the friendship of Benjamin Franklin and George Whitefield', *William and Mary Quarterly*, 3rd series, 50 (1993), pp. 535, 542.

47 Quoted in Lambert, *Pedlar in Divinity*, p. 46.

48 GW to SH, 25 February 1750, *Select Letters*, 2:333.

49 Rowland Hill to anon., n.d., F1/1330, CF.

50 For example, Isaac Creswell and John Wilkes to SH, 24 September 1787, F1/684, CF.

51 CW to SH, 4 August 1752, PLP 113/2/5, Rylands.

52 Robert Harris to SH, 15 February 1772, Francis, 'Selina, Countess of Huntingdon', p. 175; Christopher Davies to SH, 11 August [1772], F1/1162; Henry Howell to SH, 19 March 1788, F1/1996 (quotation). CF.

53 Thomas Skinner to SH, 12 October 1782, F1/486, CF.

54 SH to Joseph Benson, [22 April 1770], Duke.

55 For contrasting examples see S. Phillips to SH, 31 October 1783, F1/562; Thomas Hutton et al. to SH, 9 August 1787, F1/645. CF.

56 David Jones, *A Funeral Sermon, preached at Spa-Fields Chapel...on the Death of the...Countess...of Huntingdon* (London, 1791), p. 17.

57 Quoted in Welch, *Spiritual Pilgrim*, p. 193.

58 SH to John Hawksworth, 9 February 1773, G2/1/6; Rebecca Spilsbury to SH, 10 August 1780, F1/470; James Lane to SH, 20 June 1780, F1/453. CF.

59 William Taylor to SH, n.d., F1/1370; S. Phillips to SH, 18 November 1783, F1/571; John Hornby to George Best, 9 March 1790, F1/895. CF.

60 S. Seager to SH, 6 September 1788, F1/765; Thomas Burgwein to SH, 23 October 1788, F1/777. CF.

61 J. Carter et al. to SH, 18 April 1788, F1/723, CF.

62 SH to Mr and Mrs Thomas Wills, April 1778, II.c.7/3, CL.

63 Thomas Haweis to Lady Anne Erskine, 16 December 1792, F1/2233, CF.

64 Seymour, *Life and Times*, 2:303-4.

65 Bristol (1775), Edwin Welch (ed.), 'The correspondence of Nathaniel Rowland and Lady Huntingdon', *Hanes Methodistiaeth Galfinaidd Cymru* 2 (1978), p. 29n.; Gloucester (1788), John Lloyd to SH, 7 May 1788, F1/2012, CF; Birmingham (1779), Abstract of Playhouse, Rayleigh ('I have bought the great playhouse at Birmingham hoping to make it a chapel to hold [five?] thousand poor Ignorant souls.' SH to [Henry Laurens], n.d., A3/12/29, CF); and two in London, at Clerkenwell (1779) and Whitechapel (1790), *Evangelical Register* 6 (1834), p. 37.

66 Several members of Bristol Chapel to SH, 4 February 1778, F1/1816, CF.

67 GW to Lady F[anny] S[hirley], 23 August 1753, *Select Letters*, 3:28; Whitefield, *Journals*, p. 63.

68 Harry S. Stout, *The Divine Dramatist. George Whitefield and the Rise of Modern Evangelicalism* (Grand Rapids, 1991). See also Nancy Ruttenburg, 'George Whitefield, spectacular conversion, and the rise of democratic personality', *American Literary History* 5 (1993), pp. 429-38.

69 Letter of 'John Bunyan, Junior', 8-10 October 1778, *St. James's Chronicle*, in Pinks, *History of Clerkenwell*, p. 644; Lord Chesterfield to FH, 13 November 1765, Stewart, *Letters of Chesterfield*, p. 126.

70 Henry Peckham to SH, 14 June 1768, F1/34 (quotation); Thomas Cannon to Thomas Wills, 15 July 1783, F1/534. CF.

71 Baker, *John Wesley and the Church of England*, p. 78; John Penrose to Peggy Penrose, 20 April 1766, Penrose, *Letters from Bath*, p. 44; ticket for Jane Cave, 3 February 1771, E.R. Hendrix MSS, Duke. Chesterfield used his influence with Lady Huntingdon to secure tickets for a noblewoman. Lord Chesterfield to FH, 13 November 1765, Stewart, *Letters of Chesterfield*, p. 126.

72 John Lloyd to SH, 2 April 1768, F1/27, CF; Spa Fields Chapel minutes, 25 May 1781, Edwin Welch (ed.), *Two Calvinistic Methodist Chapels 1743-1811* (London, 1975), item 156.

73 Sellon against Haweis, Personal Answers Book 1761-1796, pp. 527-28, in Francis, 'Selina, Countess of Huntingdon', pp. A146-47.

74 Spa Fields Committee to SH, 9 August 1781, Welch, *Two Chapels*, item 159.

75 Abraham Gadd to SH, 12 September 1788, F1/766; John Bradford to SH, 10 December 1783, F1/1919. CF.

76 Spa Fields Chapel Minutes, 11 April 1780, Welch, *Two Chapels*, item 125.

77 For example, Richard De Courcy to SH, 8 July 1769, F1/73, CF.

78 John Child to SH, 23 July 1789, F1/2090, CF.

79 Mortgage for Birmingham Chapel, 23 February 1789, F1/815, CF; Welch, *Spiritual Pilgrim*, p. 198; Case of Sellon against Haweis, Francis, 'Selina, Countess of Huntingdon', p. A147; SH's power of attorney for Bath Chapel, 12 July 1783, F1/533, CF. For a general discussion of the social make-up of the chapels see Harding, 'Countess of Huntingdon', pp. 82-83; C.D. Field, 'The social structure of English Methodism: eighteenth – twentieth centuries', *British Journal of Sociology* 28 (1977), pp. 199-225.

80 Lady M. Manners to SH, 7 January 1773, F1/209, CF.

81 Walter Wilson, *The History and Antiquities of Dissenting Churches* 4 vols. (London, 1808-14), 4:560, 561.

82 Robert Carpenter et al. to SH, 10 April 1788; James Beale et al. to SH, 1 May 1788, F1/722, 725, CF.

83 Several members of Bristol Chapel to SH, 4 February 1778, F1/1816, CF.

Chapter 10

'O to pour my wants & needs into your kind and friendly bosom'

Early Methodists often found heavenly and earthly love difficult to distinguish. 'Falling in love' and being 'born again' risked confusion in a fervent evangelical mind.[1] One of Lady Huntingdon's most ardent female followers wrote that her soul was 'strugling and panting after its dear Redeemer and can't be satisfied till He is all mine and I am all His. . . . O my Beloved now take full Possession and . . . let no thing enter my breast but God alone that I may be fill'd with thy fulness.' She yearned to be

> nearer to Him whom my soul is athirst after . . . to give [me] the fleshy Heart with His divine love writen on it, my Love my Lord my Jesus when shall I Love Thee and only Thee, these Tast[e]s won't satisfy the strugling desire thou hast given me. Nothing will do but thy whole self made over to me and seal'd by thy Holy Spirit The Key to unlock the Hiden mistery of Redeemers Love to my hungry Soul where I should imbrace the Rod as Egarly as I now do [the] sweet Caresses of my Lord. . . . I never wish them lessen'd but throw my self prostrate with desire to be made wiling in the Day of His Power.[2]

The use of this imagery was not confined to females. One of the Countess's clerical associates wrote to her that in a vision Jesus, after whipping him smartly with a rod, 'opened his Robe . . . [and] gave me a hasty Glance of his Person. It was divinely Sweet & Glorious, & exceeding Humane. So that I fell in Love with Him. . . . Nothing will content me but a Wedding. . . . Let him Kiss me with the Kisses of his Mouth.'[3]

During the turbulent early years of her attachment to the Methodist movement, Selina Hastings was deeply devoted to the Wesleys and depended especially upon Charles. 'This I know, that if you have one grain of Charity for me it must be because you excell all others in this Grace & that because you WILL NOT know how worthless a worm she is who knows herself more oblig'd to you than to any creature living.' 'I think you so uncommonly Blessed that I know NONE besides like unto you.'[4] Most tantalising are letters to Charles from her family home at Donington: 'I found such a rebellion of heart upon every thought of coming to this place that I have never yet known in any instance.' 'I had some secret hope that you would write to me for I sit alone as a sparrow upon the house top weary & faint in my mind.' While with her husband and children, this correspondence with

Charles was free enough for her to issue a warning: 'Things dont go here so well as usual. Dont write upon. Be carfull what you write.'[5] Perhaps no more than the *cri de coeur* of a religious neophyte isolated by her family's indifference to her spiritual zeal, these letters reflect the potential for crossing the fragile line between discipleship and amorousness. The Earl certainly had no reason to resent the roués of his circle. He may have felt differently about some of the evangelicals frequently closeted with his wife, engaged in mutual soul-searching. There was the possibility for the weakening of family bonds. One of the Countess's male correspondents wrote to her, while Theophilus was still living, that if he 'had not a Family, wch I was in duty bound to help to support, I wd. soon contrive to spend the remainder of my life at but a little distance from you'.[6] However empty the rumours that circulated about her relationships with these new-found religious colleagues, they were rumours numerous and 'scandalous'.[7]

In the aftermath of the Bethesda débâcle, William Piercy fell to writing Lady Huntingdon astonishing letters, shifting tone from preacher to suitor. Having been ill, he wrote to her: 'When I had kept my Bed about 5 or 6 Days one Night for four or five Hours you seemed so present with me & in such a remarkable manner that I never found before. Jesus was with us & we conversed most freely & happily of his Love.' 'I want you here instan[t]ly. Sure the Lord will call you with his own powerful Voice of Love.' Piercy cannot 'help believe the dear Jesus will yet accompany you in these Parts & that I shall be led by the Hand by you'. 'I want you to write more & more to me about your Heart.' All he desires is 'to act with, to suffer live & die with you'. 'My dearest, my best, my only, most, & ever desirable Friend', 'I want, O I want to be nearer to you that I might unbosom my whole soul upon every private and public Experience, & as it were, pour my wants & needs into your kind & friendly Bosom.' His enemies were motivated by jealousy of their 'Bosom Friendship'. It was God 'who first formed that Union & sacred Friendship'.[8]

Adversaries often find it convenient to fall to mutual accusations of moral turpitude. These charges are most poignant in the context of religious conflict since it is supposed that serious religious commitment involves a striving after goodness. Yet eighteenth-century Methodists sent out conflicting and complicated signals regarding their personal goodness. In the first place, Methodism had not arisen as a statement against moral collapse in the Church of England. On the contrary, the new-birth movement challenged what it considered to be Anglicanism's preaching that salvation was won by individuals being and doing good. However, the Methodist movement itself had been rent asunder by the 1770s owing to the age-old theological dispute over what role, if any, is played in an individual's salvation by the fulfilling of moral laws. Since the Wesleyan branch espoused the possibility of personal perfection, it was clear that, whatever the theological glosses applied to this doctrine, a life of moral probity was to be considered of utmost importance and to be taken as having some significance for how one stood – not just temporally, but in relation to eternity as well.

For those, like the Countess of Huntingdon, who had vigorously slammed the door on good works making any contribution to a person's salvation – lest the ultimate power of God in choosing his elect be in any way compromised – the problem was acute. To be sure, the Calvinistic commitment to the doctrine of predestination, with people having no say in or contribution to make to their salvation, was hardly new. At an earlier stage it had been at home in standard Anglican teaching, had formed the very sinews of seventeenth-century Puritanism and then had persisted in the theological teaching of much of eighteenth-century Dissent. Yet early Anglicanism, later Puritanism and now Dissent had a practical advantage in working out this rejection of personal goodness contributing to salvation: their adherence to stable local congregations overseen by resident ministers. Regularly exercised church discipline – combined with a localised social control – would dissuade Christians from immorality. If they stumbled they would be swiftly censured. Neither Calvinistic Anglicanism, Puritanism nor Dissent posed any ostensible threat to social morals.

Calvinistic Methodism undercut this. By combining with predestination an ardent demand for constantly mobile preaching, Lady Huntingdon and her colleagues left themselves open to the charge of de-stablising communities. Unsettled ministers, many claimed, would unsettle individuals and, by extension, society. It was the Countess's aim, of course, that individuals should become unsettled: unremitting preaching, forcing a person's unceasing anxiety over salvation, demanded it. Whatever their theological differences, all the revivalist leaders espoused the technique of itinerant preaching. The novelty, excitement and new-found freedom offered to many, leader and led alike, a heady and dangerous brew. Traditional religious cords, and inhibitions, were being strained. A young female wrote to Whitefield after hearing him preach in Edinburgh that she blessed 'the Lord for the Good I have by your Ministry, yet I find there is always a hankering in my Heart after the Instrument'.[9]

Moravian terminology presented the advocates of new-birth with a dramatic and earthly form of expressing things divine. Not only the 'love feast' (a term and practice adopted by Lady Huntingdon and all other Methodists) but other forms of words combining religious aspirations with human appetites had a decided influence on the spiritual frame of mind of many eighteenth-century new-born Christians. Some of the Moravian correspondence is startling: 'I kiss the[e] and salute thee in the warm hot jowcy soft wounds of the Lamb. The Love w[h]ich I have to thee I think I need not tell you.'[10] Mercifully, such correspondence reveals only the extremes to which this particular form of religious imagery could aspire. Yet the themes are unmistakable, and the mixing of images of love divine and human fitted well the exuberance of the Methodist revival in general. Either through the ridicule or incomprehension of those outside the movement, or through the heady excitement that drew together those who had experienced what others had not, the correspondence of countless Methodists bespoke a love for one another that could leap the bounds of propriety, or at least of good judgement. The new-birth message led some to 'play together at

Blindman's buff. . . . Their Holy Kiss . . . has much more the appearance of wantoness, than of sobriety.'[11]

> Let me simply tell you a dream I saw last night. I thought you come to me & s[ai]d I cant hold out any longr. I am persuaded & with that stands before me face to face reachd out yr. right Hand (cross my left) & to my Right Hand giving yr self to me & with that I was humbled to the Dust w[i]th thankfulness &c. & we went together our way. This . . . dream & so many strange occurrences seem to speak a voice of Providence in this.

'I trust I shall be assisted to meet you & enjoy God in you & Wrestle together for each other, & for the Church of God. . . . O wt. shall we do, to set forth his Praises. O support me with Aples. I am full of Love. O do somwht. for this glorious Jesus.'[12] Thus Howell Harris, who married the object of these letters but, as has been observed, went on to become deeply involved with a married Welsh 'prophetess'.[13] John Wesley fared no better in affairs of the heart. Inappropriate liaisons from his early years, his brief sojourn in Georgia (where his letters to a young lady contained 'an olio of Religion and Love'), through his astonishing relationship with Grace Murray ('inflamed with love and lust') to his disastrous marriage all reflect emotional immaturity.[14] James Hutton believed that the Wesleys, 'both of them, are dangerous snares to many young women; several are in love with them. I wish they were married to some good sisters, but I would not give one of my sisters if I had any.'[15] Charles Wesley was charged with adultery during his abortive stay in Georgia,[16] and a similar accusation was made against him to the Bishop of London in 1744. The Countess boldly determined to support him publicly and a month after the accusation had been laid attended a West Street Chapel service, at which he was officiating, 'thus contenancing him'. Moreover, she made a direct appeal to the Bishop, and the affair was pursued no further, although she appears to have stopped attending the chapel.[17] When he married three years later, Charles Wesley became an uxorious husband and made the only truly successful marriage of any of the main eighteenth-century Methodist leaders.

When Lady Huntingdon ceased her attendance at the Wesleys' London Chapel, she turned to George Whitefield's Tabernacle, then under the supervision of Howell Harris. Whitefield, conveniently in America, bewailed the fact that it was proving to be a hotbed of antinomianism, which is the belief that by virtue of faith a Christian is released from the obligations of moral law.[18] At the very time she had started attending this chapel, Harris was being accused of tolerating terrible practices amongst its members. There were those who got 'in to Men's Houses . . . adulterating their Wives, fornicating their daughters, sodomitically abusing their Boys'.[19] It was not long before James Relly, one of Whitefield's most trusted preachers, took a mistress, while assuring his wife that it was 'no sin before God'.[20] John Wesley's rejection of the theological position of the Calvinistic version of Methodism was not a little influenced by what he perceived as a resulting indifference to moral laws. Referring to some of the ministers most intimately involved in the Countess's preaching plans, including Whitefield,

Wesley lamented their 'amorous way of praying to Christ' in public.[21] Lady Huntingdon's drawing room services had attracted some 'scented beaus', who were 'hoping to see a young wench in a religious frenzy'. But Trevecca students presented special problems. One revival meeting there saw male and female displaying 'unruly Passions'.[22] In nearby Cardiganshire it was observed in 1778 that two young Methodist women who 'did jump & keep a noise above the rest are now turned whores, to the great scandal of jumping'.[23]

It was when away from Trevecca that the most serious difficulties arose. The Countess was informed that rumours were being spread in Brecon of 'some Indecencys between the Students and my Daughters'. The master at the college complained bitterly that a student whom Lady Huntingdon had sent out to preach was 'a shocking hand at kissing young women &c.' Upon his return to Trevecca, the young man installed himself in the housekeeper's room, from which he could not be removed 'neither day nor night. . . . She pretends that she cannot do it, but that cannot by any means be the case.'[24] Another student on his preaching rounds had 'most shamefully formed such a connection' with a member of one of the Countess's chapels 'as to be wicked with her for almost all the time he was there'. For a while it had been hushed up, 'but at last it had vent, and out it came to the wide world, to the no small reproach of the Gospel at that place. He did not promise to marry the girl at any time, but persuaded the deluded creature that there was no manner of sin in Fornication.' The young man on his return informed the master that 'your Ladyship ... maintained the same sentiments'. Astonishingly, the student had since been sent out again to preach: 'I make no doubt but he has some woman at present.'[25] Another student, sent to preach in Cumbria, instead spent his time following 'a Young guidy Girl in the Neighbourhood'. Towards the end of her life, the Countess received news that one of her students had become a rank antinomian. The disease was spreading unchecked, the accounts 'shocking'. The student wrote to her that he considered this teaching 'the simple Truth, and the Old Light of the Prophets and Apostles and that which Jehovah Jesus himself Taught'. A man not unsympathetic to the Countess remarked on the great 'immodesty' of her students.[26] The impressionable young men had been seduced by example, some apparently believing that they had been licensed for mischief.

Lady Huntingdon attempted to counter the problem through rigorously tightened control. When first settling the arrangements for her Trevecca college, she persuaded Howell Harris to give up his housekeeper, Hannah Bowen, for the new establishment.[27] Yet six months later the Countess had second thoughts. Bowen was 'too young a woman [she was forty] & being rather more amiable than the generality of her order it might be a great temptation to her & more so to Twenty young men that she must of necessity be much with'. Therefore, Lady Huntingdon chose a much older woman as housekeeper, who with a cook of similar age and a young boy would be all the permanent staff required. By this means, her students 'will [be] Cutt of[f] all women coming near them which I think will have many advantages as any thing of this sort would bring much & grievious reproach on the Gospel'.[28]

Yet Hannah Bowen did come to the college, and events quickly proved the Countess's earlier inclination to have been correct. The master of the college soon became involved with both Harris's daughter and Hannah Bowen and in so doing showed his students how 'to turn to courtship'. Hannah had 'grown so big that she could not bow'. In a fury, Lady Huntingdon turned both out, refusing the pregnant Hannah any wages and informing the master that he was eternally damned.[29]

This disquieting turn of events, together with the parallel Cosson affair, hardened the Countess's resolve to keep her students free from temptation. However, to the extent that was possible at Trevecca it clearly was beyond her power to control their actions when they had the freedom of the road with frequent preaching assignments. Peripatetic preachers with a lively message of divine love on their lips had far greater temptations, and opportunities, for misdeeds than a man rooted in his local charge.[30] Her refusal to allow students to marry[31] was based in the belief that the restriction would provide greater time for their studies – or, more strictly speaking, their preaching. Yet this unmarried state left them more open to sexual temptations. Later, if John Wesley is to be believed, she extended the prohibition against marriage to all preachers in her Connexion,[32] except, of course, to that tiny handful of episcopally ordained clerics who assisted in her work. Ever seeking to nip the bud of her students' romantic inclinations, she wrote to one, enquiring if his 'intercourse with that woman was at an end?' The incensed young man replied: 'My Lady that woman is a good, a gracious God fearing woman and I am bold to say, she has not her Fellow for Godliness in all the Town of Dover.'[33] One of the two students who came briefly to Trevecca upon expulsion from Oxford concluded that he could not remain under her supervision, not least because he 'did not think it a crime to marry'. In the case of one who actually proceeded to marry without her knowledge, the Countess was livid. The young man, who by his action had severed all relations with her, asked her not to treat them 'as children being both between 22/23 years of age'.[34] The indignation is understandable, but he missed the point that Lady Huntingdon's student preachers were her children.

Over the years the chapel at Bath provided more than its share of heartache. Not least among the trials were shocking reports the Countess received in 1788. She had recently appointed a new member of the chapel committee, one P.A. Saxby. Yet Saxby had been keeping a young mistress, who was already carrying his child, and his appointment had been a 'matter of astonishment to most people of the Chapel'. When Saxby began openly parading his mistress about the Pump Room, his wife upbraided him, upon which he 'beat her unmercifully so that the whole street was in an uproar crying out, "These are Lady Huntingdon's People"'.[35]

Lady Huntingdon's efforts were hindered not only by misconduct heterosexual. In the last year of her life she found it necessary to initiate investigations into the activities of a preacher she had prided herself in having induced to leave Wesley. 'He has in time past, too near approach'd a Line of Conduct, unnatural in itself, and too indelicate to mention.

Rom.1.27.'[36] She probably took special pains in securing the truth, given the dreadful uncovering some years earlier of the activities of one of the leading laymen in her main London chapel. As a member of the committee, Morris Hughes held power of attorney for Lady Huntingdon and was superintendent of the chapel society which met weekly. Claiming that he had been 'made free', Hughes 'exposed his person' to a chimney sweep, a baker, a plumber and a cabinet-maker. Moreover, he had engaged in 'playing at blindmans-buff with the boys in the neighbourhood, and making a barber's boy thrust his curling irons up his nostrils to make his nose bleed'. Most serious, all this had become common fame, gleefully reported in the press. The hapless man was stripped of all his chapel responsibilities and, excommunicated, fled London.[37]

It is little wonder that Lady Huntingdon was herself charged with being an antinomian. Even Charles Wesley, who despite their growing differences sought to see her in the best possible light, concluded that 'her Ladyship approaches too near the Antinomian extream'. Many years earlier, apparently fearing the results of her new-found Calvinism, he had sent her 'some of my Brother's sermons on the Law, an excellent antidote against Antinomianism'.[38] It likely had come to his attention that, astonishingly, the Countess was energetically distributing among her friends and religious acquaintances copies of a newly-reprinted collection of sermons by Dr Tobias Crisp, a notorious seventeenth-century antinomian.[39]

A clergyman who earlier had been her supporter wrote to 'inform your Ladyship of an affair which for some years has griev'd me much. Your Ladyships Name is made use of to countenance the rankest Antinomianism, & the most ungodly practices.' He went on to give several examples. One man who had led a 'suitable life, after he had heard the Doctrines of final perseverance, finish'd salvation & complete Righteousness in Christ ... at length openly wicked & profane, gave way to Drunkenness & other Immoralities'. When reproved, 'he replied, Don't preach your legal stuff to me. I am not in Bondage. I am for my Lady's Gospel. Being ask'd if he thought he was doing right, he answered, No. Yet it cannot hurt me; for I know that I have a finish'd salvation a complete Righteousness.' Many such men were using the phrase 'my Lady's Gospel ... & I have heard it laughed at in several places'. One had said: 'Let him commit ever such wickedness, it could not make a hole in his Righteousness.' In short, her Calvinistic theology was producing 'pernicious' fruits.[40] Indeed, in one of the sermons preached on the occasion of her death it was reported that Lady Huntingdon 'was almost cried down as an Antinomian; but none could prove her one in her practice: and as to the law, she felt, from long experience, that she could neither get life nor comfort from it'.[41] At the very outset of her Calvinistic orientation, she had been counselled that there was a 'pipe of faith ... which reaches from the soul of the true believer up into the highest heavens from whence God is pleased to communicate all his gifts & graces. ... Whoever is thus born of God cannot committ sin because [of] the Holy Ghost.'[42]

Over the years the Countess encountered a cascade of problems from those who found in her gospel what they considered an open invitation to disregard moral restraint. They enjoyed the comfort of the conviction that whatever they did could not hinder their election to salvation. It was a mischievously attractive doctrine. In 1776 one of her students reported 'very grievous trials in Devon', where many of her followers were 'drinking in Antinomian principles, and I fear their practices will follow'.[43] This was precisely the Wesleyan theological concern that brought matters to a head in 1770. Perceived widespread moral laxity among Lady Huntingdon's branch of Methodism was driven home by her erstwhile Trevecca Superintendent, John Fletcher, who vigorously defended Wesley's 1770 minutes in his six *Checks to Antinomianism*. Fletcher feared that by avoiding any reference to good works, the Countess was 'verging very fast towards Antinomianism'; therefore, he 'judged the propositions contained in those Minutes ought rather to be confirmed rather than revoked'. Wesley wrote: 'I find no such sin as Legality in the Bible: the very use of the term speaks an Antinomian.'[44] One of the Countess's leading students at Trevecca later departed her Connexion to settle as a Dissenting minister. He reflected on her itinerant preachers 'wandering from county to county, and from diocese to diocese', preaching 'in meeting-houses, and fields, and barns, the flesh-pleasing doctrines of the antinomian error'.[45]

To the end of her life, Lady Huntingdon found it impossible to shake-off this label. On one occasion at Trevecca, when her birthday and the college's founding were being celebrated, the festivities suffered an electrifying interruption by a man screaming that she was 'a whore'.[46] It did not help that during the 1780s she appointed as one of her chaplains John Bradford, an Anglican cleric who espoused unmistakable antinomian views. It was widely stated that 'your Ladyship as well as Mr Bradford maintained the same sentiments', yet it took an unconscionable length of time before she finally expelled him.[47] Lady Huntingdon's eccentrically incisive watchdog, John Berridge, felt impelled to write to her words of strong caution:

> Though Believers are under the teaching of God's Spirit, they often fall into their own; and thereby slide into sad doctrines, and sometimes into sad practices; and how must you deal with such people if there is no rule of life to appeal to? You may tell them that Jesus, by his Spirit, teaches you so and so; and they will tell you that Jesus teaches them quite the contrary. And if they are led by their own spirit, they will be more violent for their mistake, than you can be for the truth. If there is no written Rule of Life of allowed authority, you can never deal with deluded Christians; they will plead inward teaching for the worst doctrine, and godly motives for the worst practices.[48]

There have, no doubt, ever been preachers of the gospel with sexual urges, and those who act upon those urges beyond the marriage bed. What some eighteenth-century new-life preachers did was not only to act but to justify such action – to give sanction to such action – by claiming it as evidence of the exercise of sanctified love. Antinomianism was far from a minor blot on the Methodist escutcheon. Perfection and Calvinism: either extreme could lead to antinomianism. If Wesley's teachings were pushed to the limit, sanctification could make one believe it impossible to commit sin. With

Calvinism, if actions could not in any way merit a salvation set by God, a person's actions were not only unimportant but irrelevant. The internecine conflict within Methodism was a theological dispute over the source of salvation. But in practical terms, and on good authority, it was not beliefs but fruits that could be judged. Therefore, Wesleyan and Huntingdonian Methodists both exerted considerable efforts in attempting to extricate themselves from charges of antinomianism while at the same time charging the other with fostering it. For these reasons, the accusation of lowering moral standards constantly dogged Methodist steps, whatever their theological commitments. The basic problem, which perhaps neither camp understood, was that passionate Christians found it decidedly difficult to respond to only one set of emotions.

Notes

1 This theme has been developed by Henry Abelove, *The Evangelist of Desire. John Wesley and the Methodists* (Stanford, 1990). See also Rack, *Reasonable Enthusiast*, p. 253; Stout, *Divine Dramatist*, p. 157.

2 [Ann Grinfield] to SH, ante-28 June 1755, Drew C5.

3 John Berridge to SH, n.d., 306, box 7, safe drawer 3, Cowper and Newton Museum, Olney.

4 SH to CW, 1743; [1741 or 42]; n.d., Black 13, 87, 89.

5 SH to CW, January 1743; ante-1746; ante-1746, Black 5, 98, 93.

6 Thomas Pointon to SH, 11 May 1746, 14D32/465, LRO. George Whitefield's printed letters to the Countess shed no light on the nature of their personal relationship. Almost no originals of their correspondence have survived.

7 Thomas Cannon, *No. 5. The Family Library, being the Substance of a Funeral Sermon...on the Death of the...Countess...of Huntingdon* (London, [1791?]), p. 120.

8 WP to SH, 11 June 1774, A4/2/10; 13 September 1774, A4/1/18; 24 January 1775, A4/2/12; 28 July 1775, A4/2/18; 15 January 1781, A4/2/21; 24 February 1781, A4/6/5. CF.

9 Margaret L-y to George Whitefield, 20 November 1741, *The Weekly History: Or, An account of the...Progress of the Gospel* (1741), p. lxii.

10 Johanna Wade to Ann Okley, 16 July 1747, Edwin Welch (ed.), 'The Bedford Moravian church in the eighteenth century', *The Publications of the Bedfordshire Historical Record Society* 68 (1989), p. 13.

11 Henry Venn to Selina Wheler, 8 April 1766, C11, CMS.

12 HH to Anne Williams, 9, 8 January 1742, Trevecka 459, 458.

13 Owen, 'Harris and Trevecka family', pp. 7-10. He had formed a 'religious-sexual affection', p. 9.

14 'Philip Thickness's reminiscences of early Georgia', *Georgia Historical Quarterly* 74 (1990), p. 691; JW to John Bennet, 23 January 1750, Baker 26:402. See also Richard M. Cameron, *The Rise of Methodism: a Source Book* (New York, 1954), pp. 109-29; Rack, *Reasonable Enthusiast*, pp. 124-34. It gives 'evidence of some deep-rooted psychological disability in his nature as regards relationships with women', *ibid.*, p. 257.

15 James Hutton to Count Nicholas Zinzendorf, 14 March 1740, Benham, *Memoirs of James Hutton*, p. 47.

16 Cameron, *Rise of Methodism*, pp. 87-88.

17 James Erskine to HH, 26 January 1744/5, Letters chiefly addressed to the Rev. C. Wesley, Vol. VI, Rylands (quotation); Jackson, *Journal of Charles Wesley*, 1:393 (26 January [1744/5]); HH to GW, 8 November 1745, Trevecka 1372.

18 GW to John Syms, 12 June [1746], John W. Christie (ed.), 'Newly discovered letters of George Whitefield 1745-1746', *Journal of the Presbyterian Historical Society* 32 (1954), p. 253. See also GW to same, 12 March 1746; GW to Thomas Prince, Jr., 24 April 1746; GW to John Cennick, 2 May 1746, *ibid.*, pp. 79, 80, 85.

19 James Erskine to HH, 20 March 1744/5, Trevecka 1306.

20 HH diary, 16 January 1750, *HHVL*, p. 261.

21 JW to JF, 20 March 1768, Streiff, *Jean Guillaume de la Fléchère*, 277n.

22 John Knyveton, 4 November 1763, Gray, *Man's Midwife*, p. 158; diaries of Thomas Roberts, 6 July 1774, Trevecca Group, no. 3154, Calvinistic Methodist Archives, NLW.

23 Diary of Edmund Jones (1778), MSS 7021-30, NLW.

24 John Cave to SH, 30 September 1770; John Williams to George Best, 12 January 1788, F1/110, 1981, CF; same to SH, 21 April 1788, Ebley MSS, D.2538/8/1, Gloustershire Record Office.

25 John Williams to SH, 5 February 1789, F1/2060. See also same to SH, July 1788, F1/2027. CF.

26 John Derbyshire to SH, 9 October 1783, F1/556; R. Lovesgrove to SH, 8 June 1790, F1/919; Thomas Jones to SH, 5 July, 30 April 1790, F1/927, 909. CF; Diary of Edmund Jones (1780), MSS 7021-30, NLW.

27 SH to HH, 17 December 1767, Trevecka 2635.

28 SH to HH, 4 June 1768, Trevecka 2642.

29 HH diary, 26 March; 24 (quotation), 17, 19 September 1769, *HHRS*, pp. 228, 229.

30 They were 'sexually active preachers on the move.' David Hempton, 'Methodism and the law, 1740-1820', *Bulletin of the John Rylands University Library of Manchester* 70 (1988), p. 98.

31 Sarah Wilks, *Memoirs of Rev. Mark Wilks* (London, 1821), pp. 50, 56. See also SH to [Thomas and Selina Wills], 1 April 1782, II.c.7/13, CL.

32 JW to John Dickins, 19 June 1790, Telford, 8:223.

33 Thomas Cannon to SH, n.d., F1/1110, CF.

34 Joseph Shipman to SH, n.d., E4/5/11; Thomas Bird to SH, 1 January 1778, F1/1810. CF.

35 J. Sheppard and G. Ford to SH, 10 October 1788, F1/773; anon. to William Taylor (via SH), 10 October 1788, F1/774. CF.

36 Thomas Young to SH, 11 April 1791, F1/2175. For another suspected case of homosexuality, this time involving one of her students, see James Glazebrook to SH, 12 August 1772, F1/189, CF.

37 Spa Fields Chapel Minutes, 10, 13 August 1782, Welch, *Two Chapels*, items 177, 178.

38 CW to Sally Wesley, 27 May [*c.* 1780], Wesley Family Letters & Papers, Folio Vol. 4, Rylands; CW to SH, 22 May 1755, Wesley Family (Charles Wesley Division) Papers, 1735-1787, Drew.

39 G. Ford to SH, 3 July 1755; Ann Grinfield to SH, 21 July [1755], Drew B27, B16. For the printing: *Christ Alone Exalted: being the Compleat Works of Tobias Crisp* (London, 1755).

40 Walter Sellon to SH, 20 November 1771, E4/4/6, CF.

41 Platt, *Waiting Christian*, p. 13.

42 Anon. to SH, 20 April 1747, Trevecka 1643.

43 Thomas Molland to SH, 15 October 1776, F1/367, CF.

44 Benson, *Life of Flechere*, p. 155; JW to Joseph Benson, 30 November 1770, Wesley Family Papers, item 18-H, Duke.

45 Mark Wilks, *Nonconformity: A Sermon, Delivered...Nov. 6, 1817, at the Monthly Association, of Congregational Ministers* (London, 1818), p. 116.

46 Diary of Edmund Jones (1780), MSS 7021-30, NLW.

47 John Williams to SH, 5 February 1789, F1/2060. As late as the spring of 1790 Bradford ordained two of her new Connexional ministers. John Bradford to SH, 27 May 1790, F1/913. CF. Upon his departure he was able to draw off 'many' from Spa Fields. David Griffiths to Mrs Bowen, n.d., Llwyngwair MSS 16988, NLW. As her chaplain, see John Bradford, *An Address to the Inhabitants of New Brunswick* (London, 1788), p. 23.

48 John Berridge to SH, n.d., *Evangelical Register* 1 (1824/5), pp. 236-37.

Chapter 11

'My privilege wanted no authority to confirm it'

The Countess of Huntingdon had developed a necessarily sharp nose for money. The chapel-building of the 1760s had been drain enough, but the establishment of Trevecca and the subsequent missionary activity which flowed from it in England and America forced her hand deep into pocket. Although she received an occasional legacy, gift or loan from some of her wealthy friends and acquaintances, on other occasions she was bitterly disappointed. When Lady Sarah Smythe died, she left her estate to her chaplain, the Countess's erstwhile colleague Henry Venn. Lady Huntingdon lamented that Lady Smythe had 'left all in private legacys but nothing to the Gospel. Vastly rich. What wise & carefull believers we find in our day.'[1]

It is impossible to quantify with any precision Lady Huntingdon's wealth or income during any period of her life. Although on paper she had been the main recipient of her husband's estates, in the aftermath of the disastrous remodelling of Donington Park she and Francis had hammered-out a detailed separation of their personal finances. That resulted in her owing him several hundred pounds, the total inheritance from Theophilus's estate.[2] In 1778 she received £1,000 '& a little place' at the death of her aunt, Lady Frances Shirley,[3] from which she sold some of the fine china, plate and linen. The long-running saga of her struggle to secure a settlement from the Ferrers family continued during the 1760s and 1770s, in which she soon was joined by her cousin and new-found ecclesiastical companion Walter Shirley. It was a matter in which she was 'very pressing',[4] continuing to threaten the then Earl Ferrers with legal action to 'oblige him to Instant Payment of the money'.[5] Not only did this lay her open to 'infamy' from Ferrers, but it involved her in the un-pretty business of conflict with her two remaining children,[6] with her son-in-law openly calumniating her character.[7] 'I have found ... it difficult to manage to keep out of debt', wrote the Countess,[8] and it was not unknown for her to be brought to selling valuables in order to raise cash.[9] By the 1780s she was regularly renting out her houses at Tunbridge Wells and Brighton to various members of the nobility, using the funds raised to support her ministers.[10] One chapel concluded 'that your present capacity is not so extensive as your inclination'.[11]

Ever since her conversion from 'good works' to faith, the Countess of Huntingdon had re-focused her giving. Although she still on occasion might make a donation to charitable enterprises such as William Dodd's Magdalen Charity during the 1760s or the St Ethelburga Society in the early 1770s,[12] such action was increasingly rare. By the 1780s it was clear that not only a threadbare purse but a philosophy of giving had brought the Countess to reject donating to traditional charitable good works. Although she received 'repeated requests' from the Bath Hospital for a contribution, she thought them 'most unreasonable', given the burden of her chapel concerns.[13] When approached to aid a distressed family, she replied that she was sorry but could do very little. 'I am obliged to be a spectator of miseries, which I pity but cannot relieve.' Lady Huntingdon had come to the conclusion that there were numerous people 'who had no religion' but who would supply such wants. Even among true Christians there were 'but few . . . who had a proper concern for the awful condition of ignorant and perishing souls'. That was her mission. That would be where her money went. In short, providing preaching was the 'greatest of all charitys I know on earth'.[14] Even in the schools established for poor children at her Bath and London Spa Fields chapels the aim was strictly religious,[15] and neither school was founded nor funded by the Countess, but by the chapel committees.[16] She became increasingly uneasy over the financial implications of the Bath school. Even though making no contribution, she began to suspect that support for it was drawing off money that should be used for the furtherance of preaching. When she insisted that all chapel contributions to the school cease, the chapel's committee resigned *en masse*, creating a crisis. One of her Bath supporters in this affair wrote to say that the committee members had been 'absurd & impertinently ridiculous' to suppose that education should compete with preaching.[17] Those were Lady Huntingdon's precise sentiments.

While many aristocratic women with whom she had drunk tea and shared faith in earlier years continued to nudge members of their class not to forget charitable responsibilities,[18] the Countess went her own way. If her attitude to American slavery is recalled, the disquieting conclusion must be that when it came to the relief of physical distress she thrust such responsibility onto God or others. This attitude implies no desire on her part for luxury or ostentatious living. Far from it. Personally frugal to a fault, she lived 'without an equipage, without a livery servant, eating her frugal meal, only by this means [that] the joyful sound may be heard'.[19] She might lavish money on decking out her chapels, but not on herself. Nor could she tolerate avarice in others. Such an instance was the conviction in 1777 of the clergyman William Dodd for the forgery of a financial bond. Extensive efforts were made to secure the man a pardon. Lady Frances Montagu informed the Countess that there was a good chance the King would grant one, and Lady Huntingdon was asked by Dodd's Magdalen charity and a number of nobles to present a petition to the Queen, as Lord Hertford was to do to the King. The Countess refused.[20] Here is an arresting illustration of the clash between her roles as a leading member of the aristocracy and a leading Methodist.

She was praised by one of her ministers for not confusing those positions. Given the delicate nature of the attempts to secure episcopal ordination for Trevecca students, her 'peculiar station', he said, made it particularly necessary for 'every of yr steps . . . to be taken with the utmost caution'. Her intercession for Dodd 'which would be highly applauded in yr Ladyship as Countess of H would as the Patroness of the Methodists be misconstrued'. It would have been portrayed as acknowledging Dodd as 'One of us'.[21] This she studiously avoided and wrote to Dodd a widely-published letter, praying for his soul and assuring him that his death would be 'the best sermon you ever preached in your life'. Her supporters hoped that God would make her letter 'obliging to his Immortal soul'.[22] The Countess of Huntingdon had established her priorities.

With all her resources and energies targeted for mission, Lady Huntingdon's attempts to secure episcopal ordination for her students continued apace throughout the 1770s. It was an uphill battle. From the earliest years at Trevecca, some believed that 'none out of your Ladyship's College should ever be ordained'.[23] Her hopes had been raised by the eleventh-hour success in securing the ordination of one of the students for the East Indies mission, and during the early 1770s a few bishops displayed a readiness to consider her requests and a kindness to those who presented themselves. She frequently involved herself with all the details of applications to these bishops, including obtaining the requisite testimonials from parish clergymen.[24] However, episcopal reflex increasingly hardened as her students' expanding itinerant preaching unsettled the work of the clergy in many parishes. Some of her aspirants for ordination went so far as to attempt to conceal from bishops their connections with Lady Huntingdon and Trevecca. One student even travelled to Sweden, thinking to secure ordination there.[25] With many episcopal doors being closed on her, she moved a rung down the ecclesiastical ladder and wrote to the Dean of Norwich, 'begging him to inform the Bishops that unless they would ordain lively & gracious ministers the dissenters must have the whole of the present work in their hands'. It was to no avail.[26]

By 1777 it was being observed that 'the Countess of Huntingdon's people are peculiarly obnoxious to the bishops in general'.[27] She had become firmly convinced of the existence of a general agreement among the bishops of the Church of England to reject men who had attended Trevecca; she appealed direct to the Archbishop of Canterbury, asking him to order that 'any Injunctions for their exclusion from the Church might be relaxed' and that the usual red tape should be cut. In return, the Archbishop informed her that such decisions lay solely with diocesan bishops; yet his most uncomfortable words were that he did not believe Trevecca 'likely to send forth very able or judicious Divines'. He was certain, however, that her intentions were good.[28]

Trevecca had reinforced Lady Huntingdon's ecclesiastical irregularities. There was even uncertainty regarding the expected length of study, variously described as either two, three or four years. After the mid-1770s the average enrolment of students was about ten.[29] During its twenty-four-year existence over two hundred men were enrolled at one time or another, yet only twenty ever secured episcopal ordination. Of these, apparently none remained within the Countess's service.[30] The bishops' anxiety over the quality of their education was justified. After Joseph Benson's dismissal, it proved decidedly difficult to secure an adequate master, and during some periods there was none. Moreover, the explicit insistence that her college be a hive of missionary outreach meant that in practice students could far more accurately be described as preachers. She would address them: 'Come, come, *Meyer*; come, *Seymour*; you are only going to a few simple souls: tell them concerning Jesus Christ, and they will be satisfied.'[31] The production of 'very able or judicious divines' was not the Countess's aim. The purpose was to try to ensure that a young man was sufficient in making public addresses, at which point he was hurried away from his studies to preach. This, more often than not, was at the sacrifice of a prepared mind, which put these young men at a distinct disadvantage. It was not even, or primarily, the absence of 'book learning' that marked out Trevecca students, but the absence of the ability to engage effectively in the theological confrontations that inevitably lay ahead of them. Even the Scripture passages that adorned every Trevecca wall could not compensate for that deficiency.[32]

At Trevecca, the philosophical disciplines were conspicuous by their near total absence. Lady Huntingdon was insisting on an education that distanced her students from the earlier Dissenting emphasis on a learned ministry. Philip Doddridge at his Northampton Academy had encouraged students to read widely and to marry head and heart.[33] His tragic early death had robbed the Countess not only of a steadying friend but also of a useful guide for her educational enterprise. Indeed, in Dissenting eyes, Trevecca 'formed a body of more injudicious Calvinists than England had ever before seen'.[34] Many students spent remarkably short periods of time in study, being kept on the move by the Countess, preaching. Their brief snatches of academic work suffered 'constant interruption'. They had no choice in this, as she held 'supreme direction in the affairs of the college and therefore claimed implicit obedience'.[35] One complained to her that in three years he had not been at the college more than a total of three months. 'Altho learning do not make ministers, it is necessary for ministers to have it.' Another protested to her that she had kept him from the college for two and a half years at a stretch, yet another that he had had 'very little oppertunity for improvement during the time I have been in your connection, being continually obliged to move from place to place'. One of her closest advisers was concerned at the brief periods students were students. 'A little smattering knowledge is apt to puff up with conceit, at the same time that it is so superficial as to be of little use to themselves or others.'[36] It was a fruitless appeal, and five years later one master was pleading with her to defer for a considerable time calling out any students to preach 'or else they will be ruined. . . . I have heard by men of knowledge and veracity very great complaints upon that score.'[37] She, however, knew what she wanted from these students, even though the quality of the Trevecca products provided added ammunition for the satirical guns.[38]

While some students might appeal for more study, many others eagerly awaited news of the Countess's preaching assignments and dropped their studies with no evident regret.[39] One student sent out to supply a chapel for five weeks was 'extremely stupid and ignorant', able to 'learn hardly any thing' and therefore happy to be 'any where better' than Trevecca. At one point the tutor reported that with only two exceptions all the students were 'exceedingly ignorant in scripture history'; indeed, the last four admitted 'are little better versed in this . . . than they are in Mahomet's Koran'. Former tutors had been scathing about the students' quality, academic and otherwise. One criticised the Countess for admitting, in effect, almost anyone who applied; he appealed that future prospective candidates should be 'properly examined, & tried respecting their characters, abilities, motives'.[40] This suggests that it was not always intellectual qualities that were lacking. One chapel bitterly complained about those sent from Trevecca to preach: the 'vilest of all R[asca]ls falsely call'd Students, for I declare from my heart, none out of ten deserve that name'; and it is evident that a number of the students were emotionally immature. Many left after a brief time, one citing 'the Strife and Contention that is dayly at College'.[41] Another read a letter in which Lady Huntingdon had reported that he was not welcome in a particular chapel, upon which he wept 'bitterly', with a 'grief . . . almost insupportable'. He soon left Trevecca, asking the Countess for a reference so that he could take a job as a household servant.[42]

The general quality of these students, the level of education they received while at Trevecca and the suspicion of or antipathy towards their activities produced insuperable barriers to episcopal ordination. Increasingly, they themselves judged such hopes futile and turned towards Dissenting groups. As chapels formed, there was a natural demand for men who could do more than preach. Congregations wanted 'to enjoy the Gospel with all its privileges, which is not afforded them till' ordination took place.[43] Lady Huntingdon was receiving a stream of such requests, and since she could not secure it for them from bishops, Dissenting churches appeared to the students their only option. This distressed her sorely. Not only would ordination by Dissenters make untenable the claim that she remained a faithful Anglican; she also feared, with some justification, that Dissenters would prove incapable of holding to orthodox Calvinist doctrines. In addition to the possibility of theological impurity, Dissenting chapels used settled ministers, and the Countess never relented in her insistence on a constantly mobile ministry. It is not difficult to understand why a growing number of her students, weary of the constant demand to act as travelling preachers, left her service to plough ecclesiastical furrows of their own with Independent Dissenting chapels. She viewed 'with grief' ministers 'confined to chapels, while thousands of souls are perishing'.[44]

Lady Huntingdon was particularly horrified by the threat of Baptists gaining ground among her chapels and men. This was not a misplaced fear, and during the mid-1760s she became convinced that they had targeted her work.[45] Over the following years she lost ministers and students to the Baptists,[46] and several of her chapels suffered serious internal conflict with members who expressed such principles.[47] In at least one chapel Baptist elements gained 'all power'. At the Birmingham Chapel, Baptists were 'dabbling in the water before & behind'.[48] For a prospective student at Trevecca the Countess laid-down two criteria: he must be unmarried and 'be clear certainly of Baptist principles'. At the college she personally presented theological arguments in defence of the baptism of infants, forcing one student to make a written declaration of his recantation of Baptist beliefs. In this she argued ardently and, presumably, persuasively. Not only from within was the threat real. Baptists were 'exceedingly diligent in fishing' around Trevecca. The students had to be fully armed 'against the encroachment & advances . . . of the Enemy'.[49] Dissenters of all stripes, she became certain, were 'watching to get Plums for themselves out of our Puddings'.[50] The Countess was expanding her enterprises into a highly competitive market.

Lady Huntingdon furthered her claim as a faithful daughter of the Church of England by her opposition to the 1771 Feathers Tavern Petition. This was an unsuccessful appeal to parliament by a number of clergymen calling for an end of the requirement to subscribe to the Thirty-Nine Articles of the Church of England. The Countess was active in opposing such a relaxation of theological statements she considered a bulwark against 'the conspiracy of Atheism'.[51] Her fervent opposition to the Petition brought her into conflict with a clerical friend of long standing. Theophilus Lindsey had been named after his godfather, the Countess's husband, and as a child had been taken under the patronage of Lady Betty Hastings and another of Theophilus Hastings' sisters. In due course, Lindsey became a chaplain to the Countess's son Francis[52] and throughout this period had maintained a friendly, but not uncritical, contact with her. Admiring her dedication but worried by its extremes, which he felt sometimes led to 'oddities & heats of passion & obstinacy', he believed that Lady Huntingdon relished religious contention and confrontation. Moreover, Lindsey became increasingly disturbed by

> the peculiarity of our popular preachers' methods in laying such stress upon particular feelings . . . because I have observed . . . this sadly misleads many; makes them mistake their own imagination for the work of God's spirit, & so go on highly his favourites, in their own opinion, whilst they belong rather to the enemy of God & all goodness, their hearts unchanged, their passions unsubdued, their affections narrowed & contracted, & damning all that have not the good luck to be clan'd & class'd with them.

He criticised Whitefield's preaching for concentrating solely on arousing emotions, with nothing 'to inform the understanding'.[53] As early as the 1750s Lindsey admitted his theological unease with certain of the Thirty-Nine Articles.[54] His doctrinal doubts, especially concerning the Trinity, increased to the extent that he it was who organised the Feathers Tavern Petition. In 1773, the year following its failure, Lindsey resigned his living in Yorkshire, moved to London, and established there the first professedly Unitarian church in England.[55] In spite of the fact that their contact appears to have ended, nearly fifteen years later Lindsey and his wife visited the Countess and were graciously received. Once again he reflected upon her self-giving labours 'to promote what she believes to be the truth', although he found her 'still in the depths of mysticism and methodism' and could but hope that Trevecca 'will be a place for more rational inquirers after she drops into her grave'.[56] Lindsey's desire for an enlightened Anglicanism and Lady Huntingdon's for an enthusiastic Anglicanism were irreconcilable.

Whatever her professed principles in upholding Anglican theological orthodoxy, the Countess of Huntingdon's practice spoke in a different voice. Here was a leader who, together with her men and movement, appeared ever at loggerheads with the church she claimed to serve. The small number of Church of England clergymen who actively engaged to assist her by occasional chapel-preaching had to tread carefully lest episcopal feathers were ruffled. The chapels themselves were brick and mortar witnesses that the Countess was outside the Church of England. Her initial chapels, during the 1760s, had dwelling-houses attached, and she maintained that these places of worship were merely extensions to her private residences. This tendentious claim could hardly be made for the new chapels erected throughout the kingdom in the following decade, in places she had never seen and often never would visit, let alone reside.[57] However, she hoped that by granting them her patronage, even these chapels would thereby be protected from official censure or interference.

The Toleration Act of 1689 had called for all places of non-Anglican worship to be registered with the proper ecclesiastical or civil authorities. Registration clearly marked-out such a building as a Dissenting chapel. The Countess's negative attitude to Dissenters, combined with her positive claim to be working from within to save the Established Church, had precluded her contemplating sheltering under the Toleration Act. Combined with this was her position as a peeress of the realm, the prerogatives of which she ever sought to exploit to the full in pursuing religious goals. Since her chapel building had commenced in the provinces, it was inevitable that London would stand at the apex of her plans. There the Wesleyans had long had chapels, and John Wesley's opening of an additional one in the spring of 1777 very likely acted to spur her in that direction. Her Mulberry Gardens Chapel was built in 1777 at Wapping, provocatively adjacent to that of a Dissenting minister fervently opposed to methodistic enthusiasm.[58] Indeed, her chapel was so close that his preaching was being drowned-out by their loud singing.[59] The voices raised within the Mulberry Gardens Chapel were discordant, and the fits and starts surrounding the establishing of this enterprise resulted from bitter internal strife among and between the people and various ministers. By 1778, Lady Huntingdon had fully exerted her authority, with the 'Lord's appearing for me in so wonderfull a manner at the Mulbury Gardens'. The iniquitous people she had put to rout there 'make the wicked as ashes under the soles of my feet'.[60]

Mulberry Gardens quickened the Countess's pulse regarding large-scale London plans. Already her eye had fallen on a large amusement house in Clerkenwell, known as the Pantheon. Built some years earlier as a place for genteel conversation, the taking of tea, coffee and wine in pleasure gardens or galleries in the rotunda, mostly on Sundays, it was not long before the establishment proved attractive to prostitutes. By 1776 the promoter of the project was bankrupt, and a new lease holder was sought for the Pantheon. Lady Huntingdon was highly excited by the prospect of 'having this temple of folly dedicated to Jehovah Jesus'.[61] Its drawbacks, however, were considerable: there would be great expense in converting the temple from pagan to Christian use. There also was its distance from central London, where it was argued by some of her advisers she would be far better positioned 'to provide a Ministry & a place of hearing for the Great & the Noble'.[62] Walter Shirley and Augustus Toplady, after applying pressure, received her grudging assent to give up the idea. She watched with mixed pleasure and envy as two Anglican evangelical clerics spent a great deal of money to embellish the interior of the building. Herbert Jones and William Taylor christened it Northampton Chapel, registered it as a Dissenting meeting house and opened its now religious doors in the summer of 1777. Also envious, for far different reasons, was the incumbent of the parish. It was highly ironic that William Sellon was the son of Walter Sellon, the man who at the beginning of the decade had taken a leading role against Lady Huntingdon's Calvinism. Now at its end, his son would prove to be her 'sure Enemy & Persecutor'.[63] William Sellon had seen a pleasure dome in his parish transformed into a competing house of worship. He wasted little time in citing Jones and Taylor before the Consistorial Court of the Bishop of London for preaching in a Dissenting chapel. The court found in Sellon's favour.

There now stepped back upon the stage the remarkable Thomas Haweis, who since the Aldwincle furore had ceased any relationship with Lady Huntingdon. She also felt betrayed that one of her former close confidantes had, in 1771, married Haweis.[64] But the Countess's expanding activities and her desperate shortage of clerical assistance led her in 1774 to re-establish connection with this man whose sermons had once made her 'tremble'. After taking services at her Bath Chapel for six weeks, he 'received her scarf' and unofficially became her domestic chaplain. She reported triumphantly that 'the Lord has sent us Mr Haweis to join our connection & indeed he is a most blessed & extraordinary minister'. Thomas Haweis was to prove truly extraordinary. His service, which he offered in spite of what he termed the Countess's 'peculiarities',[65] came not unattached with certain strings. He refused to have anything to do with Trevecca. He happily agreed to preach frequently at her Bath Chapel, 'the most important in the Kingdom', but only if he had a 'constant assistant' to lead the worship. He said that when he had to take the entire service there he perspired so profusely that the keys in his pocket rusted. Moreover, he would preach only in those of her chapels which were preserved 'inviolate for the Ministers of the Establishment whom the Laws of this Land empower you to protect' and where houses would be at his disposal.[66] He extracted from her a general promise that in future her religious services would be 'as distinct as possible to the dissenters' and set about cleansing all her chapels of anything that could appear irregular to episcopal authority.[67] In this she advised him to take 'secret & quiet means' and doubted 'his success much'.[68] In the process, Haweis stepped on a number of clerical toes that had walked Lady Huntingdon's path much longer; these men took a more pragmatic view of the maintenance of her work. One such was Thomas Wills, an evangelical clergyman from Cornwall who had married her niece and frequently served her chapels. Wills felt that Haweis was working against the Countess's best interests, but she wrote to counter any suggestion that he was doing anything other than her own bidding. Haweis tightened the knot of the Countess's obligation by informing her more than once that he had been refused a doctorate at Cambridge solely because of his connection with her and of the resulting 'enmity against me on your Ladyship's account'.[69]

Two days after receiving word that ecclesiastical authority had moved against William Taylor and Herbert Jones at Northampton Chapel, Lady Huntingdon leapt at the opportunity to fulfil her original intentions and set out from Bath 'to take possession'.[70] The round brick structure of three storeys, with a large tiled dome, was quickly altered and re-fitted according to her taste. The interior contained two complete circular galleries which incorporated an organ, box pews and an elevated pulpit fronted by a huge black eagle. Hard against the building stood a three-storey private dwelling, where she immediately took up residence and had a door knocked into the wall between house and chapel.[71] (See illustration 15.) No longer, as for the past decade, would she make her London lodgings at the home of an apothecary on Oxford Road. As for Taylor and Jones, following a brief period she planned that they re-emerge as leaders in the chapel under her dispensation. When she negotiated the lease with the owners of the building, she agreed to reimburse Taylor and Jones the several hundred pounds they initially had laid-out to convert the Pantheon.[72]

As with former such enterprises, Lady Huntingdon hoped that her presence and her peerage would protect from ecclesiastical challenge what she now called Spa Fields Chapel. However, the omens were not good, and she recognised the highly provocative nature of the venture. There was little doubt in her mind that enemies of the project were ready to attack 'the miserable maid servant'. However, she mused that 'a good man has often said to me "you often put me in mind of a Catt. Do what they will with you, you always light upon your feet."'[73] Supposing that her official chaplains were immune from ecclesiastical prosecution, with imaginative audacity she signed, on the 27th of March 1779, a document formally appointing Haweis to that position,[74] and the following day he presided and preached at the reopening of the chapel. Supposing it best to force the issue at once, she initiated a correspondence with the Bishop of London. Her argument was that by taking the chapel under her wing she was preventing it from defecting to the Dissenters. Thus she had 'agreed to take it, & to protect it regularly under the church', which would be ensured by its being 'a regular chapel of my own'. Of course, 'my privilege of having a chapel united to my own House wanted no authority to confirm it', yet she hoped that she could count on the Bishop's approbation. To put his mind at ease she assured him that 'nothing has ever caused any unhappy or unchristian differences wherever she has been'. The Bishop informed her that he was not in a position to judge how far her protection would be effective and that he would deeply regret being placed in the position of having to take any action that would offend her. But within a fortnight he wrote again to tell her that although he had been planning to visit her, he had been informed that the chapel 'will shortly be opened for the performance of Divine Service, as before; in which notice your Ladyship's name was used'. It was therefore 'too late for me to remonstrate on the impropriety of your Ladyship's interposition in this affair'.[75] The Bishop was quite correct in perceiving the Countess's action as ecclesiastical legerdemain – an attempt to thwart the decision taken against Northampton Chapel by the Consistory Court. The chapel had been closed for two Sundays; its name and patronage changed; attenders had exchanged their admission tickets for new ones, bearing the name of the Countess of Huntingdon.[76] Nothing basically had changed.

Events now followed an inexorable course. Sellon immediately took the matter back to the Consistory Court. Lady Huntingdon persisted in the claim that Spa Fields, in spite of being capable of seating over 2,000, was her private chapel as a peeress. Attenders were admitted only by ticket and, by implication, at her personal invitation. Haweis, she said, was only performing private, not public services. Besides, she and Haweis argued that the Consistory Court had no competence in a matter which concerned the rights of a peeress of the realm. 'Ten thousand enemies are around me & many of the professing world are daily setting their faces against me.' Yet neither enemy nor fearful friend was able to dissuade her from taking over the chapel or to 'shake my Confidence'. She naively believed that 'it not being in their power to affect my privileges' the matter would be thrown out by the court, 'and thus we shall tread upon the serpent'.[77] The case dragged on for over a year, when finally Haweis was found guilty and forbidden to preach in the chapel until he received episcopal authority to do so; he also was ordered to pay costs.[78] Futile letters were fired off to the Bishop of London, all the bishops and the Archbishop of Canterbury; proposed appeals to the House of Lords and the King were abandoned.[79]

Even before this inevitable outcome, Lady Huntingdon's attitude had changed from optimism to truculence. She arrived at the conclusion that 'unless they allow me my right I will secede being resolved that Christ shall be magnified. . . . If they are permitted to turn us out woe woe be to them. Death & Hell will follow fast upon' them.[80] She was beset with 'Satans malice, the enmity of the world, false Brethren, & . . . thousands of snares & difficultys'. Seeing that the only alternative to breaking the law or giving up 'all my engagements' was to secede from the Church of England and register Spa Fields as a Dissenting chapel, she chose the latter. All other evangelical enterprises in England appeared to her to 'be in peace', and she had been singled-out for persecutions which 'are each hour arising against me & only at me seems all the bitterness express'd'.[81] The reason she was being singled-out was, of course, her provocative action regarding Spa Fields, in spite of persistent friendly advice to desist. Thus she became the first English Methodist to secede from the Church of England.

Much of the bitterness came from the Countess's own ranks. Many within her chapels opposed secession. Bath, for example, was horrified by the turn of events in London. Chapels such as Bath, 'properly & originally protected by your Rank', should not be dragged into a general secession.[82] Much more awkward was the position of Anglican clerics she had patronised and who had served as preachers in her chapels. She had little difficulty in securing the agreement of her niece's husband, Thomas Wills – who had been serving for several months at Spa Fields – to secede from the Church of England. He registered as a Dissenting minister and signed Spa Field's application for registration as a Dissenting chapel on the same day, 12 January 1782.[83] Yet one minister was hardly enough. In spite of claiming that she had put no pressure on any to secede,[84] she did exactly that. She demanded it of men like Cradock Glascott,[85] and when he refused she wrote to tell others of his 'misarable fall' and expected him 'now to turn out an enemy & persecutor'. To Glascott she wrote: 'Never Never Never forget that in the height of God's greatest honours upon you, you have the misery of knowing you have declined his services.'[86] When Herbert Jones, one of the two clerics who had established the Northampton Chapel, refused, she accused him of 'villeney'. He was 'so fatal a proof of approaching apostasy that I tremble at his name'. She was convinced that 'he means a life of sensual ease'. She had 'done with him for life'.[87] Thomas Pentycross strung her along for two years, finally refusing her entreaties, which had included a 'costly present' sent to his wife. By deciding to remain within the Church of England he had 'fallen', while his wife was a 'Vixon'.[88] Henry Peckwell, who also had served the Countess's work for many years, refused, while suggesting that only Spa Fields become a Dissenting chapel, leaving all her others as before. The egregious William Piercy, late of America, while assuring Lady Huntingdon that 'every Step taken by me has been artless, & without either Duplicity, Hypocrisy or Guile', also refused and thus added the final piece of fuel to the conflagration of their relationship. His rejection of secession triggered her finally to conclude that he had been 'the most Corrupt for ten years past' in his stewardship of Bethesda. She and her lawyers now pored over fifty or so of his letters from across the years, just as one might turn a bitter eye on the correspondence of a love affair long since gone wrong.[89]

All these clergymen who refused to follow the Countess into secession she treated with fastidious contempt. They were 'plausible pleaders for Satan only',[90] driven now from her purse and presence. As the wheels of secession ground forward, she pinned her hopes on securing a mass exodus of Welsh evangelical clergy in support of her action. Her hopes were high: 'The whole association of Wales was to offer their all in supporting my cause.' Her hopes were dashed when the Welsh Association reported that it would be as possible 'to perswade the *Pope* to become *Lutheran*' as to get them to agree to secede from the Church of England.[91] Following secession, her only 'constant support' was the prospect that she might soon die, for she knew of 'no one single minister' other than Wills 'that will secede'. William Taylor, Herbert Jones's colleague, finally agreed but insisted that she make special provision for his maintenance.[92] Thomas Wills and William Taylor were the only Anglican clergymen to follow Lady Huntingdon into secession.

Before then, many, such as Joseph Townsend, William Jesse, John

Berridge, Richard de Courcey and Henry Venn had ceased preaching in her chapels. So had William Romaine, one of London's most noted evangelical preachers. He had never been a favourite with those to whom she had increasingly turned in the 1770s. Toplady had been shocked that Romaine, arguing that 'we have Rebellion enough amongst us already', opposed a reprinting of Foxe's *Book of Martyrs*. He accused Romaine of being 'so conversant with Papists . . . that he speaks, both in the Pulpit, & out of it, just what they wd have him. . . . He begins to smell of the Dead.' Others of her supporters had had bitter fallings out with Romaine during the 1770s and found in him an 'open enemy'.[93] By the mid-1770s the Countess had developed a strong distaste for this man who officially still stood as one of her chaplains.[94] Taking over Spa Fields, she wrote to him explaining her actions and intentions. She received in return a scrappy note on scrappy paper: 'Madam, I am an entire stranger to the report you mention, & do not know, nor desire to know, one single step you are taking in this matter. I wish to mind my own business & not to interfere in the least with yours.' She at once formally revoked his appointment as her chaplain.[95] Her cousin and chaplain, Walter Shirley, who had been desperate to leave Ireland ('a dreadfull Country . . . unprincipled & lawless'. 'Like a deliver'd Bird' he had longed 'to fly to the Dear People of God in England') at the secession flew back to a parish in Ireland where he soon died.[96]

None other than Thomas Haweis freed himself from his new-found association with the Countess, lest the dust of Dissent cling to him. Claiming that on principle he could no longer assist her under the new dispensation, he departed from Spa Fields before the end of 1780. Haweis believed that others had precipitated the crisis, but the impending secession 'was indeed thro' her own impetuosity, and much against my advice'. His reflections upon the matter contain this astonishing comment: 'I am persuaded if her Ladyship had then finished her course, there would have been no division or breach of communion. Another noble would have been found to afford the same patronage.'[97]

It is clear that her Ladyship was far better off with some of these clerical losses, but the cumulative effect was devastating. Moreover, the departure from her service of Haweis, Piercy, Shirley and Romaine left her without a single chaplain. Martin Madan, of course, had long since been de-scarfed, but just as the Spa Fields crisis hit its height in 1780 he published *Thelyphthora*, a notorious defence of polygamy. Fearful of guilt by such a close previous association with Madan, she had called on Haweis and Shirley to publish works rebutting him; this they immediately did, in effect their final service before departing from her.

Although a handful of Anglican clerics continued over the years on occasion to supply her chapels, any notion of maintaining, let alone expanding, the Countess's work depended upon securing new ministers. With further Anglican Orders now impossible, Lady Huntingdon and her advisers laid plans for their own connexional ordination. As with most new religious denominations, this event marked her Church's true birth. It took place at Spa Fields on the 9th of March 1783, when during a five-hour service

Wills and Taylor ordained six Trevecca students as ministers of the 'Countess of Huntingdon Connexion'. All the candidates were obliged publicly to sign a newly-drafted Confession of Faith, consisting of fifteen articles resting on a firm Calvinistic foundation and maintaining 'the infallible truth' of the Scriptures.[98] There was one notable and unexplained absence from the service, 'wanting to make it compleate': the Countess of Huntingdon.[99]

Notes

1 SH to Thomas Haweis, 29 March 1790, SMU 119.

2 General Account of Financial Separation, 9 January 1759; Lady Huntingdon's Particular Account; A General Abstract, 9 January 1759. Rayleigh.

3 SH to Thomas Wills, 7 August 1778, English MSS 338, Rylands.

4 Mr Masterman to anon., 6 November 1762, 26D53/2114. See also Suit of Walter Shirley, 26D53/1910; Lord Ferrers to anon., two letters, *c.* 1770, 26D53/2108,9. LRO; FH to EH, 11 May 1769, T3765/M/2/14/71, PRONI.

5 SH to FH, 5 October 1775, Drew A80.

6 SH to FH, 10 September 1775, Drew A78; Edward Dawson to [Lord Moira], 4 September 1775, HA 2178.

7 Walter Shirley to SH, 14 October [1775], F1/1365, CF. See also SH to FH, 28 September 1775, Drew A79.

8 SH to Sir Eardley Wilmot, n.d., Drew A110.

9 For example, Account of plate sold, 1787, E4/15/3, CF.

10 For example, SH to Lord Donegal, 15 December 1780, E4/10/2; Sir Gilbert Heathcote to SH, 28 May 1783, F1/530; M. Wills to SH, 24 September 1779, F1/1843. CF.

11 Thomas Tuppen to SH, 24 July 1777, E4/2/37, CF.

12 *An Account of the rise, Progress, and Present-State of the Magdalen Charity* (London, 1766. 3rd edition), p. 237; Vouchers, early 1770s, A2/9, CF. For examples of her occasional benevolence to individuals during the 1740s and 50s see Welsh, *Spiritual Pilgrim*, p. 93.

13 SH to Mr Carpenter, 11 December 1785, English MSS 346/185a, Rylands. In 1766 a collection for the Bath Hospital was taken in all Bath's churches and chapels, except Lady Huntingdon's. John Penrose to Peggy Penrose, 27 April 1766, Penrose, *Letters from Bath*, p. 59.

14 Recollections of John Eyre, *The Order Observed at the Countess of Huntingdon's College, at Cheshunt* (London, 1792), p. 79; SH to Spa Fields Committee, 22 July 1785, Miscellaneous letters, Rayleigh.

15 At both, the children were 'in particular' to be instructed in the Bible, taught Calvinistic doctrine and publicly catechised in the chapel. *Rules for Conducting a School for the Education of Poor Children in the Protestant Religion and Useful Learning; instituted at the Countess of Huntingdon's Chapel, Spa-Fields, Clerkenwell, 1782* (London, 1790), rule I; *Rules for the Education of Poor Children in the Protestant Religion and Useful Learning Instituted at the Countess of Huntingdon's Chapel, Bath. 1784* (Bath, 1784), rule VI.

16 Welch, *Two Chapels*, item 189. The Spa Fields school was built largely through the benefaction of one chapel member. [F.W. Willcocks], *Spa Fields Chapel and its Associations* (n.p., *c.* 1886), p. 109.

17 R. Carpenter et al. to SH, 10 April 1788, F1/722; T. Jones to George Best, 26 September [1788], F1/1334; John Lloyd to SH, 27 May 1788, F1/2021 (quotation). CF.

18 Paul Langford, *Public Life and the Propertied Englishman, 1689-1798* (Oxford, 1991), p. 570.

19 Henry Venn to J. Stillingfleet, 13 November 1769, C14, CMS. See also Theophilus Lindsey to SH, 9 May 1769, F1/62, CF.

20 Lady Frances Montagu to SH, 12 June 1777, F1/394, CF; SH to Mr and Mrs Thomas Wills, April 1777, II.c.7/3, CL.

21 Thomas Wills to SH, 21 June 1777, F1/1765, CF.

22 'A Letter from...the Countess of Huntingdon, to the Rev. Dr. William Dodd, While under Sentence of Death', *Authentic Memoirs of the Life of William Dodd* (Salisbury, [1777?]), p. 48; J. Newson to SH, 31 June 1777, F1/396, CF. 'Did you see Lady Huntingdon's absurd

letter to the Dr.? she tells him if he feels an assurance of being saved his tribulation will become matter of glory and triumph.' Elizabeth Montagu to ?, July [1777], Blunt, *Mrs. Montagu*, 2:26.

23 Edward Davies to SH, 22 May 1770, F1/94, CF.

24 For example, SH to HH, 18 May 1771, Trevecka 2695.

25 James Glazebrook to SH, 16 December 1771, F1/153; Henry Mead to SH, 16 August 1776, F1/401. CF.

26 SH to anon., [1776], SMU 113a. For their correspondence see SH to Philip Lloyd, 23 July 1776; Lloyd to SH, 17 November 1776, E3/2/9, 10, CF.

27 Diary of Henry Bourne, 13 May 1777, Aveling, *Memorials of Clayton*, p. 33.

28 SH to Frederick Cornwallis, 24 June 1777; Cornwallis to SH, 3 September 1777, E3/2/1, 2, CF.

29 Brown, 'Evangelicals and education', pp. 135-36.

30 Harding, 'Countess of Huntingdon', p. 271n.

31 Meyer, *Saint's Triumph*, p. 40.

32 Cullum, 'Synopsis of a tour', p. 54.

33 Alan P.F. Sell, 'Philosophy in the eighteenth-century dissenting academies of England and Wales', *History of Universities* 11 (1992), pp. 87, 91, 106.

34 D. Bogue and J. Bennett, *History of Dissenters from the Revolution in 1688 to the Year 1808* 4 vols. (London, 1810), 3:79. Trevecca's lack of commitment to intellectual endeavour 'casts an unfavourable light upon the whole evangelistic movement'. Deryck W. Lovegrove, *Established Church, Sectarian People. Itinerancy and the Transformation of English Dissent, 1780-1830* (Cambridge, 1988), p. 70.

35 Aveling, *Memorials of Clayton*, p. 17.

36 Thomas Suter to SH, 14 September 1782, E4/4/12 (quotation); William Dunn to SH, 22 September 1777, F1/407; Thomas Parish to SH, 4 December 1782, F1/494 (quotation); Thomas Wills to SH, 7 December 1783, F1/1918 (quotation). CF.

37 John Williams to SH, 14 December 1787, F1/1972; same to George Best, 12 January 1788, F1/1981. CF.

38 See Lyles, *Methodism Mocked*, p. 65.

39 William Aldington to SH, [1773 or 1774], F1/1290, CF.

40 John Williams to SH, July, 21 February 1788, F1/2027, 706; Samuel Phillips to SH, 31 October 1783, F1/562. CF.

41 S. Seager to George Best, 12 November 1788, F1/782; A. Dixon to SH, November 1783, F1/572. CF.

42 Robert Parsons to SH, 20 November 1771, F1/145; George Baylis to SH, 10 July [1772], F1/1297. CF.

43 William Aldridge to SH, 29 April 1775, F1/1715, CF.

44 SH to Thomas Pentycross, [1781], Countess of Huntingdon letters, Rayleigh.

45 SH to Judith Wadsworth, 27 December 1765; SH to anon., 5 July 1766. SMU 57, 73.

46 Thomas Green to SH, 14 March 1781, F1/1860, CF; Edmund Jones to SH, 15 May 1789, Ebley MSS, D.2538/8/1, Gloucestershire Record Office.

47 For example, John Child to SH, 23 July 1789, F1/2090, CF; *Memoirs of Thomas Wills* (London, 1804), pp. 199-200; Wilks, *Memoirs of Mark Wilks*, p. 56.

48 T. Morley to SH, 22 June 1789, F1/841; Richard Munn to SH, 19 August 1789, F1/853. CF.

49 SH to Selina Wills, 1 April 1782, II.c.7/13, CL; G. Meller to SH, n.d., F1/1229; John Williams to SH, 23 August 1788, F1/760. CF.

50 SH to Mr Carpenter, [2 November 1785], Black 133.

51 Edmund Burke to SH, [late 1771 or early 1772], Seymour, *Life and Times*, 2:287.

52 Thomas Belsham, *A Sermon, Occasioned by the Death of the Rev. Theophilus Lindsey* (London, 1808), p. 41; Registers of Peers Chaplains, FV/1, Vol. XI, f. 196, Lambeth Palace Library.

53 Theophilus Lindsey to Lord John Rawdon, 25 July, 9 November 1758, 21 April 1759, T3765/M/2/20/5, 7, 8, PRONI.

54 Theophilus Lindsey to SH, 11 August 1755, Drew B30.

55 *Admissions to the College of St John the Evangelist in the University of Cambridge* 2 vols. (Cambridge, 1893, 1903), 2:516-18; Martin Fitzpatrick, 'Heretical religion and radical

political ideas in late eighteenth-century England', in Eckhart Hellmuth (ed.), *The Transformation of Political Culture* (Oxford, 1990), p. 351.

56 Belsham, *Memoirs of Theophilus Lindsey*, p. 2n.

57 Harding, 'Countess of Huntingdon', p. 292.

58 Thomas Gibbons to SH, 5 June 1777, F1/1761, CF. This minister, Henry Mayo, had at the time of the Aldwincle affair argued that the 'extraordinary gifts of the Holy Ghost ceased' since the New Testament era. He also depicted Thomas Haweis as an utter rogue. [Henry Mayo], *Aldwinckle. A Candid Examination* (London, 1767), pp. 3-4, 56-57.

59 Dissenting Deputies Minutes (1778), MS 3083/2, pp. 278, 280, Guildhall Library.

60 SH to Mr and Mrs Thomas Wills, April 1778, II.c.7/3, CL.

61 Pinks, *History of Clerkenwell*, pp. 141-44; SH to anon., [1776], quoted in 'History of Spafields Chapel', *Evangelical Register* 9 (1837), p. 3.

62 Walter Shirley to SH, 28 October 1776, F1/368, CF.

63 SH to Thomas Haweis, 13 July 1790, SMU 126.

64 Judith Wadsworth (the surname actually was Wordsworth, although Lady Huntingdon always addressed her as Wadsworth) and the Countess had undergone an acrimonious 'separation' over some failed attempt they had entered into 'for promoting...the Gospel among the Quakers'. Haweis began to pay his court in 1768, at the height of the Aldwincle controversy, and candidly made it clear that he had his eye on her family's interest in rich mining holdings in Wales. But Martin Madan vigorously opposed the relationship and was instrumental in dividing her family to the extent that she was 'disinterited'. Haweis had even been planning to give up the ministry in order to move to Wales to superintend these mines. In the event, Madan 'refused all intercourse with us and after our marriage continued in a state of irreconcilable Enmity to the Day of his death'. Thomas Haweis, MS autobiography, pp. 111-12, 117-19 (quotations from pp. 112, 119, 124), ML B1176, Mitchell.

65 SH to Judith Wadsworth, 24 January 1767, SMU 75; SH to John Hawksworth, 2 April 1774, G2/1/11, CF; Thomas Haweis, MS autobiography, pp. 123-24, ML B1176, Mitchell.

66 Thomas Haweis to SH, n.d., n.d., F1/1189, 1192, CF; SH to Haweis, 21 March 1777, SMU 94. For the rusted keys see Haweis, MS autobiography, p. 125, ML B1176, Mitchell.

67 SH to Thomas Haweis, 20 February 1777, SMU 93.

68 SH to Thomas Haweis, 17 October 1777, SMU 96; SH to Mr & Mrs Thomas Wills, April 1778, II.c.7/3, CL (quotation).

69 SH to Thomas Wills, 1 April 1777, Letters of SH, 1774-1784, English MSS 338, Rylands; Thomas Haweis to SH, 23 June 1777; n.d. (quotation), F1/395, 1190, CF.

70 SH to John Hawksworth, 16 February 1779, Letters of SH, 1774-1784, English MSS 338, Rylands.

71 Dowling, 'Countess of Huntingdon's chapels', p. 104.

72 SH to Mr & Mrs Thomas Wills, 16 February 1779, Letters of SH, 1774-1784, English MSS 338, Rylands; Articles of Agreement for Spa Fields Chapel, 22 March 1779, Rayleigh.

73 SH to John Hawksworth, 16 February 1779, Letters of SH, 1774-1784, English MSS 338, Rylands; SH to [Thomas] Beale, 9 March 1779, G2/2, CF.

74 Registers of Peers Chaplains, FV/1, Vol. XV, f. 40, Lambeth Palace Library. Legally, she could only maintain two domestic chaplains, though she frequently flouted the rule by appointing several without registering them. See Langford, *Polite and Commercial People*, p. 270; Welch, *Spiritual Pilgrim*, pp. 151-52.

75 SH to Robert Lowth, 25 February, 19 March 1779, E3/2/4, 8; Lowth to SH, 26 February, 11 March 1779, E3/2/5, 7. CF.

76 Note of lease, n.d., E3/2/12, CF.

77 SH to [Thomas] Beale, 6 April 1779, G2/2, CF; SH to Selina Wills, 11 May 1779, Letters of SH, 1774-1784, English MSS 338, Rylands.

78 Records of the case are printed in Francis, 'Selina, Countess of Huntingdon', pp. A131-49, taken from Libels and Assignations, 1776-81; and Personal Answers Book, 1761-96, Greater London Record Office. For the legal struggle see also Harding, 'Countess of Huntingdon', pp. 309-18; Welch, *Spiritual Pilgrim*, pp. 155-59.

79 SH to Bishop of London, n.d.; Thomas Wills, Cradock Glascott, William Taylor to Archbishop of Canterbury and Bishops, 30 June 1780; SH, note, n.d., E3/3/7,10, E3/2/16, CF; Nathaniel Rowland to Thomas Wills, 9 June 1779, II.c.10/4, CL.

80 SH to Selina Wills, 3 September 1779, Letters of SH, 1774-1784, English MSS 338,

Rylands. As early as 1776 she expressed the fear that she might be turned out of the Church of England. SH to anon., [1776], SMU 113a.

81 SH to [Thomas] Beale, 20 August 1779, 13 August 1780, G2/2; SH to John Hawksworth, 4 August 1780, G2/1/21. CF.

82 Thomas Pentycross to SH, [*c.* 1780], F1/1252, CF. Bath was not registered as a Dissenting chapel until 1788. Harding, 'Countess of Huntingdon', p. 329.

83 Spa Fields Minutes, 11, 12 January 1782, Welch, *Two Chapels*, item 175.

84 SH to John Hawksworth, 4 August 1780, G2/1/21, CF.

85 Spa Fields Minutes, 19 April 1781, Welch, *Two Chapels*, items 144, 145.

86 SH to Thomas Wills, 8 February 1782, II.c.7/11, CL; SH to Cradock Glascott, 12 October 1781, E4/10/18, CF.

87 SH to Thomas Wills, 8 February 1782, II.c.7/11, CL.

88 Mrs Pentycross to SH, 11 February 1784, E4/13/10; John Lloyd to SH, January 1784, E4/13/25; William Taylor to SH, 18 March 1784, F1/1934. CF.

89 Henry Peckwell to SH, 31 July 1780, F1/469; WP to SH, 4 December 1782, A4/2/28 (quotation); SH to anon., n.d., A4/5/9 (quotation). Piercy threatened to publish her letters to him, unless she paid him £500. Piercy to SH, 21 January 1784, A4/6/18. CF.

90 SH to Mr Evans, 10 June 1782, E4/10/19, CF.

91 SH to anon., 17 September 1779, SMU 102; Peter Williams to SH, 18 August 1780, F1/1856, CF.

92 SH to Mr and Mrs Thomas Wills, 7 May (quotation), 1 April (quotation), 23 July, 10 September 1782, II.c.7/14, 13, 15, 16, CL.

93 Augustus Toplady to SH, 30 July 1776, Augustus Montague Toplady Papers, Coll. 98, Emory University Library; Henry Peckwell to SH, 5 May 1774, F1/288. See also Walter Shirley to SH, 28 October 1776, F1/368. CF.

94 SH to Judith Haweis, 7 October 1775, SMU 86. Upon learning that he was increasingly dismissive of Christians who claimed to be led by the Holy Spirit, she wrote to Romaine a highly critical letter, informing him that his position had 'abundantly griev'd me'. SH to William Romaine, September 1776, SMU unnumbered.

95 William Romaine to SH, [February or March 1779], E3/3/12, CF; Registers of Peers Chaplains, 23 March 1779, FV/V, Vol. XV, f. 37, Lambeth Palace Library.

96 Walter Shirley to SH, 14 September 1779, F1/448 (quotation); same to SH, 17 September 1782, E4/1/24. CF.

97 Thomas Haweis MS autobiography, pp. 124, 131 (quotations), 176, ML B1176, Mitchell.

98 *An Authentic Narrative of the Primary Ordination* (London, 1784), p. 77. The Fifteen Articles are printed in Welch, *Two Chapels*, pp. 88-92, with the quotation from Article 2. Roughly one-third of the Confession was derived from the Thirty-Nine Articles, and a half from the Westminster Confession of Faith. Kenneth Morey, 'The theological position of the Countess of Huntingdon's Connexion', B.A. dissertation, C.N.A.A., 1990, pp. 26, 31. Those portions of the Thirty-Nine Articles that did not appear to validate a Calvinistic position were scrupulously excluded.

99 William Hodson to SH, 10 March 1783, Welch, *Two Chapels*, item 187.

Chapter 12

'He honours me most by my living a martyr'

With ordination in its own hands, the new Church now added to England's religious map was able to produce sorely needed manpower. However, for the Countess of Huntingdon this advance was counterbalanced by a growing demand from ministers and congregations for a much greater say in the conduct of affairs. The new denomination proved to be constantly haemorrhaging towards Dissent. In 1771 the recently-formed chapel at Dover had hymned the Countess's praise during their services:

> Give reward of grace and glory
> To thy faithful handmaid dear,
> Let the incense of our hearts be
> Offered up in faith and prayer
> Bless, O Bless her, Bless, O Bless her
> Now henceforth, for evermore.[1]

Twelve years on, in the wake of secession, Dover sang a different tune, producing 'incendiary Verses' against her, referring to her as 'Old Pope' and anxious 'to throw off my Ladys Government'. When she wrote angrily to a student, demanding that he fulfil her orders to keep itinerating, he replied:

> I think it is very hard that a person who has a providential call from a Church which is destitute of a pastor must be obliged to refuse it merely because he had taken a rash step at his Entrance into the Connection and had entered into an Engagement for four years merely to range up & down the country & have no settled place to the disturbing frequently of settled churches & unsettling them.

When she accused him of being unfaithful, he responded: 'I am quite unconcerned on that account, being fully convinced of my right to go where the Lord is pleased ... to lead.'[2] Never was the problem stated with more precision. Her men increasingly yearned to settle, and their obedience would be to God, not Countess. The worst possible had occurred: Lady Huntingdon could no longer pretend to be a faithful Anglican, and her absolute authority over men and chapels was being threatened by a rising tide of self-assertion. Protected now by the Toleration Act, preachers and people realised that they had also gained protection from their patroness. Her only answer was to attempt to assert authority ever more decisively. The result was a permanent rupture in her relations with literally dozens of her former supporters, along with a number of chapels. 'Owen is discharged the Connection. . . . Half hearts & designing views can do us no good.'[3]

As Lady Huntingdon's Connexion assumed its shape, many of those preachers whose loyalty she demanded had cause to seek alternative routes to their ecclesiastical destinies. There was change, development, even decay in the fledgling denomination. Yet the Countess lacked any sense of historical development, or of the altering or maturing needs of individuals. Once committed, any subsequent evidence of a slackening of loyalty to her personal command branded them in her eyes as turncoats. It was all very well for her to insist that her followers forsake everything to follow the way of self-sacrifice; but she had nothing else to which to devote her life, her time, her capacious energies. Those who supported her had other considerations: families, earning money, self-fulfilment, status. They indeed could appear to her far too worldly. She had been their patron, yet such men felt increasingly patronised. Quite simply, the walls of her authority became increasingly porous.

The choice of Spa Fields as Lady Huntingdon's permanent residence had serious repercussions, not least of all at Bath, which along with Trevecca hitherto had served as centre of operations. With her absence, Bath Chapel – not a stranger to strife – was thrown into unremitting turmoil. Not only was there the contention with her regarding the school, which created a 'flame of fury',[4] but her secession from the Church of England had produced havoc. The Bath people had been delighted with the services of Thomas Pentycross, but she disowned him when he refused to secede. One member wrote to her, wondering if 'you have the Glory of God or your own Fame most at Heart' by demanding it of Pentycross. Another, a member of the chapel committee, informed her that they were 'sick & tired of such Duplicity as . . . found in your Ladyships conduct'. Her 'sophistry is plainly seen through by a great number of the Congregation'. Her plan now was to give the Bath Chapel to William Taylor as his 'private property', presumably as a reward for his agreeing to secede. She had told them of her 'right to dispose' of her chapels 'as a Guinea' from her 'pocket to any . . . person'. For his part, Pentycross 'incriminates yr Ladyship wth a severity very unbecoming'. Four years later, in 1788, she was told from Bath that 'for a long time past we have had great confusion amongst us and it still continues to increase. . . . Most of the principal subscribers have resigned their seats.'[5] Attacks from the likes of John Wesley were galling enough; yet when her spiritual children became men and proceeded to mount successful challenges to her authority from within her own ranks, the Countess was thrown into confused agitation. Such treachery was a marked result of the decided hardening of her attitudes during the 1770s which solidified in the following decade. Her path was now littered with broken relationships, as she futilely fought to exercise an ever-tightening grasp of men and missions.

Lady Huntingdon's retirement to Spa Fields, 'quite fatigued out of my life',[6] put further miles between her and her college at Trevecca, where securing – let alone retaining – a resident master had proved increasingly difficult. By 1784 she was receiving plaintive letters: 'We are now ready to conclude you have forgotten your little, poor, afflicted Family, at the College.'[7] When she departed Trevecca in the spring of 1787 after a six-weeks stay, it was for the last time.[8] In fact, as early as 1782 she was thinking of uprooting the college, urged by Wills to move it close to London. Then for a time it was planned to move it to a site adjoining the chapel in Swansea.[9] Nothing came of these schemes.

Meanwhile Trevecca was left to wither on the vine. In 1785 the Countess removed the master for engaging in theological disputation, which was strictly against her instructions, and for becoming so agitated in the heat of the discussion that blood rushed to his face, burst through his nose and onto the tablecloth, which was certainly against her sense of propriety.[10] By now the unfocused nature of the institution's objectives was patently painful. The opinion of the final Trevecca master regarding the students' quality has been noted. 'Indeed the senior students that are here now are by far more stupid upon the whole than any I ever had', he reflected.[11] Apart from the raw quality of the students, their constant displacement to pursue itinerant preaching throughout the kingdom wreaked havoc with any sense of academic continuity. A number of chapels were increasingly unimpressed by the student-preachers. With regard to one, 'it is the opinion of us & all Judicious hearers that if your Ladyship would take him into the College till he makes a greater Proficiency in his Learning it may be much to his advantage'. This chapel went on to ask her not to send any further students. Even she came to reflect, looking back over all the students 'under my hands' since the founding of Trevecca, that 'I have been offended' with them.[12] In other words, she had failed to find a single dutiful son. In fact, during the late 1780s she had virtually abandoned them. Numerous letters begged her to pay the long overdue accounts of local tradesmen clamouring for their money.[13] Rent for the college building and lands had not been paid for two years; the tax authorities were threatening to seize Trevecca's goods; and the Countess had made not a single reply to the college's urgent letters. 'O that the Lord wood please to permit and strengthen your Ladyship . . . to come once more to College then I wood think that all things wood be well.' She firmly insisted that her students walk to Bath to attend a service of ordination, so that 'no expense may be incurred by horses'.[14] The ten students in 1788 were virtually in rags. The college was down to two horses, one lame the other totally blind. 'It would grieve any man's heart to see our poor horses undertaking such journeys as they do.'[15] Effectively, the college had been hobbled. Yet the students attempted to keep up their spirits. At a preaching service they 'did nothing but jump cry sing and pray till it was near 12 a clock. At other times they are the same.'[16]

The secession crisis contributed significantly to a bunker mentality, yet Lady Huntingdon's belief that she was being persecuted from many directions was worn as a badge of pride. Her Spa Fields cathedral became for her a castle. Drawing from her arsenal further alarming military metaphors, she wrote that God would not be satisfied with 'Pigmys in his Cause of War & the Lord is a mighty man of valour a mighty man of war – his soldiers must be of the Prus[s]ian order.' 'I will be the Pla[gue] of all that want to sleep in a whole skin.' 'Almighty strength is ours, it is all engaged to defeat the devil's purposes. . . . I think I see him bruised under my feet, begging hard for life, but . . . the Lord shall give him his death's blow, and my soul triumph in the strength [of the] Lord.'[17] With 'very much land before us yet to be possessed', only true dedication could 'rid some of the evil beasts out of our land'. It would be 'war to all that are at ease in Zion'. 'Faith & fighting must make churches & ministers that will meet with an all Hail from our dear master in the great day of accounts.' As for those evangelical Christians who had broken with her, 'let us pray & believe they will be "as the ashes under the souls [*sic*] of our feet"'.[18] These were contagious metaphors, unfortunately method as well as metaphor. Supporters assured her that they had 'drawn the sword' and in God's defence 'having thrown away the scabbard, cannot sheath it, but in the Bosom of his Foes & yr Ladyship's'.[19] The stage upon which the Countess of Huntingdon acted was rarely less than cosmic.

On the eve of her secession from the Church of England, the Countess mounted a momentous mission. She sent three ministers on extended preaching tours throughout England during the summer of 1781, 'for a universal publication of Good News to Sinners over this land'. She expected at least a million people to hear and 'rejoice to all eternity'. This gospel barnstorming she believed to be England's only hope: 'This people by this <u>may</u> have a chance to prevent the measure of their Iniquity being filled & so not fitted for destruction.' With, in her view, every other religious agency in the nation having failed, the 'Lord gives us thus to stand in the gap & with my poor old arms of weakness'.[20]

Over the life of Spa Fields Chapel the Countess brooded with commanding eye. Ever refusing to allow any of her ministers to settle in one place, to the end of her life with an increasingly shaky hand but deep well of ink, she continued to write constant letters, exercising a meticulous control over their movements. Indeed, believing that any unpregnant moment was a faithless one, if nothing else was to hand she wrote her letters, frequently devoting six or seven hours a day to the task. 'I have been writing since ten this morning & so fatigued I am ready to faint.'[21] Often these letters passed the line between exhortation and incantation, and, as in the past, they served as a means for emotional release. On occasion, her appalling handwriting meant that her men were incapable of deciphering instructions,[22] and it became nearly frantic during times of high tension. (See illustration 16.) Yet her letter-writing often provided her companionship.

Spa Fields received her special care regarding preaching. She ensured that the people heard such sermons as that preached by a former Trevecca student, now a minister in her Connexion:

> How will you, gospel despisers, who have heard Christ preached in Spa-Fields Chapel, and elsewhere, be alarmed to see Jesus sitting upon his

> judgment throne, in the clouds, preparing vengeance for you who have despised his word, neglected his gospel, and blasphemed his name! . . . you daring sinners [with] your secret sins, and midnight impurities; your sins committed in the dark. . . . How will the presumptuous soul be alarmed to see the bottomless pit open its insatiable mouth; and with an horrid visage and greedy eye looking, gaping, yawning, to swallow him up!

Warming to this theme, the preacher described what awaited them:

> Rivers of fire, in which wicked spirits are plunged, rolled, tormented, and burned after death. . . . You have heard from this pulpit many times, by many of God's ministers, that the day of account will come. . . . It is at the peril of your souls that you speak one word against the things which you have heard.[23]

Lady Huntingdon received the delicious news that, as punishment from God, William Sellon had been struck with palsy, 'his mouth so distorted as to be unable to speak'.[24] Yet the sense of her standing alone was further undergirt by her broken relationships with all other Christian groupings and denominations. Not only Wesleyans, not only the authorities of the Church of England, not only those of the older Dissenting bodies: now she angrily cut-off all contact with Whitefield's London Tabernacle Chapel and others in relationship with it. In earlier days, induced by Whitefield, she had assisted the Tabernacle. But to her displeasure it and Whitefield's other London chapels had been registered in 1764 as Dissenting places of worship, while he was absent in America.[25] By 1785 she was persuaded that the Tabernacle and others in the Whitefieldian Connexion were making strenuous efforts to steal her men and thus were 'universally to be rejected'. She also fell out with one of the managers of the Tabernacle who was supporting William Piercy's financial claims against her.[26]

The Countess's arrival at Spa Fields, the subsequent secession and her increasing triumphalism also dug a wide chasm between her and the emerging Evangelical wing of the Church of England. Some of these men 'have set their faces in open war against me & will join heartily with any evil adversary. But my cause is in the Lords hands.'[27] Others, such as John Berridge, Henry Venn and John Newton, pursued their course more quietly, redoubling efforts to invigorate the parish life of the Established Church.[28] Thus the philanthropic 'Clapham sect' of Evangelicals, centred round the layman John Thornton, developed apart from Lady Huntingdon.[29] Her active support of slavery further widened the division. Hannah More took pains to show that she had never attended services at any of the Huntingdon chapels. The effort of John Venn, the clerical leader of the Clapham group, to explain his father's earlier relationship with the Countess and 'irregular' clergy as a temporary aberration, is further vivid illustration of the attitude within Evangelical circles. Her correspondence with Thornton ended soon after the secession, when he informed her that his efforts must be directed towards the work of parishes.[30] Prior to the secession his wife had written to John Newton about the difficulties caused in Lady Huntingdon's chapels by the constant turnover of ministers and concluded that 'the people seem to need a more stated ministry which [I] am persuaded more & more, is best to abide by'. And soon after Lady Huntingdon had most bitterly dismissed one of her ministers, Thornton befriended him.[31]

In this context, the Countess's connection with the Earl of Dartmouth is instructive. She began to harbour doubts regarding his commitment to Calvinistic doctrines and, amazingly, sent a minister on what proved to be a frustrated attempt to drive the point home.[32] When she sought to have a clergyman 'quit the regular service of the Church, and to preach out', Dartmouth's chaplain and incumbent of his parish church informed Dartmouth that he had strongly advised against it, 'as you know I have always disapproved of irregular Doings'.[33] These ecclesiastical differences donned a political dress when in 1774 Dartmouth laid the Quebec Act before the House of Lords. To many of Lady Huntingdon's religious circle it was 'astonishing ... how good Ld Dartmouth c[oul]d ever be prevailed upon to produce such a Bill' since it established Roman Catholic rights in Canada.[34] She was by no means unusual in her abhorrence and fear of Roman Catholicism, but her intensity in the matter brooked no competition. The Countess's words against Catholics were harsh,[35] and when they built a chapel and school in Bath she was beside herself: 'Papists over England threaten terrable days against this land & the Church of God', although she found some hope in the prophecy that 'Popery and Babylons downfall will be in the year of 1790'.[36]

A year after the Countess took over Spa Fields, London experienced the turmoil of the Gordon Riots. In 1779 a 'Protestant Association' was formed in Scotland to protest at the proposed limited repeal of penal laws there against Roman Catholics, repeal that had been peacefully accomplished for England the preceding year with the Catholic Relief Act. This Association was successful, through rioting and civil disobedience, in having the proposal abandoned in Scotland; and, savouring this success, the Association turned its attention to the south, seeking to force repeal of the freshly-passed English legislation. To that end, the eccentric young Lord George Gordon was dispatched to London at the end of 1779, where he commenced gathering signatures for a petition. He told parliament that the 'indulgences given to Papists have alarmed the whole country'. If parliament needed any persuading, Gordon said that they 'will find 120,000 men at my back'.[37] By June 1780, he had collected a petition containing 44,000 signatures. More ominously he had collected in St George's Field some 60,000 supporters of the Protestant Association. Over the next several days London was thrown into chaos, with Catholic chapels and homes destroyed to the piercing cries of 'No Popery'. The mob violence spilled-over into the successful freeing of prisoners from several gaols, and unsuccessful attacks on Lambeth Palace and the Bank of England. At one point, well over thirty fires raged in the City alone. Ten thousand troops were poured into the capital, turning Hyde Park into an armed camp. During that dreaded first week in June, 300 people were killed in the London rioting, twenty-five eventually executed for their roles and substantial property damage sustained. Between the Great Fire and the Blitz it was London's most devastating destruction.[38]

Although the rioters were active in Clerkenwell, they took deliberate care that no damage be done to Spa Fields when one of their leaders announced that his mother worshipped there. The chapel was spared, it was said, because it was deemed to be a 'No Popery place'.[39] The Countess was assured that it had been 'providence which delivered & preserved you from sharing in the dreadful devastations occasioned by the mob'.[40]

At his trial in 1781 Gordon's serving barrister was his cousin, Thomas Erskine, the brother of Lady Huntingdon's permanent companion, the lot-drawing Lady Anne.[41] Gordon's chief defence witness was the Reverend Erasmus Middleton, one of the six students expelled from Oxford in 1768 and a protégé of Thomas Haweis.[42] Middleton had been one of three expellees who went on to receive episcopal ordination and in 1778 was preaching at the Countess's Mulberry Gardens Chapel in Wapping. Moreover, he had just taken over as editor of the periodical she supported, the *Gospel Magazine*, on the death of Augustus Toplady. A member of the Protestant Association committee and related to Gordon by marriage, Middleton argued that any thought of creating violence had been absent from their intentions; in spite of the prosecution's serious questioning of Middleton's veracity, for lack of any hard evidence Gordon was found not guilty.[43]

Immediately following the riots the *Gospel Magazine* published a fulsome defence of the Protestant Association, while distancing all concerned from the depredations of the rioters. This they published along with a lurid description of how 200,000 'inoffensive' Protestants in Ireland during the reign of Charles I had been 'inhumanly butchered' at the instigation of the 'Romish priests'. 'This was but a little above a century ago, and . . . Rome is still the same. . . . Her bigoted zealots would not shudder at the like cruelties, if their priests required them at their hands.' A month following the Gordon riots the Countess wrote that 'Popery, if ever established, must involve the body of the Church in all its absurdities of faith & practice'.[44]

However, with ecclesiastical authority bearing down on her as the secession crisis reached its head, Lady Huntingdon hardly wished to incur the additional wrath of civil authority, and the riots had made her extremely fearful of guilt by association. Shortly after Lord Gordon's acquittal, he made plans to stand as a Member of Parliament for the City of London, but anxieties regarding renewed rioting forced him to withdraw. This relieved 'your Ladyship from many fears and cares'. The Countess implied that Gordon had been among 'our best friends'; but she now instructed her Spa Fields Committee to arrange a secret meeting with the Mulberry Gardens Committee '& inform & enforce caution & care in publick matters. . . . I consider this way in private to you to be most effectual that the pulpit may be kept for the Lords services, & not as the medium of Politics.'[45] How her London pulpits had been used during the recent crisis can only be imagined.

It was a member of Theophilus Lindsey's Unitarian chapel in London who initiated the Catholic Relief Bill in 1778. Lindsey had long been uneasy with bitter anti-Roman Catholicism, and by the 1780s he and a large number of Dissenters had come round to espousing the cause for univeral toleration, including Roman Catholics.[46] To her ladyship, 'to give toleration to papists & dissenters' was 'to attack . . . [the] way of God'. The Church of England had been worth fighting for, worth saving, since it had stood as a bulwark against the Church of Rome. Yet now even the bishops appeared willing to contemplate religious toleration, while at the same time 'fall[ing] on me with such violence, [I] that contended all her life for the Church'. This toleration was simply too much for her to grasp, let alone contemplate: it was 'against the truth itself'.[47]

Whichever way she now turned, the Countess saw the crumbling of certainties, and she focused especially on what she perceived to be a devilish and deadly Church of Rome. Following the end of the American War of Independence, she projected new plans to reclaim and resuscitate Bethesda, to build colleges for Indians and towns for British settlers, all under her tight control. When a suspicious new America rejected all these schemes and the Countess was left with her Georgia lands apparently to no purpose, the authorities of that state asked her to donate them to the university they were planning. They sent her the plan. She sent her refusal, shocked that full freedom of religion was to be allowed to both staff and students. That would mean, she wrote, that 'even Popish Bishops & Tutors may become the Guardians of the youth & their instructors'. The result would be 'the most wretched', a result inevitable when Roman Catholicism was tolerated. She insisted that she must remain faithful to Whitefield as well as to her witness to Protestantism.[48]

Three months later, in April 1787, the Countess, now in her eightieth year, was busily preparing to take her first step outside the United Kingdom. She had received news that 'above six Hundred Protestant familys are now in Brussells, & much expectation is raised for my Establishment there'. Indeed, they had 'a large Chapel taken for me', which could be used for all her ministers. This opportunity had created 'envy, malice & jealousies' among her religious competitors in England, but she asked God to pity them and thanked him that 'to the most unworthy he yet shews his loving kindness & tender mercies'. Truly remarkable reports were circulating. Charles Wesley had been told that she had secured a Jesuit college in Brussels as her chapel. A correspondent delighted in the fact that Lady Huntingdon was going to 'attack the enemy in his strongholds'.[49] For this venture she had chosen Thomas Wills to accompany her, but the day before the planned departure she received the first of his apparently frenzied letters: 'Oh, my dear Madam, trust to no intelligence you receive from . . . Brussels.' Wills claimed to have uncovered 'a deep Plot laid' by 'our popish & hellish adversaries . . . to get you out of this kingdom, to defeat your work and usefulness here; & to get you into their own hands'. The plan was to snatch her up on the continent and murder her. Although it might not have been done by

> gunpowder, poison would have effectually removed you out of the way & who knows but the popish Massacres would have been acted over again? . . . [You have] been delivered from assassination, or Poison, & death, to put in execution their infernal purposes. . . . But depend upon it, my dear Madam, tho' this Project is frustrated, another will be soon hatched. . . . The devil & the Papists will be contriving some other Plan to get us all into their Trap.

'Every Congregation in your whole Connexion should be called upon to join in public thanksgiving. Pray, my dearest Madam, charge them to do it in London; as I will here [at Bath] & at Bristol.' She must reject the voices of others who may be 'pressing your dr Ladysp still to go'. Wills would 'chearfully' have gone, but the Papal plot clearly showed that 'the Lord has not given you a special Call' to make the journey. Besides, he seriously doubted 'the information of the hundreds of Protestants longing for your coming'.[50]

It may be suspected that Wills's commitment to the journey had from the beginning been somewhat less than wholehearted. As for the supposed warm welcome awaiting the Countess in Brussels, rather than a cruel plot it far more likely had all along been a cruel hoax, a 'joke' along the lines of the muff-enclosed cuckoo at the Spa Fields service. Moreover, her supporters were highly disturbed by the practical implications of the intended shift of her gaze to Europe. She had, in fact, made it clear that she would have diverted all her financial resources away from England while she was in Brussels, where she had planned to be for 'some time'. This would have thrust the full weight of financial burden upon her chapels.[51]

Thomas Wills had already become uneasy regarding his position. He had sacrificed his place in the Established Church in order to lead the work at Spa Fields as well as to handle many of the numerous negotiations with existing and potential chapels in the expanding Connexion. As one of the two clergymen who had seceded from the Church of England, he now was alarmed by a plan put forward by the Countess only months before the Brussels débâcle, a plan to give clergymen who had remained within the Church of England authority over the Connexion's affairs.[52] Wills had not seceded to endure such an ironic, and to him unfair, turn of events. He had believed that he would be Lady Huntingdon's closest clerical supporter during her life and her successor as leader of the new denomination after her death.

There were other differences between them. Lady Huntingdon's insistence that only constant preaching would produce people's salvation left little room for the development of Christian nurture, which to her smacked of Wesleyan perfectionism. Wills, on the other hand, saw a desperate need in her chapels for a programme of patient growth in grace. Moreover, as she attempted to provide for the continuance of her work after her demise, the Countess proposed that her college have only laymen as its trustees. Wills could not accept what he considered a further slight to his position. All these differences pointed to the inevitable. In confidence, he communicated his growing concerns and, possibly, observations regarding her gullibility over Brussels, in letters to his colleague William Taylor. It was a confidence grossly misplaced, as Taylor took the opportunity of settling scores with a man who had always taken precedence over him at Spa Fields. Wills's letters were spread before Lady Huntingdon. He had accused her of antinomianism and 'as if my Intellect was gone'.[53] Needless to say, Wills was expelled from her service and her sight, supplanted at Spa Fields by the inadequate, and antinomian, John Bradford. Upon his dismissal, Wills sought permission to preach one last sermon, which she roundly refused. Within three weeks he published a 'farewell address' to the people, stressing that the Countess had dismissed him: he had not resigned. An uproar followed, especially when some of his Spa Field's supporters handed copies to all members as they left the chapel, and the Countess stepped in to stop their distribution.[54] Departing with Wills was his wife, Lady Huntingdon's niece, goddaughter and namesake. Selina Wills had been a steady helper and supporter for a decade, 'my dearest creature' as the Countess had been wont to address her, but whom she now snubbed in public.[55]

Lady Huntingdon had in the past severed relationships with ministers – a list would be tedious – but Thomas Wills had a wide following within her Connexion. This he now cultivated by personal visits and the distribution of his printed *Farewell Address*. At Bristol he 'spits his Venom like a Viper'. There he was able to muster much support among people who were ready 'to prejudice the minds of the Society against your Ladyship'. She was advised to send a letter to be read at the chapel, to explain why she had dismissed him. Bristol was in serious confusion: 'I must . . . inform your Ladyship I think the Connection will be sensibly affected by the removal of your most valuable & much respected Minister Mr Wills.' The Countess was profoundly distraught. Wills's 'rage increases daily', and he was abusing her from pulpits, 'labouring day & night by every artifice to breed division'.[56] Not only was Spa Fields in crisis, Wills having drawn-off substantial numbers of its members, but several Connexionally ordained ministers left in sympathy with him.[57] Once again she sought comfort in prophecy, sharing with others a 'Millennium Poem'. One man responded by assuring her that the Second Coming was imminent and that Christ 'shall be revealed from Heaven with his Mighty Angels in flaming Fire, taking vengeance on them that know not God'.[58]

William Taylor had set in motion Lady Huntingdon's expulsion of Thomas Wills. Three months after that dismissal a wall next to the Bath Chapel was daubed with a large graffito: 'THE METHODIST TAYLOR TAKEN IN ADULTERY.' Although Wills's expulsion produced 'mental sufferings' from which he never fully recovered,[59] to suppose that he personally scrawled this message would be to project too ludicrous a picture. However, he certainly capitalised on the accusation in order to exact his revenge, a revenge complete when Taylor had to admit the charge.[60] Lady Huntingdon issued instructions for Taylor to be 'put out of the Connection for good'. His response was to demand of her payment of £600, but she was informed that for three years past he had been involved in 'criminal practices' regarding the Connexion's finances. For his part, Taylor accused her of refusing to pay what he was owed and ultimately, and hollowly, threatened to sue her for it. In the end, he even had to negotiate with her to secure the removal of his personal effects from chapel premises.[61]

The Countess's Connexional headquarters at Spa Fields was in disarray. There she lived in the chapel house with her constant companion, Lady Anne, and though the drains were 'often so offensive as scarce to be endured',[62] and despite her recurring bouts of gout and gallstones and one or two more serious and prolonged complaints, Lady Huntingdon's physical health was not unreasonable for her age. Yet it was during one of those prolonged periods, at the end of 1789, that she had to bear the added burden of the news of her son Francis's sudden death. It is a measure of the extent to which her firm theological orientation had the potential for bending in the face of a passionate concern for her own flesh and blood that three years earlier she had grasped at a gossamer glimmer of hope that her son might avoid damnation. The Unitarian Theophilus Lindsey told her that 'possibly the state of future punishment might be only a process of severe discipline, and that the greatest sinner might ultimately find mercy'.[63] It was a message she desperately yearned to believe, but it was a message her theology ultimately reminded her she dare not. A year before Francis's death it was clear that she was as anxious as ever, and one woman argued that he not only would be converted to Methodism but 'also be a promoter of the Gospel of Christ'. It might appear unlikely, opined the woman, but 'it shall ashuredly come to pass'.[64] It did not come to pass. Even though hurt by his frequent indifference, the Countess continued to love Francis with a dull desperation. Yet when he died he left his extensive estates and income to various members of his family, except to her. She received one bequest: his 'best enamelled gold snuff box as a token of my Gratitude and affection'.[65] As soon as she had recovered from the illness, in January 1790, she wrote a statement 'regarding her family'. It has not survived, but she concluded it by saying that 'all my present peace, & my future hopes of glory, either in whole or in part, depend wholly, fully, & finally upon his merit alone'.[66]

Although the Countess found Welsh clergymen 'slippary', she made one last effort to induce the Association of evangelical clergymen in Wales to unite their work with hers. It came to nothing, as they judged it 'impracticable'.[67] A new aspect of her character now emerged: an undisguised cynicism. Not only was she disparaging of the students she had nurtured at Trevecca for over twenty years; it was worse than that. She reflected on 'the sad experience I have had of ministers; from their want of sound principles; from pride; from interestedness, & wicked practices of all kinds'. She had had to endure 'the vilest of men' in her service, who had only assumed the 'characters of ministers . . . of Jesus Christ'. 'Alas! where my best confidence has from time to time been placed, the Lord has confounded it.'[68] One of her correspondents wrote that had he 'been in your Ladyships situation' over the many years he had known her, 'my grey hairs by this time would have been brought down with sorrow to the Grave'. What, though, could she do but soldier on? God 'honours me most by my living a martyr'.[69]

During the course of the doleful events at Spa Fields at the close of the 1780s, Lady Huntingdon had refused to correspond with William Taylor, instructing him to refer his claims direct to Thomas Haweis.[70] Truth to tell, Haweis, who like an ecclesiastical butterfly had dodged in and out of her sphere of influence, now re-entered. His wife, the Countess's former confidante Judith, had died in 1786, and two years later he married another of the Countess's boon companions, Janetta Payne Orton. Haweis discovered that it had been she, not Lady Huntingdon, who had provided the £1,000 for the purchase of the Aldwincle advowson. The wealthy Miss Orton brought to the marriage her extensive property interests in the West Indies, which included the slaves that Haweis would long continue to own. In the spring of 1789, Lady Huntingdon's desperate need for clerical leadership and the chaos created among her leading chapels from the fall-out over the Wills affair, together with Haweis's new marriage partner, brought the Countess to send him a letter 'importuning in the strongest terms my return to her help'. His wife was 'very willing to renew her old attachment'.[71]

Thomas Haweis believed that he now held every card. He agreed immediately to take over his prize, the chapel at Bath, but only after receiving from Lady Huntingdon 'the strongest assurances that the chapel should be put entirely into my care'. Moreover, he utterly refused even to be present at any ordinations undertaken by the Connexion.[72] There was, of course, no question of his seceding from the Established Church, and he continued as the frequently non-resident rector of Aldwincle. Haweis was set fair to win in one of the eighteenth-century's most dramatic struggles over church management and control. However, no sooner had he assumed the clerical leadership of Lady Huntingdon's enterprises than he discovered a lay-led movement within several chapels, centred on Spa Fields, to produce a structured and orderly form for the Connexion following the Countess's death. In fact, it was during her serious illness at the end of 1789 that several men from her London chapels met to draft such a plan, which was in distinct contrast to the single-handed leadership that had guided her enterprises. A broadly conciliar form was proposed, providing for an Association, with a significant majority of laymen in decision-making processes. It was this democratising provision that particularly horrified Haweis. He wrote to the Countess at the beginning of 1790 that he saw a 'strong attack made on your Ladyship's efforts'. He succinctly stated his vision for the future of her work: 'Where you might not chuse yourself to be the immediate Person . . . I am your servant.'[73]

Lady Huntingdon had been persuaded, however, that when she had gone the conciliar plan was the way forward. It would mean that her Connexion would be put 'into such a line of general usefulness that when the Lord calls for me my absence will not make more than an old shoe cast aside'. Haweis's approbation of the plan was 'important to my ease', and she wanted him to agree to be present at the first meeting of the new body.[74] Days later, a clearly set-out and balanced *Plan of an Association* was published 'By order of the Countess of Huntingdon', dividing her sixty-four chapels throughout England into twenty-three districts, each with a committee composed of ministers and laymen. Each district was to send one minister and two laymen to an annual General Association which would govern all Connexional affairs, including those of the college. Provision was made for regular and systematic collections to maintain all the work.[75]

Haweis, however, was adamant: he 'cannot concur in the proposed association . . . because . . . I should not chuse to be in Bondage to Laymen, or committees'. Lady Huntingdon was thrust into a dreadful position. She felt that under no circumstances could she afford to lose Haweis. Replying at once, she assured him that 'except your generous services I know of none like minded'. His 'choice in avoiding all laymen & committee men I agree to'. She appears to have believed that she could proceed with the Association plan, while allowing him alone to operate totally outside its control. At the same time, he would continue to serve her work, 'considered as my principal & justly deserved minister' and with all others in her Connexion showing him 'that honour you most heartily claim'. For three months she bombarded him with such remarkable ideas, combined with fulsome praise. 'You flatter me extremely by allowing me any name united with yours', she wrote. 'You have but to name your wishes ever as my ready commands.'[76] In the past, the Countess might at times have entreated, but never grovelled. Yet Haweis would have none of it and in June gave his ultimatum. If the plan went ahead, 'your Ladyship will love me, bless me, & dismiss me. . . . I shall wait with solicitude your Ladyship's determination. . . . While you alone direct, I wish'd & asked for no more than to serve you.' If she persists, he 'shall submit to the decision in silence, & cordially wish well to every [person?] tho' my active services may be no longer employed'. Once again, Haweis revealed his major concern to be control of the Bath Chapel. He was 'astonished' to find that Bath, always in his mind different from the rest of her enterprises, was to be brought under the control of the Association. He held one last card, and it was a trump: 'Your Ladyship has not a truer friend than Lady Ann, consider this Subject again my dear Madam I intreat you.'[77]

Lady Anne Erskine and Thomas Haweis were closely leagued in this contest, and the threat of losing not only Haweis but her close companion tipped the scales. Three weeks after Haweis's uncompromising letter, and after what must have been almost unimaginable turmoil involved in having to dismantle the well-advanced and well-publicised plan for the Association, Lady Huntingdon capitulated.[78] Haweis wasted no time in exerting his authority. 'I am much rejoiced your Ladyship never made any irrevocable engagement to any of the Ministers who have assisted you, & it is my cordial wish that during your life you never will.' Subtly calling into question her powers of judgement and addressing her as one might a somewhat senile relation, Haweis told her: 'You know the singleness of your own Eye in every confidence reposed in others you may be disappointed.' He now was free to assure her that he 'shall be proud to have my name go down coupled with your Ladyship's Patronage to another generation' and that she had from his wife and himself 'the most respectful deference I hope you will ever find'.[79]

These start-stop struggles over the nature of the future leadership of the Countess's enterprises took place in 1790. The more cynical she became about her work in England the more ready she was to project highly romanticised projects further afield. Sensing that her own time was short, she yearned to taste fruits of successful overseas missions sweeter than those she knew had been accomplished at home. Her American ventures had collapsed, along with some fleeting missionary efforts in Canada.[80] But there was a new hope. At the outbreak of the French Revolution a clerical friend had written to her joyously: 'Wonderful things in France! – what has the Lord to do for his cause! It is all for the Messiah's Kingdom.'[81] Hoping to take advantage of a France in chaos, she devised an astonishing scheme: she would approach Jacques Necker, the French minister of finance, and offer £1,000 to purchase 'the finest Church in Paris. Their finances are so low that they will rejoice to have me ... purchase it.' 'France will be for the English prodistants if I succeed.' 'A good & gracious man says I shall not die till I have a chapel in Paris.' 'The warmth of my heart to have a chapel ... at Paris fills my many moments with joy & delight.' 'Madrid may also stretch out her Hands.' She 'could drive the globe for our Immanuals kingdom to come'.[82]

Ultimately, however, the prospect of a mission to the South Seas laid claim to the Countess's ebullient zeal and highly-tuned romanticism.[83] The idea was planted in her mind by Haweis, who went so far as to approach Captain William Bligh, then planning a new voyage of his *Bounty*.[84] Haweis assured her that 'millions, if so it might please of the Lord, of Heathen to the latest posterity, might have cause to bless God for your Ladyship's zeal for their salvation'. They planned together to send two young Trevecca students. With every pulse beating hope, the Countess stated that 'the ship & all expenses attending their mission must be from me', but at the very last moment the two prospective missionaries balked, and the scheme was scuppered.[85] Yet as she lay upon her deathbed at Spa Fields, Lady Huntingdon refused to give up hope for dispatching missionaries to Tahiti.[86] In her last letter, written in her own hand eight days before her death, she was 'immersed in the great business of preparing missions for the south seas'; at the end, choking with the phlegm that was to kill her, it was her dying concern.[87]

Three months after John Wesley's death, Lady Huntingdon died, aged eighty-three. The 17th of June 1791 was the day Mozart completed 'Ave, verum corpus'. It was the same month that the Catholic Dissenters Relief Bill became law. Apparently, at the very end she did not make an ideal display of her faith, yet it was argued by those about her that 'her state did not depend on her last moments'. The doctor who attended her wrote that she had exhibited 'the greatest degree of Christian composure that ever I witnessed',[88] and his statement was made public, likely in an attempt to counter a number of negative reports that were circulating.[89] Ten days after her death, a funeral cortege of a hearse and three coaches moved from Spa Fields through Islington and Highgate. The hearse and one coach then continued all the way to Ashby de la Zouch, where the Countess of Huntingdon, dressed in a suit of white silk which she had worn at the opening of one of her chapels, finally joined her husband.[90]

Public reactions to Lady Huntingdon's death were varied in the extreme. The satirical 'Tears of Methodism' is an example of one extreme. Then, too, it was observed that 'many have, do, and will talk dishonorably of her; reproach and vilify ... her. ... How have many, the comparatively moral, as well as the prodigal and debachee, told of her death with a kind of triumph, and said, I am glad *that old devil is dead – she is gone to hell*.'[91] Three days after her death *The Times* reported: 'LADY HUNTINGDON, of pious memory took her departure from this world at her house in Spa Fields last Friday. ... By her death, and that of the no less methodistically celebrated John Wesley, the Methodists and Swadlers lose the two best pillars of their Church.'[92] The other extreme was one of the numerous sermons preached and printed on the occasion of her death. The preacher, a former Trevecca student, developed the parallel between the Countess and various notable women, holding her up as a noble successor to Queen Elizabeth in the preservation of the true faith. However, biblical women provided the best comparisons. She had been like Deborah. Improving on his theme, he compared the Countess with the humble Mary, anointing Jesus' head and feet. Yet 'Selina excelled her in all', since she had to spend more money on her work than Mary did for her ointment. Although forced to admit that 'the Lord has not personally spoken of *Selina* in the scriptures', the preacher assured his auditory that she had none the less been included in the Bible, hidden there in predictions of future saints who would bring inestimable blessings to God's people. Best of all, those who had been foolish enough to be 'her particular enemies' would receive their comeuppance. They should ponder in 'terror' the fact that in reality 'she is not dead, but sleepeth' and 'will rise up in judgment against thousands'.[93] One man had no hesitation in concluding that 'she was the greatest Woman, in the cause of the Gospel of Jesus Christ, that ever lived in the world'.[94] Yet another broke into Welsh verse, with an assurance that Lady Huntingdon had been welcomed to and escorted into heaven by George Whitefield and Howell Harris.[95]

When he heard of the passing of the Countess of Huntingdon, John Berridge reflected upon their differences but trusted to a reunion in heaven: 'For the Lord washed our hearts here, and there He will wash our brains.'[96] Indeed, it may have been Berridge who penned an anonymously-published single-sheet elegy which, while highly praising her dedicated piety, weighed that piety's cost:

> On wealth, fame, friends, as on vile dirt you trod,
> Enough for you that souls were won to God.[97]

Notes

1 Joseph Cook to SH, 21 December 1771, F1/158; Thomas Cannon to Thomas Wills, 15 July 1783, F1/534. CF.

2 Thomas Green to SH, 14 March 1781, F1/1860, CF.

3 SH to Selina Wills, 1 April 1782, II.c.7/13, CL.

4 SH to Thomas Wills, 17 March 1784, II.c.7/17, CL.

5 Anon. to SH, February 1784; Thomas Parry to SH, 5 March 1784; John Lloyd to SH, 9 March 1784; G. Ford and J. Sheppard to SH, 25 November 1788. E4/13/27, 30, 22; F1/791. CF.

6 SH to Selina Wills, 1 June 1784, II.c.7/20, CL.

7 Samuel Phillips to SH, 19 March 1784, F1/609, CF.

8 Harding, 'Countess of Huntingdon', p. 250n.

9 Thomas Pentycross to SH, 28 August 1782, F1/480; Thomas Wills to SH, 7 December 1783, F1/1918; C 18/1, p. 1. CF.

10 D.E. Jenkins, *The Life of the Rev. Thomas Charles* 3 vols. (Denbigh, 1908), 2:87. 1785 saw the publication for the use of her students of *A Copy of a Letter from the Countess of Huntingdon to One of Her Students Who had Desired Her Ladyship's Opinion and Advice with Respect to the Ministry* (Trevecka, 1785). It contains pious exhortation.

11 John Williams to SH, 3 April 1788, Ebley MSS, D.2538/8/1, Gloucestershire Record Office.

12 Thomas Watson to SH, 14 June 1788, F1/734, CF; SH to [Thomas Haweis], 13 April 1790, SMU 122.

13 For example, John Williams to George Best, 9 June 1788, Ebley MSS D.2538/8/1, Gloucestershire Record Office.

14 Averina Powell to SH, 2 October, 27 November, 23 May (quotation) 1788, F1/2043, 2051, 728, CF; SH to Mr Carpenter, 31 March 1785, Trinity Presbyterian Church Collection, Bath Record Office (quotation).

15 John Williams to SH, 29 September, 15 November 1788, F1/769, 2049, CF; same to SH, 3 April 1789, Ebley MSS D.2538/8/1, Gloustershire Record Office (quotation); same to SH, 15 April 1789, F1/2070, CF.

16 Averina Powell to SH, 21 August 1788, F1/2032, CF.

17 SH to Mr & Mrs Thomas Wills, 16 February 1779; SH to John Hawksworth, 16 February 1779. Letters of SH, 1774-1784, English MSS 338, Rylands; SH to Hawksworth, 21 October 1781, G2/1/22, CF.

18 SH to Mr Langston, 18 February 1784, Letters of SH, 1774-1784, English MSS 338, Rylands; SH to Thomas Charles, 12 March 1790, II.a.17/20, CL; SH to anon., 17 September 1779, SMU 102; SH to Mr Green, 8 October 1784, MSS 7005C, NLW.

19 John Lloyd to SH, 25 May 1788, F1/2020, CF.

20 SH to Thomas Pentycross, [1781], Countess of Huntingdon letters, Rayleigh. For the preaching tours see *Extracts of Journals of Several Ministers*.

21 Aldridge, *Funeral Sermon*, p. 22; SH to Thomas Wills, 29 April 1785, II.c.7/22, CL (quotation).

22 For example, S. Phillips to SH, 23 June 1780, F1/454, CF.

23 George Waring, *The End of Time. A Sermon, preached at the Countess of Huntingdon's Chapel, Spa Fields, Clerkenwell, London, on Sunday Evening, August 22, 1790; by George Waring, one of Her Ladyship's Ministers* (n.p., n.d. 2nd edition), pp. 28-29, 33, 41.

24 Thomas Wills to SH, 8 October 1783, F1/1909, CF.

25 GW to SH, 14 February 1754, *Select Letters*, 3:63; Bebbington, *Evangelicalism in Modern Britain*, p. 30.

26 SH to Mr Carpenter, [2 November 1785], Black 133 (quotation); SH to Henry Laurens, 19 January 1787, A3/12/11, CF.

27 SH to [Thomas] Beale, 20 August 1779, G2/2, CF.

28 Henry Venn to J. Stillingfleet, 16 September 1783, C14. Venn said that he and Berridge had been 'of one mind for over twenty years'. Venn to Thomas Atkinson, 1793, C5. CMS.

29 For example, John Newton to Mary Newton, 31 August 1775, C66, CMS.

30 Hannah More to Bishop of Bath and Wells, 1801, George W.E. Russell, *A Short History of the Evangelical Movement* (London, 1915), p. 45; John Venn's memoir of his father, in Henry Venn (ed.), *The Life and Selection from the Letters of the Late Henry Venn* (London, 1837. 5th edition), pp. 176-77; John Thornton to SH, 7 October 1783, F1/554, CF.

31 Lucy Thornton to John Newton, 25 August 1777 (quotation); John Thornton to John Venn, 6 February 1790. C68, CMS.

32 Walter Shirley to SH, n.d., F1/1264, CF.

33 Edward Stillingfleet to Lord Dartmouth, 21 June 1773, Dartmouth Manuscripts, D (W) 1778/III/294, Staffordshire Record Office.

34 R. Chapman to SH, [1774], F1/1538, CF.

35 For example, SH to Mrs H. Leighton, 19 December 1768, Duke.

36 SH to [Thomas Haweis], September 1778, SMU 100; T. Watkins to SH, 25 February 1790, F1/889, CF.

37 Quoted in J.P. de Castro, *The Gordon Riots* (Oxford, 1926), p. 17.

38 In addition to de Castro, *Gordon Riots*, see John Stevenson, *Popular Disturbances in England 1700-1870* (London, 1979), pp. 76-90; George F.E. Rudé, 'The Gordon riots: a study of the rioters and their victims', *Transactions of the Royal Historical Society*, 5th series, 6 (1956), pp. 93-114; Anthony Babington, *Military Intervention in Britain from the Gordon Riots to the Gibraltar Incident* (London, 1990), pp. 21-27; Christopher Hibbert, *King Mob. The Story of Lord George Gordon and the Riots of 1780* (London, 1959); Colin Haydon, *Anti-Catholicism in Eighteenth-century England* (Manchester, 1993), pp. 204-44.

39 Quoted in Hibbert, *King Mob*, p. 90. The rioter whose mother attended Spa Fields was one of the twenty-five later executed. Pinks, *History of Clerkenwell*, p. 146.

40 J. Harris to SH, 15 July 1780, F1/460, CF.
41 Hibbert, *King Mob*, pp. 146-47.
42 Tyerman, *Life of John Wesley*, 3:34.
43 T.B. Howell (comp.), *A Complete Collection of State Trials...to 1783* 24 vols. (London, 1809-28), 21:610-11, 641; Hibbert, *King Mob*, pp. 147-64.
44 *Gospel Magazine* 7 (1780), pp. 266-70; SH to Mr Way, 26 July 1780, E3/3/2, CF.
45 Spa Fields Committee to SH, 24 September 1781, Welch, *Two Chapels*, item 163; SH to Spa Fields Committee, 11 September 1781, E4/10/15, CF.
46 Theophilus Lindsey to Lord John Rawdon, 16 December 1757, T3765/M/2/20/2, PRONI; Fitzpatrick, 'Heretical religion', p. 357.
47 SH to [Thomas] Beale, 20 August 1779, G2/2, CF.
48 SH to Trustees of the University of Georgia, 15 January 1787, A3/12/10, CF. Immediately upon her death, Georgia confiscated all her property in the state. For her post-Revolution attempts to renew Bethesda and pursue new American projects see Boyd Stanley Schlenther, '"To convert the poor people in America": the Bethesda orphanage and the thwarted zeal of the Countess of Huntingdon', *Georgia Historical Quarterly* 78 (1994), pp. 245-51.
49 SH to John Bidwell, 10 April 1787, B4/3, CF (quotation); CW to anon., 9 April 1787, Welsh Methodist (Wesleyan) Archives D/D/23, 870E, NLW; R. Herdsman to SH, 17 April 1787, F1/621, CF (quotation). See also Samuel Beaufoy to SH, 27 April 1787, F1/623, CF.
50 Thomas Wills to SH, 27, 30 April 1787, F1/622, 624, CF. See also *Memoirs of Thomas Wills*, p. 205.
51 SH to Henry Laurens, 18 January 1787, A3/12/11 (quotation); SH to John Bidwell, 10 April 1787, B4/3. CF.
52 Thomas Wills to SH, 12 October 1786, F1/1941, CF.
53 SH to Nathaniel Rowland, 25 July 1788, Deposit 350A, NLW.
54 *A Farewell Address from the Rev. Mr. Wills to the Various Congregations and Societies in the Countess of Huntingdon's Connection; Particularly those at SPA-FIELDS, his late More Immediate Charge* (London 1788). For his expulsion see Edmund Jones to SH, 9 January 1788, Ebley MSS D.2538/8/1, Gloucestershire Record Office; Spa Fields minutes, 7 July 1788, Welch, *Two Chapels*, item 211; Introduction to records of the Apostolic Society, C5/2, CF; *Memoirs of Thomas Wills*, pp. 210-21.
55 Lady Catherine Maria Wheler to SH, 5 February 1731, HA 13233 (as goddaughter); SH to Selina Wills, [10?] June 1784, II.c.7/20, CL (quotation); *Memoirs of Thomas Wills*, p. 217.
56 J. Jenkins to SH, 10 May 1790, F1/911; William Gardener et al. to SH, 16 August 1788, F1/755; Abraham Gadd to SH, 12 September 1788, F1/766. CF; SH to [Thomas Haweis], 9 June, 29 January 1790, SMU 125, 112.
57 David Griffiths to Mrs Bowen, 24 March 1791, Llwyngwair MSS 16988, NLW.
58 Robert Moody to SH, 11 July 1788, F1/2026, CF.
59 J. Sheppard and G. Ford to John Lloyd, 9 October 1788, F1/772, CF; *Memoirs of Thomas Wills*, p. 210.
60 Thomas Haweis to Lady Anne Erskine, 25 November 1789; same to William Taylor, 1 January 1790. A3023, Mitchell; J. Jenkins to SH, 10 May 1790, F1/911, CF.
61 SH to anon., 3 February 1790, SMU 104 (quotations); William Taylor to George Best, 26 February 1790, 25 January 1791, n.d., F1/2120, 2167, 2182, CF.
62 Thomas Haweis, MS autobiography, p. 127, ML B1176, Mitchell.
63 Belsham, *Memoirs of Theophilus Lindsey*, p. 2n. Lindsey had long known that Francis was, at best, a religious sceptic. Theophilus Lindsey to [FH], 4 September 1770, HA 8324. Charles Wesley observed that Francis constantly delighted in 'impious talk'. Jackson, *Journal of Charles Wesley*, [ante-1763], 2:258.
64 John Williams to SH, 4 August 1788, F1/750, CF.
65 FH will, 9 August 1779, HAP Box 32, folder 29.
66 George Best to Thomas Charles, 20 June 1791, B5, Methodist New Room, Bristol.
67 SH to Selina Wills, n.d., II.c.7/25, CL; Nathaniel Rowland to SH, 25 September 1790, F1/939, CF.
68 SH to Ely Chapel, 19 May 1790, MSS 9231 0/38, NLW; SH to Thomas Haweis, 6 March 1790, SMU 116; SH to Spa Fields Chapel, 19 May 1790, *Countess of Huntingdon Connexion Circular* (1846), p. 50.

69 Nathaniel Rowland to SH, 25 September 1790, F1/939; SH to Robert McAll, 13 September 1788, E4/17/2. CF.

70 William Taylor to George Best, 5 April 1790, F1/2126, CF.

71 Thomas Haweis, MS autobiography, pp. 95, 161, 173, 176 (quotations), ML B1176, Mitchell. For his continuing ownership of slaves into the next century see George D. Nankivel to Haweis, 18 February 1801, F1/1088, CF.

72 Thomas Haweis, MS autobiography, p. 177, ML B1176 (quotation); Haweis to Bishop of Peterborough, 30 December 1808, A3023. Mitchell. Even Haweis's sycophantic biographer is at a loss to explain his 'strangely inconsistent' acceptance of the Countess's entreaty. Arthur S. Wood, *Thomas Haweis* (London, 1957), p. 169. What had been unpalatable in 1780 now appeared fully to his taste.

73 Thomas Haweis to SH, 6 January 1790, F1/2115, CF.

74 SH to [Thomas Haweis], 25 February 1790, SMU 108.

75 *Plan of an Association for Uniting and Perpetuating the Connection of the Right Honourable the Countess Dowager of Huntingdon* (n.p., 1790), with the quotation from p. 14.

76 Thomas Haweis to SH, 27 February 1790, F1/2121, CF; SH to Haweis, 6 March, 9 June, 13 April 1790, SMU 116, 125, 122.

77 The quotations are taken from two versions of the same letter: Thomas Haweis to SH, 12 June 1790, F1/2134, CF; and A3023, Mitchell. Lady Anne gave the Countess 'no rest until the Plan was recalled'. James Bridgman, *An Address to the Ministers, Deacons, and Friends of the Countess of Huntingdon's Connexion and College* (London, [1857]), p. 10.

78 She had written to her chapels in May, strongly supporting the plan. Circular letter of SH to her chapels, 19 May 1790, DC1/1, CF. See also SH to Spa Fields Chapel, 19 May 1790, *Countess of Huntingdon Connexion Circular* (1846), pp. 50-51.

79 Thomas Haweis to SH, 5 July, September 1790, F1/2137, 2145, CF; same to SH, 20 November 1790, A3023, Mitchell.

80 See Schlenther, 'To convert the poor people in America', pp. 245-51.

81 David Jones to SH, 18 August 1789, F1/851, CF.

82 SH to Thomas Haweis, 24 March, 13 April, 15 March, 8 April 1790, SMU 118, 122, 117, 121; SH to Thomas Charles, 8 July 1790, Thomas Charles MSS, 13,354, Calvinistic Methodist Archives, NLW.

83 For the impact of the South Seas on the romantic vision of Calvinistic Methodists, which marked them out from the Wesleyans, see Johannes Van Den Berg, *Constrained by Jesus' Love: an Inquiry into the Motives of the Missionary Awakening in Great Britain in the Period Between 1698 and 1815* (Kampen, Netherlands, 1956), pp. 98, 109-110.

84 Thomas Haweis to anon., n.d., B1178; same to Sir James Wright, 6 June 1791, A3023. Mitchell.

85 Thomas Haweis to SH, 12 June 1790, F1/2134, CF (quotation); SH to Haweis, 12 February 1790, SMU 113b (quotation); A. Skevington Wood, 'The failure of a mission: 1791', *Congregational Quarterly* 32 (1954), pp. 349-50.

86 Thomas Haweis, *A Short Account of the Last Days of the...Countess Dowager of Huntingdon* (London, [1791]), p. 10.

87 SH to Thomas Charles, 9 June 1791, C15 (quotation); George Best to Thomas Charles, 20 June 1791, B5. Bristol New Room; same to [David Griffiths?], 20 June 1791, Additional Manuscripts 894c, f. 17, NLW.

88 George Best to [David Griffiths?], 20 June 1791, Additional Manuscripts 894c, ff. 16, 17, NLW.

89 Haweis published his *Short Account of the Last Days* in order 'to confute the falsehood, and silence the misrepresentations, already obtruded on the Public' (p. 3) regarding her state of mind at the end.

90 Welch, Two Chapels, item 226; Shirley, *Stemmata Shirleiana*, p. 192.

91 Cannon, *Family Library*, p. 120.

92 *The Times*, 20 June 1791.

93 Cannon, *Family Library*, pp. 104, 111, with the quotations from pp. 112, 119, 125.

94 Jones, *Funeral Sermon*, p. 17.

95 John Thomas, *Marwnad, ar Farwolaeth yr Anrhydeddus Arglwyddes Waddolog, Huntingdon* (Trevecka, 1791), p. 4.

96 Quoted in C.E. Vulliamy, *John Wesley* (London, 1931), p. 288.

97 *Elegy to the Memory of the...Countess Dowager of Huntingdon* (n.p., [1791]).

Conclusion

Lady Huntingdon's leadership and care of her chapels had involved her in 'almost continual sorrow'.[1] By any measure the agitated accents swirling around her and the resulting personal conflicts were inescapable in both their persistence and their intensity.

Why did all the Countess's enterprises produce an inordinate amount of internal strife? First, there was her demand that people be kept on a constant religious cusp. The ethos of her religion was the seeking out of the most potent emotive experience, the divine fire that was her holy grail ever since her own awakening. She lived ever in a state of high tension, always fostering the creation, or re-creation, of some magic religious moment. This demand, this need, never slackened. As an appeal it might produce an enlivened spirit but lacked religious milestones by which a believer could judge measured progress. She demanded that preaching centre solely on the need for utter dependence upon God's forgiveness. Yet where was the room for development in that faith? For growth? For Christian maturity? That, however, would smack of the 'moral' preaching Lady Huntingdon so heartily rejected. Her demands thus contributed to an immaturity of faith, the constant seeking of new birth or re-birth rather than a growing up following that birth. Perhaps eighteenth-century Methodists in general and the Countess in particular laid far too much ironic weight on external signs: tears, sobs, shouts. She demanded that her preachers always stress the 'feeling part of the Gospel'.[2] Indeed, her own eyes were often curtained with tears, a display which was noted throughout her new-born religious life. To her, tears were the litmus test of sincerity. What 'refreshed her dear heart in the Lord . . . [was] if some poor sinner had been cut down under the Word, and sent away weeping'. When her Trevecca 'sons', her 'family', were gathered round her, she frequently had 'many tears running down her . . . cheeks'. This 'dissolved all about her into a flood of weeping, till some have sobbed again'.[3] These tenuous tests all could and did pass away, and she was unable to grasp the fact that sensational religious experience is not a bird that will sing in every bush; that perhaps it is not enough merely to feel.

Eighteenth-century evangelicals such as John Fletcher and John Berridge certainly were passionate, but tears were not their homiletic hallmark. They were generally coherent, striving to find that mysterious balance between instinct and intellect. To them, true evangelicalism did not seek to manipulate people but to set before their hearts and minds a cogent message of the gospel. Perhaps Lady Huntingdon most overlooked the appeal to a changed inner-heart, even the quiet assurance, the heart of the heart. She was intent not on planting and nurturing, but harvesting. Time after time congregations besought her to send back former preachers to revive what had fallen dead. The Countess distrusted any Christians who, rather than evangelising the kingdom, were content quietly to maintain their religious traditions. She sang the sentient songs of a different Kingdom. There was nothing quiet about her faith, nor was there anything content. Least of all was she content. This was her contribution to the new-birth movement, and in full and fervent flow it might hold for a period all the excitement of a virgin enterprise. But it was also a toxic contribution, since her impulsive heart and hand turned from one new project to another. When these schemes faltered, as assuredly they did, she had neither the inclination nor the ability to organise the unexciting means by which they might have been maintained. The resultant never ceasing uncertainty and confrontation wearied most of those who wished her well, and many gave up the struggle in order to seek more peaceful, and to them, productive plateaux. Moreover, her religious zeal did not direct her or her people towards works of charity; if anything, the reverse was true. Such solid yet unspectacular achievements as some might make in daily practical service did not impress her. At least, they were not the stuff of Christianity as she understood it. She had not been converted from a profligate life to one of good works, but from good works to one of wrestling faith. At its worst, this produced a fearful, negative, even aggressive religion that lacked the discipline of ethics. That, quite literally, was the burden of her faith.

A second basic cause for ceaseless contention was the Countess's ambiguous role as an ecclesiastical leader. Eighteenth-century women were expected to submit to their superiors. A titled lady certainly would expect to receive social deference; but could that deference be demanded of religious followers? Since she was also, perforce, a member of the laity, how could such a person command and direct clerics? In practice, her authority was potentially more draconian than any bishop's, not least because it was exercised *ad hominem*. She had too much work and too much power. However, some men saw this as an opportunity. She could prove an alternative to episcopal power who, because she was a woman, might more easily be swayed. She might more readily be bent to a man's personal ambitions. For some, like William Piercy, it was a risk worth taking. Thomas Haweis's sharp and greedy eye put him in a class of his own. Her anomalous role as religious leader immersed her in increasingly treacherous waters.

There was a third, related, reason for bruising clash and conflict. The Countess of Huntingdon expected imperfect men to serve her to perfection. Curiously, she frequently failed to apply her central religious belief regarding fallen human nature to the men she chose. Time and again she supposed that she had found a man 'quite after my own heart',[4] a perfectly obedient son in the service of the gospel, as if such a thing were possible. Thus Calvinistic caution was thrown to the winds of a ceaseless desire to discover those who would follow her unerringly and unswervingly. As it was observed at her death, she had been far 'too credulous respecting reports, especially when brought or sent by some supposed choice friend'. Given the quality of a number of her students and ministers, 'she rather merited our pity than our scorn: Seeing that she was often greatly imposed upon by snakes in the grass, whom she generally found out in the end'. As another colleague put it after her death, 'her predilections for some, and her prejudices against others, were sometimes too hastily adopted – and by these she was led to form conclusions not always correspondent with truth and wisdom'.[5] It was only very late in her life and after a most painful evolution that she bitterly discovered that the same evils she saw in the society about her were just as liable to be present within her followers.

There is a further consideration. The Countess of Huntingdon's programme for the salvation of others was fatefully woven into the web of her own personality and how she attempted to manage facing the predicament of life. At the very outset of her pilgrimage Thomas Barnard had advised that 'according to your Ladyship's spirit' would be her religious progress.[6] Yet hers was a cyclothymic temperament, with wide, even wild swings between elation and depression. In its extreme form this manifests itself in fluctuation from excitement and hyperactivity to the self-deprecation and feelings of unworthiness and hopelessness which are characteristic of a depressive state of mind. She lacked that inner peace which is the basis of good judgement. In the parallel universe she occupied, the Countess was ever consumed either by the fire or by the ice of God. It was natural enough that this dominant aspect of her personality provided potent ammunition for those who attacked her, but it was just as evident to those who attempted to stand by her. 'She had her clouds' and 'sometimes very dark ones indeed'. 'Low in the dust her soul would prostrate lie, while her full fir'd affections dwelt on high.'[7] Her trials, she wrote, 'often make me ready to faint'; and when she referred, as often she did, to 'this miserable world'[8] she was speaking of her own misery, which though attempting to control she never managed to conceal. Serenity forever eluded her. Those who proved her best friends were drawn to her not because of any winsome quality of her faith but by her vulnerability. Those who proved less than friends were attracted by the same quality.

Her unquiet heart, her misery, her 'disturb', her demons of disorder, offer sobering examples of the connection between physical and mental/spiritual health; or, more precisely, the influence of poor physical health upon spiritual and mental anguish. 'I never have had an event in my life prosperous or usefull respecting the Gospel but heavy has been the Cross laid & that the most often on my misarable body.'[9] Yet one of Thomas Haweis's notions brought a startling and strangely liberating message: that Satan had the power to inflict physical illness.[10] Previously, the Countess had perceived frequent and intense illnesses only as God-given, as evidences of her faithlessness and thus markers to point to further introspection and soul-searching. However, if illness could be Satan-given, a device of the Devil to thwart what actually were godly intentions and enterprises, then she was free to assume a posture of unblinking boldness. Here was all the more reason to attack Satan head-on, to frustrate his plans, rather than to bewail how she had failed to fulfil God's plans. It was a liberating notion. It was also an extremely dangerous notion. The more she fulfilled God's will, the greater her physical suffering would be – a sure measure of just how seriously Satan took her role in the regeneration of England. Yet however interpreted theologically, her illnesses always produced the mixed adrenaline of faith and fear. It was a terrified faith. Another of her ministers taught that Satan had the power to counterfeit God's promises – that is, that Satan could make a faithful Christian accept as a true message from God what actually was a devilish device. That was truly unsettling, as one of her female friends discovered: 'This Idea drove all comfort from my mind. . . . If it is possible for the Devil to apply the word of God with comfort to the Heart, I'm sure we may ask, & (in my opinion) never know, what is Truth.'[11]

Driven and held captive by fear and hatred of alien forces, Lady Huntingdon lacked inner freedom – the freedom from fear. This illimitable dread contributed directly to her 'temper warm', and her inner disharmony was often revealed in outward enmity. Even into the nineteenth century, leaders in her denomination would recall her as an intolerant person, whose 'natural temperament' was 'bigoted'.[12] She was a combustible figure who lacked a sense of proportion. At her most inflamed, she assumed more than a tincture of infallibility, to which she was capable of giving distinctive voice with her verbal and written fusillades – although seen through the Countess's eyes her judgements on others were frequently not intended to be vindictive but corrective. After the death of her daughter Selina, when there was no hope of influencing her two remaining children, nothing was to be gained by self-restraint. Thus the establishment of Trevecca, the clash during the 1770s with Wesley and the related impact upon her of hard line predestinarians, all fuelled her forward movement to the inevitable clash with the Church she professed to love. This entombed rather than enshrined her lasting usefulness in the new-birth enterprise. It must be observed that her affection was not given unconditionally. As one of her ministers observed, 'she bore a particular affection to all her students who turned out well, especially to those whose ministry the Lord smiled upon'.[13] Such success would be the measure of love's endeavour.

In revealing the story of her volatile relationship with a volatile century, it is impossible to avoid being caught up in Lady Huntingdon's emotions and dreams, her exquisite personal tragedies and hopes. Harsh judgements are as unwise as they are potentially unjust. Her patent need and capacity for affection carried with it such a fragility that judgement can give way to pity. Hers was a sad fate, and given her personality she was highly unfortunate in having to seek her footing in faith at the very outset of the new-birth revival. The numerous choices open to her were unstructured and ill-focused. That only added to the excessive fluctuation she and other seekers experienced, an instability in English church life that would not become relatively more settled until the period after her death. Meanwhile, there was an unrootedness that her life and actions only seemed to reinforce.

While not everything she did was benignly intended, there were a number of men and women who found the Countess's character at least as alluring as it was alarming. They were both held by her strength and touched by her frailty; seeing so much good intention in her, they risked rejection by patiently attempting to aid in the effort to have her humility honed, in the process finding it necessary to convey their message to her in studied opacity. A typical balanced observer wrote that 'some good I hope is done where much is intended, by this praiseworthy lady, who has, for full forty years, devoted her fortunes, time, and labours to promote what she believes to be the truth'.[14] She was a decent, despairing woman, and nothing that has been here written should be taken to suggest that her dedication was in any sense insincere. Her capacity to see and seize opportunities was arresting, and from the extensive evidence available it is reasonable to suppose that she was never consciously self-seeking in her activities as a Methodist leader. Moreover, she was breathtakingly brave. Her readiness to sail to America or to venture to Brussels and her willingness to deprive herself of physical comforts to put herself in the front line of battle with those she was certain meant her harm, all suggest that she would never allow her men to face dangers she herself would shirk.

However, while Lady Huntingdon's personal relationship with her God is not capable of evaluation, her relationships with others and the fruitfulness of her enterprises are. It is no disparagement of the Countess of Huntingdon to conclude that her passionate promotion of evangelical preaching and the celerity with which she frequently acted in seeking a purchase on English religious life was driven by an unconscious personal need for inner fulfilment. Unsettled as the child of a loveless marriage, she condemned her errant mother and comforted her offended father. It is to be hoped that a sense of discretion constrained her son Francis from revealing to her the awful 'secret' he discovered many years later: her mother had left her father because from him she had contracted syphilis, the ultimate cause of her painful death.[15] Selina Hastings had thrown herself into her husband's arms and sought emotional fulfilment and certainty there. In subsequent years, as the icons of her life altered, she veered distractedly, only finding grounding in a belief system where she could exert firm control over others. It was a system of beliefs that brooked no compromises, tolerated no shading of colour.

It appears likely that the Countess's own uncertainties remained, making her all the more forceful in her certainty. The results of her efforts were as disappointing as her dedication was remarkable. It may be suggested that although she had failed in her enterprises, she had none the less failed diligently. That, of course, begs the question. Her diligence is not in doubt, but can there be a doubt that diligence so forcefully exerted contributed to the fruits produced? The eighteenth-century new-birth movement had thrown the age-old problem of ecclesiastical authority into sharp relief. Upon the ever-changing canvas of English religion emerged many colourful figures, but none combined the potentially volatile and confusing elements of laity, feminineness and aristocracy found in the Countess of Huntingdon. It was a potent recipe. For a lay person to assume the direction of religious affairs, let alone for a woman to assume the leadership of men, excited confusion and conflict. Her leadership was a complicated, mixed and for very many a painful blessing. Moreover, in a new age in which local leadership increasingly sought to control or influence ecclesiastical affairs, a movement whose soldiers were expected to obey commands without question was passé. She was forcefully dedicated to carrying the gospel forward in the teeth of all opposition, and her taste for conflict had a sharper edge than most. Lady Huntingdon's recourse to *force majeure* was fateful, for in the process the devils she trampled upon were not only godless devils but also the godly devils of other Christian persuasions. It was just as well for her that she did not live into the new age of religious accommodation, a crucial generation of religious change which was being born just as she died. By 1790 there probably were more Roman Catholics in Great Britain than there were members of Methodist societies.[16]

Perhaps the lust for certainty is the original human sin. Perhaps faith best offers a thoughtful walk with God, a way of living at peace without certainty. In what were the most startling words she ever wrote, the Countess of Huntingdon said that when she had achieved the true faith she desired for herself the result would be 'the conversion of the world'.[17] Apparently neither was achieved. The eighteenth-century's new-birth impulse had a potent impact upon society and individuals. The resultant instability is nowhere better illustrated than in the troubled and uneasy reign of the Queen of the Methodists.

Notes

1 Cannon, *Funeral Sermon*, p. 126.
2 Laurence Coughlan to SH, 15 March 1776, F1/348, CF.
3 Aldridge, *Funeral Sermon*, p. 18.
4 SH to Thomas Haweis, 13 September 1790, SMU 128 (referring to John Johnson).
5 Cannon, *Funeral Sermon*, p. 118; Haweis, *Impartial and Succinct History*, 2:416-17.
6 Thomas Barnard to SH, 13 August 1739, DE23/1430, LRO.
7 Platt, *Waiting Christian*, p. 16; Thomas Young, *A Tribute of Gratitude, to the Memory of the...Countess...of Huntingdon* (Newark, 1791), p. 5.
8 SH to HH, 4 June 1768, Trevecka 2642; SH to Henry Laurens, 6 February 1784, A3/10/18, CF.
9 SH to [Thomas Haweis], September 1778, SMU 100.
10 Lucy Thornton to John Newton, 25 August 1777, C68, CMS.
11 F. Montague to SH, 14 July 1773, F1/236, CF.
12 Haweis, *Impartial and Succinct History*, 2:414; Willcocks, *Spa Fields Chapel*, p. 16.
13 Aldridge, *Funeral Sermon*, p. 24.
14 Belsham, *Memoirs of Theophilus Lindsey*, p. 2n.
15 FH to EH, 11 August 1783, T3765/M/2/14/123, PRONI.
16 See David Hempton, *Methodism and Politics in British Society 1750-1850* (London, 1984), Chapter 3. For Roman Catholics see Hempton, 'Religion in British society', p. 217; John Bossy, *The English Catholic Community 1570-1850* (London, 1975), Chapter 13.
17 SH to John Hawksworth, 5 December 1778, G2/1/20, CF. Elsewhere, she wrote regarding Trevecca that God had 'favour[e]d me with this...college where many more voices than mine could breath[e] still better the longing of my heart'. SH to [Thomas Haweis], 20 February 1777, SMU 93.

EPILOGUE

In her will, the Countess of Huntingdon bequeathed all her possessions to a group of four self-perpetuating trustees: Lady Anne Erskine, Thomas and Janetta Haweis and a long-serving layman, John Lloyd.[1] These possessions included six chapels she owned outright, among whose number was, to Haweis's joy, Bath. Less to his joy was the discovery that she had left overall debts of £3,000.[2] She left nothing to endow her college or chapels.

Lady Anne Erskine sought life as a Lady Huntingdon *redivivus*, slipping into an attempt to exercise a like control of affairs, until her death in 1804. As the leading Trustees, she and Haweis continued Lady Huntingdon's style of paternalism. On one notable occasion, a number of local Jews were induced to attend a service at Spa Fields. As it progressed, they decided to leave, but without reckoning with Lady Anne: 'I will not let you go', she proclaimed and extended her arm to forbid their exit. She was assured that none escaped 'at that door'.[3]

After the death of Janetta Haweis in 1799, her husband married, at the age of sixty-eight, his twenty-four-year-old secretary.[4] Retiring from Aldwincle to Bath, Haweis for a time conducted services at the chapel. Yet his manner 'was high, and not sufficiently courteous to the common people'. Moreover, displaying 'a peculiar confidence in himself', he was increasingly careless in preparation, his sermons 'commonplace and unctionless'. His style was 'invariably terrific', with preachings constantly based on such texts as 'Who among us can dwell with everlasting burnings?', or 'Depart, ye cursed'. He appeared to take '*pleasure*' in delivering such sermons. It was a pleasure not reciprocated by the 'dissatisfied congregation', who finally 'induced him to decline his ministry among them, and also his attendance at the chapel'. Haweis spent the remainder of his days worshipping at another Dissenting chapel in Bath.[5] From Ireland, the Countess's erstwhile daughter Elizabeth wrote of Haweis's 'Lies'. Knowing 'a good deal of his past character I shd. not be surprised at any thing in his future'.[6]

As soon as Thomas Haweis died in 1820, the Connexion attempted to put into place the Plan of Association he had forced the Countess to jettison thirty years earlier. It was too late. The Trustee form of church government had set a pattern for religious strife which would continue for several further decades, with ecclesiastical disruption and civil law suits draining the denomination of resources and spirit. It was nothing other than 'the decay of our Connexion', stemming from Haweis's and Lady Anne's refusal to accept the Countess's proposed presbyterially-based plan of government. Subsequent Trustees therefore professed to have derived from her their power, a 'despotic power'. The resulting 'chronic dispute' had 'nearly terminated both the usefulness and the existence of the Connexion', according to one of its leading mid-nineteenth-century ministers.[7] With the best will possible, it would be difficult to maintain that the denomination made any distinctive or enduring contribution to Dissent. At the close of the twentieth century its twenty-five congregations continue under a modified form of Trustee government.

The simultaneous deaths of John Wesley and the Countess of Huntingdon placed punctuation marks against English Methodism: his a comma, hers for all intents a full stop. In 1811, London had forty-six Wesleyan and two Countess of Huntingdon chapels.[8] Wesleyan leaders took pleasure in reporting the atrophy in her Connexion, large numbers of whose ministers and congregations left to join the Independents.[9] 'Huntingdonianism', as it was sometimes called, remained totally unconnected with the Evangelical movement within the Church of England.[10]

In her will, Lady Huntingdon named six clergymen who, she stipulated, must never be allowed to preach in any of her chapels. This remarkable parting command reveals how deep and how bitter her divisions had run. Predictably, one of the six was her Whitefield *manqué*, William Piercy who, in a quirky twist, in 1797 demanded from the State of Georgia several thousand pounds to recompense his unpaid services to the Countess. Later, he appeared in Savannah, sued the Trustees of Bethesda in a United States federal court and finally grudgingly accepted £500.[11]

Whereas Wesleyan Methodism had geared for a new century through a carefully-wrought ecclesiastical system, Lady Huntingdon's enterprises now became occluded without the only hand they had ever known to control and to command. Those who had benefited most by her efforts became Dissenters. This she had always feared and firmly resisted. Dissenters inhabited a localised world. They settled. They developed long-term and consistent relationships. Her personality and her movement were unsettled. The itinerating she demanded of preachers mirrored the lack of stability in the life and labours of the Countess of Huntingdon.

Notes

1 Lloyd, who admitted that he was somewhat mad, was a pitiful figure. An emotionally unstable man with a bitterly caustic gossiping tongue, he had been in the thick of events at the Bath Chapel, but then moved about the country attaching himself to several of her chapels at different times, separated from his wife and children, who had rejected his religious orientation. See, for example, John Lloyd to SH, 16 April 1774, 3 April 1788, F1/1687, 2003, CF.

2 SH will (copy), Rayleigh; Welch, *Two Chapels*, item 227. Her personal annual income of £1,200 ceased at her death. C4/1, p. 79, CF.

3 Lady Anne Erskine to Thomas Haweis, 31 August 1796, NLW 7794E.

4 Wood, *Thomas Haweis*, p. 244.

5 Jay, *Autobiography*, pp. 477-80. His elder son became a clergyman and studiously disowned his father's evangelicalism.

6 EH to Walter Shirley [junr], 22 January 1801, 14D32/2119, LRO. She does not elaborate on these comments. Lady Huntingdon's last remaining child, Elizabeth continued as a *grande dame* in Irish society and political life until her death in 1808. Henry Nugent Bell, *The Huntingdon Peerage* (London, 1821. 2nd edition), p. 153.

7 Bridgman, *An Address*, pp. 3-20, with the quotations from pp. 3, 8; D3/2, CF (quotation). See also Welch, 'Lady Huntingdon's plans', pp. 36-40; Willcocks, *Spa Fields Chapel*, pp. 22-31; *Evangelical Register* 6 (1834), pp. 105-8, 418-21; *Countess of Huntingdon New Magazine* (1850), pp. 270-72, 279.

8 R.J. Helmstadter, 'The Reverend Andrew Reed', in R.W. Davis and R.J. Helmstadter (eds.), *Religion and Irreligion in Victorian Society* (London, 1992), p. 13. In 1790 Wesleyans in America had 228 preachers and nearly 60,000 members. Sydney G. Diamond, *The Psychology of the Methodist Revival* (London, 1926), p. 49. The Countess had none.

9 John Hustus Adams to Jabez Bunting, 4 July 1821, W.R. Ward (ed.), *The Early Correspondence of Jabez Bunting 1820-1829* (London, 1972), p. 79; John Walsh, 'Methodism at the end of the eighteenth century', in Davies and Rupp, *History of the Methodist Church*, 1:283, 292-95; Ward, *Protestant Evangelical Awakening*, p. 352.

10 Henry Thornton to John Venn, 25 September 1795, C68, CMS.

11 Minutes of Trustees of Bethesda College (typescript), pp. 12, 20, 31, 37-39, Georgia Department of Archives. Doubtless, Bethesda would have collapsed without Piercy's action, but this financial settlement executed the *coup de grace*. He spent the final years of his life as the rector of an Episcopal church in Charleston, South Carolina.

Bibliography

Manuscripts

Bath Central Library
MS AL 2062

Bath Record Office
Trinity Presbyterian Church Collection

Bridwell Library, Southern Methodist University, Dallas
Countess of Huntingdon Letters

Birmingham University Library
Church Missionary Society Manuscripts: Venn MSS
Hole MSS

Bodleian Library, Oxford
MS St Edmund Hall

Bristol University Library
Bristol Moravian Church Diaries

British Library, London
Additional Manuscripts 36,190

Cheshunt Foundation, Westminster College, Cambridge
College Archives
Connexional Archives
Countess of Huntingdon Correspondence
Hawksworth Collection
Murray Papers

Congregational Library, at Dr Williams's Library, London
Letters of Countess of Huntingdon II.c.7
Miscellaneous Letters II.a.17, II.c.8, II.c.10

Countess of Huntingdon Connexion Archives, Rayleigh
Letters of Countess of Huntingdon
Letters of John Berridge
Miscellaneous Letters and Manuscripts

Cowper and Newton Museum, Olney
Letter of John Berridge

Drew University Library, Madison, New Jersey
Letters to and from the Countess of Huntingdon
Wesley Family (Charles Wesley Division) Papers

Duke University Library, Durham, North Carolina
E.R. Hendrix MSS
Frank A. Baker Collection
Wesley Family Papers

Emory University Library, Atlanta, Georgia
Augustus Toplady Papers
John Wesley Collection

Evangelical Library, London
Letters to George Whitefield

Georgia Department of Archives, Atlanta, Georgia
Transcript Minutes of Bethesda College

Georgia Historical Society, Savannah, Georgia
John Johnson's Letterbook (transcript)

Gloucestershire Record Office, Gloucester
Ebley Manuscripts

Guildhall Library, London
Dissenting Deputies Minutes

Hereford and Worcester Record Office, Worcester
Ordination Papers

Historical Society of Pennsylvania, Philadelphia
Letter of George Whitefield

Huntington Library, San Marino, California
Hastings Correspondence
Hastings Family Correspondence
Hastings Legal Papers
Hastings Personal Papers
HM Manuscripts

John Rylands University Library of Manchester
English Manuscripts
  Countess of Huntingdon Letters, 1774-1784
  Letters to and from George Whitefield
  MSS 346
  Rylands Charters
Methodist Archives
  Countess of Huntingdon Black Folio of Letters
  Diary of John Bennet
  John Fletcher Letter Books
  Letters Chiefly Addressed to the Rev. C. Wesley

MAM JW
PLP 7; 59; 116
Tyerman/Everett Transcripts
Wesley Family Letters and Papers

Lambeth Palace Library, London
Registers of Peers Chaplains

Leicestershire Record Office, Wigston Magna, Leicester
Hastings Letters
Letters from the Earl and Countess of Huntingdon (copies of Panshanger Manuscripts, Hertfordshire Record Office)

Library of Congress, Washington, D.C.
Papers of George Whitefield

Lichfield Joint Record Office, Lichfield
Bishop's Subscription Book

Methodist New Room, Bristol
Manuscript Collection

Mitchell Library, Sydney, Australia
Thomas Haweis Letters
Thomas Haweis Manuscript Autobiography

National Library of Wales, Aberystwyth
Calvinistic Methodist Archives
Howell Harris Manuscript Diaries
Thomas Charles Manuscripts
Trevecca Group
D.T.M. Jones Collection
Llwyngwair Manuscripts
NLW 350A
NLW 894C
NLW 7005C
NLW 7021-30A
NLW 7794E
NLW 9231C
Trevecka Letters
Welsh Methodist (Wesleyan) Archives

Public Record Office of Northern Ireland, Belfast
Granard Papers
MSS D3531
Rawdon Family Letter Book

Smethwick Library, Smethwick
Records of All Saints Church

Society for Promoting Christian Knowledge, London
Society Letters and Minute Books

Staffordshire Record Office, Stafford
Dartmouth Manuscripts

The Upper Room, Nashville, Tennessee
Letters of the Countess of Huntingdon (copies in Cheshunt Foundation, G2/2)

Yale University Library
James M. and Marie-Louise Osborn Collection

Printed Primary Sources

An Account of the Execution of the Late Lawrence Ferrers. London, 1760.

An Account of the Rise, Progress, and Present-State of the Magdalen Charity. London, 1766. 3rd edition.

[Adair, James Makittrick]. *The Methodist and the Mimick*. London, 1766.

Admissions to the College of St John the Evangelist in the University of Cambridge. 2 vols. Cambridge, 1893, 1903.

Aldridge, W[illiam]. *A Funeral Sermon Occasioned by the Death of the...Countess...of Huntingdon*. London, 1791.

Andrews, Cyril B., ed. *The Torrington Diaries*. 4 vols. London, 1934-38.

'Anecdotes of John Henderson, B.A.' *Arminian Magazine*. 16 (1793), pp. 140-44.

Argyll, Duke of, ed. *Intimate Society Letters of the Eighteenth Century*. 2 vols. London, n.d.

Authentic Memoirs of the Life of William Dodd. Salisbury, [1777?].

An Authentic Narrative of the Primary Ordination. London, 1784.

Aveling, Thomas W. *Memorials of the Clayton Family*. London, 1867.

Baker, Frank, ed. *The Works of John Wesley*. Vols. 25 and 26. Letters 1721-55. Oxford, 1980, 1982.

Barnard, Thomas. *Life of Lady Elizabeth Hastings*. Leeds, 1742.

Belsham, Thomas. *Memoirs of the Late Reverend Theophilus Lindsey*. London, 1873.

_____. *A Sermon, Occasioned by the Death of the Rev. Theophilus Lindsey*. London, 1808.

Benham, Daniel. *Memoirs of James Hutton*. London, 1856.

Bennett, John. *The Star of the West; being Memoirs of the Life of Risdon Darracott*. London, 1813.

Benson, Joseph. *The Life of the Rev. John W. de la Flechere*. London, 1838.

Beynon, Tom, ed. *Howell Harris, Reformer and Soldier*. Caernarvon, 1958.

_____. *Howell Harris's Visits to London*. Aberystwyth, 1960.

_____. *Howell Harris's Visits to Pembrokeshire*. Aberystwyth, 1966.

Bingley, William, ed. *Correspondence Between Frances, Countess of Hartford, and...Countess of Pomfret*. 3 vols. London, 1805.

Blunt, Reginald, ed. *Mrs. Montagu 'Queen of the Blues.' Her Letters and Friendships from 1762 to 1800*. 2 vols. London, [1923].

Bogue, D., and Bennett, J. *History of Dissenters from the Revolution in 1688 to the Year 1808*. 4 vols. London, 1810.

Bradford, John. *An Address to the Inhabitants of New Brunswick.* London, 1788.

Bridgman, James. *An Address to the Ministers, Deacons, and Friends of the Countess of Huntingdon's Connexion and College.* London, [1857].

Cameron, Richard M. *The Rise of Methodism: a Source Book.* New York, 1954.

Cannon, Thomas. *No. 5. The Family Library, being the Substance of a Funeral Sermon...on the Death of the...Countess...of Huntingdon.* London, [1791?].

Cartwright, J.J. *The Wentworth Papers.* London, 1883.

Candler, Allen D. et al., comps. *The Colonial Records of the State of Georgia.* 26 vols. Atlanta, 1904-1916.

Cheyne, George. *Essay on Regimen. Together with Five Discourses, Medical, Moral, and Philosophical.* London, 1740.

Christie, John W., ed. 'Newly discovered letters of George Whitefield 1745-1746.' *Journal of the Presbyterian Historical Society.* 32 (1954), pp. 69-90, 159-86, 241-70.

Cobbett, William, comp. *Parliamentary History of England from...1066 to 1803.* 36 vols. London, 1806-20.

A Copy of a Letter from the Countess of Huntingdon to One of Her Students Who had Desired Her Ladyship's Opinion and Advice with Respect to the Ministry. Trevecka, 1785.

Cottingham, John. *The Righteous Shall be in Everlasting Remembrance.* London, 1791.

[Cullum, Sir Thomas Gery], 'Synopsis of...[tour] made in Wales in 1775.' *Y Cymmrodor.* 38 (1927), pp. 45-78.

Curnock, Nehemiah, ed. *The Journal of the Rev. John Wesley.* 8 vols. London, 1938. Reprint edition.

Elegy to the Memory of the...Countess Dowager of Huntingdon. n.p., [1791].

Extracts of the Journals of Several Ministers of the Gospel...in a Series of Letters to the Countess of Huntingdon. London, 1782.

Eyre, John. *The Order Observed at the Countess of Huntingdon's College, at Cheshunt.* London, 1792.

A Farewell Address from the Rev. Mr. Wills to the Various Congregations and Societies in the Countess of Huntingdon's Connection; Particularly those at SPA-FIELDS, his late More Immediate Charge. London, 1788.

George, Mary Dorothy. *Catalogue of Political and Personal Satires.* Vol. 6. London, 1938.

George Whitefield's Journals. Edinburgh, 1960.

Gill, Eric. *Autobiography.* London, 1940.

Gill, Frederick C., ed. *Selected Letters of John Wesley.* London, 1956.

Gillies, John. *Memoirs of the Life of the Rev. George Whitefield.* London, 1772.

Graves, Richard. *The Spiritual Quixote.* London, 1926. Original edition London, 1773.

Gray, Ernest, ed. *Man's Midwife.* London, 1946.

Halsband, Robert, ed. *The Complete Letters of Lady Mary Wortley Montagu.* 3 vols. Oxford, 1965-67.

Hargreaves-Mawdsley, W.N., ed. *Woodforde at Oxford.* Oxford, 1969.

[Harris, Howell]. *A Brief Account of the life of Howell Harris.* Trevecka, 1791.

Harris, Howell. Diary. *Journal of the Historical Society of the Presbyterian Church of Wales.* 39 (1954), pp. 43-48.
_____. Diary. *Transactions of the Calvinistic Methodist Historical Society.* 29 (1944), pp. 45-53.
Haweis, Thomas. *An Impartial and Succinct History of the Rise, Declension, and Revival of the Church of Christ.* 3 vols. London, 1800.
_____. *A Short Account of the Last Days of the...Countess Dowager of Huntingdon.* London, [1791].
[Hill, Richard], *Pietas Oxoniensis.* London, 1768. 2nd edition.
Historical Manuscripts Commission. *Reports on Manuscripts.*
Mrs Frankland-Russell-Astley. London, 1900.
Earl of Dartmouth. Vol. 3. London, 1896.
Reginald Rawdon Hastings. 3 vols. London, 1928-34.
Duke of Portland. Vol. 6. London, 1901.
Calendar of the Stuart Papers. 7 vols. London, etc., 1902-23.
'History of Spafields chapel.' *Evangelical Register.* 9 (1837), pp. 1-4, 49-52.
Howell, T.B., comp. *A Complete Collection of State Trials...to 1783.* 24 vols. London, 1809-28.
Humphreys, John D., ed. *The Correspondence and Diary of Philip Doddridge.* 5 vols. London, 1829-31.
Jackson, Thomas, ed. *The Journal of the Rev. Charles Wesley.* 2 vols. London, 1849.
Jones, David. *A Funeral Sermon, preached at Spa-Fields Chapel...on the Death of the...Countess...of Huntingdon.* London, 1791.
Jones, William. *Memoirs of...Rowland Hill.* London, 1834.
[Kimpton, John]. *A Faithful Narrative of the Facts, Relative to the Late Presentation of Mr H s, to the Rectory of Al w le.* London, 1767.
[King, William]. *The Art of Cookery In Imitation of Horace's Art of Poetry.* London, [1708].
'The letters of Hon. James Habersham.' *Collections of the Georgia Historical Society.* Savannah, 1904.
Lewis, W.S., ed. *Horace Walpole's Correspondence.* 48 vols. New Haven; Oxford, 1937-83.
Little, D.M., and Kahrl, G.M., eds. *The Letters of David Garrick.* 3 vols. London, 1963.
Llanover, Lady, ed. *The Autobiography and Correspondence of Mary Granville Mrs Delany.* First series. 3 vols. London, 1861.
Lloyd, Evan. *The Methodist. A Poem.* Los Angeles, 1972. Original edition London, 1760.
The Love-Feast, A Poem. London, 1778.
Macdonald, James. *Memoirs of the Rev. Joseph Benson.* London, 1822.
Madan, Martin. *An Answer to a Pamphlet, Intitled, a Faithful Narrative of Facts Relative to the Late Presentation of Mr H s, to the Rectory of Al w le.* London, 1767.
[Mayo, Henry]. *Aldwinckle. A Candid Examination.* London, 1767.
Memoirs of the Life of Laurance Earl Ferrers. London, 1760.
Memoirs of the Life of the Rev. Thomas Wills. London, 1804.

Meyer, John Henry. *The Saint's Triumph in the Approach of Death...a Sermon Occasioned by the Death of the...Countess of Huntingdon.* London, [1791].

Minutes of the Methodist Conference 1744-. Vol. 1. London, 1862.

Morgan, Edward. *The Life and Times of Howel Harris.* Holywell, 1852.

Mullett, Charles F., ed. *The Letters of Dr. George Cheyne to the Countess of Huntingdon.* San Marino, Calif., 1940.

Nowell, Thomas. *An Answer to a Pamphlet, Entitled Pietas Oxoniensis.* Oxford, 1768.

Nuttall, Geoffrey F., *Calendar of the Correspondence of Philip Doddridge DD (1702-1751).* London, 1979.

Owen, T.E. *Methodism Unmasked.* London, 1802.

Parkinson, Richard, ed. *The Private Journal and Literary Remains of John Byrom.* Vol. II, Part II. [Manchester], 1857.

Penrose, John. *Letters from Bath.* Glouster [*sic*], 1983.

'Philip Thickness's reminiscences of early Georgia.' *Georgia Historical Quarterly.* 74 (1990), pp. 672-98.

Pierce, Samuel. *A True Outline and Sketch of the Life of Samuel Eyles Pierce.* London, 1822.

Plan of an Association for Uniting and Perpetuating the Connection of the Right Honourable the Countess Dowager of Huntingdon. n.p., 1790.

Platt, William Francis. *The Waiting Christian: being the Substance of a Discourse Occasioned by the Death of the...Countess Dowager of Huntingdon.* Bristol, 1791.

Priestley, T[imothy]. *A Crown of Eternal Glory...a Funeral Sermon, Occasioned by the Death of the late Right Honourable and Most Respected Lady, Selina, Countess of Huntingdon.* London, 1791.

Redford, George, and James, John A., eds. *Autobiography of William Jay.* London, 1854.

Rogers, James E.T., ed. *A Complete Collection of the Protests of the Lords.* 3 vols. Oxford, 1875.

Rules for Conducting a School for the Education of Poor Children in the Protestant Religion and Useful Learning; instituted at the Countess of Huntingdon's Chapel, Spa-Fields, Clerkenwell, 1782. London, 1790.

Rules for the Education of Poor Children in the Protestant Religion and Useful Learning Instituted at the Countess of Huntingdon's Chapel, Bath. 1784. Bath, 1784.

A Satirical Dialogue between the Celebrated Mr F—te, and Dr Squintum. London, 1760.

A Select Collection of Letters of the Late Reverend George Whitefield, M.A. 3 vols. London, 1772.

Sellon, Walter. *The Church of England Vindicated from the Charge of Predestination.* London, 1771.

Seven Sermons, by the Learned and laborious Servant of Christ, The Rev. William Bridge...Particularly Recommended by the Countess Dowager of Huntingdon, to Congregations in Connection with her Ladyship. London, 1789.

Shirley, Walter. *A Narrative of the Principal Circumstances relative to the Rev. Mr. Wesley's Late Conference, held in Bristol, August the 6th, 1771.* Bath, 1771.

Some Account of the Proceedings at the College of the Right Hon. the Countess of Huntingdon, in Wales Relative to those Students called to go to her Ladyship's College in Georgia. London, 1772.

Stewart, A. Francis, ed. *Letters of Lord Chesterfield to Lord Huntingdon*. London, 1923.

Stock, Leo Francis, ed. *Proceedings and Debates of the British Parliaments Respecting North America*. 5 vols. Washington, D.C., 1924-41.

Taylor, George, ed. *Plays by Samuel Foote and Arthur Murphy*. Cambridge, 1984.

Telford, John, ed. *The Letters of the Rev. John Wesley, A.M.* 8 vols. London, 1931.

Thomas, John. *Marwnad, ar Farwolaeth ye Anrhydeddus Arglwyddes Waddolog, Huntingdon*. Trevecka, 1791.

Tovey, Duncan, ed. *The Letters of Thomas Gray*. 3 vols. London, 1909-12.

The Trial of Lawrence Earl Ferrers. London, 1760.

Venn, Henry, ed. *The Life and Selection from the Letters of the Late Henry Venn*. London, 1837. 5th edition.

'Walpole's visits to country seats.' *The Walpole Society*. 16 (1927-28), pp. 9-80.

Ward, W.R., ed. *The Early Correspondence of Jabez Bunting 1820-1829*. London, 1972.

Ward, W. Reginald, and Heitzenrater, Richard P., eds. *The Works of John Wesley*. Vols. 18-23. Journals and Diaries 1735-86. Nashville, 1988-95.

Waring, George. *The End of Time. A Sermon, preached at the Countess of Huntingdon's Chapel, Spa Fields...August 22, 1790; by George Waring, one of Her Ladyship's Ministers*. n.p., n.d. 2nd edition.

_____. *A Sermon Occasioned by the Death of the...Countess of Huntingdon*. Birmingham, [1791].

[Warner, Richard]. *Bath Characters*. London, 1808. 2nd edition.

Welch, Edwin, ed. 'The Bedford Moravian church in the eighteenth century.' *Publications of the Bedfordshire Historical Record Society*. 68 (1989).

_____. 'The correspondence of Nathaniel Rowland and Lady Huntingdon.' *Hanes Methodistiaeth Galfinaidd Cymru*. 2 (1978), pp. 26-37.

_____. *Two Calvinistic Methodist Chapels 1743-1811*. London, 1975.

Wesley, John. *A Collection of Moral and Sacred Poems*. 3 vols. London, 1744.

_____. *Thoughts Upon Slavery*. London, 1774.

Wheatley, Phillis. *Poems on Various Subjects, Religious and Moral*. London, 1773.

Wheler, George Hastings, ed. *Hastings Wheler Family Letters 1704-1739*. Wakefield, 1935.

Whitefield, George. *A Letter to the Reverend Dr Durrell*. London, 1768.

_____. *Sermons on Important Subjects*. London, 1825.

Whittingham, Richard, ed. *The Whole Works of the Rev. John Berridge*. London, 1864. 2nd edition.

Wilks, Mark. *Nonconformity: A Sermon, Delivered...Nov. 6, 1817, at the Monthly Association, of Congregational Ministers*. London, 1818.

Wilks, Sarah. *Memoirs of Rev. Mark Wilks*. London, 1821.

[Willcocks, F.W.]. *Spa Fields Chapel and its Associations*. n.p., *c*. 1886.

Williams, William. *An Elegy on the Reverend Mr. G. Whitefield...Presented to Her Ladyship*. Carmarthen, 1771.
Wilson, Walter. *The History and Antiquities of Dissenting Churches*. 4 vols. London, 1808-14.
The Works of John Wesley. 14 vols. London, 1872.
The Works of the Reverend William Law. Vol 9. London, 1762.
Young, Thomas. *A Tribute of Gratitude, to the Memory of the...Countess...of Huntingdon*. Newark, 1791.

Newspapers and Magazines

Arminian Magazine
Countess of Huntingdon Connexion Circular
Countess of Huntingdon New Magazine
Evangelical Register
Free Church of England Harbinger
Gentleman's Magazine
Gospel Magazine
Methodist Magazine
The Times
Town and Country Magazine
The Weekly History: or, An Account of the Progress of the Gospel

Secondary Sources

Ablove, Henry. *The Evangelist of Desire. John Wesley and the Methodists*. Stanford, California, 1990.
Addison, G.W., ed. *The Renewed Church of the United Brethren, 1722-1930*. London, 1932.
Andrews, Malcolm. *The Search for the Picturesque*. Aldershot, 1989.
Babington, Anthony. *Military Intervention in Britain from the Gordon Riots to the Gibraltar Incident*. London, 1990.
Baker, Frank. *John Wesley and the Church of England*. London, 1970.
Baker, G. *The History and Antiquities of Northamptonshire*. London, 1822.
Beaumont, Cyril W. *A Miscellany for Dancers*. London, 1934.
Bebbington, David. *Evangelicalism in Modern Britain*. London, 1989.
Belden, Mary Megie. *The Dramatic Work of Samuel Foote*. New Haven, 1929.
Bell, Henry Nugent. *The Huntingdon Peerage*. London, 1821. 2nd edition.
Bloch, Ruth H. *Visionary Republic: Millennial Themes in American Thought, 1756-1800*. Cambridge, 1985.
Bossy, John. *The English Catholic Community 1570-1850*. London, 1975.
Brown, Dorothy E.S. 'Evangelicals and education in eighteenth-century Britain: a study of Trevecca College, 1768-1792.' Ph.D. dissertation, University of Wisconsin-Madison, 1992.
Chamberlain, Jeffrey S. 'Moralism, justification, and the controversy over Methodism.' *Journal of Ecclesiastical History*. 44 (1993), pp. 652-78.

Chilcote, Paul W. *John Wesley and the Women Preachers of Early Methodism.* Metuchen, New Jersey, 1991.

Clarke, D.F. 'Benjamin Ingham and the Inghamites.' M.Phil. thesis, University of Leeds, 1971.

Colley, Linda. *In Defence of Oligarchy: the Tory Party 1714-60.* Cambridge, 1982.

The Complete Peerage of England, Scotland, Ireland, Great Britain and the United Kingdom. 13 vols. London, 1910-40.

Connely, Willard. *The True Chesterfield.* London, 1939.

Crane, Arthur. *The Kirkland Papers 1753-1869.* Ashby de la Zouch, 1990.

de Castro, J.P. *The Gordon Riots.* Oxford, 1926.

Diamond, Sydney G. *The Psychology of the Methodist Revival.* London, 1926.

The Dictionary of Welsh Biography Down to 1940. London, 1959.

Dowling, Frank. 'The Countess of Huntingdon's chapels.' M.Sc. dissertation, Oxford Polytechnic, 1992.

Durden, Diane Susan. 'Transatlantic communications and literature in the religious revivals, 1735-1745.' Ph.D. thesis, University of Hull, 1978.

Edwards, Maldwyn. 'John Wesley.' In Rupert Davies and Gordon Rupp, eds. *A History of the Methodist Church in Great Britain.* 4 vols. London, 1965-88. Vol.1, pp. 35-79.

Elliott, Marianne. *Wolfe Tone.* New Haven, 1989.

Field, C.D. 'The social structure of English Methodism: eighteenth – twentieth centuries.' *British Journal of Sociology.* 28 (1977), pp. 199-225.

Fitzpatrick, Martin. 'Heretical religion and radical political ideas in late eighteenth-century England.' In Eckhart Hellmuth, ed. *The Transformation of Political Culture.* Oxford, 1990, pp. 339-72.

Francis, Matthew. 'Selina, Countess of Huntingdon (1707-1791).' B.Litt. thesis, University of Oxford, 1957.

Gill, Frederick C. *Charles Wesley the First Methodist* London, 1964.

_____. *The Romantic Movement and Methodism.* London, 1937.

Harding, Alan. 'The Anglican prayer book and the Countess of Huntingdon's connexion.' *Transactions of the Congregational Historical Society.* 20 (1970), pp. 364-67.

_____. 'The Countess of Huntingdon and her connexion in the eighteenth century.' D.Phil. thesis, University of Oxford, 1992.

Harris, Frances. *A Passion for Government. The Life of Sarah, Duchess of Marlborough.* Oxford, 1991.

Hatch, Nathan O. *The Democratization of American Christianity.* New Haven, 1989.

Haydon, Colin. *Anti-Catholicism in Eighteenth-century England.* Manchester, 1993.

Helmstadter, R.J. 'The Reverend Andrew Reed.' In R.W. Davis and R.J. Helmstadter, eds. *Religion and Irreligion in Victorian Society.* London, 1992, pp. 7-28.

Hempton, David. 'Methodism and the law, 1740-1820.' *Bulletin of the John Rylands University Library of Manchester.* 70 (1988), pp. 93-107.

_____. *Methodism and Politics in British Society 1750-1850.* London, 1984.

_____. 'Religion in British society, 1740-1790.' In Jeremy Black, ed. *British Politics and Society from Walpole to Pitt 1742-1789*. London, 1990, pp. 201-21.
Hibbert, Christopher. *King Mob. The Story of Lord George Gordon and the Riots of 1780*. London, 1959.
Hill, Bridget. *Women, Work, and Sexual Politics in Eighteenth-century England*. Oxford, 1989.
Holmes, Geoffrey, and Szechi, Daniel. *The Age of Oligarchy*. London, 1993.
Hughes, Hugh J. *Life of Howell Harris the Welsh Reformer*. London, 1892.
Hull, James E. 'The controversy between John Wesley and the Countess of Huntingdon.' Ph.D. thesis, University of Edinburgh, 1959.
Jenkins, D.E. *The Life of the Rev. Thomas Charles*. 3 vols. Denbigh, 1908.
Jones, Marsh W. 'Pulpit, Periodical, and Pen. Joseph Benson and Methodist Influence in the Victorian Prelude.' Ph.D. dissertation, University of Illinois at Urbana-Champaign, 1995.
Kelly, J.N.D. *St Edmund Hall*. Oxford, 1989.
Lambert, Frank. *"Pedlar in Divinity"; George Whitefield and the Transatlantic Revivals, 1737-1770*. Princeton, 1994.
_____. 'Subscribing for profits and piety: the friendship of Benjamin Franklin and George Whitefield.' *William and Mary Quarterly*. 3rd series. 50 (1993), pp. 529-48.
Langford, Paul. *A Polite and Commercial People. England 1727-1783*. Oxford, 1989.
_____. *Public Life and the Propertied Englishman, 1689-1798*. Oxford, 1991.
Lawson, A.B. *John Wesley and the Christian Ministry*. London, 1963.
Lovegrove, Deryck W. *Established Church, Sectarian People. Itinerancy and the Transformation of English Dissent, 1780-1830*. Cambridge, 1988.
Lyles, Albert M. *Methodism Mocked. The Satiric Reaction to Methodism in the Eighteenth Century*. London, 1960.
MacCarthy, Fiona. *Eric Gill*. London, 1989.
McCaul, Robert L. 'Whitefield's Bethesda college.' *Georgia Historical Quarterly*. 44 (1960), pp. 263-77, 381-98.
MacDermot, Frank. *Theobald Wolfe Tone*. London, 1939.
McLynn, Frank. *The Jacobites*. London, 1985.
Malcomson, A.P.W. *John Foster. The Politics of the Anglo-Irish Ascendancy*. Oxford, 1978.
Marini, Stephen A. *Radical Sects of Revolutionary New England*. Cambridge, Mass., 1982.
Medhurst, C. E. *Life and Work of Lady Elizabeth Hastings*. Leeds, 1914.
Monod, Paul K. *Jacobitism and the English People 1688-1788*. Cambridge, 1989.
Morey, Kenneth. 'The theological position of the Countess of Huntingdon's connexion.' B.A. dissertation, C.N.A.A., 1990.
Noverre, Jean G. *Letters on Dancing and Ballets*. London, 1930.
Nussbaum, Felicity A. *The Autobiographical Subject. Gender and Ideology in Eighteenth-Century England*. Baltimore, 1989.
Nuttall, Geoffrey F. 'Continental pietism and the evangelical movement in

Britain.' In J.P. van den Berg and J.P. van Doren, eds. *Pietismus und Reveil.* Leiden, 1978, pp. 207-36.

_____. 'Howel Harris and "the grand table": a note on religion and politics 1744-50.' *Journal of Ecclesiastical History.* 39 (1988), pp. 531-44.

_____. *The Significance of Trevecca College 1768-91.* London, 1969.

Ollard, S.L. *The Six Students of St. Edmund Hall.* London, 1911.

Owen, Alun Wyn. 'Howell Harris and the Trevecka "family".' *Transactions of the Calvinistic Methodist Historical Society.* 44 (1959), pp. 2-13.

Page, William, ed. *The Victoria History of the County of Leicestershire.* Vol. 1. London, 1907.

Pinks, William. *The History of Clerkenwell.* London, 1865. New edition.

Poole, David R., Jr. 'Bethesda: an investigation of the Georgia orphan house, 1738-1772.' Ph.D. dissertation, Georgia State University, 1978.

Rack, Henry. *Reasonable Enthusiast. John Wesley and the Rise of Methodism.* London, 1989.

_____. 'Religious societies and the origins of Methodism.' *Journal of Ecclesiastical History.* 38 (1987), pp. 582-95.

_____. 'Survival and revival: John Bennet, Methodism, and the old dissent.' In Keith Robbins, ed., *Protestant Evangelicalism: Britain, Ireland, Germany and America c. 1750 – c. 1950.* Oxford, 1990, pp. 1-23.

Reynolds, J.S. *The Evangelicals at Oxford, 1735-1871.* Oxford, 1953.

Rivers, Isabel. *Reason, Grace, and Sentiment. A Study of the Language of Religion and Ethics in England, 1660-1780.* Vol. 1, *Whichcote to Wesley.* Cambridge, 1991.

Rudé, George F.E. 'The Gordon riots: a study of the rioters and their victims.' *Transactions of the Royal Historical Society.* 5th series. 6 (1956), pp. 93-114.

Russell, George W.E. *A Short History of the Evangelical Movement.* London, 1915.

Ruttenburg, Nancy. 'George Whitefield, spectacular conversion, and the rise of democratic personality.' *American Literary History.* 5 (1993), pp. 429-58.

Sangster, Paul. *Pity My Simplicity. The Evangelical Revival and the Religious Education of Children, 1738-1800.* London, 1963.

Schlenther, Boyd S. '"To convert the poor people in America": the Bethesda orphanage and the thwarted zeal of the Countess of Huntingdon.' *Georgia Historical Quarterly.* 78 (1994), pp. 225-56.

Scott, Beatrice. 'Lady Elizabeth Hastings.' *Yorkshire Archaeological Journal.* 55 (1983), pp. 95-118.

Sedgwick, Romney, ed. *The House of Commons 1715-1754.* 2 vols. London, 1970.

Sell, Alan P.F. 'Philosophy in the eighteenth-century dissenting academies of England and Wales.' *History of Universities.* 11 (1992), pp. 75-122.

[Seymour, Aaron C.H.]. *The Life and Times of Selina Countess of Huntingdon.* 2 vols. London, 1839.

[Shirley, Evelyn Philip]. *Stemmata Shirleiana; or the Annals of the Shirley Family.* London, 1873.

Shuttleton, David. 'Methodism and Dr George Cheyne's "More enlightening principles".' In Roy Porter, ed. *Medicine and Enlightenment.* London, 1994, pp. 323-42.

_____. '"My owne crazy carcase": the life and works of Dr George Cheyne 1672-1743.' Ph.D. thesis, University of Edinburgh, 1992.

Sidney, Edwin. *The Life and Ministry of the Rev. Samuel Walker.* London, 1838. 2nd edition.

Smith, John C. *British Mezzotinto Portraits.* 4 vols. London, 1883.

Stevenson, John. *Popular Disturbances in England 1700-1870.* London, 1979.

Stout, Harry S. *The Divine Dramatist. George Whitefield and the Rise of Modern Evangelicalism.* Grand Rapids, 1991.

Streiff, Patrick P. *Jean Guillaume de la Fléchère.* Frankfurt, 1984.

Sutherland, L.S., and Mitchell, L.G., eds. *The History of the University of Oxford.* Vol. V. Oxford, 1986.

Turberville, A.S. *The House of Lords in the XVIIIth Century.* Oxford, 1927.

Tyerman, Luke. *The Life of the Rev. George Whitefield.* 2 vols. London, 1876-77.

_____. *The Life and Times of the Rev. John Wesley.* 3 vols. London, 1878. 4th edition.

_____. *The Oxford Methodists.* London, 1878.

_____. *Wesley's Designated Successor.* London, 1882.

Van Den Berg. *Constrained by Jesus' Love: an Inquiry into the Motives of the Missionary Awakening in Great Britain in the Period Between 1698 and 1815.* Kampen, Netherlands, 1956.

Vulliamy, C.E. *John Wesley.* London, 1931.

Walsh, John. 'Methodism at the end of the eighteenth century.' In Rupert Davies and Gordon Rupp, eds. *A History of the Methodist Church in Great Britain.* 4 vols. London, 1965-88. Vol. 1, pp. 277-315.

_____. '"Methodism" and the origins of English speaking evangelicalism.' In M.A. Noll et al., eds. *Evangelicalism. Comparative Studies of Popular Protestantism in North America, the British Isles and Beyond.* New York, 1994, pp. 19-37.

_____. 'The origins of the evangelical revival.' In G.V. Bennett and J.D. Walsh, eds. *Essays in Modern English Church History.* London, 1966, pp. 132-62.

_____ et al., eds. *The Church of England c. 1689 – c. 1833.* Cambridge, 1993.

Ward, W. R. 'Anglicanism and assimilation; or mysticism and mayhem.' In W. R. Ward, *Faith and Faction.* London, 1993.

_____. 'Power and piety: the origins of religious revival in the early eighteenth century.' *Bulletin of the John Rylands University Library of Manchester.* 63 (1980-81), pp. 231-52.

_____. *The Protestant Evangelical Awakening.* Cambridge, 1992.

Welch, Edwin. 'Lady Huntingdon's chapel at Ashby.' *Transactions of the Leicestershire Archaeological and Historical Society.* 66 (1992), pp. 136-42.

_____. 'Lady Huntingdon and Spa Fields chapel.' *Guildhall Miscellany.* 4 (1972), pp. 175-83.

_____. *Spiritual Pilgrim. A Reassessment of the Life of the Countess of Huntingdon.* Cardiff, 1995.

Wood, A. Skevington. 'The failure of a mission: 1791.' *Congregational Quarterly.* 32 (1954), pp. 343-51.

_____. *Thomas Haweis.* London, 1957.

Woolverton, John Frederick. *Colonial Anglicanism in North America.* Detroit, 1984.

Young, B.W. 'William Law and the Christian economy of salvation.' *English Historical Review.* 109 (1994), pp. 308-22.

INDEX